THE CANADIAN PROFILE

People, Institutions, Infrastructure

Second Edition

edited by

JERRY DERMER

York University

STRATEGIC BRIEFINGS FOR CANADIAN ENTERPRISE SERIES

CAPTUS PRESS

Strategic Briefings for Canadian Enterprise Series
The Canadian Profile: People, Institutions, Infrastructure, 2nd ed.

ISBN 1–895712–43–2

Canadian Cataloguing in Publication Data
Main entry under title:

The Canadian profile: people, institutions, infrastructure

(Strategic briefings for Canadian enterprise series)
2nd ed.
Includes bibliographical references.
ISBN 1–895712–43–2

1. Canada — Economic conditions — 1991–   .*
2. Canada — Social conditions — 1971–   .*
I. Dermer, Jerry. II. Series.

HC115.C283 1994   330.971   C94–932748–4

York University Campus, 4700 Keele Street, North York,
Ontario M3J 1P3 Canada
Phone: (416) 736–5537   FAX: (416) 736–5793
EMail: CAPTPRES@IO.ORG

0 9 8 7 6 5 4 3 2 1
Printed and bound in Canada

Table of Contents

Series Introduction

JERRY DERMER

Is a general knowledge of the business environment necessary for every Canadian manager today? Many still believe it is not. After all, competition in global and local marketplaces still takes place among individual firms, not among industries, countries or governments. Furthermore, a business can be successful in a declining market or a stagnant industry, or even in an uncompetitive country. Given these realities, as well as the difficulties of dealing with ambiguous and complex socioeconomic issues, it is not surprising that many Canadian managers still prefer a narrow, domestic focus to a global one.

Yet in this age of political and economic upheaval, there seems little need to argue that the environment in which Canadian business finds itself is changing. The world economy is becoming more homogeneous and more competitive as market capitalism is increasingly accepted as the universal organizing mechanism. The countries of the former USSR have renounced communism. China and India are embracing free enterprise. Other nations are climbing on this bandwagon, increasing trade and negotiating agreements in fear of being left behind. Economic growth made possible through international trade and foreign direct investment is the new political ideology because it will outpace domestic growth even for the most developed economies. The potential is mind-boggling. If the 850 million Indians and 1.1 billion Chinese can raise their per-capita income levels to that of Spain today, the increase in the size of the world economy would exceed what is now produced in North America.

Because Canada is an open economy, the importance to managers of understanding international opportunities and threats must not be underestimated. The ability of business to create and trade goods and services on favourable terms determines the material standard of living of Canada's residents. Enjoying, for example, fresh fruits and vegetables all year round; the best products — cars, clothing, etc. — that the world can provide, and easy access to international travel requires that Canada be able to reciprocate by producing competitively priced goods that other countries want.

This relationship between global competitiveness and Canadian standard of living is the key to many of the issues prevalent today and so serves as a focus for our exploration of the Canadian business environment in this series. The challenge to managers lies in finding the best ways of achieving economic success in a sociopolitically acceptable manner, while sustaining, if not improving our quality of life. Much of the discussion in the Canadian business environment emanates from disagreements about how serious this challenge is and what, if anything, should be done about it.

ECONOMIC CROSSROADS AND SOCIAL RESPONSIBILITY

The motivation for these books is the belief that increasing global competition requires managers to broaden the scope of their observations and shorten the time of their responses in order to handle successfully the external issues that affect the long-term direction and performance of their organizations. Issues are changes and choices that confront decision makers. They arise out of the opportunities and threats, and the sources of weakness and strength that exist in the economies in which an organization operates. And since the factors that generate issues also help or hinder their resolution, strategic managers must consider not only the issues themselves but their context as well.

The scope of their observations must include both the domestic and global environments, as well as the way the two interrelate. Countries, like people, have unique personalities and abilities that cause them to focus on certain concerns and to react in particular ways. It is essential for managers to have some awareness of the Canadian personality, since it will affect the way issues are perceived and handled domestically.

Frameworks and background knowledge sharpen this awareness. The volumes of this series and the papers within them provide a framework for identifying and analyzing in context the issues that make up today's business environment. Each paper contributes relevant background by offering a succinct yet comprehensive briefing on one aspect of the global or domestic scene. The series is targeted at managers seeking to improve their knowledge of the most relevant issues external to their firms and the most significant contextual factors that will facilitate or inhibit successful resolution of those issues.

Do today's issues represent economic crossroads? History might easily lead one to dismiss any long-term concerns about Canada's ability to sustain its standard of living. It can be argued that the problems that exist today are of the kind to be expected in any normally fluctuating economy, that they are not portents of an economic doomsday that will occur unless a massive restructuring is undertaken. After all, no one can deny that Canada is still a great place to live and work or that life has been relatively good for us. Even education and training have not really mattered. While those with post-secondary education or a skilled trade have generally earned high returns on their educational investment, even those with little formal training have been able to enjoy such benefits of Canadian economic growth as home ownership, travel, cars, etc. They have lived well thanks to high-paying jobs in manufacturing, resource-related, and even some service industries, particularly in the public sector. Our affluence has also made possible a social assistance safety net of which we are justifiably proud. Little wonder, then, that Canadian embassies around the world daily face long lines of potential immigrants eager to gain access to the many benefits of our society.

A stark contrast to this view is provided by those who argue that change is needed, claiming that this description applies to the Canada of the past but not necessarily the Canada of the present, much less of the future. In the past thirty years the world that allowed Canadian business to enjoy its considerable success and the residents of Canada to benefit accordingly has been significantly reshaped. Hence, these critics question whether the Canadian economy is changing quickly enough to keep pace with global change; whether it can change enough to succeed in the world as it now exists; and whether Canada is even giving such concerns appropriate consideration.

Regardless of what managers believe about global competitiveness and living standards, social responsibility demands that they look beyond the scope of their own narrow interests to confront these three questions.

CANADA'S UNIQUE PERSONALITY

As they face the economic and sociopolitical challenges of the nineties and beyond, Canadians must carry the "baggage" of Canada's economic history. This history has played — and continues to play — an important part in shaping the business environment and our perceptions of that environment.

During its first 125 years of existence Canada has grown as an essentially open economy (with some significant exceptions), trading internationally primarily in resources. Foreigners have played a big part in the way the Canadian economy has developed, a fact that has shaped both the public's expectations and the way Canadian managers manage. Business, labour and government have all been affected.

Business

Our financial system has been dominated by five large, multi-branch chartered banks, complemented by separate trust, securities and insurance firms. Through a branch system these institutions were able to serve the needs of a widely dispersed population, especially in locations where independent operations would not have been economically feasible. The banks also had enough of a foreign presence to channel the funds needed to finance our survival and growth. The large government projects (the railroads, the CBC, the St. Lawrence Seaway, etc.) they financed helped to unite a sparsely populated country threatened by a large and powerful neighbour to the south. They also provided backing for the large export-oriented, resource-based industries that are a major component of our economy. In return, through the provisions of the Federal Bank Act, they were protected from foreign competition.

Manufacturing industries, while never emphasized as an important ingredient of Canadian economic development, were also protected, especially from the United States, which was not only the most powerful economic force in the world but also Canada's closest neighbour and largest trading partner. A system of tariffs on imports raised the prices of foreign goods to the point where the outputs of the more diversified, lower-volume Canadian manufacturers could be competitive. This in turn led foreign firms to establish branch plants within Canada in order to escape such penalties.

Because of the historical willingness of foreigners to provide capital, Canadians were never called upon to make significant sacrifices in current consumption in order to have sufficient investment funds for development. We were free to spend and enjoy the fruits of our labours immediately without forgoing growth. But foreign financing of resource development and the establishment of branch plants have combined to produce a Canadian economy that is 30 per cent foreign owned.

Because of this path of development, entrepreneurship and the ability to create value through technological know-how are not strengths of Canadian managers. A strong demand from foreign countries lacking natural endowments allowed Canadian resource companies to succeed without having to do much more than simply harvest and ship the resources at their disposal. Little value was added as Canadian industries were satisfied to export resources in an unprocessed state: logs and lumber, pulp and newsprint, unrefined minerals, agricultural crops, etc.

Branch plants had access to the much larger research-and-development (R&D) facilities of their parents and so saw little need to re-invent wheels in Canada. Nor, beyond some small differences in standards, was the Canadian market sufficiently unique to warrant individual attention. Canadians, after all, do watch American TV, travel extensively in the United States and live a comparable lifestyle. Branch plant managers tended to be assigned to Canada as one stop in a rotational program and operated during their brief sojourns more as administrators in a caretaking mode than as entrepreneurs. Branch-plant-management initiatives, such as securing the world product-mandate rights for an exportable product for a Canadian plant, although not unknown, were rare.

It must be noted, however, that although foreign ownership has been criticized for almost three decades, there is little evidence to suggest that Canadian-owned firms behave much differently. They do not spend more on R&D, develop new products or enhance productivity with any higher degree of vigour. Canadian rates of small business formations and failures, for example, and of adoptions of new product and processing technologies, are nowhere near those of countries such as Singapore and Mexico. And, protected by tariffs, these companies have tended to compete almost exclusively within Canada.

Labour

Organized labour in Canada also has a unique history in that it is a hybrid of U.S. and European traditions. Although associated with the Democratic Party, American unions are essentially non-political. Their focus is on improving economic conditions for workers. Those in Europe, however, grew out of political movements agitating for greater equality in a class-structured society where rights had historically been denied to the working class. Unions there are more concerned with social activism, more widespread, more closely linked to politics and more powerful. Canada, where organized labour is highly active in politics (note the labour-supported NDP provincial governments), union strength in the public sector is growing, and U.S.-affiliated unions (such as the teamsters) are strong, reflects the best and worst of both traditions.

Work disruptions and antagonism between unions and management are two clear problems in our economy today. The most recent example of distrust surfaced during the Canada-U.S. free trade debate. Business and labour clearly expressed different preferences and concerns, each showing a seemingly unshakable determination not to hear what the other was saying. The result of this continuing antagonism is that of all developed countries only Italy has lost more days to strikes. Canada also has one of the highest incidences of industrial accidents in the developed world.

Government

During the growth years the Canadian government taxed and spent to provide the services it believed the public wanted, whether the economy was strong or not. Our physical infrastructure — roads, bridges, utilities — is among the most developed in the world. Educational institutions and programs designed to secure social justice (medicare, housing, welfare, day care, etc.) have also made large demands on the public purse. Canada's percentage contribution of government to R&D spending, both through government-run laboratories and universities and medical institutes, equals that of the most advanced nations in the world (although, because of the lower investment intensity of the private sector, our overall R&D investment is only about half that of other advanced nations). More recently, policies aimed at fostering bilingualism and multiculturalism and at securing protection for minorities have begun to consume public funds. Whatever the merits of these programs, the problem is that in order to provide them government has fallen into a pattern of deficit financing. This has led to

The Free Flow of Capital

The development of telecommunications has also integrated the world's financial markets, allowing capital to flow unimpeded to where returns are highest. In addition to its implications for securing industrial financing for emerging global competitors, this mobility of capital also allows governments access to a world market for funds. They are therefore under no restraint to limit their spending to the funds their own economies generate; as long as there are foreign sources willing to supply capital, they can go on spending and increasing deficits. Capital flow to a country has thus been decoupled from its economic performance.

Some believe that this has decoupling has led to a situation where government actions are often divorced from economic reality. Regardless of how one views such behaviour, with increased borrowing comes the significant risk of dependency on foreign lenders who can quickly and easily switch their funds elsewhere in the world. Government deficits, caused at least in part by trade imbalances, also reduce the amount of funds available both for private industrial investors and to the government itself to serve the public in new ways. Without such discretionary funds, governments are extremely limited in what they can do.

Trading Blocs

One way in which countries have sought to protect themselves from the negative consequences of these changes has been by forming trading blocs. Three trading blocs — the so-called Triad — have emerged: the European Union (EU), the Asia Pacific Economic Community (APEC) and the North American Free Trade Agreement. Canada now faces the challenge of developing new trading relationships within this triad configuration, as NAFTA expands to include Latin America at a time when its traditional trading strengths — commodities and low-skilled, labour-intensive manufactured products — are increasing in supply and decreasing in price world wide.

CANADA'S POSITION TODAY

The world within which Canada exists today, where new standards of economic performance are required in order to meet the competitive challenge of Japan and other new economic realities, is thus considerably different from that of a generation ago. But the way Canada is reacting to these changes is a source of much concern.

To many observers there appears to be a leadership vacuum. Those who purport to lead, whether in government or the private sector, often seem to be more concerned with their own self-interest than with the greater good of the country as a whole. To maintain power, for example, governments mitigate the negative consequences of falling behind competitively by increasing the debt. This, in turn, has left our leaders without the discretionary resources needed for effective action, and the country increasingly dependent on foreigners. That the public is dissatisfied and mistrustful is demonstrated by its readiness to change governments with each election and by wide fluctuations in opinion polls seeking to measure satisfaction. Nor is confidence in business any higher. The decade of takeovers and insider trading that defined the corporate greed of the 1980s also increased the public's skepticism about business ethics and corporate social responsibility.

The result of this dissatisfaction and skepticism is a society where all are adamant about preserving or increasing their rights and privileges — where sacrifices are not considered lest one find oneself taken advantage of.

Where then does Canada stand? Who will emerge to lead this nation? What are the major strengths and weaknesses of Canada as a place in which to do business? What types of businesses are most and least affected by these factors? Where are prospects brightest and where dimmest? What decisions have to be made and by whom? What will happen if they are not made? The proliferation of these types of questions demonstrates the need for a systematic approach to today's issues.

ANALYZING AND RESPONDING TO STRATEGIC ISSUES

One could examine these changes in any number of ways — for example, by subdividing the environment according to economic, social, political, technological, ecological, demographic and cultural dimensions; or by using the firm, market, industry or nation as units of analysis. But whatever the scheme used for studying them, it is clear that the changes engender a host of perplexing and paradoxical opportunities and threats: perplexing in that some things that help one business can be fatal to another; paradoxical in that what improves a country's standard of living and makes it a desirable place to live may, at the same time, make it a disadvantageous place to operate a business.

The approach strategic managers take toward issues and their context in attempting to cope with today's realities must therefore differ from that taken by their counterparts of a generation ago in at least three ways:

Global Scope The identification of issues must begin with the assumption that significant change can originate anywhere in the world. The time span between the occurrence of an apparently distant event and the appearance of significant local consequences has decreased to the point that geographic distances have become largely irrelevant. The world is a much smaller place today. In such a world it is naïve to imagine that we or any nation can be immune to or insulated from significant changes. Patterns of managerial behaviour based on denial, insularity and nostalgia are simply no longer tenable.

The continual collection and analysis of comparative global data are necessary if we are to confront rather than shrink from reality. Issue identification requires scanning globally, not just locally, and searching for causality through many levels and convoluted linkages.

Comprehensive Conceptualization The manner in which issues must be analyzed has now also changed. Phenomena are more complex and systemic, and rarely lend themselves to a single, simplistic explanation. Valid single-factor models and direct explanations of cause and effect are now the exception rather than the rule. Many variables interrelate: within each business, markets must be matched simultaneously with people, technology and money in order to produce products that can acquire and sustain a competitive advantage. Opportunities come in increasingly narrower windows; timing is critical. Within industries, labour, management and government must co-operate to form systems of interrelated suppliers and producers able to meet strict timetables. Competition is now among systems — therefore firms, industries and economies collectively form the most relevant units for analysis. When the whole can be significantly different from the sum of the parts, analytical frameworks must assume an appropriately holistic perspective if questions of change are to be understood.

Consensual Response In Canada today, change can only be effected through co-operation. Managerial approaches based on the ideas of command and control are now more unacceptable than ever. In our pluralistic society, power is widely distributed among different segments of the population. Rights are protected by checks and balances; the authority of any one segment to act independently is limited and never free of consequences and accountability. No longer can ideologies and positions simply be prescribed and commanded. Nor, with the population increasing in education and sophistication, are experts automatically heeded as authorities.

These realities require new ways of managing, ways that may well be uncomfortable to many now in, or aspiring to, positions of responsibility. Change desired by any institution or interest group must now be advanced and promoted in a manner that is cognizant of its political palatability. Consultations, consortia, co-operation through partnerships, etc. — these are the most effective modes for achieving sustainable change.

The books in this series contribute by providing a framework for identifying strategic issues and analyzing the factors that help or hinder their resolution. The approach combines two models frequently used at the level of the firm. One of these matches productive capabilities to market needs in accordance with stakeholder expectations so that the three are internally consistent, with any imbalance implying the need for adjustment. The other analyzes each situation to identify strengths, weaknesses, opportunities and threats — the so-called SWOT analysis — and uses these as diagnostic tools for creating a competitive strategy that builds on strengths and mitigates threats.

The intent of the series' creators is not to lead the reader to a position of agreement with the thoughts of the editor or any of the contributors. It is rather to have made the reader a better manager — a manager who is more aware of the global scene, more motivated to engage in the processes that will shape Canada's future and more capable of doing so.

Introduction

JERRY DERMER

Implementation is now a key concern of strategic management theorists: strategy is only meaningful if it can be converted into action. Recommendations are plentiful: the challenge is making things happen. Accordingly, this book provides the capability assessment component of this series' strategic analysis of the Canadian business environment. Its nine papers identify the developmental issues that must be resolved if Canada is to adjust structurally to economic trends and global market opportunities. The book probes Canada's demographics, institutions and infrastructure, assessing its ability to continue to provide the standard of living Canadians have come to expect.

In the first paper, David Foot, one of Canada's foremost authorities on demographic changes, begins this analysis with a briefing on just what the population figures mean. Based on the latest census data, his conclusions are provocative in that he disagrees with many of the "experts" on the marketing and employment implications of these trends.

For example, David provides data on the Canadian population and its growth rate in the form of a Population Pyramid, and then relates this analysis to the types of decisions that are influenced by such life style phenomena. He identifies the members of the baby boom and the baby boom echo generations, states when the latter era will end, and what are its implications. These are discussed both in terms of the market opportunities of the future, as well as in the types of organizations in which we will be working. This is all important information for anyone concerned with tomorrow's economy.

John Saywell, in a fast moving yet easily digestible paper, tackles the difficult task of explaining "The Socio-Political Environment: Discord and Fragmentation." Jack integrates and analyses the effects of such disparate topics as the foundations of Canada's economic, social and justice systems; francophone and multicultural issues; the effects of the Charter of Rights and Freedoms; and the Constitutional debate. His exploration of the issues of abortion and environmentalism leave us with a much clearer understanding of the constraints to be overcome if change is to be accomplished.

It seems that the number of critical socio-political issues is growing exponentially in Canada and each has significant implications for the ability to compete globally. For example, Charter rights to freedom of association do not necessarily include the right to strike. Thus, labour disputes and Charter conflicts intersect to make the achievement of labour-management harmony more difficult to achieve. Similarly, the resolution of other pressing socio-political issues such as aboriginal rights or equalization payments continually collide with structural economic adjustments. Jack's paper is essential background for the understanding of these conflicts.

It has been said that nothing so characterizes contemporary Canadian affairs as the multiplicity of active interest groups. Bill Stanbury reinforces this view in his look at the fabric of interrelationships needed to make any policy initiative workable. His paper "Interest Group Behaviour and Policy Making in Canada" is a succinct yet comprehensive appraisal of just what makes things happen. Although research studies have repeatedly pointed out that harmonious interrelationships among the public, private and organized labour sectors are requisite for enhanced economic capability, Bill rejects tripartism, opting instead for a more situationally-specific and issue-oriented approach. His paper supplies a wealth of valuable information on many of the special interest stakeholder groups that continually intervene into the pubic policy process in Canada to influence policy-making behaviour to their advantage.

More specifically, Bill explains that interest groups operate in the policy arena for a variety of reasons. For example, government actions have the effect of creating interest groups and as government activity expands, more people are affected. Sections of his paper cover the set of actors and institutions involved, and the nature of the exchanges between interest groups and political parties. He briefs us on the activities of the growing number of government relations consulting firms. He leaves it to the reader, however, to decide who in Canada has power.

Sociologist Ed Grabb complements the analyses of Professors Saywell and Stanbury by offering his perspective on the values that are alleged to differentiate Canadians from Americans. In his paper "Democratic Values in Canada and the United States," he examines North American history, searching for factors that can help explain the presumed differences. His comparison of the two populations with respect to attitudes and values makes for intriguing reading. Ed offers his answer to the question of whether Canadians are as different from Americans as many would like to believe.

The three sectors associated with a tripartism perspective — corporate, government and organized labour — are each covered in a separate paper briefing us on its makeup, history and pressing issues. Contributors Tom Wesson, David Siegel and Graeme McKechnie explain how the outlooks and attitudes, policies and performance, of each, help or hinder economic development and the satisfaction of society's expectations.

To be more competitive and to achieve higher performance, does Canada have to change the composition and operation of its corporate sector? Briefing us on this overriding question, Tom Wesson first provides a short history of corporate development in Canada. He begins his article, "The Structure of Canada's Economy," by describing the sectoral transformation of the Canadian economy, tracing its evolution from agriculture through manufacturing to services, and provides a brief background on the makeup of the modern corporation and the role of their boards of directors. The chapter focuses primarily on describing the composition of the corporate sector, highlighting the characteristics of industry and ownership concentration, and foreign ownership. His analysis includes Canada's unique corporations — those owned by the Crown and the Caisse de Dépôt.

David Siegel explains the workings of the government sector, appraising its capability to meet the challenges it faces in helping to reshape Canada. He explains the advantages and disadvantages of the federal parliamentary system that exists in Canada. His paper briefs us on how power is distributed in a governmental structure and process that features both career civil servants and political appointees, numerous multilevel co-ordinating committees with overlapping memberships, and powerful central agencies.

Issues arising from such broad concerns as enhancing global competitiveness, maintaining national identity, and adapting to changing demographics do not map neatly into the mandate of a single department. Dave explains the organizational mechanisms that governments are using to respond to these issues and to vocal external stakeholders.

Requisites for productive, internationally-competitive economies invariably include a well-educated, well-trained, industrious labour force, working harmoniously with management. Japanese and European practices are invoked as role models to which North Americans should aspire. Clearly, closing the gaps between contemporary practice and these ideals is one of the most profound challenges facing Canada today. Graeme McKechnie's paper, "The Organized Labour Sector" briefs us on the historical background and current happenings so that we can assess the likelihood of achieving these objectives.

Graeme outlines what are the types and sizes of unions operating in Canada, which are growing, which are declining, and where we can expect future growth. As a highly experienced mediator and arbitrator he is well qualified to describe and comment on the labour relations process at the level of the firm. He lays out for us the stages through which labour and management proceed before a strike/lockout decision is made. He also traces the labour movement's history to its European and American roots and shows how these still influence how it operates today.

Graeme's paper is especially topical. It seems that every new day brings on a new labour-related issue. For example, the Ontario NDP government is seeking jurisdiction over job training in the constitution. Unions oppose this move stating that Canada needs a national job retraining program, not ten provincial ones, and that it threatens Canada's unemployment insurance program. How will this be resolved?

In his paper on financial infrastructure, Peter Campbell helps us to understand Canada's position in world capital markets, its ability to attract capital for investment, and the recent transformation of the financial industry itself. Included is a description of the forces that have transformed the financial sector into a globalized industry. Peter explains for us the role the financial sector plays in helping or hindering Canada's economic growth. Of particular interest was his explanation of why the four-pillar financial system was a sound and effective structure to aid Canada's development, and what were the global forces that led to its demise. He argues that the financial services sector in Canada is entrepreneurial and innovative, well managed and solidly positioned to meet the global challenges of the 1990s.

Technology is an essential ingredient and there are few in Canada as experienced as Charles McMillan on these issues. His review "Technology and Competitiveness: A Canadian Strategy" traces the history of this topic and compares Canada's performance to the best global performers. His analysis points out many of the recent changes at both the federal and provincial levels attempting to improve these abilities, and he offers a host of policy suggestions to improve the situation. Charlie is very persuasive and so the reader must decide if he overemphasizes the importance of technology in discussions of international competitiveness and industrial growth.

McMillan's article lays out the components of science and technology policy and provides the background to allow the reader to decide if government should become actively involved in establishing and implementing such policies in Canada. It also describes what it is about the Japanese system of bringing technology to market that makes it so effective, and so difficult to compete against.

The articles in this book thus allow the reader to decide whether Canada has the wherewithall to compete and the structures and systems in place to effect winning response to the global challenge.

The Effect of Changing Demographics: Marketing and Human Resource Trends

DAVID K. FOOT

INTRODUCTION

Demographic trends in general, and population aging in particular, are important issues affecting the external environment of all organizations in North America and elsewhere, whether they be in the private or public sectors. As a discipline, demographics can be described as the "scientific study of human populations." Hence, demographics is about people — both as customers or clients and employees. Therefore, demographic trends have important implications for both the marketing and personnel functions in any organization.

This chapter explores the interrelationships between demographic trends, marketing and human resource planning, with particular emphasis on the future trends in North America and especially Canada. The analysis highlights the importance of the post-war baby-boom generation in influencing the external environment within which organizations have operated, and must continue to operate. Since individual organizations have almost no influence on demographic variables such as births, deaths, immigration and so on, demographic trends are truly external to the organization. It is not possible to use organizational decisions to internalize or modify these trends. They are inherently part of the external environment that must be monitored for the organization to be successful.

Interesting implications emerge from these observations. First, since people — and hence demographics — are the crucial element in both marketing and human resource planning, these two functions should be closely linked in any organization. Yet for many organizations it is often difficult to conceive of two more disparate areas, both physically and conceptually. An implicit message of this chapter is the need for a closer linkage between marketing and personnel functions.

Second, demographics is concerned with long-term trends. In Canada annual population growth is around 1 per cent. Thus, incremental changes to the population are small compared to the total. This means that demographic shifts occur slowly and hence are easy to ignore — especially for those organizations with predominantly short-term goals, such as surviving to the next payroll, interest payment or annual general meeting! Moreover, management styles and practices in North America have tended to reward and reinforce predominantly short-term goals. Salary and bonus packages tied to current (one-year-term or less) performances are one example. Consequently, demographic trends have tended to be ignored in corporate decision-making.

Third, and perhaps a corollary to the short-term orientation in the corporate sector, has been the perceived need to be "more competitive". This goal tends to be associated with corporate downsizing (or "right-sizing") which so often resulted in the devolution of corporate functions to the front line. Emphasis is placed on moving these functions and their employees "closer to the customer" to make them "more accountable". While there may be undisputed benefits to this management practice, it does effectively downplay corporate functions such as strategic planning. Under this management style, trends that affect product performance are emphasized, and environmental monitoring tends to be product or niche-market oriented. To answer the bigger questions like "which markets should we be in and why?" requires not only a longer-term perspective but also a much broader, or corporate, perspective. Since demographic trends are probably more relevant to these types of corporate questions, these trends have tended to be ignored or to only receive "lip service" in the streamlined corporations of the past decade.

There is evidence that the tide may be changing again. Futurists like John Naisbitt and Faith Popcorn have re-emerged in the early 1990s with bestselling visions of future trends.[1] The short-term, predominantly inward-looking management style that dominated the 1980s is gradually being replaced by a more longer-term, outward-looking style in the 1990s. In this emerging management style, corporate functions like environmental planning take on more dominant roles.

It is within these various management styles and practices that demographic trends are positioned, interpreted and used. The management priorities of the 1980s, which focused primarily on short-term, product-oriented goals, resulted in the relative neglect of demographic trends in corporate decision making. The 1990s appear to be different. Longer-term, corporate-oriented goals give greater emphasis to the role of demographic trends in corporate decision making.

This paper provides two illustrations of the use of demographic trends in organizational decision making. After a necessarily cursory review of demographic trends in Canada, it examines the impact of demographic trends in marketing (people as customers or clients) and human resource planning (people as employees). While the focus is on the emerging trends in the 1990s and beyond, historical evidence is presented to provide the long-term perspective so crucial to understanding and using demographic trends appropriately in the modern organization.

HISTORICAL DEMOGRAPHIC TRENDS: A REVIEW

Sources of Demographic Data

In Canada, the sources of major demographic data are the decennial censuses (1871–1941) and the quinquennial censuses (1951–1991) currently conducted mid-year by the federal statistical gathering agency Statistics Canada. The censuses provide details not only on the number of people but also on a variety of characteristics such as age, gender, location, marital status, ethnicity and so on. Additional information on related topics, such as labour-force status and housing, are also gathered at the same time. Thus the results of a census provide a "snapshot" of the Canadian population.

To fill in between the census years, Statistics Canada gathers additional data from a variety of other sources. Vital statistics on births, deaths, immigration, marriages and so on are collected from appropriate administrative registry authorities, while sample surveys are used to collect information in other areas (for example, the Labour Force Survey). In this way, consistent time series can be constructed to monitor the changes over time in the Canadian demographic, economic and social landscape. In many cases, the censuses provide useful periodic information that serves as a benchmark for these ongoing surveys.

Before reviewing historical Canadian census data, it is useful to be acquainted with the basic population identity that underlies these data and the future projections based on them. At any point in time (t), a country's population (P) is the population at a previous time period (t–1) plus births (B) minus deaths (D), plus immigration (I) minus emigration (E) over the intervening time period. (Births minus deaths is called the net natural change, while immigration minus emigration is called net immigration.) This means that the change in population (P) can be expressed as the following identity:

$$\Delta P \equiv P_t - P_{t-1} \equiv B - D + I - E$$

or

$$P_t \equiv P_{t-1} + B - D + I - E.$$

In Canada, data on births, deaths, and immigration are collected from appropriate administrative sources, but since it is not necessary to get permission to leave the country (that is, exit visas are not required) or to inform the authorities when doing so, there is no administrative source for emigration data. Consequently these data must be estimated, and the census provides an important benchmark for such estimates. In essence, the above identity is reversed to read

$$E \equiv B - D + I - \Delta P$$

to obtain estimates of emigration. These "residual" estimates of emigration ensure that the population identity is satisfied empirically.

For sub-national divisions within a country, such as provinces, the population identity must be modified to include movements of people within a country. Conceptually, this can be accomplished by defining (I – E) to include all net immigrants to the population, both international and intra-national. The census is also useful in identifying intra-national movements of persons both between provinces and within provinces.

Results of Recent Censuses

Figure 1 displays the results from the 1971 and 1981 censuses in Canada to provide a historical perspective. This figure is called a "population pyramid". It shows the number of persons in each age-gender group for each census year.

A number of features of the Canadian population are apparent from Figure 1. Consider first the pyramid for 1971. Perhaps the most notable feature is that by 1971 the base of the pyramid had collapsed — there were fewer one-year-olds than ten-year-olds in the population. This reflects the declining numbers of births during the 1960s after the commercial introduction of the birth-control pill and as women entered the paid labour force. As a result, the increasing numbers of births that followed the Second World War came to an end, creating what is commonly referred to the "baby-boom" and "baby-bust" generations. From the 1971 population pyramid, the baby-boom generation in Canada can be conveniently defined as ranging from ages 5 to 24 years — that is, those born over the period from 1947 to 1966.

To assess the extent of the baby-bust, it is necessary to move forward to the 1981 population pyramid. In so doing, note that the 1981 pyramid looks like the 1971 pyramid moved up ten years. Not surprisingly, ten years later people are ten years older! (This represents one of the truisms of demographics — indeed of life in general, since we prefer not to contemplate the alternative!) Yet, while individuals may get a year older each year, this is not true for a group of individuals, such as a country. This difference is primarily attributable to net immigration, which augments the population in certain age groups. The very young and the elderly tend not to migrate as much as those of working age and especially not as much as those in their early working years. Consequently, countries with large immigrant populations, such as Canada, the United States and Australia, will not age at the same pace as those with populations born solely within the country. While perhaps obvious in retrospect, this is one of those demographic "facts" that is not always easy to comprehend.

Turning to the 1981 population pyramid, note that those in the baby-boom generation are aged 15 to 34 years. There are more than 400,000 people in each single-year cohort. The baby-bust generation is under 15 years. Other parts of the population pyramid are also of interest. The indentation around age 65 years represents the impact of the First World War when fertility dropped in Canada. "The boys" came home — the Roaring Twenties were obviously good times — and the number of births increased. This was followed by the Depression years of the 1930s and, once again, fertility and the number of births declined. Those born between 1930 and 1939 were aged 42 to 51 years in 1981 and these were not larger cohorts. Because of this relatively long period of low fertility, further postponement of childbearing did not take place during the Second World War. In fact, births started to rise over the war years, although the substantial increase was delayed until the advent of the post-war baby boom.

FIGURE 1
Population Pyramid, Canada
1971 and 1981

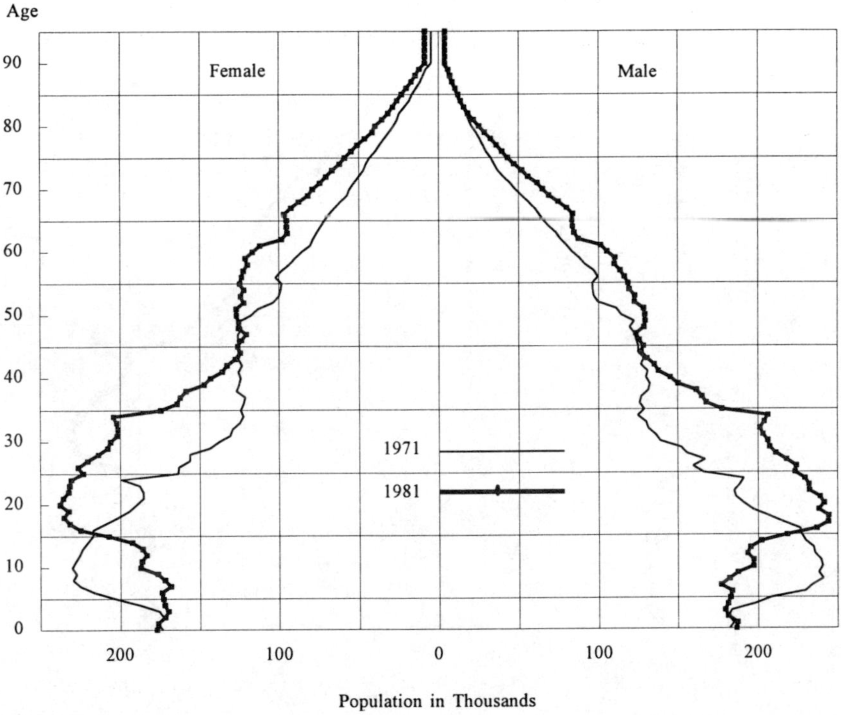

While every year these generations have become one year older, a new anticipated phenomenon emerged in the 1980s. This is apparent from the 1991 population pyramid (Figure 2), which suggests that the base of the population pyramid has been expanding slightly. After a period of decline, the youngest age groups started to grow again in the 1980s. This phenomenon is not attributable to a rise in fertility. Rather, it occurred because over the 1980s the massive baby-boom generation entered the prime childbearing period of the mid-twenties to mid-thirties. Even though, on average, baby boomers continued to have somewhat fewer children, over the 1980s there were so many of them having children that the numbers of births increased. This generation — the children of the baby boomers — is often called the "baby-boom echo" generation. Just how long this trend can be expected to continue is a topic for debate and will be examined in the projections outlined in the next section. However, it is probably useful to note that, by 1991, early baby boomers were in their forties and even those peak boomers, born in 1960, were 31. Consequently, this massive generation was entering the ages when infertility starts to increase and it

FIGURE 2
Population Pyramid, Canada
1991

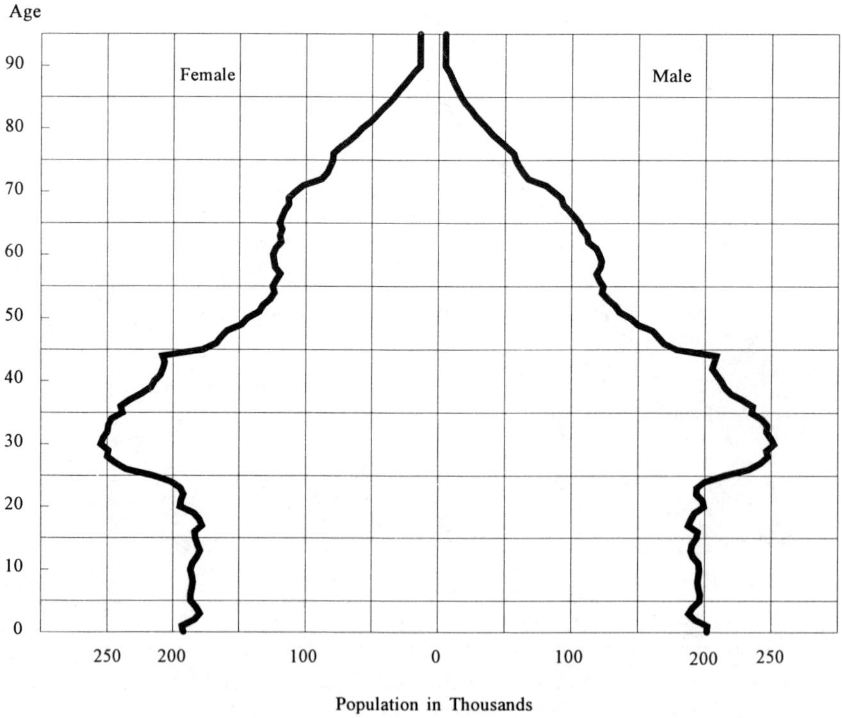

becomes increasingly difficult to bear children. For this reason, most population projections anticipate a decline in births sometime in the 1990s, thus signalling the end of the echo generation. The issue will be more fully outlined in the next section.

As postscripts, it should be noted that initial census results were adjusted for an estimated undercount — an adjustment that was larger in 1991 than in past censuses — and that the decision to now include "non-permanent" residents (primarily immigrant refugee claimants currently in Canada awaiting decisions on their applications) in the population count, both increased the population from initial estimates. The 1991 Canadian population was 28.1-million, well above the previous estimate of 27.0-million. Moreover, as might be expected, these non-permanent residents are concentrated in the younger age groups, particularly those in the 15 to 34 age group. Historical data consistent with this new definition are available back to 1971 (Figure 3), resulting in modest changes to population numbers and the implied growth rates.

Figure 3 summarizes these historical data. By 1991 in Canada:

- the relatively large group born prior to the First World War were aged 76 years and over;
- the small group born during the First World War were aged 72 to 75 years;
- the relatively large group born during the "Roaring Twenties" were largely in the early retirement ages of 62 to 71 years;
- the small group born over the Depression years of the 1930s were aged 52 to 61 years;

FIGURE 3

Canadian Population by Age (1961 to 1991)

Age Group (years)	*Population (millions of people)*			
	1961	*1971*	*1981*	*1991**
0 to 14	6.192	6.381	5.482	5.653
15 to 24	2.616	4.004	4.659	3.831
25 to 34	2.481	2.890	4.215	4.770
35 to 44	2.390	2.526	2.968	4.300
45 to 54	1.879	2.291	2.499	2.927
55 to 64	1.289	1.732	2.159	2.370
65 to 74	0.889	1.077	1.477	1.870
75 and over	0.502	0.667	0.883	1.271
Total	18.238	21.568	24.342	26.992

*Estimated population (excludes temporary residents).
Source: Statistics Canada.

- the Second World War babies were aged 45 to 51 years;
- the massive, 9-million-strong post-war baby-boom generation was aged 25 to 44 years;
- the subsequent smaller baby-bust generation was aged 12 to 24 years;
- the relatively larger baby-boom echo generation consisted of pre-teens.

These historical demographic facts have had important implications for the development of the Canadian marketplace both in terms of outputs (products and services) and inputs (labour). Both the marketing and personnel functions of all Canadian organizations have experienced the impacts of these demographic changes. But perhaps more importantly, with the absorption of the massive baby-boom generation into the Canadian labour force over the 1960s and 1970s completed, new trends emerged over the 1980s. Population aging has had an important impact on the marketplace as both the consumer and the worker have become noticeably older — a trend that can be expected to continue. In this sense, the new trends of the 1980s have been the watershed between the rapid-growth, youth-oriented decades of the 1960s and 1970s and the new slow-growth, older external environment of the 1990s and beyond.

But, perhaps most important of all, these are not unanticipated or unpredictable trends. The basic demographic truism that as individuals "every year we get one year older" provides an unassailable foundation on which to build a vision of the future of the Canadian marketplace and labour force. As the 1980s so clearly signalled, any Canadian organization that ignores these emerging demographic trends is likely to be ultimately destined to be at the "back of the pack" — if not at the "bottom of the harbour". After a cursory review of the population projection methodology, the following two sections provide a guide to a future, based on these historic demographic developments.

POPULATION PROJECTIONS

Population projections are based on the previous population identity and on the demographic truism outlined above. By making assumptions regarding the components of population growth, usually based on historical data, future populations can be derived. This is called the cohort component method, because it examines each of the components of population growth on a cohort (age) basis. By choosing different assumptions, alternative population projections are derived. This is the projection method employed by Statistics Canada.

In this approach, assumptions regarding fertility focus on the total fertility rate, a convenient statistical construct that provides an age-dependent measure of fertility for an entire population at a point in time. Since each couple needs two children to replace themselves, a minimum replacement fertility level of 2 is established. However, since some members of the population cannot, or choose not to, have children, the replacement fertility rate for a population is slightly higher — around 2.1 children per woman. Canadian fertility peaked at almost 4 children per woman in 1960 at the height of the baby boom and thereafter declined dramatically to under 2 children per woman by the 1970s. Currently, the total fertility rate is around 1.7 children per woman, a figure used by Statistics Canada in its current "medium" population projection. This assumption determines the total number of births in each year.

Similarly, the number of deaths is determined by another convenient statistical construct called life expectancy at birth, which provides an age-independent measure of mortality for an entire population at a point in time. Life expectancy has been rising in Canada from around 60 and 62 years for males and females respectively in the 1920s, to 74 and 81 years respectively by 1991. In the projections of Statistics Canada, these increases continue, although at reduced rates — to 78.5 and 84 years respectively by 2016 in their "medium" projection.

Perhaps the most controversial and important assumption concerns immigration. The average annual level of immigration to Canada over the 1960s to 1980s (1960–89) was approximately 135,600 persons a year. Then, in the 1990s, annual immigration levels consistently exceeded 200,000 persons, a figure that had only previously been exceeded in 1967 and 1974. Without exploring the reasons for this dramatic change in policy, it is important to note that these new immigration levels are incorporated into the latest population projections from Statistics Canada; the "medium" population projection uses an annual intake of 250,000 persons, considerably higher than the previous assumptions of 140,000 and 200,000 persons a year.

Finally, the Statistics Canada projections assumes that 50,000 people leave Canada each year. This is consistent with historical data, derived by the residual identity method noted above.

These assumptions, which reflect current data, result in a net immigration that approximately equals the current net natural increase in the population; that is, the difference between immigration (250,000) and emigration (50,000), approximately matches the difference between births (400,000) and deaths (200,000). Moreover, in future years, births are projected to decline and deaths to increase, resulting in the assumed net immigration becoming the more important component of population increase. This underscores the importance of the immigration assumption in the population projections.

PEOPLE AS CUSTOMERS

There are many theories and approaches to marketing. A common theme that runs through almost all of these marketing concepts, whether they are broadly based or more narrowly focussed on niche markets, is the need to know and understand your customer. Often psychographic information is assembled to provide suitable definitions of customers, but there are numerous other approaches to this problem as well.[2]

A useful and simple categorization of marketing is to view it as either volume-oriented or growth-oriented. Although these are not necessarily mutually exclusive categories, they require somewhat different strategies. Volume-oriented marketing usually implies mass-marketing in a mature market that is focused on small margins and large turnover. On the other hand, growth-oriented marketing usually focuses on new-product markets, where the competition may not yet be established, and so the margins can be higher on a smaller turnover, but with significant potential for enlarging the turnover. Demographic trends can be an important input into both volume- and growth-oriented marketing strategies.

Marketing is often seen as proactive — advertising, promotions, sponsorships and so on, are used to convince the customer to purchase the product or service. In the first instance, it is concerned with convincing the customer of the need for the item being offered. In the second instance, it is concerned with convincing the customer that, given this need, one particular brand or organization will best satisfy that need. The focus is often on recruiting new customers; although, organizations are increasingly directing marketing programs towards retaining existing customers. Nonetheless, marketing is often conceived as creating or changing customer preferences.

In many regards, this proactive approach to marketing can be a bit like "hitting your head against a brick wall so that it feels good when you stop!" At least in the first instance of identifying basic needs or wants, surely it is not cost-effective to go to all the effort and expense of creating or changing a market in which customers often already have well-defined preferences. By using a life-cycle approach to demographic trends, it is possible to identify existing requirements and to concentrate marketing strategies on satisfying them.

Since product or service development is not an "overnight" achievement, many organizations need to take a long-term view of the marketplace. In this long-term realm, marketing can afford to be — and may have to be — more reactive than proactive, since customers' needs and wants change over their lifetimes. A life-cycle approach to marketing is particularly attractive in a marketplace in which the age structure of the customer base is undergoing significant changes.[3] Once again, it requires a long-term, more reactive to marketing than has traditionally permeated the discipline.

Figures 1, 2 and 3 provide information on the customer base in Canada. The most populous age cohorts in Canada are the baby boomers, so this is where volume marketing can be directed. This generation were children in the 1960s, youths in the 1970s and young adults in the 1980s. Those born at the peak of the baby boom in 1960 were 11 in 1971 and 21 in

1981. This helps to explain the young and active orientation of many marketing strategies in past decades. Baby foods gave way to sports products and services, and dynamic downtowns offering active events and nightclubs flourished in this era.

By 1991 the peak boomers were aged 31 — getting attached, if not married, and moving to their own abodes in the suburbs. Sports facilities were gradually replaced by fitness facilities, and baby foods and toys regained their importance as these boomers began raising families. Housing demand gradually moved from rental to ownership, mini-van sales leaped and gardening began to appear as an important leisure activity.

Where are the volume markets of the 1990s? Because of the shape and distribution of the baby-boom generation, the Canadian population profile provides a unique opportunity to examine the volume markets a decade before. The twenty-year boom period has a skewed distribution with a peak (or mode) well to the left of centre; that is, the baby boom peaked 15 years after it began, and ended five years following the peak. The first decade of boomers, therefore, provides a leading signal for where the larger, second decade of boomers will be a decade later.

Figure 4 outlines the decadal growth rates by age over the period 1971–2011. The most rapidly growing market in Canada in the 1960s was youths (15 to 24 years). By the 1970s (1971–81), they had become young

FIGURE 4
Canadian Population Growth by Age
1961 to 2001

Age Group (years)	*Population Growth (per cent)* 1961–1971	1971–1981	1981–1991	1991–2001*
0 to 14	3.1	–14.1	3.1	–0.7
15 to 24	53.0	16.4	–17.8	1.8
25 to 34	16.5	45.9	13.2	–11.6
35 to 44	5.7	17.5	44.9	13.9
45 to 54	22.0	9.0	17.1	45.1
55 to 64	34.3	24.7	9.8	21.0
65 to 74	21.2	37.1	26.5	14.9
75 and over	32.9	32.4	43.9	42.9
Total	18.3	12.9	10.9	10.2

*Projected growth.
Source: Figure 3 and Statistics Canaada, *Population Projections for Canada, Provinces and Territories 1989–2011* (Ottawa: Statistics Canada, 1990), projection No. 3.

adults (25 to 34 years); over the 1980s (1981–91), they matured into 35 to 44 year olds. Not surprisingly, in the 1990s the most rapidly **growing** marketplace will be populated by customers aged 45 to 54 years, while the biggest **volume** marketplace will be the second-half boomers, who are ten years younger. In the first decade of the new millennium, the most rapidly growing marketplace will be customers in their early-retirement ages (55 to 64 years), with the biggest volume marketplace, once again, ten years younger. It does not require a crystal ball to develop this vision of the future marketplace, since every year people **will** get one year older (although an increasingly number will be confronted by the unattractive alternative).

Given this information, it should not be surprising that the rental housing market boomed in the late 1970s, since it is dominated by 25- to 34-year-olds, or that the owner-occupied housing market boomed in the late 1980s, since in Canada, the age of the first-time house buyer tends to be in the early- to mid-thirties. What is next? The 1990s and beyond, could see a **growth** of demand in cottage country, as some of the boomers seek recreation properties. The remainder will probably be renovating the city and suburban homes to accommodate their predominantly teenage families. However, in the rental market, vacancy rates are likely to continue to rise and with the consequent softening in rents, apartments will no longer provide a good investment. The rental housing market will probably continue to decline in the 1990s, because the smaller cohorts of the baby busters will be leaving home to seek their own rental units. This downward trend, however, will likely end in the first decade of the next century as the baby-boom echo generation starts leaving home to move into their first apartments.

Given the unique Canadian demographic profile, the example of the housing market illustrates the way that a combination of life-cycle and demographic information can be used to identify growth, mature and declining markets in the Canadian marketplace. Moreover, this is likely to provide a very solid foundation, since the aging trend is both well established and inevitable. Yet it is only a foundation. Other factors, such as economic cycles and changing consumer preferences, must also be monitored and included in a complete analysis. To focus on these factors to the exclusion of demographic trends, is to build long-term analysis of the external environment on a cracked foundation. In general, these other factors either determine the variations around the demographic life-cycle, or modify it slightly. They seldom reverse a trend established by the combination of life-cycle and demographic information. For example, a declining standard of living experienced in the 1990s might mean that consumers are not able to afford a recreation property. Such economic conditions would modify the housing trends mentioned above, but they are unlikely to reverse them.

Figure 4 also contains additional useful information. The baby-boom echo generation is projected to be largely a phenomenon of the 1980s and early 1990s. Births will decline over the mid- to late-1990s, resulting in less growth in the young people's market by the end of the 1990s and, especially, in the first decade of the next century. The declining youth market of the 1980s is anticipated to be a slow growth market in the 1990s as the echo generation reaches its youth. Products and services oriented to young adults (25 to 34 years), (such as rental housing, sports and life insurance), are likely to be declining markets in the 1990s. This youth market growth is projected to continue into the first decade of the next century as a result of above-average immigration levels. The declining group at that time will be the 35- to 44-year-old market.

Perhaps even more surprising in an aging population, the growth of the seniors market will slow down in the 1990s, especially the "young seniors" market (aged 65 to 74 years). Why? Because those entering this market in the 1990s were mostly born during the Depression of the 1930s and there are very few of them. However, although the young seniors market is slower-growing in the 1990s, it is a relatively affluent market. Not only are young seniors at a point in their lives when their net worth is the highest, they are also likely to be the richest group in Canada as a result of having relatively little competition from within their age group. On average, having four children increased the value of many of their investments (e.g., bigger houses, stocks, etc.). They provide a low-volume, high-margin, niche market. One cannot help but question the appropriateness, from society's standpoint, of continuing senior-citizen discounts in the 1990s for this new group of relatively affluent young seniors.

Note, however, that the growth of the "senior seniors" market (75 years and over) continues unabated into the 1990s and beyond. It is growing at over three times the rate of the young seniors market, and is second only to the boomers in growth, as it was in the 1980s. This helps to explain the rapid growth in pharmaceutical products aimed at this group, and increasing concerns over the viability of health care plans, both public and private.

Appropriate health care and housing for senior citizens will be a rapid-growth market in the 1990s. Out-of-hospital delivery of health care to nursing homes, or other, more innovative housing options, is likely to be in increased demand. But while this may be a high-growth market, it is not necessarily one in which high margins can predominate. Many of the senior seniors are quite poor. For one thing, much of this activity is being offered through the public sector in Canada, which often limits the size of margins. For another, many of these seniors are women (since their life expectancy is seven years longer than for men), many of whom did not have their own careers or who were married to men whose pensions, if they had them, were not automatically transferrable. Consequently, the slower-growing seniors' market of the 1990s is likely to bifurcate into a much more slowly growing "rich young seniors'" and a rapidly-growing, dominantly-female "poor senior seniors'" market. Private and public policies for seniors in general, should be adjusted to reflect this changing seniors' marketplace.

This section has barely scratched the surface of the potential contribution of demographics to marketing priorities and policies. It has outlined how the use of life-cycle information, for which age is the suitable proxy, can be combined with population projections, developed on the basis of historical trends, to provide a vision of the emerging marketplace of the 1990s and beyond, in Canada. Growth, mature and declining markets are all part of the future marketing landscape, and each in its own way offers marketing opportunities and challenges for all organizations.

PEOPLE AS EMPLOYEES: THE HUMAN RESOURCE IMPLICATIONS

Another area in any organization directly affected by demographic trends is personnel. The traditional approach to personnel management focuses on recruitment, selection and training. Recently, corporate downsizing has made out-placement increasingly important. Just as environmental factors influence an organization's structure, conduct and performance, they also influence these human resource functions.[4] So, not surprisingly, if demographics is one of the most important environmental factors, it influences not only human resource planning, but also an organization's structure and conduct.

This section investigates the impacts of changing demographics not only on personnel policies, but also on the structure and conduct — or culture — of organizations. This analysis involves a combination of personnel management with organization behaviour, viewed through the eyes of a demographer. This is because organizational behaviour and personnel management are uniquely intertwined and both are being driven into new directions by changing demographics. From this point of view, personnel management is no longer purely individually based, but becomes an essential part of the strategic planning of any organization. Hence, it can be more accurately referred to as human resource management — a description that will be used throughout the remainder of this section.

With the first baby boomers entering the Canadian labour market in the 1960s and the bulk of them entering in the 1970s, labour force growth in Canada exceeded that of all other developed Western countries, and youth employment soared to record levels by the early 1980s. Over the course of that decade, as the first boomers entered their forties, and the bulk of them entered their thirties, there appeared to be an abundance of qualified candidates for middle-level positions in most organizations. Moreover, a shortage of entry-level workers emerged, and youth unemployment rates declined noticeably as the smaller generation of the busters entered the labour market. Consequently, labour-force growth dropped to one-half the previous rates over the 1980s. Organizations that maintained traditional hierarchical structures were faced simultaneously with a surplus of qualified candidates for middle-level positions and an emerging shortage of candidates for starting-level positions. The traditional functions of personnel management were thrown into increasing chaos as these labour market characteristics emerged in the 1980s. It became increasingly clear that problems initially dismissed as being attributable to "unrealistic expectations" of employees, had in fact a much more fundamental basis for their expression.

Keyfitz was the first to anticipate the problem. In 1973 he noted the direct relationship between population growth and promotional prospects, and concluded that decreased population growth associated with declining fertility, must inevitably lead to delayed promotion in organizational hierarchies.[5] Ten years later, Cantrell and Clark applied the analysis to the Canadian labour force.[6] The overwhelming conclusion from this research is that, to the extent that age matters in promotion, the baby-boom generation suffers a disadvantage as a result of its large size.

The impacts of these demographic trends on human resource management in specific organizations has also been recognized. Morgan documents the problem of blocked career paths in the federal public service in Canada.[7] Bardwick refers to these promotional blockages as "the plateauing trap". She emphasizes the impersonality of environmental factors, especially demographics, and the consequent frustration for the individual employee — often compounded by the employer's failure to fully realize, and honestly address, an employee's long-term prospects. Declining morale, increased psychological stress, absenteeism and decreased productivity are all likely outcomes of this phenomenon.[8]

Implicit in these analyses are the dual assumptions of linear career paths and pyramidal organizational hierarchies. Driver argues that these two concepts are linked.[9] The linear career path, which has been the most prevalent one for most employees, is characterized by continued mobility up the hierarchy towards the top of the organization. Achievement and power are the motives, promotion and recognition the rewards. In this world, promotional blockages are very threatening. These career paths are best fostered in tall pyramidal organizational structures with many occupational or employment levels. The culture in such organizations focuses on salary and bonuses, evaluation of performance potential and training for the next level.

Driver suggests that those born in the small generation of the 1930s experienced high demand and mobility as a result of their small numbers and the post-war economic recovery and, hence, have developed a strong commitment to the linear path. This then provided the role model for the career expectations of the boomers. Since those born in the 1930s are currently dominating the top levels of organizations, it is not surprising that the most common organizational structure in the post-war period in North America became the tall pyramid.[10]

Increasingly, the baby boomers found the linear career focus to be at odds with reality, as they experienced promotional blockages. Bardwick noted that while plateauing was inevitable for most employees, it was occurring sooner for the boomers due to their large numbers and to organizational restructuring that eliminated middle-management positions.[11] Driver contended that a "linear career crisis" had emerged as the boomers' expectations clashed with reality.[12]

This problem can be readily envisaged by noting that the baby-boom generation has almost a rectangular shape in the population profile and that, as it aged in the labour force over the 1980s, managers in hierarchical organizations were faced with attempting to promote a rectangle up in the organizational triangle — an impossible task. Boomers were working ever-longer hours in an attempt to distinguish themselves as worthy of the limited number of available promotions. This is why the average work week lengthened during the 1980s, and the increased leisure time promised in the 1970s did not materialize.

Moreover, population aging resulted in increasing scarcity of candidates for entry-level positions as the baby-bust generation entered the labour market in the 1980s. Consequently, two types of mismatches between the triangular organizational hierarchy and the barrel-shaped labour force in Canada simultaneously emerged in the 1980s — too few younger employees and too many middle-level employees. Foot and Venne have estimated that the closest fit between the labour force and a representative organizational hierarchy occurred over the late 1970s and that, over the course of the 1980s, a mismatching problem emerged that reversed the trend of the previous two decades when the baby boomers entered the labour force. Moreover, from a demographical perspective, this trend of increasing mismatching can be expected to continue into the future unless corrective action is taken.[13]

Corrective action can be located both within individual organizations and within society at large. An economic environment that encourages appropriate organizational change will likely impose less pressure on individuals and society to take the necessary corrective actions, than an economic environment that impedes organizational change. Consequently, in the booming 1980s, corrective action was gradually taking place in many forward-looking organizations. However, the recession-prone 1990s have impeded this initial progress, and more of the adjustment appears to have fallen on individuals, and, increasingly, on societal mores, laws and policies. The underlying trends are still the same — their manifestation takes different forms in different settings. The concern of this paper is with organizational change, but the section concludes with a few observations on complementary corrective actions outside the individual organization.

FIGURE 5
Career Paths and Associated Characteristics

Career Path	*Direction of Job Movement*	*Number of Occupations*	*Organizational Structure*	*Reward Systems*
Steady State	None	One	Rectangule	Tenure, Fringe Benefits
Linear	Upward	Two	Tall Pyramid	Promotion, Power
Spiral	Lateral/ Upward	Five (?)	Flat Pyramid	Re-education, Retraining
Transitory	Lateral	Many	Temporary Teams	Variety, Time Off

Source: D.K. Foot and R.A. Venne, "Population, Pyramids and Promotional Prospects," *Canadian Public Policy* 16:4, 387–98.

To understand what that corrective action for the individual organization might be, Foot and Venne employ Driver's idea that individual career-path and organizational-structure concepts are linked. Figure 5 summarizes these linkages. Four general career paths and their characteristics are identified and linked to four organizational structures and cultures. The following provides a brief summary of these linkages.

The first two career paths are the most familiar. The steady-state career represents a lifelong career path where an employee is committed to an occupation for life (for example, a minister of religion or a professor). Since there are many employees at the same level, the associated organizational structure is almost flat (that is, rectangular). The accompanying culture emphasizes tenure, seniority and fringe benefits. The linear career is perhaps the most pervasive in North America. Here, the employee seeks upward movement towards the top of a tall, increasingly narrow, pyramid structure with numerous salary levels. Changes in occupation are infrequent, the most common being from a line occupation (such as an engineer or accountant) to a managerial one. Promotions and accompanying salary increases and bonuses are the main measures of career success.

The next two career paths many be less familiar. The spiral career, which combines mainly lateral moves with a few vertical moves, is associated with a moderate number of changes in occupation over a lifetime. The supporting organizational structure is a flat pyramid with a few, broad salary levels. Here the emphasis is on occupational flexibility with liberal opportunities for lifelong re-education and retraining. Last, the transitory career is characterized by frequent occupational change and lateral mobility. The associated organizational structure consists of temporary teams, such as a management consulting team or a royal commission; the organizational culture revolves around variety and possible breaks between assignments.

While the steady-state and transitory career paths are likely to remain applicable to certain organizational environments, such as the church and management consulting respectively, population aging will intensify the movement from tall organizational structures and linear career paths, to flattened organizational structures and spiral career paths.

The Foot and Venne findings provide dramatic verification of Driver's contention that "organizations are geared to reinforce precisely the wrong career concept — the linear concept."[14] While it is likely that some organizations will continue to maintain structures and cultures that foster the linear career path, many linear-oriented organizations have adapted to this new reality by flattening their pyramidal organizational structures. One motivation for this may be the desire to reduce the importance of promotions, by reducing the number of hierarchical levels.[15] When there are fewer levels, less upward movement is possible, and much of the employee's attention is directed laterally rather than vertically. In other words, employees are encouraged to move from the linear career path towards the spiral career path. Technological change, retrenchment during recessions and increased global competition are other reasons often cited for corporate flattening and eliminating middle management. These all serve to intensify the process.

The emergence of the spiral career path in North America, where the pressures from the baby-boom generation are the most intense, encourage the view of education as a lifelong process and the emergence of the "generalist" employee. The multi-skilled employee with a solid training in basic skills and a variety of experiences who can be flexible and move laterally into new positions, is likely to be the most challenged and productive to her employer. Lateral swaps or exchanges are likely to become much more common. For example, three employees plateaued as directors of marketing, communications and human resources, might well be rotated to provide new challenges for each of them. Lateral moves can be a solution both to an individual employee's plateauing problem, and to the entire cohort of employees at that particular organizational level.

The "sensible" employer will recognize these employee contributions and reward the employee appropriately, even though no promotion to the next hierarchical level has taken place. In other words, employers who wish to keep their potentially plateaued employees challenged and productive will make sure that lateral as well as vertical moves are reflected in the financial rewards of the employees. With fewer levels in the hierarchy, each level will carry a much broader compensation range.

Both employers and employees will have to make other changes as well. Employers will likely have to provide more information and support services to assist employees in establishing career "paths" (as distinct from career "ladders") as they adapt to the new work environment. In addition, it will be increasingly necessary for employers to provide more training and education to help employees prepare for the occupational changes associated with lateral moves. For their part, employees will find it advantageous to encourage and use these services, rather than to resist their introduction. On the human resource planning side, far more attention will need to be paid to programs designed to encourage lateral movement. Information bases must be expanded to include data on employees' other skills and interests; policies to encourage the use of educational and training opportunities outside of the employee's current responsibilities will need to be developed; exchange programs must be designed so that employees are encouraged to seek out other employees and positions that may be of interest for lateral moves; and salary structures that position employees in the organization hierarchy may have to be abandoned, because an employee who has been rewarded for three lateral moves, may well have a slightly higher salary than the "boss" who may be in the higher-level position as a result of one vertical move.

Other changes within organizations are likely to be more subtle. Success in the workplace is likely to be redefined to include the variety of positions held, as well as their level in the organizational hierarchy. Reducing hierarchical levels may reduce formality, make leaders more accessible, improve communication and information flows, and lead to a more participatory style of management. Emphasis will need to be on the opportunities for increasingly independent and challenging work. Embracing challenge and mastering it will have to be rewarded. Extended study leaves or sabbaticals may become necessary to achieve these goals, as may employee access to improved health and recreation facilities.

This is only a representative, and by no means exhaustive, list of the changes that are required. The key item is the likely transformation of the workplace in North America over the 1990s and beyond, from tall hierarchies and linear career paths, to flatter hierarchies and spiral career paths. This transformation is likely to be accompanied by a much greater emphasis within organizations on human resource management issues, than has been the case in the past.

Finally, changes are also likely outside the individual organizations. Several public-policy issues dealing with the baby boom in the labour force will need to be addressed. For example, to facilitate the spiral career path it may be increasingly necessary for educational institutions, especially post-secondary ones, to offer timely and relevant courses. These will need to be scheduled at times that do not conflict with work (for example, on evenings or weekends) or redesigned into compact, modular courses that can be completed during short-term leave (such as three weeks). Teaching methods must be modified; older students often have different expectations and different learning skills than younger students. Not only do they have more life experiences to draw on, they are also more likely to place a higher value on their time — especially if the workload continues to pile up back at the office. In addition, since employers are likely to pay the fees for these students, educational institutions will be provided with an opportunity to broaden and increase their funding bases. The myriad possible effects on all educational policies deserve careful consideration and cannot be adequately explored here.

In the case study of the federal public sector, Morgan recommends early retirement as one measure to ease the career blockage problem.[16] Early retirement incentives and flexible retirement policies, such as easing employees into retirement by allowing them to become part-time mentors or consultants, are becoming more common. Bardwick refers to the latter as "transitional retirement" policies, and recommends that these part-time employees receive a proportional fraction of their salary and benefits.[17] Of course, the removal of mandatory retirement provisions and the introduction of various flexible retirement policies, such as has been introduced into the U.S. pension policy and the Canada/Quebec Pension Plan, could work in the opposite direction by allowing employees to remain longer in the senior levels of organizational hierarchies. However, Foot and Gibson note that this may be very appropriate in a slower growing workforce where, increasingly, the retraining of existing older workers is likely to provide one source of labour-force renewal.[18]

Changing demographics is inevitably driving these workplace changes, whether they are taking place within organizations or outside. If individual organizations cannot, or do not, adapt to the more flexible workplace, society will bear the brunt of this adaptation. In North America in the 1990s, many individuals have found it necessary to retrain on their own, either in traditional educational institutions or elsewhere. Impediments to lateral moves between organizations must be reduced, once again raising the need for universally portable pensions, or some other innovative solution to this problem. Lateral mobility between occupations can be increased by simultaneously holding more than one part-time position in different organizations, perhaps in quite different sectors of the economy. This requires rethinking the traditional "job" as a full-time commitment to one occupation, if not one organization, with all the flexible pension, taxation and social service contribution arrangements that this requires. Increasingly, workplace flexibility is the key issue emerging from these long-term trends, and people, whether as employees, employers or voters, will find it necessary to develop strategies and policies to facilitate these inevitable workplace trends.

CONCLUSIONS

Demographic trends, and population aging in particular, have been, perhaps, the most neglected environmental trends affecting all management in all organizations in Canada and elsewhere. People are both customers and employees, so demographic trends have important implications for both the marketing and human resource planning functions in any organization. The Canadian demographic profile is dominated by the massive baby-boom generation, born between 1947 and 1966. This generation has had an enormous impact on all organizations, as it has aged over the post-war period, and these impacts can be expected to continue into the 1990s and beyond. Marketing will be increasingly dominated by products and services offered to those between their thirties and their fifties, although other market segments, such as seniors, will also offer challenging opportunities. Demographic trends are also cementing the unique relationship between changing organizational structures and human resource planning policies. The simultaneous emergence of plateauing and recruiting problems (in a non-recessionary environment) lead to the flattening of organizational hierarchies, and the move from linear to spiral career paths. The age of the "generalist" is arriving and organizations must pay increasing attention (and money) to re-education and retraining, if they are to successfully adapt to the new organizational alignments. A strong emphasis on human resource planning, carefully integrated into other corporate functions, such as marketing, is needed to accommodate the inevitable aging of the Canadian labour force. Finally, it is important that public policies, such as education, retirement, pension and other workplace policies, be consistent with the changes taking place as a result of these predictable demographic developments.

Notes

1. J. Naisbitt and P. Auburden, *Megatrends 2000* (New York: Avon Books, 1990); F. Popcorn, *The Popcorn Report* (New York: Doubleday, 1991).
2. D.R. Lehmann and R.S. Winer, *Analysis for Marketing Planning* (Plano: Business Publications Inc., 1988).
3. D.J. Luck and O.C. Ferrell, *Marketing Strategy and Plans*, second edition (Englewood Cliffs, N.J.: Prentice-Hall Inc., 1985).
4. W.L. French, *Human Resources Management* (Boston: Houghton Mifflin Co., 1986).
5. N. Keyfitz, "Individual Mobility in a Stationary Population," *Population Studies*, 27: 2, 335–52.
6. R.S. Cantrell and R.L. Clark, "Individual Mobility, Population Growth and Labour Force Participation," *Demography*, 19: 2, 245–63; F. Denton and B. Spencer, *Age Structure and Rate of Promotion in the Canadian Working Population*, QSEP Research Report No. 210 (Hamilton: McMaster University Faculty of Social Services, 1987).
7. N. Morgan, *Implosion: An Analysis of the Growth of Federal Public Service in Canada (1945–1985)* (Ottawa: Institute for Research on Public Policy, 1985).
8. J. Bardwick, *The Plateauing Trap* (New York: Amacom, 1986).

9. M.J. Driver, "Demographic and Societal Factors Affecting the Linear Career Crisis," *Canadian Journal of Administrative Studies*, 2: 2, 245–63.
10. Ibid.
11. Bardwick, *The Plateauing Trap.*
12. Driver, "Linear Career Crisis."
13. D.K. Foot and R.A. Venne, "Population, Pyramids and Promotional Prospects," *Canadian Public Policy*, 16: 4, 397–98.
14. Ibid.; Driver, "Linear Career Crisis."
15. Bardwick, *The Plateauing Trap.*
16. Morgan, *Implosion.*
17. Bardwick, *The Plateauing Trap.*
18. D.K. Foot and K.J. Gibson, "Population Aging in the Canadian Labour Force: Changes and Challenges," *Journal of Canadian Studies*, 28: 1, 59–74.

QUESTIONS FOR DISCUSSION

1. Are demographics predictable in Canada? What types of decisions are really influenced by such a slow changing phenomenon?
2. What features of the Population Pyramid presented in Figure 1 are of greatest significance to industrial policy-makers?
3. Who are the members of the baby boom echo generation? When will this era end? Is this a significant event?
4. If demographics are so predictable, why are there so many demographics-related mistakes such as building facilities like public schools, prisons, and religious meeting places which now have become unnecessary and unused?
5. Is demographic analyses most relevant to volume or growth-oriented marketing? How does a life style approach to marketing based on demographic data differ from other approaches?
6. What is the largest consumer market segment in Canada today? How will it change over the next decade? What does the author see as the growth markets of the 1990s? What are some of the implications of an aging population? How reliable are these predictions?
7. How do the demographic trends cited in this paper influence the personnel policies, structures and cultures of future organizations?
8. What organizational career paths does the author see as most likely to emerge?
9. What do demographic trends say about the work period in which you expect to be employed? What, if anything, could change these predictions?

Professor David Foot's current research interests lie in the numerous interrelationships between economics and demographics, and in the implications for both private and public policy, especially in the Canadian context. Following his undergraduate degree in Australia and his doctorate in economics from Harvard University, Professor Foot's research involved projections and analysis of the Canadian and Ontario economies, mainly under the auspices of the University of Toronto's Institute for Policy Analysis. Subsequently, Professor Foot focussed on Canada's declining population growth and associated population aging as one of the fundamental and often neglected determinants of the challenges to economic performance and policy. His research has resulted in findings that have often been neglected in the discipline or that challenge widely held, but usually untested, views regarding the economic impacts of demographic changes. In addition, his research has resulted in contributions to a variety of specific policy areas, such as education, youth unemployment, housing, recreation and leisure, promotion and retirement, savings, labour force growth, immigration, interprovincial migration, government expenditures and intergovernmental relations. A number of these themes are contained in his 1982 book, ***Canada's Population Outlook: Demographic Futures and Economic Challenges*** *and in his latest book (co-authored with Blossom T. Wigdor),* ***The Over Forty Society*** *(1988).*

The Socio-Political Environment: Discord and Fragmentation

JOHN SAYWELL

Once described as "the peaceable kingdom," Canada today is a bewildered society, a nation seemingly blind to the reality that has seized it. Individual and group rights overwhelm any sense of community; the state is torn by the divisiveness of history and geography; the economy is less and less able to bear the burden placed upon it. There is no longer any distinction between what is economic and social, market-based and non-market-based, private and public, federal and provincial, national and international, perceived and real. Politicians seem unable to lead and find nothing to follow. Canada has never been an easy country to govern, but success seldom has seemed so distant. The intelligentsia would call the situation "post-modern": we might say with less pretentiousness that everything is interactive, interdependent, volatile and unpredictable. That is the environment in which would-be planners — government, social, economic or corporate — must operate.

Whenever the sad state of the Canadian economy is on the agenda, the discussion seems to turn to Japan. Japan is the nation that got it right — the nation that achieved, indeed far surpassed, its objective of global competitiveness with a combination of state and private sector planning and co-operation, labour-management collaboration, corporate concern for the long, rather than the short term, the primacy of collective over individual interests (or the assumption that they were the same) and the primacy of those same collective goals over any external interests. The process has not been easy — or nice — or governed by the canons of post-mercantilism economics.

Some of the mechanics of the Japanese system can be imported, but reproducing it is an impossible task, because Canada's sociopolitical culture and its economy, are profoundly different. Japan is an essentially homogeneous society based on consensus in matters of public policy and social organization. The collective — national, corporate or familial — takes precedence over the individual, and responsibilities are more important than rights. Canada is a heterogeneous society, where consensus is elusive, and rights and entitlements are placed above responsibilities. The Japanese like co-operation and collaboration, even in settling legal disputes. Canadians are far more adversarial, and prefer litigation to accommodation. When Canadian auto workers reject proposals to increase the competitiveness of their plant (which would allow them to keep their jobs and their homes), or a walkout by twenty clerks brings all shipping in Vancouver to a halt for weeks, the Japanese view the occurrence as another demonstration of the bizarre nature of Canadian society.

The problem with Canada, Japanese people have told me, is that we have had it too good. With our vast space and abundant natural resources, our economic and cultural integration with the Western world, and our ready access to flows of labour, capital and technology, we have had life handed to us on a platter. We could be self-indulgent — and we have been, at least until relatively recently when the foundations of our economy began to crumble and our tenuous political and social consensus began to unravel.

It is — has always been — difficult to make Canada work as a country. It has too much geography and a history that has done as much to divide us as to unite us. The process of governing this country of diverse regions and peoples has been one of accommodating the diversity — of seeking strategies, policies and programs that can achieve unity, however precarious, across the broad face of the land. The objective of the state has not been efficiency or rationality in the use of our physical and human resources, but the resolution of conflicts among regions or provinces, religions, languages and cultures, occupations and social classes and, recently, between genders.

THE POLITICIZED ECONOMY

In the ideal (and unreal) world of the classical economist, a national economic strategy with global competitiveness as its objective would be based on efficiency, rational (market-driven) allocation of resources, due diligence in state support of winners and, perhaps, reduction of pain for losers. But these principles have never been the determinants of Canadian economic policy. And the economy, as it evolved, became hostage to too many fortunes to be easily transformed — or even marginally modified — by economists or other advocates of a market-driven economy. Not until the 1980s did a combination of globalization, the GATT, the Free Trade Agreement (FTA) and the ascendancy of privatization, force a radical transformation of the Canadian economy. That transformation, however, is not being carried out as part of a national industrial strategy, but in response to the dictates of a global economy dominated by powerful trading blocks. Both the public and private sectors in Canada are reactive, not proactive. The role of government is not planning but damage control, and caring for the dead and the wounded with soaring unemployment insurance benefits and welfare payments.

Canadian nationalism was not the dynamic behind the creation of the state in 1867, but nation-making was the objective of the pragmatists who brought it into existence. Their goal was to create a political structure within which a national economy could develop, a structure strong enough to ensure the economic and political survival of the northern half of North America. Success demanded, so it seemed, an interventionist central government to offset the apparently predictable dictates of geography and the market. An open-door immigration and capital investment policy, more or less free land in the West for staple production, tariff protection to force import substitution, and a state-nourished integrated railway system, were the components of the National Policy implemented in the decades after Confederation. The benefits were to be extensive growth in the GNP, economic integration, and political survival; the costs, modern economists remind us, were economic inefficiency and a lower GNI per capita.

However hesitant its beginnings, by the 1920s the policy had achieved its objectives: the railways were built (and overbuilt); the West was oversettled; staple exports from the farms, the forests and the mines had mushroomed; and secondary manufacturing, much of it in American branch plants and services, had grown in Central Canada to serve a protected domestic market. But success created its own dialectic. Farmers' grievances against the perceived unequal incidence of the National Policy, burst forth in a political revolt in 1921. Maritimers, left behind in the heady economic expansion, spoke sullenly of secession. The rise of new staples — mining and forestry — strengthened the economies of Ontario, Quebec and British Columbia, while the north-south flow of these new staples weakened the older east-west and trans-Atlantic axis. The power of the provinces, enlarged by judicial review, was further enhanced since many major new state functions that emerged, such as economic regulation, education, social services, highways and urbanization, fell within provincial jurisdiction.

The precarious equilibrium thus created, broke down with the depression of the 1930s. By the end of the 1920s all levels of government carried a heavy debt burden. The booming '20s had been accompanied by enormous surplus capacity in such industries as automobiles and pulp and paper. A precipitous decline in exports, a drop in commodity prices — often to levels below the cost of production — and prairie drought shattered the economy. By 1933 the unemployment rate was 26 per cent and 1.5-million people — one person in four in the cities — lived on relief. When the drought hit Saskatchewan, two-thirds of the population was dependent on government relief. Not only had the economy collapsed, so had the capacity of governments.

Even if they had had the will or the knowledge to act, Canada's governments could not have done so; they were paralyzed by the federal system. Responsibility for social distress lay with local and provincial governments. Many cities went bankrupt and could not even pay the interest on their debts. Before the worst was over, the Prairie provinces were in default and British Columbia had teetered on the brink. Direct taxes were levied both federally and provincially, but the worst-hit provinces were the least able to raise revenues.

Although a central bank was established, it was not given a mandate to use monetary policy to combat the depression. The courts had effectively denied Ottawa control over economic regulation, industrial relations and all trade but international trade; in 1937 federal legislation concerning unemployment insurance, marketing and wages and hours of work, was ruled unconstitutional.

Faced with this complex crisis, Mackenzie King appointed a royal commission (Rowell-Sirois) to examine the interlocking economic and constitutional problems.[1] The report recommended a restructuring of revenues and responsibilities within the federation. Although the recommendations — such as total federal control over unemployment and the direct tax field — were not accepted, they were the beginning of what has been described as the second National Policy. Slowly implemented after the Second World War, this "New National Policy" — part political, part social and part economic — did much to reconstruct the Canadian state. It also initiated debates over public policy that are still with us today.

Put hopelessly simply, the "New National Policy" called for Canada to remain a capitalist federal state where the role of government was to encourage factor flows — investment, labour and technology — but to intervene to stabilize the economy, offset sharp differentials in regional income and protect Canadians against economic and social misfortune. Keynesian stabilization of fiscal and investment policy, equalization payments and regional development programs and a complex social security and welfare system all involved fundamental changes in the Canadian state system and the relationship between the state and the individual.

They also increased the burden the economy was to bear: in 1950, even with the heavy war debt, governments reaped only 20 per cent of the GNP; a generation later they took close to 50 per cent. Economics and politics became even more inseparable.

There had always been tension and conflict between Ottawa and the provinces as each pursued its perceived self-interest, dictated sometimes by conflicting economic interests, and at others by partisan political interests. But implementing of the "New National Policy" brought the two levels of government into constant jurisdictional conflict over access to fields of taxation and legislative and administrative power. No longer was there a clear distinction in fact between the two levels of government. The buzz-words of the new era were stabilization, equalization, regional development and shared cost programs. Political scientists and politicians spoke of "co-operative federalism," but the reality more often resembled a battlefield.

When Ottawa adopted Lord Keynes as its own in 1945 and explicitly committed the federal government to counter-cyclical fiscal and investment policies to maintain a high and stable level of employment and income, the scenario was predictable.[2] A successful counter-cyclical fiscal policy demanded a centralized and rationalized direct tax system in a state where both levels of government had constitutional access to all direct taxes, including all personal and corporate income taxes.

Ottawa had taken over the taxes during the war, and in 1945 proposed to "rent" them permanently in the interests of rationalization, efficiency, equity and stabilization. Quebec refused the offer outright; Ontario was reluctant to part with corporation taxes; and all the provinces demanded an ever-larger share of the tax proceeds. As a result, federal-provincial fiscal relations underwent a bewildering series of agreements — tax rentals, tax sharing, tax abatements and finally, tax collection. This ad hoc process led to the many different tax systems we have today. For all provinces, except Quebec, Ottawa collects the personal income tax at a standard rate, but each province adds its own tax, in addition to that which it receives back from Ottawa. Quebec, Ontario and Alberta, which together account for 75 per cent of corporate income, all levy their own corporate income taxes. By 1992 there was talk of ending tax collection and letting each province go its own way. Thus ended the bold hope of the war years for a single, sensible, national tax system.

Keynesianism may have been dead, but the arguments for a rational tax system were not. Separate tax systems only reinforce the sharp differences in regional development and income. There are few industrialized countries where regional diversity is so great, and the unifying and equalizing forces so weak. The 1940 Rowell-Sirois Commission recommended that, in return for surrender of the direct tax field by the provinces, Ottawa should provide national adjustment grants that would enable every province to provide an average level of services with an average level of taxation.

The arguments in favour of this system were threefold: that direct taxes were not levied where the income was earned; that a cost-benefit analysis of Canada's economic policy showed it to favour Central Canada (although true quantification was impossible, there was undeniably some truth in this assertion); and that greater equality in the standard of living was essential to a common citizenship.

Despite these arguments, the principle of equalization payments was not implemented until 1957, under Louis St. Laurent. Although the formula has changed repeatedly since then, the policy has remained a part of Canada's federal structure, and the principle was entrenched in Section 36 the 1982 Constitution:

> Parliament and the Government of Canada are committed to the principle of making equalization payments to ensure that provincial governments have sufficient revenues to provide reasonably comparable levels of public services at reasonably comparable levels of taxation.

In 1987–88 Ottawa transferred six billion dollars in equalization payments to the poorer provinces, with Ontario, Alberta and British Columbia paying the bill.

Described as "the glue that holds Confederation together," or the lubricant of the federal system, economists would argue that on the grounds of economic efficiency, equalization is a dubious, if not a downright insane, policy. By providing an artificially high standard of living (for example, in PEI, where the province's revenue was 55 per cent of the national average before equalization, and 83 per cent after), the payments inhibit outward migration and other factor flows from the poorer regions, and divert revenue from the richer areas into less productive uses.

The same argument has been made about the vast array of regional development programs financed by the Central government in an attempt to remove the cause of regional disparities. The government had always attempted to subsidize projects or sectors through bonuses, freight rates, tax benefits and other measures, but it was only when John Diefenbaker arrived on the scene in 1957, that the war on regional disparities really began.

Over the past 30 years there has been a bewildering variety of programs (represented by a dazzling array of acronyms: ADA, ARDA, FRED, RDIA and many more) reflecting various approaches and objectives. While these programs were all based on some form of economic analysis, there has always been little doubt that their implementation had a very strong political motivation. Critics were quick to observe that as the threat of separatism grew in Quebec, so did the amount of regional development assistance. By 1982 the entire province was eligible for grants and the province was spending 40 per cent of the total.

Yet the billions of dollars spent to combat regional disparity in almost all areas but southern Ontario, British Columbia and Alberta, has not lessened regional disparities, although it may have prevented them from becoming worse. And economists argue that the cost of thus artificially distorting resource allocation is great. It delays adjustment and, because it reduces national economic efficiency, could in fact lead to greater disparities in the long run. But attempted equalization has become a sacred trust, and half the MPs in Ottawa would sound the alarm bells if that trust was betrayed.

THE POLITICS OF THE PROTECTED SOCIETY

"At the most general level, capitalist economies and democratic politics are rendered compatible by the welfare role of the state," declared the Royal Commission on the Economic Union and Development Prospects for Canada in 1985. It continued:

> There are debates at the margin. The particulars of how the state-welfare role should be handled in the interests of values pertaining to economic efficiency, to human dignity, and to evolving conceptions of equity, including the relationship among risk, innovation and reward, are always controversial.... [However] without the stabilizing integrating contribution of the welfare state, support for the relative autonomy of capitalist markets would crumble.[3]

The origins of the present-day welfare state — or the "protected society" as Tom Courchene more appropriately described it — can also be traced back to the depression and Second World War. The provinces (and their agents, the municipalities), within whose jurisdiction social policy fell, had already created a primitive, ad hoc security net: workmen's compensation; allowances for single mothers, the blind and other disadvantaged citizens; and assistance for the unemployed and unemployable. In 1927 the federal government agreed to help finance provincially-administered old age pensions.

The depression revealed the hopeless inadequacy of this security net. Ottawa's attempts to introduce unemployment insurance and national labour regulations were ruled unconstitutional by the courts. In the later 1930s and during the war, professionally trained bureaucrats in the federal civil service, supported by liberal-minded politicians, began to develop plans for a comprehensive social security system for the new and better post-war world. Threatened by the surging popularity of socialism, Mackenzie King was persuaded to move cautiously to the left as the war neared its end. The 1944 Speech from the Throne bluntly stated that the

> objective of our domestic policy is social security and human welfare.... plans for the establishment of a national minimum of social security and human welfare should be advanced as rapidly as possible. Such a national minimum contemplates useful employment for all who are willing to work; standards of nutrition and housing adequate to ensure the health of the whole population; and social insurance against privation resulting from unemployment, from accident, from the death of the breadwinner, from ill-health and from old age.

In the same session, Ottawa introduced family allowances as both an income security measure and a Keynesian stimulus to post-war consumer demand.

With the war over, the federal government put its "New National Policy" proposals before the provinces. It had no choice, because most of its proposals fell within provincial legislative jurisdiction. Unemployment insurance had been placed under Ottawa's control by a constitutional amendment in 1940; given that Ottawa has the power to make direct payments to individuals, family allowances did not require provincial legislation for their implementation. But the bulk of social security and welfare programs, including old age pensions, health insurance and welfare programs, fell within provincial jurisdiction.

Social security and welfare programs financed by the state are always controversial since they create a division between left and right. In Canada, they also created a division between Ottawa and the provinces — sometimes a few provinces and sometimes many, often rich provinces like Ontario, and always Quebec, which consistently opposed any federal encroachment on its legislative or financial jurisdiction.

Gradually, however, through seemingly endless negotiations, conflict and compromise, the elements of the "New National Policy" were put in place between 1945 and 1968. In 1951, constitutional amendments permitted Ottawa to finance old age pensions out of taxation and, in 1964, to establish contributory old age pensions (CPP — Quebec established its own). But the other elements were achieved with the use of shared cost programs: hospital insurance (1957); welfare assistance (the Canada Assistance Plan, 1966), which incorporated existing and new assistance programs for the blind, the disabled, the unemployed without benefits, as well as child welfare and mothers' allowances; and medicare (1968). Ottawa offered to pay roughly half the cost of these programs if the provinces agreed to implement a scheme that met Ottawa's conditions. In the case of medicare, for example, the conditions were that the plan be comprehensive in scope, universal in coverage, accessible, portable and publicly administered. Since 1951, the federal government had also been assisting universities financially, and in 1966, it agreed to pay the provinces half the operating costs of universities without conditions.

Although there were warnings that the country was embarking on an income security system it might not be able to sustain, everything seemed possible in the heady decade of the 1960s. Not only were the above programs implemented, but the unemployment insurance scheme was so expanded as to become almost a guaranteed annual income; tax credits and deductions for old and young added to the cost through revenue forgone; in the public sector, where compensation was ultimately limited only by the ability of governments to tax, workers secured the right to bargain collectively and strike.

By the 1970s the illusions had gone. Faced with spiralling costs it could not control, the federal government put a lid on its spending, forcing the provinces either to control spending or pay a larger share. But costs continued to rise — health-care costs in particular, which became the largest single item of public expenditure. By 1981 transfer payments to the unemployed, the elderly, families and the ill, amounted to 13 per cent of the GNP. With the population aging rapidly, the future looked bleak.

Attempts to change the system — to cap expenditures, introduce user fees, lower benefits — met with howls of protest from the affected regions, provinces, groups or individuals. What began as a measure of social justice had become an entitlement — to unlimited health care, to generous regionally beneficial unemployment benefits, however economically unsound and susceptible to inventive manipulation, and to welfare benefits that were continuously relaxed, and did little to address the root causes of unemployment and poverty.

As the pressure to control government spending grew, so did the demands that the welfare system be protected. By 1992, when the entire constitution was once again being debated and everything seemed up for grabs, a coalition of interest groups and NDP provincial premiers were demanding the insertion of a "social charter" into the 1982 Charter of Rights and Freedoms. The federal government's March 1992 proposals included a social covenant that would require governments to commit themselves to universal health care, adequate social services, high-quality education, collective bargaining rights and a clean environment. A special commission would police the covenant, but would have no legal power to enforce it. It was not clear whether the courts would enforce such a general covenant.

Who can dispute our right to a clean environment? No one would deny that global warming and the destruction of the ozone layer, the threat to the Brazilian rain forest, the dangers of nuclear fallout from disasters such as Chernobyl and water pollution in the Great Lakes endanger our lives. But the closer we come to home, the more complex and personal such issues become.

Only 27 per cent of Canadians believe that the forest industry is sufficiently important to justify any environmental damage. Yet pressure for more stringent environmental controls on the logging industry threatens the international competitiveness of an already beleaguered sector of the economy. Many Canadians applauded the international lobby that dramatically reduced the export of Canadian furs. But to the 85,000 Canadian trappers, half of them aboriginals, the ban was a disaster. Governments forced the pulp and paper industry to refurbish mills to use recycled paper. Not only was the recycling process economically inefficient, but since 90 per cent of Canadian newsprint is exported, companies found that they had to buy back hundreds of thousands of tonnes of used paper from the United States to supply their mills. Environmentalists and Cree Indians lobbied intensively in the United States against the Great Whale hydro-electric development in Quebec, a project that promised a massive transformation of the landscape and economy of the northern half of the province. When, partly in response to that pressure, the state of New York cancelled its agreement to purchase power, and Massachusetts banned the purchase of Hydro Quebec bonds, the Quebec government warned that thousands of jobs were at risk, and government revenues threatened. And when Ottawa passed a new environmental bill in the spring of 1992, Quebec and other provinces accused the federal government of being "totalitarian" and warned that the law jeopardized the delicate negotiations for a new constitutional agreement.

The "clean environment" issue transcends both national and international territorial boundaries. Canadians have been unconscionably reckless in their exploitation and degradation of their natural resources, and the environmentalists' call to arms was long overdue. However, implementing environmental protection policies, whatever agreements there may be in principle, or over the long term, demands a delicate short-term balancing of competing interests and values. It is easier to "think globally" than to "act locally" if the cost may be the demise of a firm or the loss of a job.

The Canadian social security system has been hailed as one of the best in the world — certainly it was far superior to the American one. It was also becoming one of the most expensive, and was certain to become more so as the population aged. While reform seemed essential, it also seemed close to impossible politically.

Even in the field of public education, where there was no jurisdictional conflict or co-operation, the picture was gloomy. Canada, it seemed, had one of the most expensive public education systems in the industrialized world — yet every international comparison suggested that the quality of Canadian students was very far from being the highest. Attempts at academic reform — higher standards, a more rigorous curriculum, etc. — again met with opposition from the educational bureaucracy. The asylum seemed securely immune to the needs of the inmates; one writer quipped, "the only way to get a high school education is to go to university." Yet the universities, too, seemed incapable of adjusting to a new era of austerity. Caught in the three-way traps of deficit-ridden governments, a mandate of accessibility and equality for all and the demands of unionized faculty and staff, they found that rhetoric about academic quality in the ivory tower, was being taken less and less seriously.

CANADA, QUEBEC AND THE CONSTITUTION

Since 1960, Canada has been convulsed by the question of constitutional reform. The problem has appeared in many forms, but the dynamic force behind the push for change has always been the the demand from Quebec for a radical decentralization of the Canadian federal state. What began as an apparently simple request for more money and more power was soon cast in the rhetoric of "special status," "associate statehood," "distinct society" or "sovereignty-association" — each term carrying with it certain (usually unspecified) alterations to the constitution. The concrete matters debated during the sixties included an amending formula, patriation of the constitution, a new division of revenues and responsibilities, language and cultural rights and reform of the institutions of the central government. By the 1970s the Western provinces had also become important participants in the debate as they attempted to increase their clout at the political centre, most notably by demanding an "elected, equal and effective" Senate. By the 1990s Canada's aboriginal people had also become key players in the game; their primary demand was for self-government, whatever form that might take. But in 1992, the main topic in the debate that put the country at risk and pre-occupied our governors was still the question of a new form of federalism or the independence of Quebec.

Historians, political scientists, sociologists and armchair experts have all attempted to explain "what happened with Quebec." None have had much success. For there **is** no simple explanation other than the glib statement that the obsession of the Québécois (as they now call themselves) and of their political and religious leaders since the conquest in 1759 has been "*la survivance*." Over the years this has meant a high birth rate ("*la revanche du berceau*"); political control of the territory of Quebec; the cementing of the French language, the Catholic religion and traditional rural, agrarian and familial values; and, after 1867, the protective shelter of a provincial government that controlled the social and cultural life of the Québecois and the institutions that enabled them to survive. But the twentieth-century forces of industrialization, urbanization and modernization weakened the cement within Quebec society, while the post-1945 expansion of the activities of the central government penetrated the walls of fortress Quebec.

The Quiet Revolution that began in 1960, was first and foremost a demand for modernization within Quebec. But it soon became a demand for a revolution in the relations between Quebec and the rest of Canada. The survival, that for two centuries had been a defensive obsession, now seemed to demand an offensive strategy. The state, which had for centuries been a somewhat passive participant in the struggle, replaced the church as an instrument to assure survival. This state was soon firmly in the hands of a new élite — of bureaucrats, academics, journalists, trade union leaders and upwardly mobile business leaders — that assumed all power within Quebec, and demanded either more power within the Canadian state system or, if that proved to be impossible, independence.

Canadians outside Quebec responded with a mixture of sympathy, bewilderment, opposition and anger. The demand for more money and power was a familiar refrain in federal-provincial relations. Few objected to allowing Quebec (and other provinces if they wished, though none did) to "opt out" of national social security and welfare systems, provided it continued to provide the same services. Few objected to Ottawa sharing Canadian tax dollars more liberally with Quebec — and other provinces — although it threatened stabilization as well as equalization policies. Most objected to Quebec's claims to warrant its own foreign relations with French-speaking countries, but accepted the compromise of allowing Quebec to be represented as part of the Canadian delegation at meetings of La Francophonie. But most anglophones condemned the language policy of the Quebec government, and rejected the very idea of Quebec being recognized as a "distinct society" if that meant it had a status legally superior to that of other provinces.

A funny thing happened on the way to the new 1982 constitution. The process had begun in 1968 largely as a response to nationalist pressures from Quebec for enlarged provincial powers. But under Pierre Trudeau, who had come to Ottawa in 1965 to fight nationalism in Quebec, and became Prime Minister three years later, the nature of the debate was slowly but surely transformed. Patriation of the 1867 constitution — a statute of the British Parliament — was made to appear as a symbol of our nationhood. The debate over power-sharing was soon eclipsed by the discussion of a Charter of (individual and collective) Rights and Freedoms. The provincial premiers in Quebec and elsewhere, Trudeau argued, wanted to increase "their" power, while he was determined to increase the power of "the people."

The irony was that the conclusion of the twenty-year debate over the demands of Quebec for a new constitution, was the emergence of a new constitution in 1982 that restricted, rather than expanded, Quebec's powers — this, despite Mr. Trudeau's promise of a "renewed federalism" when he appealed to the Québécois to vote *non* in the 1980 referendum on independence. There was no re-distribution of legislative powers; there was only a modest limitation of the federal government's power to offer the provinces new shared-cost programs in areas of provincial jurisdiction; and the new amending formula did not give Quebec a veto over constitutional change. In short, Quebec did not receive the special status it had demanded since 1960. In fact, the Charter of Rights and Freedoms restricted the power of Quebec, as it did that of every other government in Canada. The section on language entrenched official bilingualism at the centre and protected some anglophone educational rights in Quebec. The courts decided that the right to "freedom of expression" protected anglophones against some other sections of Bill 101, such as the prohibition against English in commercial advertising.

Recognizing these limits for what they were, the Parti Québécois government, led by René Lévesque refused to endorse the new constitution — and so began the long journey to Meech Lake and beyond.

THE POLITICS OF LANGUAGE

Language, perhaps the most inflammatory of the issues that have bedevilled Canada over the last generation, was a crucial element in the debate over constitutional reform. Unlike the distribution of powers which can seem arcane to the the uninitiated, language is not just an issue but a fundamental part of everyone's daily life. Language is part of our identity — we are, to a certain extent, what we speak. New Canadians urge their children to retain their language, for it is the key to retaining their cultural heritage. Conversely, language can be a barrier to complete assimilation by the host culture. The importance of language, as both a reality and a symbol, is readily understood by virtually anyone.

The critical importance of language to identity was best stated by Bernard Lee Whorf, the eminent linguist:

> And every language is a vast pattern system, different from others, in which are culturally ordained the forms and categories by which the personality not only communicates, but also analyzes nature, notices or neglects types of relationships and phenomena, channels his reasoning, and builds the house of his consciousness.[4]

René Lévesque, founder of the Parti Québécois, put it more bluntly:

> We are Québécois.... Being ourselves is essentially a matter of keeping and developing a personality that has survived for three-and-a half centuries. At the core of this personality is the fact that we speak French. Everything else depends on this one essential element and follows from it or leads infallibly back to it.[5]

Language has been a contentious issue throughout Canadian history; by the 1960s it was more contentious than ever — seemingly unsolvably so. The only language rights guaranteed in the 1867 constitution were the rights of Canadians to speak English or French in the Parliament and courts of Canada and Quebec. Where more extensive language rights were protected by law (as in Manitoba) or existed in practice (as in Ontario), they were soon eroded by the sheer size of the anglophone majority.

By the 1960s most of Canada outside Quebec was unilingually anglophone; francophones who left Quebec had discovered that they had to learn the language of their new hosts to assimilate. Inside Quebec, most francophones were unilingual and few anglophones could function in French. On the whole, social class and language in Quebec were closely related: French was the language of the factory floor and English of the boardroom. Upwardly mobile francophones had no choice but to become bilingual — and even then their chances of success seemed remote. In Ottawa, the language of work was basically English. It was a bad joke to note that French was the language of the elevator, and English of the executive offices.

To stem the tide of Quebec nationalism and separatism in the 1960s, Pierre Trudeau concluded that the federal government — in Ottawa and across the country — had to accommodate francophones as well as anglophones. If francophones could feel at home in the national capital and across the country, he reasoned, Quebeckers would be less interested in independence. The Official Languages Act of 1969 declared French and English to be the official languages of Canada "for all purposes of the Parliament and Government of Canada, and [to] possess and enjoy equality of status and equal rights as to their use in all the institutions of the Parliament and Government of Canada."

The civil service, at least in its upper echelons, was to be truly bilingual. Civil servants were packed off to language schools and bonused for their bilingual proficiency; a language commissioner tracked the success of bilingualism in the civil service, Crown corporations, and boards and agencies. Trudeau also embarked on a campaign to encourage the provinces to move towards bilingualism in their operations and to create or expand francophone schools.

Although it achieved limited success in Ottawa, Trudeau's policy aroused bitter opposition among anglophones who, not understanding the policy and believing that they had to become bilingual, protested that they would not have "French crammed down their throats." Meanwhile, this nationwide crusade for bilingualism did little — or nothing — to dampen the nationalist fires in Quebec. Indeed, if anything it fanned the flames.

In 1976, anglophone pilots and air traffic controllers went on strike, refusing to accept French as the language of communication over Quebec. The support for the strikers from anglophone Canada was strong and included a measure of venom in its criticism of the bilingual policy. The federal government was forced to back down, but many Québécois went to the polls that November with buttons reading "Il ya du Français dans l'air" to cast their votes for the victorious Parti Québécois.

Language became even more important as other traditional elements of Québécois culture weakened. Quebec in the 1960s was becoming increasingly secular; the Church was losing its two-hundred-year-old hold on society. There was less and less room for traditional rural and agrarian and familial values in an increasingly urban society.

Moreover, as the birth rate dropped from one of the highest in the industrialized world to one of the lowest, and immigrants to Quebec usually assimilated to English rather than French, demographic projections pointed to a declining francophone population in Quebec — to the point where it was conceivable that, in some distant future, the majority of Montrealers might be anglophones.

In the face of all this, members of the francophone élite that had gained power in 1960, whatever their political affiliations, were determined to be "*maîtres chez nous*." Their primary weapon was to be language: French would be the language of the province of Quebec at all levels, right up to, and including, the corporate board rooms.

Introduced in stages, the largely unilingual language policy reached its fullest — to some, its most draconian form — in 1977 when the Parti Québécois introduced Bill 101. French became **the** official language: the government would operate in French; business and the professions would operate in French (Eaton's had to drop its apostrophe to provide a *visage française*!); all advertising would be in French; immigrant children would be educated in French — only the children of Quebec anglophones were to be excepted from the French-only education policy.

Bill 101 aroused intense opposition in anglophone Canada. The Supreme Court of Canada ruled that the provisions making French the only official language of government were unconstitutional because they violated the guarantees of the 1867 Constitution. In 1988, the court further ruled that the French-only sign law violated the freedom-of-expression clause in the Charter of Rights. When Quebec used the Charter's "notwithstanding clause" to override the court decision, anglophone protests reached a hysterical pitch. Just as many Québécois had voted for the Péquistes over the language of the skies, many anglophones rejected the idea of a "distinct society" in the Meech Lake Accord after the crisis over the language of signs.

THE CHARTER OF RIGHTS AND FREEDOMS

The Charter of Rights and Freedoms in the 1982 Constitution is destined to be Pierre Trudeau's most lasting — perhaps his only lasting — legacy. For the first time, basic rights and freedoms were entrenched in the constitution; only with difficulty could they be overridden by any government. Before 1982, criminal law in Canada was whatever the federal government declared it to be, despite traditional assumptions about the right to counsel or the right to be presumed innocent until proven guilty. The Charter explicitly stated the rights and freedoms Canadian enjoy and endowed the courts with the power to police them. The only avenue by which the democratic process could prevail against the courts was the legal capacity of a government to invoke the "notwithstanding" clause in the Charter, openly declaring that a law was to operate **notwithstanding** the constitutional limitation.

The Charter was designed to provide a base for a common Canadianism, to serve as a unifying doctrine of rights. To some extent it has done so. But perhaps it has done more to divide us by introducing another element of conflict into Canadian society. As Alan Cairns put it, the Charter constitutionalized a profound social transformation:

> Various social transformations in the sixties and seventies that initially had no obvious connection to our constitutional agonies were pulled into the constitutional arena... by the Charter project. The essence of the social change of the period is catapulted by the powerful phrase "coming out," initially employed by the gay community. The ambit of the phrase can appropriately be extended to include the coming out of women, of aboriginal peoples, of third force Canadians, of visible minorities, of linguistic minorities, and of the disabled. In each case, their coming out challenged the comfortable assurance by which yesterday's dominant élites and majorities had defined the boundaries of acceptable, normal behaviour, and had transmitted their definitive cures of who was significant and who was not.[6]

The Charter did not end questions about rights by entrenching them — or some of them; in fact, it was the beginning point of many new questions. What precisely did the rights in the Charter mean? Did "freedom of association" entrench the right to strike? Did the right to "life, liberty and security of the person" entrench the right of a mother to have an abortion or the right of a foetus to live? Did the right to equality mean the right of any group or person previously disadvantaged on grounds of race, colour or sex to see that inequality erased? What aboriginal rights did the Charter confirm? Did the instruction to the courts to interpret the Charter "in a manner consistent with the preservation and enhancement of the multicultural heritage of Canada" establish some kind of "multicultural rights?" And, more generally, if some rights were guaranteed, why not others? To some the missing right was the right to property; to others it was the right to economic and physical well-being.

The debate over rights changed the nature of the Canadian **community**. Canada became a society driven by the vocabulary of rights, not community. Most issues that reach the public policy agenda are capable of compromise, and politics, the art of the possible, is the art of compromise and consensus. But rights, once asserted, become absolutes, strongly and intractably held. It is hard to bargain over rights, or among them. Rights fragment society and paralyze politicians for whom there is no correct choice other than personal conviction or party discipline. What Leslie Pal wrote of abortion might also be said with equal truth of other less contentious issues regarding rights: "To a government obsessed with the bottom line, with jobs and trade, with global competition and the budget, abortion policy is an unsavory agenda item, something that wins no friends and makes many enemies."[7]

WOMEN'S RIGHTS: UNITY AND DIVISION

The modern movement for women's rights emerged as a political force in the late 1960s. Earlier movements had sought to establish the legal or political equality of women — as symbolized by the right to vote, or membership in the Senate — and were in part, based on the doctrine of moral superiority: the idea that a female presence in the political arena would bring the supposed virtues of maternal feminism to such issues as temperance and moral reform. The movement that began in the 1960s, by contrast, reflected the post-war emergence of women as part of the labour force. While only 16 per cent of workers were women in 1901, the figure had risen to 38 per cent by 1970. A decade later, it was 50 per cent — and 41 per cent of these women were principal wage earners who had never been, or were no longer, married.

At the same time, however, it was obvious that income in the labour force was segregated by gender — women earned, on the average, 60 per cent as much as men. Women not only predominated in occupations that tended to be lower paid, but were often paid less than male counterparts doing the same job — the doctrine of equal pay for equal work did not exist.

In the beginning, the demands were for equality of opportunity and affirmative action programs designed to achieve economic equality. But the issues changed during the seventies. The leaders of the movement became more strident, and raised such issues as the unequal power of women and the need for a feminist perspective on many public and private matters. The agenda no longer focussed solely on economic equality but encompassed a broad range of issues in which the private person was not seen as separate from the public or political one. The role of women in society, day care, single-parent social services, reproductive freedom, rape, wife and child abuse and pornography, were all items on the new feminist agenda.

The appointment in 1970 of the Royal Commission on the Status of Women — which wrote a blueprint for social change on issues ranging from pay equity to abortion — led to the creation of the National Action Committee on the Status of Women to oversee the implementation of the commission's recommendations. A host of other organizations emerged over the course of the next two decades, representing woman professionals, women in sports, native women, black women, disabled women, and others. Sometimes such groups pursued their own unique interests; at other times they acted in concert as a single feminist lobby group. And they had strong links to other, non-feminist, organizations in areas such as health, the family, religion, literacy advocacy, multiculturalism and labour. Other women's groups existed outside of, or even opposed to, the thrust of the mainline groups, such as those who opposed abortion, and some religious and professional women's organizations.

Women had become a powerful lobby group. Their concerted and persistent pressure led to the insertion into the Charter of Rights and Freedoms of Section 28, which states: "Notwithstanding anything in this Charter, the rights and freedoms referred to in it are guaranteed equally to male and female persons." The section was originally subject to the provisions of the "notwithstanding clause" (Section 33), but again formidable lobbying in the last stages of Charter fine-tuning led to this section being removed from the list of those that could be overriden.

With the Charter experience behind them, women became a far more powerful presence than ever before. On many issues, really all women were united: affirmative action, pay equity, wife and child abuse and the protection of victims of sexual abuse (as in the case of a law forbidding questions at trial concerning a defendant's previous sexual experience). But on some rights-related issues women were deeply divided. Such was the case with abortion.

Abortion is a lens through which we can watch the politics of social fragmentation and political paralysis. In most societies, abortion is, and has been, a contentious issue, because it involves profound questions of morality and conscience, usually in the context of legal and religious prohibitions. Until 1969, the Canadian Criminal Code stated that abortion was an offence punishable by life imprisonment (or two years if the convicted person was the mother), unless it had been deemed necessary in order to save the life of the mother. Despite a general trend in Western countries toward relaxing abortion laws after the Second World War, there was little organized pressure in Canada to liberalize the law — although there was pressure from lawyers and doctors to clarify it. Nevertheless, the Trudeau government modified the law. The new provisions did not actually "get the State out of the bedrooms of the nation," however; they left abortion as a crime punishable by life imprisonment, unless performed by a doctor in an accredited hospital, after a decision by a committee that continuation of the pregnancy "would or would be likely to endanger" the mother's "life or health" (Criminal Code, Section 251). The new law was only moderately less restrictive. Many hospitals (including all religious hospitals) did not establish such a committee, and many doctors remained reluctant to perform abortions because of moral or medical reasons, or because they feared the legal consequences, particularly through suits by third parties.

But the introduction of the new law served to mobilize opinion both for and against abortion liberalization. In particular, it brought Dr. Henry Morgentaler into the open as a determined advocate of an unrestricted right to abortion. Just as the stirrup revolutionalized the history of medieval warfare, Morgentaler's adoption of the vacuum aspiration technique for abortion, revolutionalized the politics of abortion in Canada. Abortions could be performed quickly, cheaply and safely, in a doctor's office or a free-standing clinic.

Morgentaler established a clinic in Montreal in 1969 and was immediately arrested and charged. Although he admitted performing 5,000 abortions, a jury acquitted him in 1973. But the Quebec Court and the Supreme Court of Canada overturned the verdict, and Morgentaler was imprisoned. Upon his release he went before two more juries and was acquitted each time. In 1976, the government of Quebec simply decided not to prosecute him or any other doctors performing abortions. (This was possible since, while criminal law comes under federal jurisdiction, the administration of justice is in the hands of the provinces.) As pro-life forces mobilized to bring about more restrictive laws, Morgentaler allied himself with pro-choice activists and other organizations, to force the issue by publicly opening free-standing clinics in Toronto and Winnipeg. As predicted, with pro-choice and pro-life militants demonstrating on the streets in Toronto, the clinics were raided, and he and his associates were arrested. Again he was acquitted by a jury, and his case was appealed to the Supreme Court of Canada, which finally took on the task of determining the constitutionality of Section 251 of the Criminal Code.

Enter the Charter of Rights. Section 7 states: "Everyone has the right to life, liberty and security of the person and the right not to be deprived thereof except in accordance with the principles of fundamental justice."

The questions before the Court were easy to frame, if difficult to answer: Did "security of the person" mean women had the right to terminate a pregnancy? Did a foetus enjoy the "right to life?"

Confronted with an issue of such complexity and a decision of such momentous and divisive consequences, a divided Court hedged. Two judges concluded that

> Forcing a woman, by threat of criminal sanction, to carry a foetus to term unless she meets certain criteria unrelated to her own priorities and aspirations, is a profound interference with a woman's body and thus a violation of security of the person.[8]

But rather than proceed with this substantive reasoning, the judges moved on to focus on process. Because Section 251 was not evenly applied in all hospitals and the criteria and process used were unclear, they concluded, its implementation violated Section 7. Although they stated that the foetus "may well be deserving of constitutional protection," they concluded that the current law was unfair and arbitrary, and could not, therefore, be sustained.

Two other judges concluded simply that the procedure in Section 251 could deny a woman access to medical services necessary to save her life. Only Madam Justice Wilson confronted the issue head on and declared that women had a right to abortion, free of criminal sanction. But she did state that at some — indeterminate — point in the pregnancy the state could establish restrictive criteria enforced by sanctions.

Another two judges, in dissent, simply said that there was no evidence that the Charter intended to establish a right to abortion, and the court had no right to reject the deliberate will of Parliament.

With Section 251 struck down and Canada without a law on abortion, with doctors unclear about the law and provincial governments determining hospital policy, the ball was in the federal government's court. Although the government promised quick and decisive action, it could not carry the party caucus on any policy and after six months of agonizing deliberations decided on a "free vote" in the Commons. The proposal before the House endorsed the principle that in the early stages of pregnancy a doctor could perform an abortion if the "physical or mental well-being" of the woman was threatened, but in the later stages termination would only be allowed if two doctors concluded that continuation would "endanger the woman's life or seriously endanger her health." Leslie Pal summarized the result in the Commons in the summer of 1988 as follows:

> The Government's main resolution was defeated 147 votes to 76. An amendment which would have left the choice of abortion to the woman in the early stages and demanded only one doctor's opinion later was defeated 191 to 29. An amendment which would have left the decision entirely up to a woman and her doctor was defeated 198 to 20. An amendment which would have restricted abortion to the first 12 weeks

> of pregnancy was defeated 202 to 17. The most successful amendment — in that it was defeated by the narrowest margin — would have prohibited abortions except on the evidence of two doctors that the continuation of the pregnancy would endanger the woman's life. None of the 29 female MPs supported this proposal.[9]

The clear gender split on the last vote suggested to many pro-choice militants that men were still determined to control women's bodies. For months the government remained silent while pro-life activists took to the streets to close down abortion clinics and invite arrest for ignoring court injunctions. During the summer of 1989, the lives of Barbra Dodd and Chantal Daigle became front-page news as they successfully fought off anti-abortion injunctions secured by the natural fathers of the foetuses they carried. Finally, in the Daigle case, the Supreme Court ruled that a foetus was not a "legal person" in either the Charter or the Quebec Charter.

The Mulroney government then introduced a new abortion law, Bill C-43, which retained the criminality of abortion, but was less restrictive in principle than Section 251 — although the criteria for securing an abortion with medical approval remained deliberately vague and ambiguous. After heated debate the bill passed the Commons (140 to 131) in May 1990. Not until January 1991 did the Senate turn its attention to the bill, where contradictory pressures from pro-choice groups, pro-life groups and the medical profession (which disliked the implicit "chill" factor in the ambiguous legislation) led to a 43–43 vote and the death of the bill.

As the country was once again without a federal law on the issue, the scene shifted to the provinces, which, since they were responsible for the delivery of medical services, could effectively take charge by permitting or prohibiting the licensing of clinics and the use of medicare fee schedules for abortions. It was not long before access to abortion was again before the courts. For over a decade a great deal of Canadian time and energy — on the part of politicians, interest groups, lawyers and judges — had been consumed by the question of abortion and rights, without reaching a final resolution. As far as abortion is concerned, politics seemed to be the art of the impossible.

The same threatened to be the case with assisted suicide. The Criminal Code makes it an offence to assist a person to commit suicide, even though suicide or attempted suicide is not itself a crime. Sue Rodriguez, terminally ill with amyotrophic lateral sclerosis (ALS), wanted a physician to assist her to die when she could no longer live with dignity, and challenged the law as a violation of her Charter rights under sections 7 and 15. Simply put, the question she asked was "Who owns my body?" In a 5 to 4 decision in 1993, the Supreme Court upheld the law, in effect implying that the state did. Despite the decision and the law, Rodriguez did secure a physician-assisted suicide in front of at least one witness, Svend Robinson, an NDP member of Parliament. The split decision and the widespread outpouring of support for Rodriguez — and the likely refusal of a jury to convict the culprit if he or she were ever arrested and charged — made it inevitable that the issue would join abortion as another divisive "right to life or death" issue on the public agenda.

THE ABORIGINAL "RIGHT" TO SELF-GOVERNMENT

In June 1990, Elijah Harper, the sole aboriginal member of the Manitoba legislature, prevented the Meech Lake Accord from coming to a vote in that province, thus effectively killing the agreement. Later that same summer, national and international television audiences watched incredulously as the Mohawks of Kanetesake, in battle dress and carrying combat guns, fought the Quebec police and then the Canadian army to a standstill in support of their claims to contested land. For centuries, native people in Canada had their lives largely determined by the Europeans who controlled the Canadian state; now it seemed the future of that state would be decided in part by an agenda written by the aboriginal peoples. Speaking on behalf of these peoples, Harper gave a clear message that no new constitutional arrangement would be acceptable unless it recognized specific aboriginal rights. Foremost among those rights, it soon became clear, was the right to be recognized as a distinct society with the "inherent right to self-government" — whatever that might come to mean.

At issue was the place in Canadian society of about 500,000 status Indians, 30,000 Inuit and 50,000 non-status Indians and Métis. Since 1700, some 500 treaties had been signed with aboriginal peoples in which they usually ceded title to their land in return for reservations, the right to hunt and fish, and annual payments. After Confederation, as western settlement proceeded, the new Canadian government, which was given jurisdiction over Indians and Indian lands, negotiated 11 treaties between 1871 and 1921 regarding vast stretches of land, including Northern Ontario, the Prairies, and parts of the Northwest Territories. But no land cession treaties were signed covering Northern Quebec, the Maritimes, most of British Columbia or much of the Arctic.

Dealing with aboriginal people has not been one of the success stories of the Canadian government. Historically, federal policy was made by the government without consultation and with little complaint. But by the 1950s, Indian organizations were becoming more active, demanding consultation and finding broad public support in their fight against poverty and general marginality. Only in 1960 did status Indians receive the right to vote. Although there were many new programs to assist Indians, none seemed to resolve the problems of poverty and marginality. Revising Indian policy in the late sixties, the federal government did consult with Indian leaders. But the new policy, when it emerged as part of Trudeau's "just society," did not recognize any special rights or historic land and treaty claims.

Rather, in a 1969 statement on Indian policy, the government proposed to remove the "Indian problem" through assimilation. The policy was to rest

> upon the fundamental right of Indian people to full and equal participation in the cultural, social, economic and political life of Canada.... To argue against this right is to argue *for* discrimination, isolation and separation. No Canadian should be excluded from participation in community life, and none should expect to withdraw and still enjoy the benefits that flow to those who participate.

The government dismissed the principle of "aboriginal rights" with the argument that claims to land and associated rights were "so general and undefined that it is not realistic to think of them as specific claims capable of remedy." Termed cultural genocide by Indian leaders, this statement prompted a massive organization among aboriginal peoples. They wanted to retain their society and culture and negotiate new terms for their membership in the Canadian community. The force of the aboriginal opposition, combined with the support from the broader community, compelled the government to drop the proposal. Several court decisions also upheld the concept of an original title to the land and aboriginal rights that could be litigated.

In the face of these developments, the government had to begin to negotiate land claims and to consider seriously the broader question of aboriginal rights. By 1982 pressure had led to the inclusion of section 25 of the Charter, which stated that nothing in the Charter limited any "rights or freedoms that pertain to the aboriginal peoples of Canada." Section 35 of the 1982 Constitution stated that the "existing aboriginal and treaty rights of the aboriginal peoples of Canada are hereby recognized and affirmed," and Section 37 committed the government to hold consitutional conferences to identify and define the rights to be included in a further revision to the Constitution.

Although a number of minor agreements were reached, three first ministers conferences over the subsequent four years, failed to reach any agreement on what had become the central issue: the aboriginal right to self-government. In two 1990 decisions, the Supreme Court of Canada provided support for aboriginal claims. In one decision the court ruled that the Hurons outside Quebec City retained the right granted them in a 230-year-old treaty, to build camp fires and cut trees in a provincial park. A week later, in *R. v. Sparrow*, the court acquitted an Indian who had fished with a drift net larger than regulations permitted, and made a strong statement that governments cannot limit aboriginal rights without consultation and agreement.

But as the deadline for the approval of the Meech Lake agreement loomed, there was no recognition of the historical and cultural distinctiveness of the aboriginal population, or their right to some form of self-government. Yet, if they were not distinct, who was? Elijah Harper spoke for the aboriginals when he refused to let Meech Lake pass until aboriginal rights had been recognized.

The aboriginal peoples' right to self-government became a critical issue in the new round of negotiations after the death of Meech Lake. The Charlottetown accord in 1992 called for a constitutional amendment which recognized the right to self-government and aboriginal governments as one of the three levels of government with the right

> (a) to safeguard and develop their languages, cultures, economies, identities and traditions, and (b) to develop, maintain and strengthen their relationship with their lands, waters and environment; so as to determine and control their development as peoples according to their own values and priorities and ensure the integrity of their societies.

The principle of native peoples' inherent right to self-government, inherited from their self-governing ancestors, might be conceded. But there were too many questions left unanswered in the accompanying text. What did self-government mean: municipal government, something like provincial status, complete sovereignty within or without the Canadian state? What lands? What about urban communities? Who would pay and how much? Many Canadians, in areas of large aboriginal populations, were not prepared to gamble and voted against the accord. The vast majority of aboriginal peoples boycotted the referendum. With the defeat of the accord, the complex issues of land rights and self-government had to be resolved by negotiations between the First Nations and the provincial and federal governments and through concrete cases brought before the courts. The only certainties were that the direction would be towards self-government and aboriginal entitlement to land, and that the process would be incredibly time-consuming and the result incredibly costly.

MULTICULTURALISM: MYTH OR REALITY?

As a historian, I have always been disturbed by the proud boast that Canada was not a "melting pot" like its southern neighbour, but a multicultural mosaic where new Canadians were not forced into the crucible of assimilation but encouraged to wear their ethnic or cultural origin on their sleeve. Through most of Canadian history — unless new arrivals wished to remain outside the mainstream of Canadian life — they had to assimilate, outwardly at least, to the language, behaviour and cultural norms of the host society. Indeed, since almost all Canadians were of European origin — 97 per cent as late at 1961 — the culture was simply not all that culturally diverse.

Canada has always been the destination of, and home to, a flow of people from other parts of the world. Some were pulled by the prospect of a better life; others were pushed by deprivation or persecution. But with some exceptions — notably Chinese, Japanese and Indian immigrants to the West coast — these immigrants were, through the 1950s, largely of European origin. Although the process of assimilation was sometimes slow and sometimes painful, over time the newcomers assimilated to the French or English culture in which they had settled. To some extent they preserved their cultural traditions and language, but in a couple of generations most had become Canadian, their national origin identifiable only by their last name and a few preserved cultural traditions. Canadians, it seemed, wanted it thus.

While Canada historically welcomed the "men in sheepskin coats," Canadian immigration policy was never an open-door policy that admitted all comers regardless of race or skin colour. Indeed, as late as 1947, Mackenzie King could state publicly that Canada did not "wish as a result of mass immigration, to make a fundamental alteration in the character of the Canadian population." At that time there were less than 100,000 Canadians, other than native people, whose origins were not British or European. Today, one Canadian in fifteen belongs to a "visible minority" — a euphemism that seeks to avoid the words race and colour. In Toronto, the ratio is almost one in six.

The change began in the 1960s when Canadian immigration policy eliminated racial considerations as a criterion for entry. At that time 80 per cent of immigrants came from Europe; by the 1980s over 70 per cent were coming from Asia, Africa and Latin America. Of these, about 60 per cent were destined for the three largest cities: Toronto (35 per cent), Vancouver (11 per cent) or Montreal (14 per cent). The new, less restrictive immigration policy was not the only reason for the change, however. With the recovery of post-war Europe, emigrating to Canada was no longer as attractive as it had been.

Immigration policy was always contentious, with governments responding to pressure from a number of different constituencies. Usually cast in economic terms, the debate often centred on labour-force needs or the need to replenish an aging population with a younger element. But there was also the more generally humanitarian argument that it was Canada's duty to provide a home for the less fortunate of the world. Any attempt to tighten the criteria for entry, or to take a more hard-boiled approach towards refugees, aroused intense opposition from humanitarian civil libertarians and members of already established immigrant communities. Governments made adjustments in the policies every few years, but the general pattern of immigration of visible minorities remained constant throughout the 1970s and 1980s.

While most economists argue that the effects of immigration are beneficial, a recent Economic Council of Canada study suggested cautiously that, although its net economic benefit to Canada was small, immigration was necessary to increase the population and the GNP. On the other hand, the study showed that, contrary to popular belief, nearly every immigrant paid for herself in scale economies and lighter tax burdens, with the possible exception of refugees, who cost the host society much more to process.

It was clear, however, that continuing the immigration pattern will continue to change the ethnic profile of the country and will test the tolerance level of already-settled communities, particularly if there is a sudden increase in the proportion of visible minority immigration or a deep economic recession with high unemployment.

The changes to immigration policy since 1960 wrought a profound change in the structure of Canadian society — and in the meaning of the word multiculturalism. Not only were the new immigrants "visible", but over 75 per cent of new immigrants were concentrated in five major urban centres, usually in compact communities that nourished their traditional cultures. It was not long before the contradictions in Canadian society began to appear. On the one hand was the rhetoric, fostered by the state, of respecting and nourishing multiculturalism; on the other, was the inevitable real or perceived discrimination and racism. As one West Indian who emigrated to Canada in the 1960s explained,

> In those days, there were very few Blacks in Ottawa. When we went to the grocery store, we were the only ones. When my sister and I went to school, we were the only ones....
>
> While 25 years ago, new immigrants were forced to fit into the mainstream of Canadian society, now many have their own established communities into which they can migrate. Thus, very little of their "back-home" culture is lost by their move to Canada. Some of these communities are so strong that there exist entire blocks in a city that can accommodate the needs of a specific ethnic groups: financial, catering, legal, entertainment, accommodation, educational and many more services are easily available. Some have little need to venture out of their communities except for employment. Many feel this is a positive aspect of multiculturalism. Few understand its implications....
>
> Our policy makers must be careful that when they develop our multicultural policies they do not alienate cultures from each other. If immigrants know that they are coming to a well-established community then they may be more apt to accept it and live within its boundaries. But, when every new group is encouraged to preserve all of its culture, that is when each group fights to attain as many rights as the next. That is when multiculturalism turns to racism. That is when the melting pot boils over.[10]

The Trudeau government officially adopted multiculturalism as a policy in 1971 and appointed a minister responsible for its implementation the following year. Twenty years later, there is still controversy over the reasons behind the new policy. Some regard it as an attempt to appease the opponents of the policy of biculturalism and bilingualism; francophones certainly opposed it as somehow diminishing their unique position in Canada. Others scoffed that it was nothing but a cynical attempt to capture the "ethnic vote." Many others, however, believed that it was an appropriate response to the changing nature of Canadian society; they watched to see if it would become something more than "folk dancing and feathers."

The verdict on the ultimate impact of multiculturalism has yet to be delivered. However, it was embedded in principle in Canadian policy when Section 27 of the Charter of Rights and Freedoms instructed the courts to interpret the Charter "in a manner consistent with the preservation and enhancement of the multicultural heritage of Canadians...."

By the 1980s, multiculturalism had been overtaken by the more sensitive and immediate issue of race relations. The increase in both the number and the concentration of visible minorities had led, inevitably, to racial discrimination. In the early 1980s race relations became a major component of the Ministry of Multiculturalism's jurisdiction with the establishment of its Race Relations Directorate. In 1988, when the Mulroney government gave multiculturalism legislative status with the passage of the Canadian Multicultural Act, this new mandate was made explicit. The act recognized "the diversity of Canadians as regards to race, national or ethnic origin, colour and religion as fundamental characteristics of Canadian society" and provided that the government should "assist ethno-cultural minority communities to conduct activities with a view to overcoming any discriminatory barriers and, in particular, discrimination based on race or national ethnic origin." The strategy to eliminate racial discrimination was to include, among other measures, public education, institutional change and support for community advocacy.

Promoting multiculturalism and countering racial discrimination are similar, but not identical, goals. Preserving Canada's multicultural heritage is not quite the same as abolishing discrimination in housing, investigating charges of police prejudice, or responding to a demand for differential university admission requirements or professional qualifications. What can we make of the 150,000 petitions to members of Parliament protesting the desire of the government to make the RCMP more representative of the community and, among other changes, allow Sikhs to wear turbans? Or of a best-selling pin that showed a white man dwarfed by a Sikh in a turban, a Chinese man, and a black man carrying a spear, with the words "Who's the minority in Canada?"[11]

By the early 1990s, many Canadians were becoming increasingly ambivalent about immigration policy and multiculturalism. A public opinion survey in the spring of 1994, revealed that although 73 per cent believed that "a mixture of different lifestyles and cultures makes Canada a more attractive place to live," most also believed that there were "too many immigrants," especially those of visible minorities. Six out of ten agreed that "too many immigrants feel no obligation to adapt to Canadian values and way of life." (*Globe and Mail*, 11 March 1994). And another survey indicated that 72 per cent believed that "the long-standing image of Canada as a nation of communities, each ethnic and racial group preserving its own identity with the help of government policy, must give way to the U.S. style of cultural absorption." (*Globe and Mail*, 14 December 1993). The debate over immigration, multiculturalism and racism is now clearly on political agendas, and only realism, not rhetoric, will produce programs and policies that will lead to accommodation, not confrontation.

THE ROAD TO AND FROM MEECH LAKE

If left alone, Pierre Trudeau boasted, the new constitution he had fashioned in 1982 would have lasted a thousand years. But it could not be left alone because Quebec had refused to accept it as morally binding — regardless of its legal status — on the grounds that it had been passed without Quebec's consent. During the 1984 election campaign, Brian Mulroney had promised a policy of "national reconciliation" and to "bring Quebec back in" by renewing the process of constitutional reform. His overwhelming victory, followed by the defeat of the Parti Québécois in 1985, placed constitutional reform once again at the centre of the national agenda.

Although the immediate object was to pacify Quebec, it was soon apparent that Mulroney had opened Pandora's box and released many voices and interests — women, aboriginals, minorities and majorities, regions and provinces — that demanded to be heard and recognized. Everyone, it seemed, had "rights" and unless **their** rights were entrenched in a new constitution, none would be. Those voices and interests killed the Meech Lake agreement in 1990 and, after two more years of agonizing, almost paralyzing, negotiations, still threatened in the summer of 1992 to make any settlement impossible, regardless of the threat to the Canadian state as we know it.

Soon after their victory in 1985, the Quebec Liberals under Robert Bourassa set out their demands for a revised constitution. After months of negotiations, in 1987, the prime minister and all provincial premiers agreed at Meech Lake, a federal government retreat in the Gatineau hills, to a set of constitutional amendments that satisfied Quebec. By far the most controversial was the recognition of Quebec as a "distinct society" and the affirmation of the responsibility of the government of Quebec to "preserve and promote" that distinct identity. At the same time the existence of a French-speaking and an English-speaking Canada was stated to be "a fundamental characteristic of Canada." Other provisions permitted provinces to opt out of new shared-cost programs with fiscal compensation if the province undertook a comparable program, gave the provinces a voice in appointments to the Senate and the Supreme Court (as Quebec has demanded), expanded provincial powers over constitutional amendments and increased the power of Quebec (and of other provinces if they wished) over immigration and the integration of immigrants. The accord had to be approved by Parliament and all provincial legislatures by June 23, 1990.

On June 23, 1990, Meech Lake was dead. Technically, the accord died when, in Manitoba, MPP Elijah Harper, an aboriginal, refused on procedural grounds to let a vote be taken by a reluctant provincial government, and in Newfoundland, a new government, opposed to the accord, did not give its assent. But more generally, Meech failed because it had aroused intense opposition among many groups within Canadian society. While many argued that the accord would fatally weaken the central government, most of the opposition focussed on the "distinct-society" and "fundamental-characteristic" clauses. Why should Quebec be regarded as a distinct society with enhanced powers? Would distinct-society status override the Charter? If Quebec was distinct, why not aboriginals, whose demands for self-government had not been accepted? If Quebec had special status, why not all the provinces? Where did the fundamental characteristic of biculturalism leave cultural minorities? Women asked — largely outside Quebec — whether the distinct-society clause would undermine the equality rights in the Charter and whether the limits on new shared costs programs would prevent new programs such as day care.

Put most broadly, Meech Lake failed because it represented an elite consensus that did not exist in a political community too fragmented by the clamour of language, culture, region and rights.

With Quebec planning a referendum on its future in 1992, and refusing to enter into more negotiations until the other governments had firm proposals on the table, the process began all over again. This was not to be another "Quebec round" but a "Canada round" in which tens of thousands of Canadians were given the opportunity to present their views and demands. What had emerged in the Charlottetown accord in the fall of 1993 was an elaborate set of proposals which went far beyond those in Meech. The ingredients in Meech, including the controversial distinct society clause, were still there. But there were strong statements concerning the aboriginal right to self-government, and gender, racial and ethnic equality. Advocates of a Triple-E Senate won the day, as did the supporters of a social charter which committed governments to maintain high levels of health care, public education, social services and environmental protection, as well as guarantees of the right to collective bargaining. Governments were also committed to strengthening the Canadian economic union by policies to reduce the barriers to interprovincial trade, maintain full employment, ensure all Canadians a "reasonable standard of living," and ensure "sustainable and equitable development." The federal government also agreed to withdraw from the fields of tourism, housing, urban affairs, forestry, mining and recreation. Culture was also recognized as an area of exclusive provincial jurisdiction, but Ottawa retained its control over national cultural institutions and agencies. No group secured everything it wanted, but there was something for everyone except the federal government — unless it was peace at any price.

Although the accord was accepted, often reluctantly, by every government, 54.4 per cent of the Canadian people voted NO in an October 26, 1992 referendum after an emotional and bitter campaign. The vote was overwhelmingly NO in Quebec and the four Western provinces, and narrowly NO in Nova Scotia. The three other Atlantic provinces voted strongly YES and Ontario went YES by a few thousand votes. While it is difficult to generalize, it would appear that those who voted YES believed that the proposals represented a reasonable set of compromises to resolve the constitutional impasse. On the other hand, there was no agreement among those who championed the NO cause. Women and aboriginal peoples voted NO because they did not get enough. Quebec separatists and nationalists voted NO because it offered too little, while sentiment in the West — led by the Reform Party — clearly believed it offered Quebec too much. The vote was indeed a crude calculation of profit and loss, whether selfish or principled. Whatever the reasons, the defeat of the accord did not blaze a trail toward the future, but left Canada deep in a seemingly impenetrable constitutional swamp.

The federal election of October 1993 confirmed the deep divisions within the country. After eight years in office, the Conservative Party was annihilated. The Liberals won all but one seat in Ontario, swept the Maritimes, and won seats in every province to win a comfortable majority. But in Quebec, the separatist Bloc Québécois, formed three years earlier in response to the defeat of Meech, won 54 of the 75 seats to form the official opposition. The Reform Party, the six-year-old vehicle for the expression of western discontent and anti-Quebec and other nativist sentiments, swept British Columbia and Alberta, and ran second in Saskatchewan, Manitoba and even Ontario. When Parliament opened in January 1994, Jean Chretien faced Lucien Bouchard's Bloc Québécois which wanted out, and Preston Manning's Reform Party which was not prepared to make any concessions to keep them in. In the fall of 1994, the Québécois returned the separatists to power with a promise to secure the independence of Quebec. In the wake of the defeat of Charlottetown, the 1993 federal election, and the 1994 Quebec Provincial election, many began to ask whether Canada was indeed ungovernable, and the academics began to debate the future of that new nation which they variously called ROC or CWOQ (the Rest of Canada or Canada Without Quebec). As never before in our history, it seemed appropriate to hope that miracles truly did occur.

SUMMING UP

The day of reckoning has come. It was long overdue. Rich natural resources, an abundance of energy, and the comforting wall of protective tariffs, enabled Canada to achieve one of the highest standards of living in the world. But the resources are dwindling and the tariff wall is coming down, leaving Canadian industry to face the global challenge on its own. Firms, sectors and regions demand that governments protect them from the chill winds of international competition. With the economy crumbling and the government deficit soaring, the "protected society" is under siege.

Long a nation in search of an identity, Canada is now torn by the assertion of a multitude of rights — individual, gender, cultural, aboriginal, provincial — and we look in vain for a sense of community. National political parties, traditionally the mediators of regional, cultural and ideological differences, are no longer able to contain the divisions within them. Where once everything seemed possible, now nothing seems certain. This is the reality of the political, social and economic context within which Canadian managers in the private and public sector must function.

Notes

1. Royal Commission on Dominion-Provincial Relations, *Report* (Ottawa: King's Printer, 1940), 3 vols.
2. See the *White Paper on Employment and Income* (Ottawa: King's Printer, 1945). A useful survey of post-war federal-provincial relations is Garth Stevenson, *Unfulfilled Union: Canadian Federalism and National Unity* (Toronto: Gage, 1989)
3. Royal Commission on the Economic Union and Development Prospects for Canada, *Report* (Ottawa: Ministry of Supply and Services, 1985), vol. 1, 46.
4. Cited in William Coleman, *The Independence Movement in Quebec 1945–1980* (Toronto, 1984), 183.
5. Ibid., 185.
6. "Constitutional Minoritarianism in Canada," in R.L. Watts and D. M. Brown, eds., *Canada: The State of the Federation 1990* (Kingston: Institute of Intergovermental Relations, Queen's University, 1990), 75.
7. "How Ottawa Dithers: The Conservatives and Abortion Policy," in Frances Abele, ed., *How Ottawa Spends: The Politics of Fragmentation* (Ottawa: Carleton University Press, 1991), 270. *How Ottawa Spends* appears annually and provides an excellent survey of a wide-range of public policy issues.
8. *R. v Morgentaler* [1988] 2 S.C.R.
9. "How Ottawa Dithers: The Conservatives and Abortion Policy," in Frances Abele, ed., *How Ottawa Spends: The Politics of Fragmentation* (Ottawa: Carleton University Press, 1991), 285.
10. See Claudette Russell, "When the Melting Pot Boils Over," *Policy Options* (November, 1991), 20.
11. David Stasiulis, "Symbolic Representation and the Numbers Game: Tory Policies on 'Race' and Visible Minorities," in Abele, *How Ottawa Spends*, 251.

QUESTIONS FOR DISCUSSION

1. Why could it be argued that the national tariff policies disadvantaged some sections of the country?
2. Discuss the costs and benefits of equalization payments.
3. The Supreme Court has decided that the right to "freedom of association" and "freedom of expression" do not include the right to

strike. Does that support the views of Charter opponents — that the Charter, as interpreted by the Courts, would prove to be a conservative element in Canadian society?

4. Aboriginal right to self-government may sound fine in principle. What could be the economic, fiscal, legal, territorial and political consequences?
5. What are the arguments for and against a Senate that is elected, with equal provincial representation, and that has real power?

John Saywell is University Professor and Professor of History at York University. A graduate of British Columbia and Harvard in History and Government, he has taught at the University of Toronto, Berkeley and York University where he has been since joining the university as Dean of Arts and Science in 1963. Author of many books and articles on history, politics and law, Saywell also worked in economic development in Kenya for much of the 1970s, and spent two years in Japan attached to the Canadian embassy. Saywell has wide experience in television as host/narrator, author of documentaries and plays, and was Tokyo correspondent for CTV News.

Interest Groups and Policy Making in Canada

W.T. STANBURY

1. INTRODUCTION

The purpose of this chapter is to describe and discuss some of the important aspects of the role of interest groups in influencing public policy in Canada.[1] Interest groups are so numerous that they are almost ubiquitous in Canada. The issues on which they focus are highly varied: civil rights, contraception, the prevention of nuclear war, tax policy, international trade policy and the preservation of everything from particular languages or cultures, to wilderness areas, heritage buildings, dairy farms and endangered species (including loggers!). The range of interests represented covers virtually all aspects of experience from conception to death — and even beyond. The widely-read columnist Jeffrey Simpson argues that

> Nothing so characterizes contemporary Canadian affairs as the multiplicity of interest groups. Not only have the groups multiplied, but their power has increased — in some cases because governments have funded them (women, natives, multicultural groups, environmental groups, artists), in others because they have devoted large sums to lobbying and public relations (business, farmers and, to a much lesser extent, trade unions and professional associations).
>
> Increasingly, citizens press their claims through interest groups rather than political parties. In a superficial sense, Ottawa has responded to these new groups by creating new ministries to deal with them. In a more profound sense, it has felt compelled to buy the groups off with the only weapons it can muster — chunks of money or, failing that, policies that make life more secure for the interest group in question (*Globe and Mail*, March 15, 1989, p. A6).

Interests may be material, or symbolic, or both. Indeed, any one of the enormous range and variety of factors that motivate human behaviour may be represented by an interest group. Salisbury (1991, p. 376) argues that "no firm or permanent line of demarcation differentiates political interest groups from those that are not political. Interests change, emerge, or are discovered; the actualization of interests is a dynamic process." He suggests that "much of the task of interest group representatives lies in discovering what their groups' interests are so as to protect and perhaps advance them" (Salisbury, 1991, p. 373).

Would-be managers and ordinary citizens need to understand how interest groups operate in the political and policy-making process for a variety of reasons. First, many interest groups make such an effort to influence public policy that different groups become rivals, both in placing their issues on the policy-making agenda, and in trying to influence policy makers. Second, many groups obtain direct financial assistance from government, although government funding has declined in recent years (see Phillips, 1991). (Business firms obtain indirect assistance because their expenditures on government relations are tax deductible.) Third, a number of interest groups **directly** lobby business firms (trade associations) as well as government — for example, some environmental groups have tried to stop the cutting of old-growth timber by B.C. forest companies by blockading logging roads (see Stanbury, 1994). Fourth, interest groups perform important functions in a democratic society, including improving the making and implementation of public policy.

Interest groups attempt to influence governments to take certain actions. But government actions have the effect of creating interests. For example, when the government established the old age pension, it created a flow of income that each pensioner has a direct interest in having continue. People quickly become accustomed to any benefit and soon form expectations about the continuation, and potential increase of a benefit. A reduction in the benefit flow is likely to provoke a hostile reaction. Thus, as government activity expands — and particularly as the amount of cash transfers expands — more people are affected and their interest or stake in government activity grows, as well. Note, however, that the motivation behind many (perhaps most) actions by interest groups is negative — to stop a proposed action by government or to reverse a recent one. The fear of the loss of an accustomed position is stronger than the anxiety over opportunity losses.

The body of this chapter is organized as follows: Section 2 describes the various types of government actions that are the focus of interest groups' efforts to influence public policy. Section 3 describes the actors, institutions and the nature of exchanges in political markets. Section 4 briefly identifies the sources of public policy issues. Section 5 defines interest groups, describes their functions and identifies several types of interest groups. Section 6 examines business firms as interest groups, and Section 7 describes the nature and activities of government relations consultants. Section 8 looks at organized labour as an interest group. Section 9 explains how interest groups attempt to influence public policy (and often succeed). Finally, the conclusions are set out in Section 10.

2. THE FOCUS OF INTEREST GROUPS: GOVERNMENT ACTIONS THAT EMBODY PUBLIC POLICY

In general terms, public policy can be thought of as various actions of a government designed to modify the behaviour of citizens. These actions are ultimately backed up by the legitimate (constitutional) coercive powers granted to a government by a democratically elected legislature. Interest groups seek to influence public policy in all of its many forms. Government actions that embody public policy include the following:

- new statutes enacted by the legislature
- amendments to existing statutes
- subordinate legislation that does not require approval of the legislature, such as regulations or orders-in-council, which need be approved only by the cabinet or a single minister
- formal decisions of regulatory agencies to grant licenses, alter the terms of licenses, set tariffs or otherwise constrain private-sector decisions
- authoritative decisions of the courts (the most authoritative are those of the Supreme Court of Canada)
- cabinet decisions on appeals from the decisions of regulatory agencies
- the exercise of discretion by line departments and regulatory agencies in day-to-day dealings with private-sector firms: budget allocations, the application of regulations and the interpretation of policy guidelines, internal policy manuals or external interpretation bulletins
- ministerial policy statements (in the legislature, or in the form of press releases or internal guidelines to bureaucrats)
- the revenue budget (changes in tax policy, including tax expenditures)
- the annual *Estimates* — expenditure allocations among departments and agencies
- central agency (Treasury Board, Privy Council Office, Comptroller General) directives to line departments that affect that department's "clients"

Public policy is most obviously embodied in new legislation or amendments to existing legislation — statutes enacted by Parliament or a provincial legislature (municipal by-laws would also be included here). A widely debated new statute is certainly the most dramatic and obvious instrument of public policy, but it is only one of many. It would be a major mistake for interest groups to concentrate all, or even much, of their efforts in seeking to influence new legislation (including amendments). The fact is that a great deal of law (let alone policy) is **not** enacted by the legislature. The consequences of many statutes are only understandable by reference to the regulations passed by the cabinet (not the legislature) pursuant to the statute. As important in many cases are the **operational** interpretations of statutes made by the public servants who direct the administration of statutes and regulations, as well as the less frequent but important formal interpretations made by the courts. Because the enactment of new statutes (or amendments) is so visible, uninformed students of government tend to spend too much time on this one expression of public policy and too little on the other less visible, more arcane, but nevertheless important instruments of public policy.

One of the least understood, but most important, instruments of public policy consists of new subordinate legislation including regulations, orders and other statutory instruments, such as orders-in-council. Subordinate legislation has the same force of law as a statute but it is usually not enacted by the legislature. Rather, it is approved by Cabinet (more precisely, the Special Committee of Council) or, in some cases, by an individual minister or even by an "independent" regulatory agency (Stanbury, 1992). Where broadly worded statutes are enacted, their real force and effect usually depends upon the regulations that are made pursuant to them at a later date. Orders-in-council are made by the cabinet and amount to legislation by fiat without reference to the elected legislature (although the legislature has given the cabinet this power in the enabling statute).[2]

Public policy is also embedded in policy announcements by a minister. These involve "official" interpretations of existing legislation (statutes and regulations) and are designed to act as guidance for departments, agencies and those currently or potentially affected by a government policy. Unfortunately, a department's policy position is often hard to determine. There may be a "policy vacuum" on certain issues (although the substance of day-to-day decision-making constitutes an implicit policy). There may be conflicting statements of policy, which is not surprising, given the multiplicity of policy objectives governments have and the fact that they pay more attention to different goals at different times.

A related type of policy statement consists of interpretation guidelines issued by specific departments or agencies. The most famous example is the *Interpretation Bulletins* of the Department of National Revenue (DNR), which now take up at least one and a half metres of shelf space. In effect, these state how DNR officials interpret the Income Tax Act and related statutes in light of decisions of the Tax Appeal Board and the courts.

Public policy is also expressed in the decisions of hundreds of regulatory boards and agencies.[3] They make decisions on thousands of individual cases, as do the regular courts of law. The regulators' task is to apply various statutes and regulations to specific cases. Thus agencies like the Canadian Radio-Television Commission (CRTC) set prices (for telephone services, cable TV etc.) and determine such things as who will be allowed to enter the industry, whether a merger can take place and whether a license should be revoked if a company fails to meet the performance guidelines established by the agency. The decisions of most federal regulatory agencies may be appealed to the cabinet. These "political appeals" are a way by which the government can modify public policy on a case-by-case basis, without having to obtain the approval of the legislature or even announce the new direction in the legislature.

Public policy is also made as the courts interpret statutes and regulations in the tens of thousands of individual cases that wend their way through the trial court, court of appeal and, eventually, the Supreme Court of Canada. While judges often say they only interpret the law, their interpretations are authoritative until a higher court provides a new interpretation, or the legislature changes the legislation. It must be recognized that the words of the Constitution, for example, are very general in many places. It is left to the courts to determine the practical meaning of those words. As a result, there has been a virtual explosion of cases requiring interpretation under the new Charter of Rights and Freedoms (see Stanbury, 1993a, chapter 12).

For most people in their day-to-day dealings with government departments, government policy is effectively embodied in the exercise of discretion by senior bureaucrats and individual ministers. Anisman (1975, p. 23) identified some 14,885 specific discretionary powers in the revised federal statutes of 1970. Discretionary powers "comprise decisions involving a choice whether to exercise a power, decisions concerning the manner in which a power is to be exercised and, as well, any matter involving judgment, for example, a decision as to whether a particular set of circumstances exists or has existed" (Anisman, 1975, p. 2).

On an annual basis, one of the most important and insightful indicators of a government's policies is how it raises and spends our money. At the federal level, the government's planned expenditures are embodied in the several volumes of the *Estimates* introduced in Parliament in the spring of each year. Currently, the federal government spends about $160-billion each year but collects only $130-billion in taxes and other revenues. Unless authorized by parliamentary approval of the *Estimates*, no planned program or activity that requires the expenditure of public funds can be carried out.[4] While approval of the *Estimates* is a formality, the document does provide a reasonably good indication of the government's priorities.

Changes to the tax system are embodied in periodic **revenue** budgets announced by the Minister of Finance (see Savoie, 1990). These are not scheduled annual events like the tabling of the *Estimates* (or **expenditure** budget), although five of the last six were presented in February. One of the most controversial changes in tax policy in recent years was the enactment of the GST (Goods and Services Tax) which replaced the federal Manufacturers' Sales Tax on January 1, 1991.

Doern and Phidd (1983, p. 103) explain that there can be "policies without resources" (money, personnel, time and political will) to support them. "Many governments find it necessary to enunciate policy to express their concern about, and support for, a particular constituency or group, since this is usually preferable to expressing no public concern whatsoever." This takes us into the world of symbolic politics, where the object is to show concern, to temporize, to husband scarce resources whose expenditure may produce little or no substantive result, but above all to be seen to be "doing something" in response to interest-group pressures or a politician's identification of a latent concern of important groups of voters.

3. ACTORS, INSTITUTIONS AND EXCHANGES IN POLITICAL MARKETS

The major actors and institutions in the policy-making process include the government, the cabinet, public servants, voters, political parties, news media, interest groups (including corporations, trade associations and unions) and the courts (judiciary). Their roles in the process are outlined in Figure 1.

FIGURE 1
Major Actors and Institutions and their Roles in the Policy-Making Process

Governments	• exercise legitimate power of coercion through governing instruments • are subject to the Constitution as interpreted by the courts (but able to amend it) • exercise social control over behaviour of business and other groups • effect income/wealth transfers through a wide variety of means • arrange for provision of many collective goods
Cabinet	• is collectively responsible for the executive • is appointed by the Prime Minister • amounts to a periodically elected collective kingship where their party has a majority in the legislature • has virtual monopoly over the supply of legislation • is able to create law by approving regulations without reference to the legislature • through its committees, "filters" major policy initiatives of individual ministers
Public Servants	• provide the government with technical knowledge/policy advice • administer public policies/programs • are a "permanent," professional cadre (not partisan) • implement policies established by politicians who are responsible for values choices

FIGURE 1 (Continued)

Voters	• select the government of the day in periodic elections • rely heavily on the news media (particularly TV) for information on policy making • create public opinion, which constrains/encourages government • join interest groups which lobby government between elections
Political Parties	• are coalitions of individuals that compete for office • act as a mediating institution between the individual and the state • seek a majority of seats to become the government of the day • organize election campaigns and develop policy promises • offer promises of policies in exchange for political support (money and votes)
News Media	• act as a communication channel among all actors • select, amplify, distort the "news" • are business enterprises (selling audiences to advertisers) • sometimes act as the unelected opposition • help to shape public opinion (primary source of political news) • are relied upon by the public for news (TV more so than newspapers)
Interest Groups (including corporations and unions)	• aggregate interests (reduce cacophony); provide information to policy makers • seek to advance interests of members by a variety of techniques • represent "values" as well as economic interests • mediate between citizens and government • use media to inform government and to influence public opinion • are not able organize all interests due to "free rider" problem
Courts/ Judiciary	• independent of executive, interest groups and voters • adjudicate private and public disputes • interpret the laws (including the Constitution) and regulations; review the actions of administrative bodies • interest groups try to use the courts to alter public policy

An important element of the public-choice approach to a positive theory of government intervention is the idea that policies are "sold" or exchanged by political parties for financial and other resources. For example, in Albert Breton's view, the trading process can be caricatured as follows: "if you will donate some money to our party, we will provide you in exchange with a tariff which will allow you to reap monopoly rents of such and such magnitude, or we will allow you to form a professional or trade association that will have the power to set standards, to define the terms of licenses, to set the rates that can be charged for services rendered, and so on!" (Breton, 1976, p. 16). In other words, political parties obtain campaign contributions from firms and other interest groups in exchange for promises of favourable policies when they gain or retain power.[5]

However, the political exchange process is rather more complicated, in reality. First of all, in Canada, the overt exchange of policy favours for campaign contributions is widely condemned as undesirable or even immoral behaviour. Second, an elected official who accepts money for actions by the government beneficial to the person paying the money may be violating the Criminal Code. Third, contributions to political parties and candidates by individual donors seldom exceed $50,000.[6] Moreover, there are legal limits on official "election expenses" and parties or candidates are required to disclose the names of persons contributing more than $100 in cash or kind (see Stanbury, 1994b).

All of this indicates that policies are not simply "sold" for campaign contributions. A richer explanation is required. What then is the medium of exchange between interest groups and political parties? First, interest groups may spend their own money (in lieu of a party's money) directly on campaigns to support candidates, parties and policies following an agreement by the party to take the actions requested by the interest group.[7] Second, the interest group can co-operate with the party in power — it agrees to go along with the party on policy A (which it would otherwise oppose) in exchange for the party implementing policy B (which the group favours).[8] A model of this exchange process is outlined in Figure 2. Where trust is well developed, the exchange may not be contemporaneous. If a **high** degree of trust exists, the governing party may agree to implement a policy desired by the interest group on the understanding that the group will "owe the party one" to be paid at an unspecified time in the future. Or the converse may occur; the interest group agrees not to protest a particular government action now and receives "a marker," which it expects in the future, to cash in when it really needs a favour. Lobbyists can persuade politicians to act in ways that advance their clients' interests by making extensive use of the norm of reciprocity.

Third, possibly the most valuable resource the interest group has to offer a politician or party is **information**, the exchange of which, is subject neither to campaign-financing legislation nor to moral strictures. The information most valuable to politicians consists of (1) knowledge of the preferences of voters, particularly uncommitted voters (those who may be persuaded to vote for the party); (2) knowledge of the likely political reactions of voters to both existing and potential policies, that the party might propose; (3) knowledge of the most efficient and effective ways to influence uncommitted voters, by means of both substantive policy actions and intentionally persuasive communications. In accepting information from interest groups, political parties and politicians appreciate the fact that what they receive is not so much likely to be wrong or untruthful, but rather selective in terms of the facts presented and in terms of the interpretation placed upon those facts. An interest group that lied or engaged in misrepresentation would soon lose its credibility with those it was seeking

FIGURE 2
Model of Exchange Processes in
a Positive Theory of Government Action

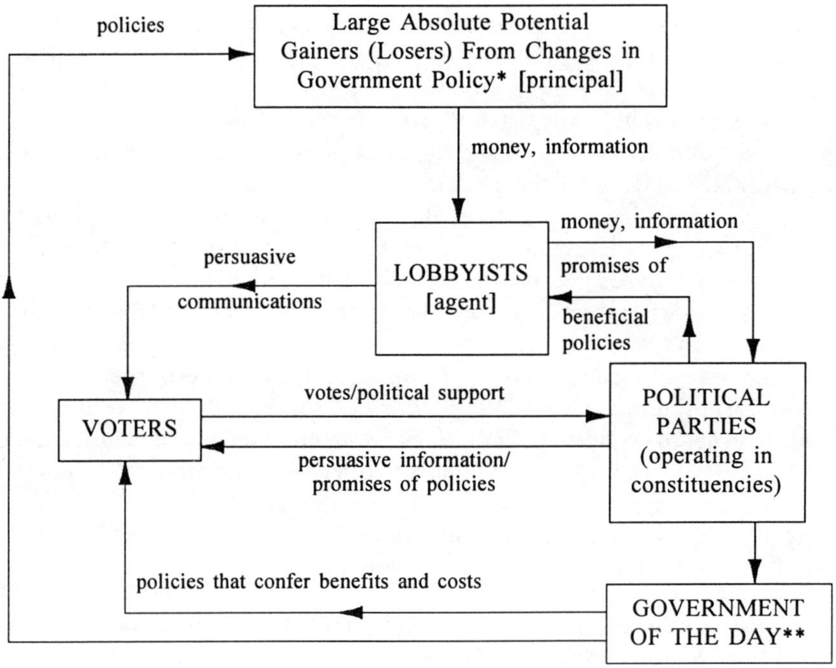

*The big "stakes" in policy outcomes may be economic and/or psychological, such as achieving an ideological objective.
**Assumed to have a majority of seats in the legislature; also controls the executive.

to influence. Virtually all writers on the politics of interest groups emphasize the importance of the credibility of interest-group representatives (see Stanbury, 1993a, chapter 8).

The fourth possible medium of exchange between interest groups and political parties relates to the capacity of the former to shape public opinion and to help define the limited number of issues that make up the public-policy agenda.

4. SOURCES OF PUBLIC POLICY ISSUES

What are the sources of policy issues? The process by which technological, economic, social or political forces lead to the perception that there is a social problem (not merely a private one) worthy of action by government, is complex. Preston and Post (1975, pp. 76–79) suggest that five factors help to explain how certain issues result in government action: public opinion, the efforts of interest groups, leadership exercised by key individuals, technical expertise and unanticipated events. Public opinion can both aid and restrain government in the development of public policy. It has long been argued that a great deal of law is the result of a change in public opinion a few years or even a decade earlier — that is, law, in the sense of changes in legislation, follows public opinion. All changes in public opinion do not result in changes in policy. Public opinion needs to be organized and mobilized to effect changes in public policy. But it is not necessary to have the support of a majority, as energetic single-issue, or narrowly-focused, groups often demonstrate. Public opinion differs in the salience of policy issues, and the intensity with which it is held. Moreover, public opinion changes over time, as the monthly Gallup Polls indicate.

The second factor is the efforts of interest groups, which consist of like-minded individuals who try to advance their interests (pecuniary or otherwise) by influencing public policy. Groups develop or even create an issue in order to change a policy perceived as unfavourable to their interests. For example, in May 1991, Canadian tobacco companies mounted a vigorous campaign against sharply rising taxes on cigarettes (see *Financial Post*, May 22, 1991, p. 5). More generally, interest groups can help define policy problems, focus public attention on them and propose solutions.

> Broadly speaking, the more political pressure [interest] groups can bring to bear on government — or the greater the political outcry if the government does not co-operate — the more likely will be their extraction of a large tithe from Ottawa. (Provinces have learned this lesson, too.)
>
> This golden rule, brilliantly followed by dairy farmers, oil companies and cable television companies, bids every occupational, linguistic, cultural and economic group to improve its organization, maximize its pressure and so increase the likelihood of receiving more funding or more favorable policy decisions from Ottawa. Each favorable decision immediately turns into a minimum acceptable contribution. Any government that tampers with those decisions risks political pain.[9]

Potential policy issues may also be generated by individuals or groups that seem to be motivated solely by what they think is in the public interest.[10] In other words, they have no pecuniary interest in the issue itself. A great many groups claim this motivation — although analysis usually uncovers more self-serving reasons.

The third factor is leadership — namely, that leadership exercised by key individuals and groups that, because of their own characteristics or association with an issue, are able to "make their mark" with respect to that issue. The role of broader, structural forces is also important, but leadership can be crucial in determining the timing of public-policy initiatives. For example, a politician may develop an issue in order to advance her campaign for office. Politicians can be thought of as political entrepreneurs in the business of obtaining votes in exchange for the promise of policy actions. How far an issue develops depends on its merits, on the ability of the politician to publicize it (gain media attention), and on whether it attracts the attention of voters.

The fourth factor in understanding the sources of public policy issues is technical expertise. This refers to the ability to understand the causes and characteristics of public-policy issues and the methods of dealing with them. Such expertise can be enormously valuable in recognizing the domains over which government action could or could not be effective. Technical expertise usually has more sway in the development and implementation of solutions after problems have been identified and a political coalition is formed that supports government action. Expertise is important also in the sense of what I have called "problem-finding" activities by officials with analytic and technical skills who focus on current or emerging problems. They have a professional interest in promoting greater awareness of problems they have detected and measured.

Fifth, an important source of issues is the unanticipated or exogenous event. An issue that has been dormant for years may be propelled into national prominence by a single unforseen occurrence.[11] Until a train derailment in Mississauga, Ontario in 1979, the Canadian public never really considered the manner in which dangerous chemicals were transported across the country. While legislation on the transportation of dangerous goods existed, the crisis stimulated rapid enactment of new legislation that had been on the back burner for some time. There is no question that sharp discontinuities perceived as crises facilitate the creation of new public policies.[12] The danger is that the result will demonstrate the wisdom of the adage "marry in haste and repent at leisure." Interest groups often try to create the sense of crisis as a justification for prompt government action without much scrutiny of the details.

These factors often combine in complex ways to put an issue on the government's agenda. But government can only manage a few major issues at any one time. The proponents of issues have to compete for the scarce space on the agenda.

5. INTEREST GROUPS: DEFINITION, FUNCTIONS AND TYPES

Definition

Jeffrey Berry (1989, p. 4) states that an interest group "is an organized body of individuals who share some goals and who try to influence public policy." Wilson (1990, p. 8) holds that interest groups are formal organizations (social movements are excluded) that try to influence public policy (although this may not be their primary activity) and have some autonomy from government and political parties.[13] Wilson (1990, chapter

2) argues that four features set interest groups apart from other forms of social organization. First, they are multi-member organizations, although the members may be individuals, firms or other organizations. Second, membership is voluntary. While interest groups may have fairly restrictive criteria for membership, members cannot be formally prohibited from leaving. Third, interest groups are highly dependent upon the active involvement of members in joining and conducting their activities. ("Staff groups" are an exception — they are discussed below.) Fourth, interest groups have a narrow focus of concern — it may be a single issue or a variety of related ones in a wider domain, but is far narrower than that of a political party, for example. In addition to these characteristics, the central or defining characteristic of interest groups is that they seek to influence public policy.

Berry (1989, p. 4) points out that "people may share an interest, a common concern, without belonging to the same interest group." Hence farmers do **not** constitute an interest group, but the Canadian Federation of Agriculture and the BC Tree Fruits Association, for example, do. The critical distinction here is that a number of farmers belong to a formal organization that, among other things, makes an effort to influence public policy. Schlozman and Tierney (1986, pp. 9–10) use the term "organized interests" rather than "interest groups" so as to include not only membership associations such as trade unions and environmental groups, but also politically active organizations that have no members in the ordinary sense (such as universities, corporations and hospitals). In their view, "organized interests" refers to "the wide variety of organizations that seek joint ends through political action."

Functions

Interest groups perform a variety of functions in a democratic society including the following:

Acting as Signalling Mechanisms Elections occur only every three to five years at the federal or provincial level in Canada, and they are relatively crude mechanisms for transforming the policy preferences of individuals into government action. Interest groups can play a valuable role in "signalling" the preferences of citizens between elections — particularly in a world that is continually changing, and thereby creating new information and issues of concern to citizens. Interest groups are not the only mechanism available for signalling preferences, of course, nor are all important interests represented by such groups. That is one of the reasons why all governments make considerable use of scientific public-opinion polls.

Aggregating Interests Groups are able to aggregate individual interests into manageable units. It is very difficult for governments to listen to millions of voices speaking independently, as the result is a cacophony. Interest groups provide a more efficient way of communicating voter preferences to governments between elections. They allow individuals to participate in policy making in a more efficient and effective manner. Participation in groups may inculcate respect for democratic values such as debate, tolerance, negotiation and compromise. Because they can represent and defend minority interests, interest groups can temper the possibility of the "tyranny of the majority."

Providing Information Interest groups provide information to government through their specialized technical knowledge and information about political support for proposed and existing policies. Stewart (1989, p. 81) suggests that the "client groups" of government departments "can be of considerable assistance to the government because of the particular knowledge and insight which they possess, and their reaction to contemplated policies and programs can be invaluable in assessing their appropriateness."

Providing Resources Interest groups help to finance the electoral activities of parties/candidates. They do so, of course, in the expectation of influencing public policy. In Canada, however, the data indicate that financial contributions from interest groups **other** than business firms and trade unions are not important sources of party or candidates' revenues (Stanbury, 1991). This is not the case in the United States, however.

Contributing to Policy Development Interest groups propose policy options and changes in public policy. Even those seeking to advance private, pecuniary interests in the policy arena,[14] may increase society's welfare, depending upon the nature of society's "welfare function," the degree of competition in the policy process, and other factors.

Acting as Agents of Government Interest groups can act as agents of government to regulate members and administer government programs, such as occupational groups. There are many voluntary agencies, some of which receive funds to provide services to citizens.[15] For example, charitable groups have established hospitals that now depend on government funding. Such groups may help implement public policies at less cost than would public servants in a government department.

Types of Groups

There are a number of ways of classifying interest groups and other entities that seek to influence public policy. This section outlines several of these.

Institutional Groups versus Issue-Oriented Groups Pross (1986, chapter 5) distinguishes between institutional and issue-oriented groups. Institutional groups are characterized as having organizational continuity and cohesion, extensive knowledge of areas of government relevant to members, easy communication, stable membership, concrete and immediate operational objectives, and organizational imperatives that are more important than any particular objective. Institutional groups are more likely to be successful because they recognize that "organization is the key to the exploitation of power in the modern community" (Pross, 1986, p. 114). The attributes of organization are as follows: a formal structure incorporating at least several people (sometimes several thousand people) — i.e., a hierarchy; a clear definition of roles (specialization and division of labour); and the ability to generate and allocate resources. In addition, an organization has a collective memory, rules governing the behaviour of members and leaders and procedures for reaching and implementing decisions.

In contrast, issue-oriented groups have the following characteristics according to Pross (1986, chapter 5). They have limited organizational continuity and cohesion; most are badly organized. They have limited knowledge of how government functions; they are often naive. Their membership is fluid, often depending on the visibility and immediate salience of particular issues. These groups have considerable difficulty in formulating and adhering to longer-range objectives. In general, they have a low regard for organizational mechanisms to achieve their goals. Perhaps because of their lack of organization, issue-oriented groups can act in ways quite different from institutional groups. Being flexible, they can generate immediate public reactions to government action. Since members have little or no pecuniary stake in the issue, they can indulge in tactics which would not be acceptable if used by institutionalized groups. They are able to command media attention, possibly embarrass the government and force a change in policy or in its short-run behaviour. Finally, issue-oriented groups may serve as more radical proxies for established interests which cannot afford to be seen to be using certain tactics.

While issue-oriented groups lack all of the characteristics of institutional groups, some do become institutionalized in time — the Canadian Federation of Agriculture and Canadian Federation of Independent Business are two examples. In between these two poles are what Pross (1986, pp. 120–121) calls the "fledgling" and "mature" interest groups.

Staff versus Membership Groups Hayes (1981) draws a careful distinction between staff and membership groups. The latter are characterized by a large number of contributors from the general public and a governing board that is controlled by the full-time staff people who "run" the group. The key distinction is whether the group seeks a membership base or not. Staff groups, such as Greenpeace Canada, do not seek an active membership base; rather, they seek contributors to causes that are defined by the staff, which forms the leadership cadre.

Most U.S. authors emphasize that the majority of new public interest or citizen's groups are not traditional, membership-based organizations. They have overcome the "free-rider" problem by limiting effective participation in the development of the organization's strategy to their small professional staffs (see Berry, 1977; McFarland, 1976, 1983). The staff has effective control; it identifies the issues to be addressed and determines the targets and tactics of the group. Staff often have a degree of commitment ranging from high to fanatical; they are ideologically committed and are willing to pursue distant and intangible goals. Further, the staff develop a strong interest in sustaining the organization as such because it is the vehicle by which they can earn an income, as well as try to achieve their non-pecuniary collective goals, such as environmental protection legislation.

Single-Issue Groups and Protest Groups By definition, single-issue groups are those organized around a single policy issue. The classic example consists of anti-abortion groups, but the category also includes animal-rights groups and those environmental groups with a very narrow focus (such as saving the whales). Single-issue groups are hard to accommodate in the political policy-making process. For members, the issue on which they focus their efforts is a matter of primary importance; it holds trumps over all other matters. There is little or no room for compromise. Moreover, negotiation is seen as moral betrayal by the most righteous supporters. Such groups are inevitably conflict-ridden as the "true believers" seek to overcome those who would compromise with policy makers.

Single-issue groups appear to be growing in importance for a number of reasons. First, they are a reaction to the growing complexity of political processes and institutions. While social and economic problems are complex, people yearn for "simple solutions." Second, there has been a decline in the influence of political parties and other mediating institutions, such as the family and the church. Third, new technologies make it easier to mobilize a constituency — direct mail and banks of telephones using auto-dialers with pre-recorded messages, can create a "long-distance constituency."

So-Called "Public Interest" Groups Jeffrey Berry (1989, p. 7) defines a public interest group as "one that seeks a collective good, the achievement of which will not selectively and materially benefit the membership or activists of the organization."[16] In his earlier book, Berry (1977, p. 137) defined collective goods as those policies for which the benefits may be shared equally by all people, independent of membership in, or support for, any given group. He excluded groups that receive their funding from governmental sources from the definition of public-interest groups because they operate under much different constraints (Berry, 1977, p. 143). Private groups receiving 20 per cent or more of their funds from government were also excluded.[17]

Phillips, Pal, Savas and Hawkes (1990, p. 1) describe a public-interest group as one whose members act together to influence public policy in order to promote their common interest and whose objective is to benefit people beyond their own membership.[18] Their intentions are not centred upon providing direct economic benefits to their members. Membership is voluntary and relatively open; restrictions are likely to be based only on the interest and identity-base of the group. Phillips et al. (1990) describe the following types of groups as being public-interest groups: ethnic or multiculturalism groups, minority language associations, aboriginal groups, women's groups and disabled persons groups. The breadth of their definition has been challenged (see Stanbury, 1994d).

The amount of resources available greatly shapes the specific objectives and activities of public-interest groups. It is common for much of the staff's time to be spent on fund-raising. Hence, the leadership may have to be responsive to different entities outside the group's membership. The ability of groups to issue tax receipts for contributions is supposed to limit U.S. groups to "education" or "technical information." In Canada some groups, such as the National Citizens' Coalition, are not able to issue receipts to make contributions eligible for the tax credit available for "charitable contributions." (see Finkle et al., 1993, chapter 6). In some cases, "advocacy groups" may use adverse publicity as a weapon — that is, take actions in order to create **visibility** for leaders, who can use it to attract members and funding.

The contrast between so-called public interest groups and other groups has been captured by humourist P.J. O'Rourke (1991, pp. 186, 187, 193–194):

> Traditionally... special interests have been frank about their political goals: they want money and privilege that other[s]... don't get... But recently special interest groups have begun dressing themselves in the clothes of altruism. And some of these groups have become so well costumed that it's hard to [determine] what their special interest is, let alone what's so special about it... When an appeal to overweening self righteousness isn't enough the [Perennially] Indignants will argue that their special interest isn't special after all; it's general. If the government does what the Indignants want, **everyone** will benefit, they claim... The Indignants thereby attempt to turn their special interest into a mass movement.

Over two centuries ago Adam Smith wisely counselled his fellow citizens to be skeptical of persons advocating various types of government action for the public good. He said "I have never known much good done by those who affected to trade for the public good." This advice seems appropriate today (see Stanbury, 1994d).

6. BUSINESS FIRMS AS INTEREST GROUPS

Business' Common and Conflicting Interests

In everyday speech, in the newspapers, and frequently in this volume, reference is made to "the business community," to "business interests" or to the power or weakness of "business." Such terms imply that business in Canada is an homogeneous or even monolithic entity. This is not true of course, but it is often convenient to speak in terms of large aggregations such as business, labour[19] and government (or governments). When we look more closely, we often find that the intra-group differences in interests (not to mention other matters) are as great as the inter-group differences. There are often disagreements, or even overt conflicts, among different segments of the business community on public-policy issues. These disagreements mean that business does not speak with one voice and that a government often receives conflicting advice on specific policy issues. Indeed, it may even receive conflicting advice from different firms in the same industry on an industry-specific issue.

Common Interests While these differences can be important, it is useful to identify and consider interests that all, or nearly all, members of the business community share. They have a common interest in having a political environment in which they have a great deal of freedom to make and sell goods and services in hope of earning a profit. More specifically, it appears that business firms have a common interest in the following characteristics of the political/policy-making environment:

- political stability — in the sense that governments change in response to democratic elections, that the decision-making "framework" and important public policies are not changed capriciously
- legal and, preferably, constitutional protections for the rights of private property (while governments must pay compensation when they formally expropriate ["condemn"] private property, property rights are **not** protected in the 1982 Constitution)
- macro-economic stability — monetary and fiscal policies that act in a contra-cyclical fashion to reduce the amplitude of economic cycles
- well-defined and practicable "framework" legislation, such as corporations, bankruptcy, intellectual property, labour, competition and contract legislation[20]
- the **process** for making public policy — it should be quite well-defined, accessible and reasonably predictable, or at least the changes should be subject to reasonable notice; further, the policy actions produced by the process should be based on rational argument, and subject to appeal to the courts
- an efficient, effective and non-partisan public service
- reasonable burden — the government should be concerned that the total net burden of its interventions on business (taxes, regulations, subsidies etc.) is comparable to that of Canada's trading partners and competitors
- an independent judiciary to settle both private interest disputes (over contracts or torts) and challenges to the constitutionality of the actions of the executive and the legislature[21]
- easy access to foreign markets (because Canada is so dependent on foreign trade, many firms have a strong interest in having the federal government negotiate and maintain trade as free of discriminatory regulatory constraints as possible)

Bases of Conflicting Interests In many cases, the "voice of business" is best described as a "tower of babble," for "there are dozens upon dozens of business associations stoutly defending viewpoints that at times clash sharply." (*Financial Post*, 1976) When he was president of the Toronto Board of Trade, A.R. Murrich observed that "...business in our society is a kaleidoscope, as diverse in its problems and aspirations as the country itself." (Board of Trade *Journal*, Christmas 1976, p. 9)

The bases of these conflicting interests begin with the fact that all firms face direct or indirect competition from domestic or foreign rivals: **intra-industry rivalry**. However, the typical industrial structure in Canada is that of a moderately to highly concentrated oligopoly — see Green (1990). In other words, firms recognize their interdependence and perceive themselves more as head-to-head rivals than do firms in an atomistic industry unaffected by the actions of any single firm. In dealing with government, firms often seek to reinforce their competitive advantage over rivals (or obtain one) by gaining discriminatory benefits that improve their position relative to their rivals. For example, a pulp and paper company whose mills are new (and less polluting) may urge stringent enforcement of across-the-board pollution controls in order to force its rivals with older mills that produce more effluent to incur higher costs in the form of expenditures on abatement, or new, less polluting production equipment. Leone (1986) emphasizes that the key competitive effects of changes in government depend largely on changes in firms' relative costs and on the type of costs (fixed versus variable) that result from policy actions.

Different industries tend to be concentrated in certain provinces or regions in Canada. The Atlantic Provinces, for example, account for about 60 per cent of the Canadian fisheries' output, while Ontario accounts for one-half of Canadian manufacturing. A large fraction of Canada's forest products exports come from British Columbia. Governments within a province or region tend to support its major industries. The effects of this are exaggerated by the important role of the provinces in Canadian federalism. The high concentration of industries in provinces or regions pits one business sector (backed by a province or region) against another (also backed by a province or region). This **interregional rivalry** is a major source of conflict within the business community in Canada. Policies that favour one industry/region (such as protectionism for Central Canada's manufacturing) impose costs on others (the resource-based industries in Western Canada).

Closely connected with conflicts brought about by interregional rivalry are those that originate between industries favouring free trade and those favouring protectionism. Manufacturing is highly concentrated in Central Canada, with Ontario and Quebec accounting for over three-quarters of the Canadian total. Canadian manufacturers have traditionally favoured protectionist policies. While tariffs have been reduced (the Canada-U.S. Free Trade Agreement [FTA] being the outstanding example), non-tariff barriers have become far more important. On the other hand, the industries concentrated in Western Canada, such as forestry (B.C.), petroleum (Alberta) and agriculture (Saskatchewan), are export-oriented. These industries have traditionally favoured a policy of freer trade for Canada, recognizing that liberalization is a reciprocal proposition. As a result, there have been conflicts and disagreements between the businesspeople of Central Canada and those of Western Canada, again with each group backed by its provincial governments.

Canadian firms that sell a substantial fraction of their output abroad, are naturally concerned about the terms of access to foreign markets and the exchange rate. Firms which focus on the domestic market, are likely to be more concerned about competition from imports and macroeconomic policies that stimulate demand.

Further, there are attitudinal differences between Canadian-owned and foreign-controlled firms operating in Canada. These include differences in attitudes toward wage, salary and benefit costs; legislation regarding competition policy; and Canadian economic nationalism. Again, attitudinal differences may contribute to conflicts within the business community over government policies and priorities.

Comparing Business Firms to Other Interest Groups

A business firm or a trade association is one of many interest groups seeking to influence public policy. It is useful to consider the characteristics of a business firm as an interest group (see Stanbury, 1994f). In general, a business firm (particularly a large one) has certain advantages relative to other interest groups. These are outlined below.

- The firm is already organized for other purposes so that the "free rider" (collective action) problem has already been solved (see Olson, 1965)
- The firm's "agency problem" is tiny compared to those of interest groups with a broadly-based membership
- Executives are familiar with strategic thinking, which is very useful in the political arena
- Business firms have a strong functional role in society, which provides them with legitimacy
- Business firms are seen to play an important role in maintaining a high standard of living in society
- Large firms have extensive economic resources, which can be used in their efforts to influence public policy. They can hire expertise in business-government relations and pay the cost of major efforts to influence public policy

- Expenditures on lobbying and other efforts to influence public policy are tax-deductible expenses

At the same time, relative to other interest groups, business firms have a number of disadvantages in their efforts to influence public policy.

- Pecuniary private interests are widely perceived to be morally inferior; business firms are deemed to be exclusively focused on increasing profits
- It is widely believed that business interests are antithetical to "the public interest," a highly evocative but ill-defined concept
- There are plenty of internal cleavages within the "business community," — large versus small business, domestic versus foreign ownership, domestic versus international focus, state-dependent versus little aid from government etc.
- Market or institutional failures (such as pollution) are often blamed on firms — they are seen to be attributable to the greed of managers, rather than as problems in institutional design
- Capitalism has an "unacceptable face"; its periodic excesses often lead to more general government intervention
- Many top executives have little training in dealing with government (and other interest groups) and fail to appreciate the differences in the political/bureaucratic arena

7. GOVERNMENT RELATIONS CONSULTANTS

Business and other interest groups may employ government relations consultants to assist them in influencing government. As we shall see, these firms can provide a variety of related services to their clients.

Government relations consulting firms (GRCs) have been growing in number and size in Canada in the last decade. Such firms have become more visible to the public and media.[22] Most firms now have senior partners with ties (past or present) to both major parties.[23] Many of the principals and staff in such firms have had experience in the bureaucracy.

As of March 31, 1994, there were 994 Tier-I ("professional") and 1815 Tier-II ("employee") lobbyists, registered under the federal Lobbyists Registration Act (which came into effect on September 30, 1989).[24] By comparison, the figures for March 31, 1991, were 658 Tier-I and 2182 Tier-II lobbyists.

Some indication of the scale of GRC, or fee-for-service lobbying firms, can be ascertained from data compiled by *The Lobby Monitor*.[25] The 14 most active government relations firms in the spring of 1994 had from 23 to 79 clients (average 44.2 each). The 10 most active law[26]/accounting firms which also act as lobbyists had from 15 to 55 clients (average 26.2 each).

What do GRCs do for their clients? Gary Ouellet, chairman of GCI, states "companies come to us when they want results. They don't want policy papers, just resolution of the issue" (*Globe and Mail*, June 5, 1989, p. B28). Can the pressure to "get results" result in unethical behaviour? The objectives of the firms hiring a GRC include:

- getting a contract (the Department of Supply and Services alone spends $10-billion annually on procurement)
- getting a favorable regulatory decision from an "independent" agency, a line department, or the Cabinet (such as getting takeovers through Investment Canada, or helping American Express to obtain the Schedule-B bank license it got in November 1988)
- obtaining or blocking new general legislation
- blocking or obtaining a change in existing general legislation (for example, tobacco manufacturers hired Bill Neville to reduce the adverse effects of the Tobacco Products Control Act, enacted in 1988)

Government relations firms offer a range of services. They can:

1. provide intelligence on what is going on in Ottawa and make predictions about future developments;
2. develop the interest group's strategy for trying to influence government, either on an ongoing basis or for a specific issue or problem by:
    - identifying and defining problems
    - identifying key people who are likely to influence the decision itself or the process by which it is made
    - generating and describing alternative influence strategies, such as traditional lobbying, public relations, advocacy ads, media campaigns, political contributions and
    - identifying and evaluating strategic alliances or coalitions
3. develop a detailed program to co-ordinate efforts to influence government
4. provide advice on the group's proposed strategic approach; and
5. prepare the persuasive materials to be used to lobby government, such as briefs, speeches, advocacy ads, press releases and internal communications programs.

In some cases, a GRC may carry out some or all of the set of persuasive activities for the client ("get into the trenches").

The larger public-affairs/government-relations consulting firms monitor social, economic and political issues relevant to their clients or potential clients. They try to identify, as early as possible, the issues that are likely to be subject to some form of policy action by government. While consultants will develop strategy and prepare briefs for clients, few make presentations directly to public officials. Many strongly believe that senior executives of their client firms are likely to be more effective. By maintaining close contact with public servants, politicians and regulators, consultants are able to indicate whom their clients should contact and what arguments are likely to be more effective. Both formal and informal contacts are used. Such contacts are based very heavily upon the exchange of information that is valuable to all participants.

One of the important steps in influencing government is gaining access to decision makers. It has been suggested that some GRCs "peddle access," that is, they use their political contacts — usually based on previous employment or party activities — to sell their firm's services as "door openers."

However, the access issue is not simple, for there are several possible definitions of "access." First, the GRC is able (for a fee) to obtain a meeting with a government official (elected or appointed) that the interest group could not have obtained itself. Second, the business firm or interest group could have eventually obtained a meeting, but the GRC greatly speeded up the process (and for some problems, time **is** of the essence). Third, the GRC is able to influence the result to the client's advantage because of past associations (not simply because it is able to make the client's argument more persuasive). This suggests GRCs are really selling **influence**, not merely obtaining or facilitating access.[27]

In terms of the objective of their efforts, the data collected under the Lobbyists Registration Act indicates, for example, the types of lobbying those registered propose to do on behalf of their clients. The most frequent activity in 1990–91, involved efforts to influence existing programs or policies (24.7 per cent).[28] The least frequent activity is supporting or attempting to defeat a bill (7.5 per cent of the total). The second most frequent activity, more than twice as frequent as lobbying on a bill, is seeking to influence a regulation (16.2 per cent of the total). Procurement-related activities ranked third (15.8 per cent), while efforts to obtain a grant or contribution ranked fifth (12.9 per cent). Arranging a meeting accounted for 13.2 per cent of Tier-I lobbyists' activities in 1990–91. This seems high in light of numerous protestations by federal cabinet ministers that firms or other interest groups do not need any help from GRCs in order to obtain a meeting with them. Similarly, virtually all senior public servants would deny that any individual, firm or interest group needs help from a professional lobbyist to arrange a meeting with them on a public-policy issue. Overall, students of lobbying should note the modest fraction of Tier-I lobbyists' time that is spent on trying to influence the development, or passage, of legislation.[29]

As extensive as the activity of lobbying firms at the federal level appears to be, it is the proverbial tip of the iceberg. The data cited above refer to Tier-I lobbyists, those consultants who operate on a fee-for-service basis, and represent various clients. Tier-II lobbyists, such as the heads of trade associations and other interest groups are not included. Further, a considerable variety of lobbying activity is exempt from the Lobbyists Registration Act (see Canada, 1993).

8. ORGANIZED LABOUR AS AN INTEREST GROUP

Unions have long recognized that they can make gains for their members, both at the bargaining table (on a contract-by-contract basis) and in the political arena (through, for example, minimum-wage legislation, various employment standards provisions). However, a large part of general labour legislation is designed to be of most help to the unorganized.

Only 36 per cent of the paid non-agricultural labour force is organized (30 per cent overall) and only 58 per cent of union members are affiliated with the Canadian Labour Congress (CLC). (See *Globe and Mail*, May 16, 1994, p. A4). The most significant growth in unionization since the late 1960s has been in the public sector. By 1992, **collective** contributions to political parties or for charitable purposes are not tax deductible or eligible for a tax credit. However, membership dues are tax deductible for members. The locals of some unions are formally affiliated with the NDP, but their membership amounts only to 8 per cent of the non-agricultural labour force (Archer, 1990). Recently, however, some unions have moved to distance themselves from the NDP, including ending the payment of affiliation dues to the party.[30]

Malvern (1985, p. 80) argues that the CLC has been selective in the issues around which it will organize a "lobbying blitz." A blitz might include the following activities: meetings with elected officials at all levels of government, meetings with public servants, letter-writing campaigns, commissioning of polls and their strategic release in the media, demonstrations, planting stories with sympathetic journalists and advocacy ads. The CLC has an annual meeting with the prime minister and cabinet (and provincial bodies have one with the premier and provincial cabinet). The CLC has commissioned studies of specific problems by holding hearings across the country. Labour organizations often try to build broadly based coalitions. They have occasionally used litigation to influence public policy (recall the constitutional challenge to 1975 federal wage-and-price controls) as well as more traditional days of protest (general strikes, political rallies, etc.).

In the late 1980s and early 1990s, organized labour in Canada was being hard pressed by foreign competition (NAFTA and globalization generally), and by what it believed to be a federal government that wanted to reduce its political and economic power.

In the spring of 1994, it was clear that there is conflict within labour ranks.[31] Some leaders believe that labour must become more active in electoral politics by being part of a "rainbow coalition" of native groups, women's groups and farmers. However, this coalition did not succeed in defeating the FTA nor NAFTA. Others believe that unions should focus on collective bargaining, but the election of Robert White as president of the CLC is likely to result in organized labour taking a larger role in politics and public-policy issues.

With the unions' backing, the NDP has gained power recently in several provinces: Ontario in 1990, and B.C. and Saskatchewan in 1991. In each case, the leaders of unions that had been actively involved in the NDP's campaign (supplying money and organizers) have pushed the new premier to deliver specific benefits. The contributions by the unions to the NDP's successful campaign in B.C. in October 1991 "were unmatched in previous elections," according to a senior labour leader. The Harcourt government in B.C. has done much in terms of policies and legislation to reward its union supporters. The Rae government in Ontario — faced with persistent recession and severe fiscal stringency — has been condemned by most unions for its social contract legislation cutting back wages of public service unions.

9. HOW INTEREST GROUPS TRY TO INFLUENCE PUBLIC POLICY

The techniques used by interest groups to influence public policy take a wide variety of forms, as Figure 3 makes clear. These techniques can be grouped into two broad categories: direct and indirect. **Direct** approaches consist of bringing organizational representatives into direct contact with public officials. Consulting with legislators or their staff, presenting committee testimony, presenting research and interacting with regulatory agency personnel, are all forms of direct approaches. **Indirect** approaches consist of more circuitous methods of influencing policy makers.[32] For example, lobbyists can pressure public officials by generating support or opposition at the local riding level. They can also launch mass media campaigns or establish opposition groups (Mahood, 1990, p. 62). Direct lobbying, the main focus of this paper, consists of efforts to communicate with decision makers and their advisors directly, to persuade them to adopt the firm's position. This may be done in a number of ways: meetings with the "target"; testimony before a parliamentary committee; the submission of a brief to a committee, government department or minister; telephone calls; contacts at social events; and participation on advisory committees. In most cases, the people doing the lobbying are employees of the interest group, but in some cases, they may be accompanied by a GRC who has been hired to assist the group in making its case.

Indirect lobbying, or what has been called "new-breed lobbying," focuses on mass marketing and the "packaging of issues." It is wholesale lobbying in contrast to the one-on-one approach of retail lobbying (Smith, 1988, p. 235). The indirect techniques of influencing public policy include efforts to influence the news media with the objective of influencing public policy by gaining visibility for the firm's (other interest group's) views and thereby influencing public opinion. Advocacy advertising is designed to sell ideas primarily to the public, but also to policy makers. The state of public opinion can make it either easier or harder for government to implement particular policies. Less direct techniques include political

FIGURE 3
Techniques Used by Interest Groups
to Influence Public Policy

Direct Influence Techniques

Direct Lobbying:

- hold formal and informal meetings with policy makers and their advisors (public servants and politicians); may be part of an ad hoc or ongoing consultative process;
- submit briefs to departments or ad hoc policy processes (for example, advisory committees);
- testify before parliamentary committees or other entities formally addressing policy/legislative issues (such as regulatory agencies);
- make telephone calls to advocate one's (the group's) position (these may also be used to acquire information about the process and other players).

Stimulation of the "Grass Roots": get "ordinary citizens" to signal their views to politicians through tactics like mass mail/fax/telegram campaigns from members of the interest group and/or other supporters.

Direct Action Activities: include demonstrations, rallies, protest marches; boycotts of the product/services of the target; planned violence (the strongest form of direct action); civil disobedience, such as blockades of streets, bridges, building entrances; the appurtenances of these activities may include placards, signs, burning in effigy, grotesque masks, speeches, spontaneous behaviour (a "happening") and strong, colourful language.

Litigation: often used to try to block some policy action, but could also compel government action, such as a full-scale environmental review of a project; constitutionality of a law may be challenged under the 1982 Charter of Rights and Freedoms.

Coalition: create an alliance among several groups and utilize one or more of the techniques.

Indirect Techniques

Media and Public Relations: getting favourable media coverage for positions, speeches and publications through interviews, press releases, video tapes, press agents.

Advocacy Advertising: selling ideas (rather than products) designed to influence public policy.

Think Tanks: trying to change the composition of the set of **ideas** in good currency (ideas can have practical consequences) by funding research and dissemination of ideas.

Election-Related Activities: political contributions to parties or candidates; running ads on specific policy issues; volunteer work for a party or candidate(s).

Doing Favours: trying to build up "credits" by helping ministers, MPs and public servants, then relying on reciprocity to achieve greater influence for the group.

contributions and the funding of think tanks, thereby trying to alter the volume and types of ideas in the policy-making political arena. Obviously, it is a longer-term approach to shaping the policy agenda.

It is impossible in the space available to discuss each of these techniques even briefly. (For more detail, see Stanbury, 1993b). Therefore, a handful have been chosen to give readers a feel for the ways interest groups go about their work.

Lobbying

Defining Lobbying: Who is a Lobbyist? The term "lobbying" most often refers to the activities of representatives of organized interest groups that are designed to influence public policy. Herb Perry, executive director of the Institute of Association Executives (the trade association for the senior personnel who run trade associations and other formal groups), points out that "there is sometimes an impression that lobbying is dirty or immoral. [Yet] every time a voter phones a school trustee he's lobbying. When the Society for Crippled Children asks for larger doorways on washrooms, it's lobbying."

In the most general terms, a lobbyist is any person who seeks to influence public policy. Hence, the term could be applied equally to the senior citizen who writes a letter urging her MP to fight the proposal to de-index the old-age pension and to a partner in a government-relations consulting firm retained by a large trade association to advise it on how to persuade the cabinet to increase subsidies and tax expenditures for the firms in that industry. Lobbyists also include the head of the Canadian Federation of Agriculture, who regularly meets with politicians (and public servants) urging them to do things like changing a regulation raising the subsidy on industrial milk, which now costs the federal treasury more than $300-million annually. Fred Moonen, then vice-president of government relations for MacMillan Bloedel, Canada's largest forest-products company, described his role as a lobbyist as "creative loitering." By this he meant that he haunted the corridors of the legislative building in Victoria waiting to catch cabinet ministers and backbenchers (including those in the opposition) for a few minutes' discussion about legislation or administrative policy (Comparelli, 1983). Therefore, lobbyists may be paid professionals representing a firm or other interest group, or they may be "amateurs" representing only themselves or a volunteer group.

Lobbyists as a Source of Information Perhaps the strongest functionalist argument for the legitimacy of firms and other interest groups to participate in the political process is that they provide valuable information to other actors in the policy-making process, notably public servants and politicians (particularly cabinet ministers).

In general, the information provided by lobbyists is of two broad types: assessments of the impact, or potential impact, of an action, or proposed action, by government (who wins and, more importantly, who loses from a policy action); and the likely **political** response of various groups to the actions proposed by government. Decision makers need to know about the potential outcomes of the policy alternatives arrayed before them, if they are to make the best choice. No one sitting in Ottawa, or in any of the provincial capitals, can predict with great accuracy how a policy action will affect those remote from the centre (although many insist that they can). Firms and other interest groups can provide (more) accurate and valuable information or expertise not available even to politicians and the bureaucracy.[33]

Obviously, politicians care a great deal about how important groups of voters are likely to **perceive** a policy action. If 90 per cent of 20,000 owners of small businesses replying to a CIFB questionnaire oppose a piece of proposed legislation thought by the federal government to benefit small business, politicians may wish to rethink the issue. It is not just the numbers of those who favour or oppose a particular measure that counts with politicians; they are also interested in the **intensity** of preferences. In particular, they want to know if there is a sizeable group of individuals who are prepared to make the issue highly visible in the media (thereby possibly influencing others) and switch their voting allegiance.

The public servants dealing with the issue are more interested in analyses that would help them assess how well a policy achieves, or is likely to achieve, its substantive (as opposed to symbolic) goals. For example, will this industrial incentive grant create jobs? How many? Where? What type? What will be the budgetary cost per job? Will competitors of subsidized firms complain? While politicians provide plenty of evidence that allocative efficiency is a low priority for them, many public servants are genuinely concerned about this objective.

Lobbyists are told that public servants who have to administer the policies and programs approved by legislators also care a great deal about their practicality, or workability, in implementation. Public servants need analytical information to assess the administrative problems associated with a policy. By avoiding administrative "snafus," public servants may save their ministers from public embarrassment, and themselves from headaches. The point is that middle-level and senior public servants take pride in their professionalism. While they may privately disagree with the objectives and substance of a particular program, they know it is their job to make it work as well as possible within the spirit intended by their political masters.

An Exchange Process At first glance, lobbying appears to be a unilateral activity: the lobbyist seeks to persuade the target to adopt his or her position and thereby influence public policy in a way that is favourable to the interests the lobbyist represents. Wise lobbyists, however, recognize and seek to benefit from the pervasiveness and power of the norm of reciprocity.

While successful lobbying is sometimes a one-way process, lobbyists are more likely to be successful if they start out with the view that lobbying is a process of exchange. Since lobbyists want something from government (a cabinet member, a senior public servant etc.), they should begin by thinking of what they can offer in exchange. This requires that lobbyists go beyond the simple exchanges posited by the public-choice approach to policy making (see Stanbury, 1993a, chapter 3). To use reciprocity effectively in the context of lobbying, an interest group has to begin by determining two things. First, what is it that the interest group wants from the various individuals and groups that are believed to have an impact on government policy? Second, what is it that the interest group has that it can offer to the targets of its lobbying efforts in exchange for what it wants from them?

Negotiating Process Lobbying is often a negotiating process, but interest groups must recognize that a lobbyist negotiating with government is **not** the same as a firm negotiating a contract with a supplier or the union representing some of its employees. Indeed, most public-policy processes are not construed by government officials, or the public, as negotiating situations at all (or even as implicit invitations to negotiate).

Negotiating with a government is different than negotiating with private parties, in a number of ways. First, lobbyists have to appreciate that, ultimately, government can exercise legitimate powers of coercion (subject to acting within the Constitution). It can force people to do what it wants. Second, government is probably more sensitive to public opinion than are most private parties.[34] This fact may be used to advantage, but the lobbyist has to be aware that information openly given or leaked to the press which is perceived as going beyond the normal range of tactics to increase pressure on a minister or the cabinet may result in a loss of access or credibility in the future. Third, government probably has a "taller" hierarchy (more steps) than most business firms, and has to consult more players than private negotiators, because policy making is more pluralistic. Fourth, wise lobbyists appreciate that a government's goal structure is usually more complex than that of business firms (or interest groups): it has more goals; many are less tangible; some goals conflict with each other; and the set of goals and their priority ranking is subject to change. Thus, agreements or understandings reached with government are often more complex, harder to reach and have more elements that are implicit, than those between private parties. Fifth, a government has no economic "bottom line" analogous to that of a firm. In some ways, this makes it easier to "cut a deal," but in others, it makes it more complicated because governments are more willing to use economic resources to achieve the political goals of the party in power (all in the name of the public interest). Sixth, lobbyists have to realize that a government probably has to be more careful about setting a precedent (which may have unattractive consequences in the future) when it negotiates. This may be due to the efficacy of demands for equity, i.e., treating people in similar circumstances in the same fashion.

A Rivalrous Process Lobbying (like efforts to influence public policy) is often a rivalrous or competitive process in which different interests are in conflict over what each is urging government to do, or not to do.[35] These conflicts stem largely from the differential impact of alternative policy actions on the income/wealth or utility of members of various organized interest groups, including firms. Conflicting claims may be couched in the rhetoric of the public interest, or in ideological terms. However, the best way to predict a group's position on an economic issue (as opposed to a non-pecuniary or "values" issue), is to determine whether its members believe they are likely to be economically better or worse-off because of a particular proposal. Even on a values issue, such as environmental protection, narrow self-interest often lurks just beneath the surface. In the case of Canadian nationalism, it is hard to avoid the conclusion that the strongest proponents of policies in the name of such nationalism also stand to gain economically from such policies. While wrapping themselves in the flag, they are also filling their pockets.

Coalitions An old maxim of warfare and politics is that there is strength in numbers. There is evidence that ad hoc lobbying coalitions are becoming more important in policy making in Canada. That is one of the reasons why MPs have recently expressed interest in legislation requiring interest groups to disclose whether they are part of a lobbying coalition[36] (see Canada, 1993). Some coalitions are very loose arrangements among groups that are moving in the same direction and keeping each other informed so that each can improve its effectiveness while acting independently. Other alliances take the form of a more formal — albeit ad hoc — coalition in which lobbying and other persuasive activities are closely coordinated.

First, a coalition, particularly one that is well organized, may represent a sizeable number of votes directly, or be able to make a credible claim to be able to influence a large number of votes. Second, coalitions can alter the distribution of potential votes so as to make the issue much more salient to politicians. One association head advises that a delegation meeting a politician should be "geographically and politically distributed.... Don't talk to half a dozen guys from Toronto or you will go down the tubes before you even speak" (*Globe and Mail*, March 10, 1983, p. B9). Third, ad hoc coalitions of groups that are perceived as "strange bedfellows" (those normally in conflict with each other), are likely to have a greater impact on both public opinion and on politicians, precisely because the alliance appears to be so unnatural. In other words, unusual coalitions or alliances may demonstrate to politicians the seriousness of the problem. Fourth, lobbying coalitions or alliances, by incorporating groups with widely differing interests, can give the appearance of "representing everybody." Therefore, it is easier for them to argue that what they want from government is "in the public interest." Fifth, lobbying coalitions are an antidote to the frequent problem of competitive lobbying by various groups on a specific issue. Competitive lobbying means that Ottawa, or a provincial government, receives conflicting advice about what it should or should not do.

Stimulating the Grass Roots

The Funk and Wagnall's *Standard College Dictionary* states that "grass roots" is an informal term of American origin, referring to "those people often living in rural areas, thought of as having fundamental, practical, and highly independent views or interests." The term has come to be used to refer to people from whom the government does not usually hear directly on public-policy issues (except perhaps on election day), because they are "ordinary folks" who are normally too busy with the practical business of making a living, tending their gardens and supervising their children. There is a clear implication that such people represent the true "voice of the people."

The firm, or other interest group, tries to produce signals from a large number of people at the grass-roots level that **appear** to be spontaneous and unorganized but that support its position. The word "spontaneous" is the key. Opinions of people at the grass-roots level can be triggered by a number of new technologies. Individuals can be "aroused" (made aware of an issue that is likely to have specific consequences for them) by mail, fax or even automatic telephone dialing machines with a pre-recorded message linked to a computer data bank of names, addresses and telephone numbers. It is usually easier to mobilize opinion at the grass-roots level when people perceive that their health, safety, primary values or income are **threatened** by a proposed policy action.

A firm can begin by making an effort to stimulate communications from its stakeholders, such as employees, stockholders, suppliers and even customers. In addition to communicating with politicians, signals from the grass roots may be focused on the news media, or on regulatory agencies, to back up a group's brief.[37] In general, the objective of generating signals from the grass roots is to show politicians that **voters** are interested and willing to act on a particular issue. The telephone calls, letters, postcards, faxes and telegrams (or mailgrams) are a means of demonstrating the organizational strength of a group and its leadership on a particular issue. A large number of messages from the grass roots is a way of showing that ordinary citizens, not just activists or paid staffers, care about the issue.

Canadians have to appreciate that differences in the design of our political institutions (notably cabinet government and the emphasis on party discipline) limit greatly the utility of generating pressure on individual members of parliament. For efforts to be effective in stimulating the Canadian grass roots, it is essential that they focus on the party in power, rather than the opposition, since it very largely determines what changes in policy will be made — provided it has a majority and that the efforts occur early in the process of developing a policy. (For an excellent example, see May, 1990.) Once the government has publicly committed itself to a specific course of action (for example, introduced new legislation or amendments to existing acts), it is very difficult to obtain other than minor changes.

Direct Action

Direct action or "expressive activity" as a technique of influencing public policy embodies a variety of specific tactics, including the following:

- verbal assault on a senior public- or private-sector executive at a conference, meeting or press conference (this is usually designed to obtain coverage in the news media)
- occupying a government's (or a firm's) office with the objective of shutting it down (or disrupting its work) and obtaining extensive coverage in the news media
- "eco-tage" — a wide range of tactics designed to inflict damage on those who oppose the goals of environmentalists, such as tree-spiking, pouring sand in the gas tanks of vehicles or logging equipment etc.
- blockades of transportation "bottleneck" points (such as bridges or tunnels), so that thousands of ordinary people become aware of the group's issue
- "bodies-on-the-line" — direct efforts to stop activities the group opposes, such as shutting down an abortion clinic, disrupting whale hunting or killing of baby seals, "tree-sitting" to prevent logging of old-growth forests etc.
- civil disobedience — actions designed to provoke the police into arresting the protesters, preferably while the television cameras roll, such as blockading an abortion clinic or violating a court order against protests in a certain area (see Stanbury, 1994c)

Illustrations of legitimate direct-action techniques are not hard to find, for example, demonstrations and rallies by pro-choice groups; a rally by students protesting budget cuts; a brief protest by fruit farmers aimed at the premier of B.C.; a hunger strike organized by environmentalists; a series of protests, rallies and other actions by farmers, to dramatize their fear and frustration with low prices and a sharp decline in their income. Legitimate tactics are usually the choice even of groups that are "outsiders" or are marginal in society, although some groups choose such tactics because, for them, they appear to be useful in both influencing public policy and in building the organization by attracting more members, providing a means for members to vent their feelings and creating solidarity within the group (see Phillips et al., 1990).

Illegitimate activities — those that violate widely held social norms about how interest groups and their members ought to behave — generate a variety of consequences. First, there is the possibility of extensive coverage in the news media, so the group's message is carried to a larger audience. Media coverage, particularly by television, is the oxygen of radical interest-group tactics. Second, such activities may reinforce the motivation of the most activist members, and assist the organization in recruiting new members seeking an outlet for their frustrations and a voice to their values. Third, illegitimate activities may stiffen the resolve of less radical or mainstream groups to ask for more and refuse to settle for less, in their efforts to obtain changes in public policy. Fourth, among more radical interest groups, illegitimate activities may boost the group into a leadership position, so that other groups will acknowledge it as the one most willing to make real sacrifices for the cause. Fifth, these activities may enhance the reputation and increase the legitimacy of the group among those relatively narrow segments of society that endorse such culturally illegitimate actions. Sixth, publicity associated with illegitimate activities, if properly managed, can indirectly enhance the group's legitimacy with broad segments of society that support its goals, if not its tactics (Elsbach and Sutton, 1991, p. 5). Seventh, illegitimate activities may **reduce** the legitimacy of the group and its demands in the eyes of the public or segments of public opinion. Eighth, one of the objectives of illegitimate activities may be to provoke opponents of the group, or the police, into extreme reactions in front of the news media, preferably television. The issue then becomes the "pornography of violence" rather than the illegitimate actions of the group. This creates a new, diversionary issue which may invest the initial action with more moral force. It also displays the "corruption" and lack of legitimacy of those who oppose the radical tactics.

Litigation

In the past decade or so, interest groups have increased their use of litigation as a technique to influence public policy. Von Clausewitz observed that "war is nothing more than the continuation of politics by other means." In the same vein, litigation can be seen as nothing more than the continuation of lobbying by other means. For example, in 1988, after they failed to prevent the Conservative government from passing Bill C–51, the Tobacco Products Control Act, which prohibits advertising in the electronic and print media, tobacco companies went to court to challenge the constitutionality of the new statute. While they succeeded at the trial level, the case went all the way to the Supreme Court of Canada.

Litigation can be used to

- stop actions by others, e.g., an injunction to stop the construction of a dam, power plant or logging road
- force positive action, e.g., make an agency establish regulations according to a schedule established in a statute
- test the interpretations of a regulatory agency by appealing to the courts
- test the constitutionality of legislation that goes against the group's interests

More generally, see Figure 4.

FIGURE 4

Outline of Possible Actions by an Interest Group
to Use the Legal System to Influence Public Policy

1. **Constitutional Challenge** A firm can challenge the constitutionality of a statute or part of a statute. This may come about in several ways.
   - A firm may seek a reference to a provincial court of appeal or to the Supreme Court of Canada
   - A firm may launch an ordinary action starting in the provincial supreme court and possibly working up to the provincial court of appeal and the Supreme Court of Canada
   - A firm may challenge the constitutionality of legislation under which the firm is the subject of a criminal charge by the Crown. The charge may be:
   - "provoked" by the firm in the sense that it deliberately violates the law in order to test the law
   - the result of an inadvertent action resulting in a charge by the Crown
   - The constitutionality of certain legislation may be raised by a firm in the context of a private action
2. **Decisions of Regulatory Agencies** The firm applies to a regulatory agency that has jurisdiction over the matter to enter a particular market, get an increase in the prices it charges its customers, discontinue service, or other action. Note that the agency is the "normal" decision maker of **first** instance in such matters.
3. **Appeal*** A firm, as a party** to a decision of a federal regulatory agency, may seek review of the decision:
   - by the Federal Court, based on an error in law or violation of the rules of natural justice
   - by the regulatory agency itself (separate appeal panel)
   - by the federal cabinet (a political appeal)
4. **Intervenor** A firm can be an intervenor in a public (or even private) action or in a case before a regulatory agency. Thus it could present evidence, file a brief and perhaps cross-examine the witnesses presented by the parties.
5. ***Amicus Curiae* Brief** A firm can submit an *amicus curiae* brief to the court in a public action.
6. **Other Actions** These include the following:
   - A firm can make an effort to influence the selection of judges. This is very difficult, since typically only the bar association is consulted by Department of Justice officials. The final selection is made by the Prime Minister
   - A firm may make a complaint to the Canadian Judicial Council about the conduct of judges on or off the bench. These have been rare
   - In a very few statutes, a firm could initiate a **private** prosecution. It might do so with a view to having the case being taken over by the Crown, or it may continue with the case. The object is to ensure that a public law is properly enforced
   - A firm can provide financial assistance to litigants to enable them to try to change public policy by means of a legal action

---

*Both parties and intervenors may launch such appeals. They may even do so on an *ex parte* basis. Further, for some agencies (such as the CRTC) the Cabinet may review (and alter) the decision entirely of its own volition.

**If a firm was an intervenor, it may also be able to appeal the case to the cabinet.

In Canada, since the Charter of Rights and Freedoms was entrenched in the revised Constitution in 1982, the number of cases in which individuals, firms and interest groups of all types have sought to use the courts to achieve their political and policy objectives has expanded greatly (see Knopff and Morton, 1992). The then-federal Minister of Justice, Kim Campbell, said that she deplored

> "the growing use of the courts" by people trying to challenge legislation they don't like. "I think this tendency undermines the ability of legislatures to work out public policy issues.... Everyone wants the courts until the courts make what people see as a wrong decision...." Campbell said the courts have a role to play with public policy issues, but should not be used "to strain the ability of the legislature to act" or to "strike down progressive legislation." She described the charter as a "pig in a poke" that was accepted without much internal debate although it ended up "dramatically changing" the country (Vancouver *Sun*, September 26, 1991, p. B9).

But the minister should not have been surprised by the growth in such litigation because the federal government has in fact been a major source of funds for individuals and public interest groups to challenge new and established statutes using the Charter and other elements of the new Constitution.

An analysis by political scientists Peter Russell and Ted Morton of the first 100 Charter cases decided by the Supreme Court of Canada, indicated that the success rate for litigants relying on the Charter after the first two years began to fall precipitously (Toronto *Star*, May 28, 1990, p. A20). During the first two years the court awarded victories to nine of 14 Charter claimants (64 per cent). Over the next four years, the success rate fell, averaging 27 to 37 per cent. Overall, the success rate of Charter claimants was 36 per cent, resulting in the Court striking down 12 provincial and eight federal laws. As for the subject matter of the first 100 Charter cases, 74 dealt with questions of Charter rights in the **criminal** justice system (Knopff and Morton, 1992, p. 22).

LEAF The Women's Legal Education and Action Fund (LEAF) was established in April 1985, the month in which the equality rights provision (Section 15) of the Charter of Rights and Freedoms came into effect. LEAF seeks to advance women's interests by using the Charter as a sword to attack existing statutes. Knopff and Morton (1992, p. 29) point out that LEAF

> "has participated in numerous Charter cases both as a litigant and as an intervenor. It intervened successfully in both the *Borowski* and *Daigle* abortion cases [and]... has enjoyed success in cases involving a boys-only hockey league in Ontario, the use of original surnames by married women and the eligibility of natural fathers for 'maternity' leave."

By mid-1990, LEAF had been involved in about 80 cases, 12 of which went to the Supreme Court of Canada. It became the most frequent non-government intervenor in Charter cases before the Supreme Court.

LEAF is financed by government grants and private donations. In 1989 LEAF spent $800,000, but a portion of this went to its legal-education programs. In addition, another $400,000 worth of legal work was donated by female lawyers. LEAF strongly objected to the federal government's announcement in February 1992 that funding for new cases under the Court Challenges Program — under which it had received money — was being ended. Shortly after they came to power, the Liberals restored LEAF's funding.

Advantages of Litigation Litigation may produce a sweeping change in operative public policy in a stroke of the highest court's pen. For example, a law may be declared unconstitutional and the government may not wish, or be able, to produce new legislation that has the same effect but is constitutionally valid — for example, the Province of Ontario moved to change its policy with respect to prayers in public schools after a Court of Appeal decision (*Globe and Mail*, October 15, 1989, p. A4).

Adversarial litigation is subject to an elaborate set of procedural rules (and customs) that limit and channel hostility into a socially accepted method of conflict resolution. One of the primary functions of the court is to resolve a variety of conflicts, including those concerning the constitutionality of legislation and the interpretation of the key terms and phrases in legislation.

On some policy issues the political process culminating in the legislature has simply not been able to resolve sharp conflicts in basic values. Thus, statutes are often vague or even contradictory. In effect, the legislature delegates to the courts the difficult task of translating principles into action. Where the principles are not clear, or are conflicting, judges are effectively forced to apply their own value judgments. Some people find this preferable to continued conflict in the political arena. Others do not, because it seriously threatens their view of the proper roles of the legislature and the courts in a democracy (see Bork, 1990).

It has been argued that the courts represent a better forum for the underdogs — if they can get there (that is, obtain standing and have the money to pay the lawyers' bills). In litigation, the grounds for battle are narrowed. There is equality of argument where facts and logic really **do** count. In litigation, the focus is often on **individual** rights. In some cases, activist judges, with a streak of *noblesse oblige*, are prepared to make decisions in terms of their views on what is desirable social policy.

The courts may provide an avenue of appeal from decisions rendered by governments, which have great powers of coercion. They are the protectors of the rights of private individuals (firms, organizations) in the sense of deciding fairly the operational scope of constitutional rights.

Disadvantages of Litigation Litigation can be extraordinarily costly, and hence, beyond the means of many individuals or organizations (including firms). For example, the National Citizens Coalition (NCC) spent some $500,000 to finance the Lavigne case, all the way to the Supreme Court of Canada, challenging the constitutionality of the use of part of a union's dues for political purposes, when some union members opposed this. This **excludes** both the costs of the other side, which won, and hence is entitled to request the Court to award costs against Lavigne/NCC (which the court did) **and** the costs of three intervenors, which the Court ordered Lavigne/NCC to pay. The total bill for this effort may be as much as $1.5-million.

Litigation involves several types of risks. First, there is the risk of losing, and hence becoming liable for the costs of the other side — and now, in light of the Lavigne case, the costs of intervenors, as well. Second, there is the risk that even if the firm or group wins the case, its own legal bills (including experts and the time of its executives) will be much more than it forecast. Such costs are hard to control short of discontinuing the action, in which case the firm could be hit with the other side's costs. Third, there is the risk that the substantive outcome will be not only negative but worse than the law which existed prior to the case. The courts may close and bar a door that was partially open but that the litigant wanted to open wider, or the litigant may win in the courts but find that the government responds by changing the law in ways **adverse** to the litigant and succeeds in making the new legislation (apparently) immune to constitutional challenge.

Most opportunities for litigation come late in the policy-making process, namely after legislation has been enacted or after a regulatory decision has been rendered. Most law (and regulation) **is** constitutionally valid, and efforts to challenge it usually have a low probability of succeeding. The critical point is that a new law (embodying a particular policy disliked by a potential litigant) may remain in force for several years, even if it is challenged immediately and is eventually overturned. In that time, irreversible changes may have occurred that limit the utility of winning in the courts.

Litigation is often a last resort by those seeking to change public policy. It may force into an inappropriate forum, a decision better determined in the political arena (through elections, intra-party debates, the legislature and the legitimate exercise of discretion by public administrators). The courts may be called upon to make value choices in interpreting a statute or the Constitution. Through strategic use of the judicial system, an elite which is unable to win election, or command the majority of the legislature, may well be able to influence judges, and gain the force of law.

Changes in public policy brought about by litigation may be an unintended consequence of defending either a private action or a criminal charge, rather than as the result of a conscious effort to reshape public policy by means of a legal decision. In the latter situation, the accused care only for their own skin and use the constitutionality sword because it is just another weapon which may work. (There is an old saw that advises that where the facts and substance of the law are against you, fight on the basis of a procedural error that violates a constitutionally protected right.) The 1982 Charter has, in effect, become a shield for the accused, although the scope of its protections are still being defined by the courts. If the constitutionality of a statute is challenged in an action in advance of any hearing on the facts, the second stage may become moot. More important, a lengthy delay will result, so that even if the case is eventually tried on its merits, from two to five years may have passed. In general, delay helps the defence and hurts the prosecution. The key point is that, in many instances, the defendant has not set out to use the Charter as a tool to change public policy. The defendant would be entirely happy to "get off" without any change in public policy at all (unless he plans a career in the activity subsequently found to be *ultra vires* of the provincial or federal government).

The decision rendered by courts (even after all appeals have been exhausted) may turn out to be very narrow, with only a limited range of applicability to other persons. In general, judges in Canada seek to render decisions on narrow, rather than broad, grounds. The point for interest groups is that the court's decision — obtained after a lengthy and costly process — may not achieve the policy breakthrough they sought. It may only have significance for the particular circumstances in the case at hand.

Wilson (1990, p. 64) suggests that extensive litigation on the part of interest groups emphasizes a process that is "inherently adversarial in character" and fails to promote compromise. Thus, "interest groups may well be obdurate, hoping to gain in court what they might fail to gain in negotiation." The conflictual nature of litigation is more problematic where the parties "have to live with each other" on a regular basis after the decision is handed down. Further, it has been argued that litigation is largely a **negative** instrument. It can rule a piece of legislation unconstitutional, but it can't directly result in new legislation, new programs or policies which are widely acceptable.

Advocacy Advertising

Advocacy advertising — paid commercial messages that seek to sell ideas rather than goods and services — is a relatively new tool in the set of techniques business firms and other interest groups can use to influence public policy. It is based largely on the assumption that an organization can influence public-policy decision makers, both directly and indirectly, by shaping public opinion through paid advertising. Sometimes called "issue" or "controversy" advertising, it is often used in conjunction with other actions designed to influence policy, notably lobbying (see Stanbury,

1986, chapter 12). Organizations, other than business and labour, are making use of such ads.[38]

Advocacy advertising can be defined as "any kind of paid public communication or message, from an identified source and in a conventional medium of public advertising, which presents information or a point of view bearing on a publicly recognized controversial issue" (Stridsberg, 1977, p. 18). The advertiser's intention is to have an influence on a matter of recognized public controversy. The results sought range from the correction of factual information to a change in the opinions of members of a target audience, the mobilization of supporters, the solicitation of financial contributions and the passage or defeat of a specific piece of legislation.[39] The main characteristics of advocacy ads are the following:

- they are paid communications in electronic or print media
- they are designed to "sell" ideas, not products or services
- they may be aimed directly at policy makers, or at some segment(s) of public opinion
- their ultimate objective is to influence public policy on an issue (or issues) that is important to the firm or organization paying for the ads

In most cases, advocacy advertising is only one of several techniques being used to influence public policy.

Stridsberg (1977, pp. 20–23) suggests there are three reasons why advocacy ads are needed by corporations. First, the corporation's constituencies (shareholders, employees, creditors, suppliers) will not tolerate silence in the face of "attacks" by its critics (such as so-called public interest groups or government agencies), or by a decline in public opinion. Second, the media are perceived by many companies as failing in their responsibilities — i.e., not giving the firm fair, accurate or complete coverage in a controversy in which the firm is involved. One critic argues that business and other "establishment" entities have frequently been the subject of "accusatory journalism." Others emphasize that the United States is an "adversary culture." Advocacy advertising, therefore, is a way of reaching large audiences "without the benefit of an editor, writer or commentator." (This ignores the fact that such ads may themselves inspire controversy in the news columns, or even counter-ads by other interest groups.) Third, firms participating in the policy-making process want maximum control over their message and the environment in which it is delivered. The "problem" with the news media is very seldom the amount of space or time, but the way the issue or information is presented. Cynics argue that big business, unlike some other interest groups, can buy space or time to deliver its message in the way it wants, while other groups are not able to do so because they lack the money.

As a technique of influencing public policy, advocacy advertising is not without some risks. Those using such ads need to be aware of them. First, the ads could cause controversy instead of helping to influence public policy in the way the sponsor intended.[40] The target audience may resent them, politicians and senior public servants may perceive the ads as "going public" on an issue that should remain in the policy community or as an effort to generate pressure from the public; others may be dismayed by the costs of an extensive campaign. Second, there is the possibility that the ads will be ineffective, thus wasting the sponsor's money. Since a major campaign could cost $500,000 to over $2-million, this is a serious matter. Third, CEOs can become enamoured with seeing their firm's position "up in lights," — in full-page newspaper ads or even in 30- or 60-second ads on television — and overlook the fact that the ads are not as effective as other, less costly, techniques of influencing public policy (the name of the game).

A variety of concerns have been raised about advocacy advertising as a technique for influencing public policy. First, it is argued that advocacy advertising favours the political interests of those with "deep pockets." It is a form of interest-group representation open only to those with larger financial resources; hence larger corporations have an advantage in the process of influencing government policy. Moreover, some argue, it adds insult to injury because the costs of advocacy ads by corporations are tax deductible. Second, critics ask, whose interests are being advanced in corporate advocacy ads? Where there is a separation of ownership and control, professional managers may be using shareholders' money in ways they would not approve. Third, potential advertisers ask, should the media have the right to reject advocacy ads? For example, on October 1990, the CBC rejected a commercial prepared (at a cost of $400,000) by the Dairy Farmers of Canada, because it expressed "a point of view or course of action on a matter of public interest." Both the CTV and Global television networks ran the ads.

10. CONCLUSIONS

This paper has focused on the nature of interest groups, their roles in the policy-making process and some of the techniques they use to try to shape public policy. Changes in public policy take many forms, from new legislation, to cabinet-enacted regulations, to the exercise of discretion by public officials in the day-to-day operation of a government program. The most effective interest groups begin by identifying those places where government actions influence their members' interests positively or negatively, and take action accordingly.

Interest groups come in all shapes, sizes and issues orientation — from ephemeral single-issue groups, to institutionalized organizations that address a wide variety of policy issues (such as the Business Council on National

Issues, the CLC and the Canadian Council for Social Development). Because they are already organized for other purposes, businesses and trade unions have some advantages when they act as interest groups, over those whose sole function is to be an interest group (such as Western Canada Wilderness Committee or Greenpeace). However, on some issues, like environmental protection, business firms are perceived as being the problem, while environmental groups are widely seen as part of the solution.

Interest groups operate in a larger political arena in which politicians exchange promises of policy action for a variety of types of political support (contributions to the party or candidates; votes; efforts to persuade others). For the party in power, however, the most valuable thing interest groups can offer is information about the likely consequences (political and economic) of proposed policies.

Interest groups can choose from a wide range of techniques (and tactics) in their efforts to influence public policy. While traditional lobbying remains important to almost all groups, it is clear that more groups are making greater use of litigation (encouraged by the 1982 Charter), advocacy ads (although these require greater financial resources) and efforts to influence public opinion by means of coverage in the news media. It is clear that the activities of interest groups in general are gaining greater visibility in the mass media. They are also the subject of analysis by policy analysts and academics.

The role of interest groups and lobbyists has become a source of greater concern over the past few years, perhaps because the perceived influence of both has increased. These concerns have prompted a reduction in federal government funding and new legislation.

The early 1990s were hard times for interest groups heavily dependent upon the federal government for grants, contributions or contracts. After they returned to power in 1988, the Tories began to reduce the funding of interest groups (see Phillips, 1991; and Pross and Stewart, 1993). Some groups, such as the Women's Legal Education and Action Fund, were cut off entirely (see Vancouver *Sun*, April 16, 1992, p. A22). In April 1993, the Minister of Finance announced that grants and contributions to all groups (only part of which funds lobbying) were to be cut 10 per cent in fiscal year 1994–95, 15 per cent in 1995–96 and 20 per cent annually for the next two years. The Liberals, elected in October 1993, adopted the Tories' strategy and cut such grants and contributions by another $45-million in 1994–95, $49-million for 1995–96 and $42-million for 1996–97 (see Chase, 1994). They did, however, restore LEAF's funding for several years.

Early in 1993, the House of Commons Standing Committee on Consumer and Corporate Affairs and Government Operations began an examination of the *Lobbyists Registration Act* enacted in 1988 (effective September 30, 1989).[41] The Liberal members of the Committee demanded extensive changes, such as the disclosure of fees by lobbyists, more detailed information about the targets of lobbying activities and more information filed by employee lobbyists (Tier-II). The Committee's *Report* of June 1, 1993, however, was less far reaching, but did propose that *all* lobbyists (fee-for-service or employee) have to disclose much more information (see Canada, 1993).

The Tory leadership campaign, followed shortly by the election, prevented the Tories from considering the *Report*. The Liberal Party's campaign platform (the so-called "red book") addressed lobbying in the chapter called "Governing With Integrity." It argued that reforms were needed in three areas: "conflict of interest, influence peddling, and selling access." It promised to implement the *Report* of the parliamentary committee.

After further consultation (164 of the 192 parties consulted were lobbyists!), the Chrétien introduced amendments to the *Lobbyists Registration Act* on June 16, 1994. The changes did *not* include all those proposed by the Commons' Committee.[42] (See Figure 5.)

One of the most difficult tasks of students of government and public policy is to ascertain the impact specific interest groups have on public policy. Particular interest groups have to compete with others, and with forces and events for space on a government's policy agenda. Thus, generalizations about how much power is exercised by particular groups — even within particular domains — are hazardous. While a framework such as the one provided here, is useful, the nature of an interest group's power is often quite specific to context. Therefore, to understand the impact of a given interest group, students of public policy must be prepared to combine theory with a knowledge of political institutions, the characteristics of the group and the policy issues the group is seeking to influence.

Notes

1. Far more comprehensive analyses can be found in Stanbury (1992a), (1993a); Seidle (1993); Sawatsky (1987a); Baetz (1993); and Cameron (1989).
2. In 1991, the federal cabinet enacted 885 pieces of subordinate legislation covering 4830 pages in the *Canada Gazette*. In 1990, the figures were 1035 and 6598 respectively (see Stanbury, 1992b).
3. Despite some deregulation in the late 1980s (see Block and Lermer, 1991), a very great deal of economic activity in Canada is subject to government regulation. In areas such as protecting the environment and human rights, the amount of regulation has been increasing (see Stanbury, 1993b).
   There are two exceptions: (1) when expenditures exceed those authorized in the Estimates, Parliament votes additional money through the *Supplementary Estimates* during the fiscal year; and (2) when Parliament is not in session, the cabinet can obtain additional spending by means of governor-generals' warrants.
4. Hartle (1988, p. 52) suggests that "donations by rent-seeking interest groups to political parties and to the election campaigns of particular candidates can be looked upon as a siphoning off of some of the rents by those who make it their business to put together coalitions of rent seekers and who

FIGURE 5

Comparison of Existing *Lobbyists Registration Act* to the Proposed Amendments (June 1994)

Existing Act	*Proposed Amendments*
TIER I: individuals who lobby for clients	**CONSULTANT LOBBYISTS**: individuals who lobby for clients
• must register within 10 days • by undertaking registration must register for: – arranging meetings, or attempting to influence legislative proposals, bills or resolutions, regulations, policies, programs, award of grants or contributions or other financial benefits, award of contracts	• must register within 10 days • by undertaking registration must register for: – arranging meetings, or attempting to influence legislative proposals, bills or resolutions, regulations, policies, programs, award of grants or contributions or other financial benefits, award of contracts
• must disclose: – lobbying firm and address – client and address – subject-matters from checklist of 52 subjects – if client is a corporation, the parents and subsidiaries – identify object of lobbying, e.g., whether it is a law, contract etc.	• must disclose: – lobbying firm and address – client and address – name and address of anyone who directs client – if client is a corporation, the parent and those subsidiaries which directly benefit – if client is a coalition, the names of the corporate and organizational members – proposed subject-matters – specific legislative proposal, bill or resolution, regulation, policy, program, contract etc. – name of each department or other governmental institution lobbied – communication techniques used
• notify Registrar in writing of changes as soon as practicable	• notify Registrar of changes in any of the above required information, new information or termination within 30 days • clarify given information on request of Registrar

garner rents on behalf of the members of the coalition through the introduction of 'appropriate' policies."

5. There are two conspicuous exceptions: Mrs. Irene Dyck has given the NDP annual contributions of as much as $453,365 (see Stanbury, 1991, p. 221). William Loewen gave the National Party, created in December 1992, over $4-million (see *Globe and Mail*, May 26, 1993, p. A6). By comparison, in 1988 the Canadian Labour Congress donated $1.01-million in cash, plus at least the same amount in kind, to the NDP. The largest corporate contribution

FIGURE 5 (Continued)

Existing Act	*Proposed Amendments*
TIER II: employees who lobby as significant part of duties	**IN-HOUSE LOBBYISTS (CORPORATE)**: employees of corporations who lobby as significant part of duties **IN-HOUSE LOBBYISTS (ORGANIZATION)**: organizations where the collective time of lobbying amounts to a significant part of one employee's duties
• annual registration – register for: – attempting to influence legislative proposals, bills or resolutions, regulations, policies, programs, award of grants or contributions or other financial benefits	• annual registration • register for: – attempting to influence legislative proposals, bills or resolutions, regulations, policies, programs, award of grants or contributions or other financial benefits
• must disclose: – employee name – employer name and address	• must disclose: – employee name – employer name and address – the parent and those subsidiaries that directly benefit – general description of employer's business activities – names of employees of organizations who lobby – general description of the membership and association activities (of organizations) – proposed subject-matters – specific legislative proposal, bill or resolution, regulation, policy, program, grant or contribution or other financial benefit – name of each department or other governmental institution lobbied – communication techniques used
• notify Registrar in writing of changes as soon as practicable	• notify Registrar of changes in any of the above required information, new information or termination within 30 days • clarify given information on request of Registrar

to the Liberals was $80,501 and to the Conservative Party $136,500 (Stanbury, 1991, Table 11-4).

6. Except for corporations and trade unions, interest groups give very little money to federal political parties in Canada (see Stanbury, 1986, chapter

10 and Stanbury, 1991). Further, under legislation enacted in 1993, advocacy groups or individuals are prohibited from spending more than $1000 on "election expenses," i.e., on activities which **directly** endorse or oppose a party or candidate during campaign periods under the *Canada Elections Act.* They can, however, advertise their views on policy issues during campaigns (see Stanbury, 1994b).

7. It should be obvious that there is a potential for deception, bluffing and other forms of strategic behaviour. For example, a group could launch a vigorous campaign against an existing policy, toward which it really was indifferent, to create a "bargaining chip" to be exchanged for an action on a policy it really cared about.
8. Jeffrey Simpson, "The pressure gauge," *Globe and Mail*, March 15, 1989, p. A6.
9. This is a notoriously difficult concept. Because it is so evocative, for strategic reasons, most groups claim that what they want is "in the public interest," and not merely of benefit to their members (see Stanbury, 1993a, chapter 13).
10. On the night of April 14, 1912, the R.M.S. Titanic — the largest passenger ship in the world — struck an iceberg on her maiden voyage and sank, with the loss of 1522 lives. Senator William Alden Smith, who headed the U.S. inquiry into the disaster, promptly introduced a bill "which radically altered the existing statues of marine legislation" (Wade, 1980, p. 406). Two other pieces of legislation related to the *Titanic* sinking were passed by the Congress shortly thereafter (p. 418). Further, the United States took the initiative in organizing the International Conference for the Safety of Life at Sea (November 1913 to January 20, 1914). It was the first such convention in modern maritime history, and it has been reconvened periodically since. Five committees were established that developed new standards of maritime safety (Wade, 1980, p. 420). Wade (1980, chapter 20) notes that the repercussions for public policy of the *Titanic* disaster were very wide ranging. For example, it blunted the thrust of women's emancipation, but the consciousness of U.S. blacks was raised by it.
11. A good example appears to be the recent federal gun-control legislation and regulations.
12. Wilson (1990, p. 6) notes that "most organizations which participate in interest-group policies do not recruit individuals with the promise to represent their views or interests politically," such as business firms, unions and professional organizations. In each case, the primary activities of the organizations do not relate to influencing public policy.
13. For example, if there is a widely-held preference for a more egalitarian distribution of income and a group succeeds in obtaining policies that redistribute income from the rich to the poor, then it may well have improved society's welfare.
14. In 1990, it was estimated that the value of labour provided on a volunteer basis in Canada was $13.2-billion. The number of hours was equivalent to six per cent of the labour force.
15. The scope and scale of the collective good pursued by public-interest groups varies greatly. "Some organizations (such as feminist, peace and environmentalist groups) seek to transform the most basic, as well as the most embracing of

human relationships: for example, the student and consumer movements" (Phillips et al., 1990, p. 16).

16. If such a criterion were applied in Canada, the set of public-interest groups would be virtually empty. For example, in 1990–91 the federal Department of Secretary of State made grants to 337 official language groups, 457 women's groups, 195 groups representing disabled persons, 160 aboriginal groups and 175 multicultural groups (Phillips, 1991, p. 200). In 1990–91, the federal Department of the Environment gave $1.11-million to eight groups (Stanbury, 1993b, Table 12). It should be noted that aboriginal groups are by far the largest recipients of grants/contributions from the federal government to assist them in their efforts to influence public policy — almost $90-million in 1986–87 (Stanbury, 1992a, chapter 14).
17. In some cases, these groups may advocate politics that produce selective benefits that go largely to their membership, but the core of their activities must be focused on the broader collective good.
18. A standard mis-generalization is to illustrate the interests of labour by quoting the statements of the senior officials of the Canadian Labour Congress. Yet only 27 per cent of the labour force in Canada is unionized, and the CLC is only one of several national or central labour bodies (albeit the largest one).
19. Business is usually concerned that labour legislation strike a careful balance between the interests of employees and employers.
20. It should be appreciated in Canada that the courts cannot be relied upon to prevent extreme acts by a majority government that might involve implicit expropriation because of the absence of constitutional protection for private property.
21. See Stanbury (1994a); Cameron (1989); Harris (1985a), (1986b); *Maclean's*, February 24, 1986, pp. 14–21; Sawatsky (1987a), (1987b); and various issues of *The Lobby Monitor* (ARC Publications, Ottawa).
22. As the Mulroney government came to the end of its second term, a number of the most prominent Tory lobbying firms moved to take on a more neutral cast, or even to appoint prominent Liberals to top positions in firms which had featured well-known Tory insiders (see *Globe and Mail*, January 25, 1993, p. A2). Not all of these "transformations" were successful with the new Liberal government (see *Globe and Mail*, November 29, 1993, p. A1).
23. When the Act was passed, the government emphasized that the purpose of the legislation was **not** to regulate lobbying, but to make the process better understood by identifying who is lobbying and on what issue. The "targets" of lobbying (politicians and bureaucrats) need not ask lobbyists if they are registered or refrain from contact with unregistered lobbyists. The Act covers lobbying directed to "public office holders." These include employees of federal departments, members of the House, Senate and their staff, cabinet members, officers and employees of regulatory agencies and tribunals, members of the armed forces and RCMP. The legislation applies to two categories of lobbyists: Tier-I consists of professional lobbyists who work for third parties. They must register their names, titles, business addresses and telephone numbers. They must register the names of clients (parents and subsidiaries) and the area of policy they are trying to influence. They must specify the nature of their work: to influence the development of the

proposal, passage or amendment of a bill; development or amendment of government policy; awarding of a grant; awarding of a contract. Tier-II consists of people whose business involves a significant amount of liaison with government officials; they need only register their own names and addresses and those of their employers. Major amendments were introduced in June 1994. See Figure 5.

24. *The Lobby Monitor*, Vol. 5(15), May 30, 1994, pp. 9, 10.
25. After he resigned as Prime Minister in June 1993, Brian Mulroney joined the Montreal law firm of Ogilvy Renault. Part of his job involved lobbying for the firm's clients, e.g., for Power Corp. in China (see Vancouver *Sun*, October 7, 1993, p. D2).
26. Wilson (1990, pp. 65–66) suggests that "to an even greater extent than for an ordinary lobbyist, the 'hired gun' cannot afford to compromise his or her reputation through duplicity or dishonesty in pursuit of short-term gain. If the contract lobbyist deliberately misleads a politician, that politician will never trust him or her again, even if he or she is working for a different client. A short-term advantage obtained dishonestly would result in long-term failure."
27. The *Annual Report* of the *Lobbyists Registration Act* for 1992–93 did not provide the same tabulation as for 1990–91. Instead, the seven categories were merely ranked. This is another example of the loss of information in official government reports.
28. In 1992–93, this activity was ranked seventh out of seven categories by the *Annual Report* of the *Lobbyists Registration Act* (p. 11).
29. See *Globe and Mail*, March 8, 1993, p. A7; *Financial Post*, March 18, 1993, p. 13; *Financial Post*, August 4, 1993, p. 10; *Globe and Mail*, November 17, 1993, pp. A1, A4; *Financial Post*, April 23, 1994, p. 4. More generally, see Stanbury (1994e).
30. See "CAW's hard-line stand grates on rivals," *Globe and Mail*, May 16, 1994, p. A4.
31. In some cases, indirect lobbying may involve foreign targets. For example, the James Bay Cree sought support in New York, the potential buyer of power from the Great Whale electric project in Quebec, in their effort to stop the Province of Quebec from building the Great Whale project. They even hired a Madison Avenue PR firm. The Cree paddled a canoe down the Hudson River and then portaged into Central Park — and received plenty of television coverage (*Globe and Mail*, September 28, 1991, p. B18). Further, Mathew Coon-Come, grand chief of the 10,000 Cree, testified at a hearing in New York City that the Great Whale project would result in "massive environmental destruction of Cree land" (*Financial Post*, October 3, 1991, p. 15).
32. Such information need not be "perfect" to be highly valuable. It need only be better than what was previously available, or else made available in a more timely fashion.
33. Thus negotiating with government over a policy issue is very seldom a strictly bilateral process. Explicitly or implicitly, other interests are involved; government has to find a solution that a number of contending interests ("stakeholders" in the relevant policy community) can "live with."
34. For case studies, see May (1990) and Stanbury (1994).

35. See Canada (1993) and more generally, see Moore (1994).
36. An alternative is a scientific opinion poll, which may focus on the total population, a region or a particular segment of the population.
37. For example, in its efforts to influence forestry practices and save old-growth forests, Greenpeace Canada published two full-page advocacy ads: *Globe and Mail*, February 9, 1994, p. A7; Vancouver *Sun*, February 12, 1994, p. A21. The two ads cost over $50,000. At the same time, Greenpeace U.K. was pressuring buyers of pulp to drop their contracts with MacMillan Bloedel Ltd. (see Stanbury, 1994c).
38. For example, the Brewers of Canada began a series of advocacy ads in 1986 designed to hold down or reduce the high and growing level of federal and provincial taxes on beer. See, for example, "Everybody benefits from fair taxation," *Report on Business Magazine*, March 1986; and "A big production number from the Brewers of Canada," *Globe and Mail*, February 16, 1986, p. B4.
39. For example, the B.C. Government Employees Union was criticized by the president of British Columbians for Mentally Handicapped People for using an "offensive, awful and unreal" advocacy ad in an effort to portray the effects of de-institutionalization of the mentally handicapped and mentally ill. A Vancouver *Sun* editorial called the ad "irresponsible almost to the point of being scurrilous." Two cabinet members called the ad "factually misleading and irresponsible." See Vancouver *Sun*, January 27, 1986, p. A1; January 29, 1986, p. A4; January 31, 1986, p. A20.
40. See *Globe and Mail*, March 4, 1993, p. A3.
41. See Ross Howard, "Ottawa to tighten lobbying rules," *Globe and Mail*, June 17, 1994, pp. A1, A4.

REFERENCES

Anisman, Philip. 1975. *A Catalogue of Discretionary Powers in the Revised Statutes of Canada, 1970*. Ottawa: Law Reform Commission of Canada/Information Canada.

Baetz, Mark C. 1993. *Readings and Canadian Cases in Business, Government and Society*. Toronto: Nelson Canada.

Berry, Jeffrey M. 1977. *Lobbying for the People*. Princeton, NJ: Princeton University Press.

———. 1989. *The Interest Group Society* 2nd ed. Glenview, Ill.: Scott, Foresman/ Little, Brown.

Block, Walter and George Lermer, eds. 1991. *Breaking the Shackles: Deregulating Canadian Enterprise*. Vancouver: The Fraser Institute.

Bork, Robert. 1990. *The Tempting of America: The Political Seduction of the Law*. New York: The Free Press.

Breton, Albert. 1976. *The Regulation of Private Economic Activity*. Montreal: C.D. Howe Research Institute.

Cameron, Stevie. 1989. *Ottawa Inside Out*. Toronto: Key Porter Books.

Canada, House of Commons Standing Committee on Consumer and Corporate Affairs and Government Operations. 1993. *Report: A Blueprint for Transparency*. Ottawa: Minister of Supply and Services, June 1.

Chase, Steve. 1994. "Means of Allocating Public Funds to Groups Must Change," *Lobby Digest and Public Affairs Monthly* 55 (May): 9–10.

Comparelli, Peter. 1983. "The Lobbyists: Creative loiterers play political street game" Vancouver *Sun* (June 22): B1.

Consumer and Corporate Affairs Canada. 1991. *Lobbyists Registration Act*, Annual Report for the year ended March 31, 1991. Ottawa: Minister of Supply and Services Canada.

Doern, G. Bruce and Richard W. Phidd. 1983. *Canadian Public Policy, Ideas, Structure, Process*. Toronto: Metheun.

Drucker, Peter. 1989. *The New Realities*. New York: Harper and Row.

Dunleavy, Patrick. 1991. *Democracy, Bureaucracy and Public Choice*. New York: Prentice-Hall.

Edelman, Murray. 1988. *Constructing the Political Spectacle*. Chicago: University of Chicago Press.

Elsbach, K.D. and R.I. Sutton. 1991. "Enhancing Organizational Legitimacy Through Illegitimate Actions: A Marriage of Institutional and Impression Management Theory" (Paper presented at the 1991 Academy of Management meetings, Miami Beach, Florida).

Finkle, Peter, Kernaghan Webb, W.T. Stanbury and A. Paul Pross. 1993. *Federal Government Relations with Interest Groups: A Reconsideration*. Ottawa: Department of Consumer and Corporate Affairs.

Fleming, James. 1991. *Circles of Power: The Most Influential People in Canada*. Toronto: Doubleday Canada.

Green, Christopher. 1990. *Canadian Industrial Organization and Policy*, third edition. Toronto: McGraw-Hill Ryerson.

Harris, Michael. 1985a. "Tory-owned consulting firm [GCI] shows clout in Fisheries switch," *Globe and Mail* (June 27): 1, 8.

———. 1985b. "Ex-premier [Frank Moores] still controversial in private-sector incarnation," *Globe and Mail* (July 22): 1–2.

Hartle, D.G. 1988. *The Expenditure Budget Process of the Government of Canada: A Public Choice-Rent Seeking Perspective*. Toronto: Canadian Tax Foundation.

Hayes, Michael T. 1981. *Lobbyists and Legislators: A Theory of Political Markets*. New Brunswick, NJ: Rutgers University Press.

Hiebert, Janet. 1991. "Interest Groups and Canadian Federal Elections." Pp. 3–76 in *Interest Groups and Elections in Canada*, ed. F. Leslie Seidle. Toronto: Dundurn Press.

Knopff, R. and F.L. Morton. 1992. *Charter Politics*. Toronto: Nelson.

Leone, Robert. 1986. *Who Profits: Winners, Losers and Government Regulation*. New York: Basic Books.

Liberal Party of Canada. 1993. *Creating Opportunity*. Ottawa: LPC.

Mandel, Michael. 1989. *The Charter of Rights and the Legalization of Politics in Canada*. Toronto: Wall and Thompson.

May, Elisabeth. 1990. *Paradise Won: The Struggle for South Moresby*. Toronto: McClelland and Stewart.

McFarland, Andrew S. 1976. *Public Interest Lobbies*. Washington, D.C.: American Enterprise Institute.

———. 1983. "Public Interest Lobbies Versus Minority Faction." Pp. 324–353 in *Interest Group Politics*, eds. A.J. Cigler and B.A. Loomis. Washington, D.C.: Congressional Quarterly Press.

Moore, Sean. 1994. "Beyond Coalitions: Using Proxy Lobbies," *The Lobby Digest and Public Affairs Monthly* 56 (June): 1–4.

Olson, Mancur. 1965. *The Logic of Collective Action*. Cambridge, Mass.: Harvard University Press.

———. 1982. *The Rise and Decline of Nations*. New Haven, Conn.: Yale University Press.

O'Rourke, P.J. 1991. *Parliament of Whores*. New York: Atlantic Monthly Press.

Phillips, Susan D. 1991. "How Ottawa Blends: Shifting Government Relationships with Interest Groups." Pp. 183–213 in *How Ottawa Spends, 1991–92*, ed. Frances Abele. Ottawa: Carleton University Press.

Phillips, Susan D., L.A. Pal, D.C. Hawkes and D.J. Savas. 1990. *Interest Groups in the Policy Process* (Unpublished study for the Department of Secretary of State, Ottawa).

Preston, Lee E. and J.E. Post. 1975. *Private Management and Public Policy*. Englewood Cliffs, NJ: Prentice-Hall.

Pross, A. Paul. 1986. *Group Politics and Public Policy*. Toronto: Oxford University Press.

Pross, A. Paul and Iain S. Stewart. 1993. "Lobbying, the Voluntary Sector and the Public Purse." Pp. 109–142 in *How Ottawa Spends, 1993–1994*, ed. Susan D. Phillips. Ottawa: Carleton University Press.

Salisbury, Robert H. 1991. "Putting Interests Back into Interest Groups." Pp. 371–384 in *Interest Group Politics*, eds. A.J. Cigler and B.A. Loomis. Washington, D.C.: Congressional Quarterly Press.

Savoie, Donald J. 1990. *The Politics of Public Spending in Canada*. Toronto: University of Toronto Press.

Sawatsky, John. 1987a. *The Insiders: Government, Business and the Lobbyists*. Toronto: McClelland and Stewart.

———. 1987b. "The Lobbyists: A Clean Operator" [re Susan Murray] *Canadian Business* (December): 32–40.

Schlozman, Kay L. and John T. Tierney. 1986. *Organized Interests and American Democracy*. New York: Harper & Row.

Seidle, F. Leslie ed. 1993. *Equity and Community: The Charter, Interest Advocacy and Representation*. Montreal: The Institute for Research on Public Policy.

Smith, Hedrick. 1988. *The Power Game: How Washington Works*. New York: Random House.

Stanbury, W.T. 1986. *Business-Government Relations in Canada: Grappling With Leviathan*. Toronto: Methuen.

———. 1991. *Money in Politics: Financing Political Parties and Candidates in Canada*, Study for the Royal Commission on Electoral Reform and Party Financing. Toronto: Dundurn Press.

———. 1992a. *Interest Groups and Public Policy: A Guide for Public Administrators* (Draft manuscript prepared for the Canadian Centre for Management Development, Ottawa, April).

———. 1992b. *Reforming the Federal Regulatory Process in Canada, 1971–1992* in Minutes of Proceedings and Evidence of the Subcommittee on Regulations and Competitiveness of the Standing Committee on Finance 23 (November 17–December 10): 23A: 1–293.

———. 1993a. *Business-Government Relations in Canada: Influencing Public Policy*. Toronto: Nelson Canada.

———. 1993b. "Notes on Environmental Issues and Interest Groups" (Vancouver: UBC, Faculty of Commerce and Business Administration, May, mimeo).

———. 1994a. "Interest Groups and Lobbying in Canada: Recent Developments, 1992–1994" (Vancouver: UBC, Faculty of Commerce and Business Administration, July).

———. 1994b. "Regulating the Financing of Federal Parties and Candidates" in *Canadian Parties in Transition*, eds. A.B. Gagnon and A.G. Tanguay. Toronto: Nelson Canada, (in press).

———. 1994c. "Protest Behaviour and Other Efforts to Influence Environmental Policy in British Columbia: The Case of Clayoquot Sound" (Vancouver: UBC, Forest Economics and Policy Analysis Unit, June).

———. 1994d. "A Skeptics Guide to the Claims of So-Called Public Interest Groups," *Canadian Public Administration* 36 (Winter).

———. 1994e. "Notes on Recent Developments in Campaign Finance in Canada and Its Regulation" (Vancouver: UBC, June, mimeo).

———. 1994f. "Assessing the Political Power of Business Interests" in *Crosscurrents: Contemporary Political Issues*, eds. Mark Charlton and Paul Barker. Toronto: Nelson Canada.

Stewart, Edward E. 1989. *Cabinet Government in Ontario: A View from the Inside*. Halifax: The Institute for Research on Public Policy.

Stridsberg, Albert. 1977. *Controversy Advertising*. New York: Hastings House.

Wade, Wyn Craig. 1980. *The Titanic: End of a Dream*. Markham, Ont.: Penguin Books Canada.

Wilson, Graham K. 1990. *Interest Groups*. London: Basil Blackwell.

QUESTIONS FOR DISCUSSION

1. What is a public policy issue? How does it arise? Are there stages to its life cycle? In how many different ways can an issue be "resolved"?
2. If you were to ask the author who has power in Canada, what do you think his answer would be?
3. What framework for analysis and what approach do you believe the author would use to analyze an issue and to predict how it would be resolved? Select an issue that interests you and apply that approach. What are its strengths and weaknesses?
4. Is tripartism a feasible model to use to address issues? Is the use of sectoral advisory groups appropriate? Is the author's assessment of organized labour's power consistent with that expressed by Graeme McKechnie in his paper?
5. Do some techniques used to influence the public policy process work better for some interest groups than for others? Can you give examples of those that have been effectively used and those that have proven to be ineffective.
6. What roles do professional consultants and advisors play in the Canadian public policy process? What changes, if any, do you see in the ways corporations will use professionals to try to influence

government? Should former politicians and public servants be allowed to become paid intervenors?

W.T. Stanbury is a Professor and a UPS Found Professor of Regulation and Competition Policy at the University of British Columbia. He received his Ph.D. from the University of California at Berkeley. He is the author of numerous books, monographs, and papers on policy issues in the public and private sectors. He was director of the Regulation Reference for the Economic Council of Canada and served on many governmental and non-governmental organizations concerned with economic policy issues.

*Democratic Values in Canada and the United States: Some Observations and Evidence from Past and Present**

EDWARD G. GRABB

Comparisons of Canada and the United States have been popular topics for discussion and speculation for a long time, probably dating back to the very beginnings of our two nations. Some of the reasons for such comparisons are obvious, of course, including our geographic proximity and our shared border, which is widely heralded as the longest undefended national boundary in the world. The relationship between the two countries in recent decades has been a close one and, apart from the occasional trade dispute, both of us have behaved like friendly neighbours, for the most part. We have been military and political allies through two world wars and countless international conferences and negotiating sessions. We also have deeply-rooted business and trading links, stemming especially from the extensive and increasing American penetration of Canada's economy during much of this century; more recent developments, most notably the North American Free Trade Agreement, have only added to the economic and other ties that bind us together. However, in spite of our close affinities and numerous connections, commentators still disagree on just how much Canadians and Americans share with or resemble each other. The opinions cover a wide spectrum, from those suggesting there are no two countries in the world that are more alike, to those maintaining that fundamental differences have always existed between the two peoples, with no clear sign that these differences have changed much over time.

*I thank Jerry Dermer, Sybil Hagerman, Richard Henshel, William Johnston, Paul Maxim, Kevin McQuillan and Cecil Van Bolhuis for their help and suggestions.

The purpose of this paper is to outline some of the major issues raised by the Canadian-American comparison, especially in regard to the dominant values and beliefs held by the two populations. While much literature has been generated on the question of Canadian and American values, the present discussion focuses more specifically on a set of themes concerning the meaning of democracy in the two nations. The analysis that follows begins with a review of historical observations and evidence on the question. The historical accounts are important to consider because they provide a basis for understanding how many of the truths and misconceptions about the two peoples began and then evolved over time. Most of the paper, however, deals with contemporary evidence comparing the orientations of Canadians and Americans to central democratic principles, particularly as these are reflected in their views on politics and government, law and order, and the role of the individual citizen in society. The paper concludes by offering some personal observations and speculations on what we really know or don't know about our two peoples and the similarities or differences between us.

HISTORICAL BACKGROUND

The British Influence

Even more than being neighbours, Canadians and Americans are, to some analysts, better viewed as "cousins" or "kin" (e.g., Stuart, 1992, p. 3; Bothwell, 1992). These characterizations stem from our numerous cultural similarities, especially those arising from the central role played by Great Britain in both of our histories. In fact, although several colonial powers, including France, Spain, Holland and others, made significant impacts on the early development of either or both of our countries (e.g., Eccles, 1972), most observers seem to agree that our common British heritage has been the major force uniting us over the years (e.g., Bothwell, 1992; Hartz, 1955; Zelinsky, 1988; see also Tocqueville, [1835] 1954).

What evidence do we have of this joint British influence? The British impact on us is probably most apparent in the use of the English language, which continues to be the mother tongue for the majority of our two populations. Britain's role is evident, as well, in the numerous parallels to be found in our legal and political systems, with their stress on such democratic principles as individual freedom, universal rights of citizenship, equality before the law and so on. The roots of these ideas, in one form or another, can be found in the tenets of British common law imported from the former mother country (e.g., Zelinsky, 1988, p. 4). According to some commentators, these and other similarities are sufficiently extensive to suggest that Canadians are "almost Americans" (Stuart, 1992), that we are much the same kind of people and diverge only to the extent that we represent two slightly different variations of a common North American cultural ethos (Granatstein and Hillmer, 1990; Gwyn, 1985).

Examining the problem from another perspective, however, several writers have argued that there are also important differences between Canadians and Americans. Supporters of this view usually acknowledge our similarities in language, laws and politics, as well as our broadly comparable economies, standards of living, religious and ethnic compositions, and so on. Nevertheless, these analysts contend that Canadian and American viewpoints remain distinct in important ways and that, paradoxically perhaps, our common British heritage is the key reason behind many of these distinctions.

In general terms, this argument states that Canada did not break away from the influence of Britain at the same time, in the same way or to the same extent as did the United States. While there are a large number of observers who agree partly or completely with this argument (see, for example, Errington, 1987; Horowitz, 1966; McRae, 1964; Merelman, 1991), the person whose work is probably most closely identified with such a perspective is Seymour Martin Lipset. Lipset is widely recognized for his extensive research in political science and sociology, but his writings on the question of Canadian and American differences are perhaps the best known, at least to Canadian audiences (e.g., Lipset, 1963a, 1963b, 1968, 1985, 1986, 1990). It is useful to consider Lipset's assessment in some detail, since his thesis captures many of the same basic themes raised by other treatments of the subject.

Lipset's Thesis of Formative Events

Essential to Lipset's comparison of Canada and the United States is his analysis of the origins of the two countries, the so-called "formative events" of our histories. Lipset perceives stark contrasts in these beginnings, once again stressing the influence of Britain on both of its former colonies. The United States is seen as growing out of a liberal democratic *revolution* against British domination and control, the culmination of which was the American War of Independence in the late 1700s. In contrast, Canada (or, more precisely, English Canada) is portrayed as the product of an opposite process, or *counterrevolution*, in which the population maintained its acceptance of British rule and allegiance to the British Crown (see, especially, Lipset, 1968).

Lipset points to a related historical event as particularly important and indicative of the revolution-counterrevolution contrast. That event was the migration of large numbers of people out of the American colonies and into Canada, both during and after the War of Independence. These people, who came to be known as the United Empire Loyalists (UELs), moved into parts of what are now the Maritimes, Ontario and Quebec, and added as many as 60,000 English-speaking settlers to the small group of about 15,000 English colonists already living in those regions (Bell and Tepperman, 1979, p. 45). Lipset's thesis suggests that this large pool of new settlers brought with them both a strong opposition to the goals of the American Revolution and a clear affirmation of the British way of life. As a result, it is argued, the Loyalists served as the historical core of what came to be English Canadian culture, a culture that embraced, more or less completely, the same British values, customs and practices that the United States of America rejected. Among the core differences in values that are said to exist, is the tendency for Canadians to be much more likely than Americans: to accept established hierarchies of authority and rule by state leaders or other elites; to take a collectivist rather than an individualist view of democratic rights; and to favour the rule of law and order, even at the expense of restrictions on personal freedoms (e.g., Lipset, 1963a, pp. 525–526; 1963b, p. 211).

Before proceeding, we should note that disagreements exist on the historical import of the Loyalist migration, at least for defining Canadian and American cultural differences. For example, research suggests that, except for certain UEL leaders and elite members, many migrants from the Thirteen Colonies to Canada at the time were not particularly pro-British or anti-American in outlook. Many were simply pioneers seeking unclaimed land or a new beginning elsewhere. More than a few may have been fugitives, criminals or adventurers of various stripes. Moreover, even those whose exodus was clearly motivated by the political issues surrounding the Revolution, probably did not see themselves as making an irrevocable bond with Britain or break with the United States. Instead, it has been suggested, most expected to maintain affinities or connections with both the Americans and the English at the end of the conflict (Bell and Tepperman, 1979, pp. 52–54; Errington, 1987, pp. 4–5; see also Jones, 1985; Upton, 1967). All of this indicates that the UEL movement may not have produced the deep divisions between the two societies that has been claimed by Lipset and other writers.

Despite such disputes over the meaning of the Loyalist migration, most commentators do seem to concur that the American Revolution played a part in establishing some initial structural and cultural distinctions between the two nations (Archibald, 1978; Clark, 1975; Crysdale and Beattie, 1973; Forcese and Richer, 1975; Horowitz, 1966; Horowitz, 1973; Porter, 1967). A key example here is the political system. Thus, although both Canada and the United States evolved into democratic nation-states, Canada retained a system of government different from the American republican form and much closer to the British parliamentary model. Among the alleged distinctions between these two systems is the tendency for Canadian democracy to be less "liberal," in other words, less committed to making individual rights and freedoms the highest government priority (see Pocklington, 1985, pp. 63, 115, 131). Taking a view similar to Lipset's, Merelman (1991, pp. 26–27) suggests that, as a result, Canadian democratic structures were marked by more deference to elite authority than their American counterparts. These and other differences probably were sustained for some time by the longer period of British colonial influence in Canada, which did not form a separate country until a century after American independence. Some would argue that, by maintaining the office of the Governor General, membership in the British Commonwealth of Nations and other connections, Canada still retains at least some allegiance to Britain today.

Such illustrations of current ties between Canada and Britain may simply be fading vestiges of the past to many observers, but they partly explain why Lipset contends that the formative events of the American Revolution not only established the original differences in American and Canadian value systems, but also ensured that the differences would be sustained right up to the present day. Lipset has argued that, once the revolution and its counterrevolutionary reaction "had formed the structure of the two nations, their institutional character was set" (Lipset, 1968, p. 61). More recently, Lipset (1990, p. 8) has reiterated the same viewpoint:

> My central argument is that the two countries differ in their basic organizing principles. Canada has been and is more class-aware, elitist, law-abiding, statist, collectivity-oriented, and particularistic (group-oriented) than the United States. These fundamental distinctions stem in large part from the American Revolution and the diverse social and environmental ecologies flowing from the division of British North America.

This strong claim, perhaps understandably, has met with a good deal of skepticism and criticism. Several researchers, including many who accept the view that the American Revolution did have an initial role in distinguishing the two countries, find it difficult to accept that the impact of this single set of events could sustain the same effects, more or less unaltered, across more than two centuries of subsequent history (for examples, see Grabb and Curtis, 1988, p. 129; Baer, Grabb, and Johnston, 1990a, p. 709). Similarly, Nevitte and Gibbins (1990, p. 3) suggest that, in general, it is "hazardous to rely on a theory about founding traditions to make inferences about the national values of populations several generations removed from founding circumstances."

Nevertheless, Lipset's original position on the issue remains largely unshaken by such criticisms. He contends that "Canada and the United States continue to differ considerably along most of the dimensions suggested in my previous work" (1985, p. 156), with "no consistent decline in the patterns of differences in behaviour and values" (1986, p. 146).

More Recent Historical Evidence

These latter comments by Lipset raise at least two key questions about the historical support for his argument. First, is it not likely that events since the American Revolution have produced significant changes in both nations? Second, have these changes not also affected the pattern of value differences between the two populations?

On the first question, Lipset agrees that Canada and the United States changed in important ways after their formative stages, with both countries being "far from where they started;" however, at the same time, he maintains that the two countries are "still separated" as much as ever, "like two trains that have moved thousands of miles along parallel railway tracks" (1990, p. 212). Thus, Lipset's answer to the second question is that later developments in the two nations basically affirmed or left intact the original differences he perceived (see also Lipset, 1963a, p. 531).

Unfortunately, Lipset provides few specific examples to support the latter conclusion. It is partly for this reason that his assessment has been characterized as often selective and incomplete by some researchers (e.g., Baer, Grabb, and Johnston, 1990a, p. 694). Lipset does mention one notable illustration from our subsequent histories to support his case. That illustration concerns the opening of the western regions of both countries during the nineteenth century. Lipset discusses, in particular, the significant role played in the Canadian West by the Mounted Police, whom he sees as the exemplars of peace, order and good, British-style government at that time (Lipset, 1963a, p. 521; 1964, p. 183; see also Lipset, 1994, p. 15). Other writers have similarly commented that Canada may be the only country in the world that has a police officer as its predominant cultural symbol (e.g., Atwood, 1972; Hagan and Leon, 1977).

The obvious contrast to the image of the Canadian Mountie, and perhaps the best known symbol of the American West in the 1800s, is the cowboy (e.g., Curtis and Tepperman, 1990, p. 46). In legend, at least, the cowboy epitomizes the self-reliant American frontiersman, the independent citizen who would rather mete out his own justice (often using his own sidearm) than rely on any police officer or government agent to do it for him.

The contrast between Mountie and cowboy is partly paralleled in another comparison drawn from the history of the West. This example concerns a specific incident involving the American Indian chief, Sitting Bull who, after taking part in the annihilation of the U.S. Seventh Cavalry and General Custer at the Little Big Horn, fled north with most of his forces and surrendered peacefully to a handful of Canadian Mounties. This event has been perceived as one instance of the generally less violent treatment of Native peoples in Canada, and is also consistent with the view that there is greater trust of, and respect for, government authority in Canada (see Lipset, 1990, pp. 174–175).

Overall, then, Lipset believes that the symbols and events surrounding the settlement of the Canadian and American Wests underscore, once again, the same core value differences that existed when our two nations began. The specific differences here centre on our beliefs regarding the proper roles of government and the individual in a democratic society. Canada is a much more "statist" society than the United States, in Lipset's terms, as reflected in the pervasive influence of government in much of Canadian life. This prevailing state presence exists, moreover, not because of repression and deterrence by the police or military, but mainly because of Canadians' own widespread belief in the competence and legitimacy of their leaders. The American population, by comparison, is said to have a serious distrust of government power, especially when it restricts individual freedom. Americans favour less state control over people's actions, even if the result is a more unstable or disorderly society (Lipset, 1968, p. 44, 49; 1985, p. 142, 144; 1990, p. 10).

Problems with Lipset's Historical Argument

The historical accounts and illustrations offered by Lipset and others are both interesting and thought-provoking. They also provide a useful background for understanding some of the possible differences between Canada and the United States. Nevertheless, there are good reasons for questioning certain elements of these historical arguments. In particular, Lipset's central claim, that the divergent nature of our national origins produced a sustained pattern of value differences that remains intact even in the present day, seems open to dispute. While it is not possible in a short paper to discuss all the reasons for skepticism on this point, some of the key problems can be briefly highlighted here.

To begin with, as noted earlier and as many critics have discussed, even if we agree about the crucial impact of the American Revolution on Canada and the United States at the time of its occurrence, it is highly improbable that this single historical event, however momentous, could have essentially the same impact on the two cultures over two hundred years later. A related difficulty is that the overriding focus on this one event makes for an incomplete and selective treatment of the question, so that other, often equally important, elements of the historical record are not adequately considered. Let us examine three criticisms that help illustrate this problem.

First, it is virtually impossible to fit Quebec and French Canada into an explanation that sees the American Revolution as the prime reason behind national differences in values. Lipset's initial writings in particular basically ignore this difficulty, concentrating almost exclusively on English Canadians in any comparisons with Americans. Only more recently has Lipset made reference to French Canadians (e.g., 1985, pp. 158–159; 1990, pp. 13, 119) and nowhere does he show how the values of this group, which he says are quite distinct from both American and English Canadian values, can be explained by the formative events thesis. Clearly, the so-called "French fact" in Canadian history is a key reason why other writers view Canadian democracy as somewhat different from Lipset's portrayal, not as a copy of the original British model, or even a composite of the British and

American systems, but as a society and culture having a unique character all its own (Merelman, 1991, p. 26; also Verney, 1986).

A second criticism to be raised about the claim that the American Revolution was the defining moment of our two nations, is that it clearly overlooks crucial aspects, not only of Canadian history, but of American history, as well. Perhaps the most important omission is the American Civil War. A convincing argument can be made that the United States did not develop according to its own founding revolutionary values, at least not until after the 1860s. The famous words declaring that "all men are created equal," and that all citizens should enjoy "life, liberty and the pursuit of happiness," were enshrined in the original American Declaration of Independence; however, there were glaring contradictions between these words and the reality of America as long as slavery was legal in "the land of the free." Because the Civil War was fought, at least in part, to resolve this fundamental contradiction, various writers have concluded that it was this event, and not the Revolution, that was more crucial for shaping contemporary American society (Foote, 1989, p. 138; Reed, 1982, p. 167; 1983, 24, 54, 85; see also Baer, Grabb, and Johnston, 1993, p. 28; Lipset, 1963b, p. 330).

Finally, the historical record after the American Revolution reveals instances where Canadians frequently showed themselves not to be the obedient and respectful subjects of authority that has been suggested. Among the most prominent and violent illustrations of popular dissent and disobedience are the revolts in Upper and Lower Canada in the 1830s and the Riel Rebellion in the 1880s. There are also many other examples from the history of labour and union strife in Canada, especially the Winnipeg General Strike in 1919 (for a review, see Russell, 1990; 1993). Some might argue that these events represent the exception rather than the rule in Canada, and that there are more such examples to be found in the American case; nevertheless, it is important not to be misled by the asumption that Canada has simply been a "peaceable kingdom" (see Kilbourn, 1970), lacking any of the dynamic disruption and discord so often associated with the American heritage.

In summary, the historical evidence suggests that Canada and the United States did have distinct beginnings, stemming in part from our different relationships with Britain. It appears, in particular, that government was given a larger role in Canada than in the United States in the early stages of our development, and that this larger state presence was sustained through much of our history. What is not clear, however, is whether the differences in state influence or structure between the two nations also gave rise to important differences in the values and outlooks of the two populations themselves. It is possible that the greater degree of statism in Canada promoted some initial differences between Canadians and Americans in their orientations to government. Beyond this, however, the case is far from conclusive. In particular, it is not apparent why any early differences in values that may have existed should still inhere in the contemporary period. The best way to assess this question, of course, is to look at the most recent evidence available on the values of Canadians and Americans. It is to that task that we now turn.

CONTEMPORARY RESEARCH ON NATIONAL DIFFERENCES

Most recent analyses of national differences in values have relied primarily on two types of evidence — measures of behaviour and measures of attitudes or perceptions. In both instances, the assumption is that what people do in various fields of activity, and what they say or think on a range of issues, provide the best available indicators for judging their fundamental values and beliefs. We cannot examine the entire array of research on behaviour and attitudes that has been done on this subject, but we can highlight a number of the major topics and issue areas that have been considered. At the outset it may be helpful to note that, while the evidence from studies of behaviour and attitudes is somewhat mixed and complex at times, in general, the findings from this research fail to offer consistent or unequivocal support for many of the presumed differences between the two populations, including those suggested by the Lipset thesis.

Behavioural Evidence

Among the spheres of behaviour that have been studied when comparing values in the two nations, there are several in particular that have received the greatest attention and that also pertain most closely to our focus on democratic values. These include education, legislative activity, criminal behaviour and involvement in voluntary associations.

(i) Education In the field of education, Lipset points out that Americans have always had higher levels of post-secondary educational attainment than Canadians. He interprets this difference to mean that Americans have a more democratic view of schooling, with a stronger emphasis on individual achievement and equal opportunity. Canadians are seen as taking a more elitist, British-style view of education, in which higher levels of schooling are restricted to a more select group and are not readily available to all people (e.g., Lipset, 1963a, pp. 523–525; 1964). At least three comments can be made about this argument.

First, while there is no doubt that a difference in educational attainment exists, it is also clear, as Lipset's own research indicates, that this difference has reduced significantly over time. In 1960, for example, the proportion of young adult Canadians involved in higher education was only half that of a comparable American group; however, this rose to about 65 per cent by 1979, and about 77 per cent by 1984 (Lipset, 1985, p. 145; 1990, p. 160). More recently, looking at all adults aged 25–64, Statistics

Canada has reported that by 1989, the proportions of Canadian and Americans with at least some post-secondary education were almost the same, at 31 per cent for Canada and 36 per cent for the United States. Canadian adults did rank behind Americans in the proportion who had completed university degrees (15 per cent for Canada versus 23 per cent for the US); even so, Canadians were second only to Americans among the 22 industrialized countries that were compared (Canadian Press, 1993).

The second point to consider is whether educational attainment actually measures value differences between the two populations or whether, instead, it is measuring a different phenomenon. For example, the higher American education levels could be a result of structural differences in the two societies, especially the generally higher incomes and standards of living enjoyed by Americans (see Curtis, Lambert, Brown, and Kay, 1989a; 1989b). In other words, it may be that Americans have higher education levels because American families, on average, have more money to cover the costs involved in getting such education, and not because Americans place a higher value on individualism or equal opportunity than do Canadians.

A third point of note is that educational attainment is only one of many potential ways to measure national differences in attitudes about education. Depending on the indicators that are used, a different picture emerges of the Canadian commitment to educational attainment. For example, recent evidence shows that as of 1992, Canada spent a larger proportion of its national wealth (Gross Domestic Product) on public and private education than any of the top 20 industrialized countries. This comparison includes the United States, which ranked near the middle among the 20 countries (Associated Press, 1992). Using this alternative measure, then, we could conclude that Canadians put greater importance on the value of education than do Americans.

(ii) Law and the Legal System One area in which there has traditionally been significant difference between Canada and the United States is the legal system. Especially prior to the 1980s, it was clear that Canadian courts and Canadian law placed greater emphasis on crime control and maintaining social order, whereas the American system placed more stress on ensuring the individual rights of those accused of crime (e.g., Hagan and Leon, 1977; Hagan, 1986; 1991). Another way of expressing this difference is to say that the American system has traditionally been weighted toward protecting the individual, even if it means a risk that guilty people will occasionally go free. On the other hand, Canadian law has placed a higher priority on protecting society from crime, even at the expense of occasionally restricting the civil liberties of individuals. There are two points that can be raised about this difference.

First, while the two legal systems are certainly distinct, we should be careful not to exaggerate their differences. For example, it has been suggested that even in the relatively early stages of their histories, the

Canadian and American legal systems were in many ways "remarkably similar"; in fact, nineteenth century Canadian legal practices were often derived from American precedents (Bothwell, 1992, p. 24). Moreover, as Lipset himself has noted, there is little doubt that, with the creation of the Canadian Charter of Rights in 1982, the Canadian legal system, for better or worse, has taken major steps to "Americanize itself," putting greater emphasis on personal rights and freedoms and more restrictions on the government's power to control individuals (1990, p. 225; see also Cross, 1992; Machado, 1991).

A second issue is the question of measurement: do differences in our laws or legal systems accurately correspond to the differences in the values of our two peoples? We might assume so; after all, both Canadians and Americans live in democratic nations where citizens have the right to vote for their political leaders and indirectly, at least, to influence how and what laws are enacted. However, it is conceivable that our legal systems are less a reflection of what most Canadians and Americans want and more a reflection of what our political leaders themselves desire. Government leaders, as well as other powerful groups in business and elsewhere, would seem to be in the most advantageous positions for either creating society's laws or influencing the people who do. Some analysts judge this situation to be especially prevalent in the Canadian political system, which is said to place less emphasis than the American system on the importance of legislators' responsiveness to the will of the voters (e.g., Pocklington, 1985, p. 115). There are also numerous examples of laws in both societies that run counter to the strong preferences of the popular majority. To take just one illustration, opinion polls have shown consistently that most Canadians favour the death penalty for certain kinds of homicide (see Grabb and Curtis, 1988; Pocklington, 1985, p. 403). Yet the death penalty was abolished in Canada in 1976 and seems unlikely to be reinstated by the government. It is quite possible, then, that the structural differences in our legal systems, as well as the laws they enact, are not the best indicators for assessing the values of the general Canadian and American populations (see also Baer, Grabb, and Johnston, 1990a, p. 695).

(iii) Crime Although crime has become an important issue of concern in virtually all modern societies, it is generally assumed that it is a more serious problem in the United States than in most other countries, including Canada. In fact, despite some evidence that Canadian crime is on the increase (e.g., Hagan, 1994, pp. 22–23), as well as opinion polls indicating a growing fear of crime among Canadians (e.g., Maclean's 1993, pp. 23–24), research does show consistently that American crime rates have been, and continue to be, higher than Canadian rates. This pattern may not be as clear for less serious or non-violent crimes. For example, statistics for the late 1980s indicate that burglary rates are only slightly higher in the United States than in Canada (Maclean's, 1989, p. 51; see also Malcolm, 1985, p. 79).

In addition, a United Nations study reports that for the period 1980–1986, the number of drug crimes per 100,000 population was 225 in Canada, only marginally lower than the American figure of 234 (United Nations, 1993). Nevertheless, in the case of more serious and violent crimes, the differences are quite large and, if anything, are growing. Thus, while homicides per 100,000 rose from 1.4 to 2.2 in Canada between 1972 and 1987, the comparable American figure almost doubled in the same period, from 4.5 to 8.3; the same pattern of an increasing gap in Canadian and American rates over time is also apparent for other serious crimes, such as rape and aggravated assault (Hagan, 1989a, pp. 363–364; 1994, pp. 22–23; also Cross, 1992, p. 304; Maclean's 1989, p. 51; United Nations, 1993).

But what do the higher levels of criminal activity in the United States tell us about value differences between the two countries? Lipset's essential interpretation is that the propensity for Americans to commit more crimes than Canadians is closely related to the higher priority given to individual rights (as opposed to law and order) in the American legal system. In addition, Lipset suggests that the different crime rates reflect fundamental differences in the two peoples' beliefs about the roles of both government and the individual in a democracy. Put simply, greater criminality in the United States amounts to proof of a stronger American belief in individualism and freedom from state control (e.g., Lipset, 1963a, p. 528; 1963b; 1964). Once again, there are several remarks that can be made about this interpretation.

First of all, Lipset's use of crime rates as a measure of commitment to the value of individualism depends on a very specific, even peculiar, definition of what is meant by individualism. Interestingly, Lipset applies the same peculiar definition in his interpretation of national differences in divorce rates, which traditionally have been much higher in the United States (though they are not so different from Canadian rates today; see Malcolm, 1985, p. 76; United Nations, 1993). Just as with the higher American crime rates, Lipset interprets higher American divorce rates as evidence of an emphasis on individualism over collectivism, in the sense that divorcing couples are putting a higher value on their own personal freedom than on such concerns as family cohesion, for example (see Lipset, 1964, pp. 178–179).

But do behaviours such as committing crimes or getting divorced really indicate a higher evaluation of individualism or personal freedom? If we borrow a conceptual distinction from the classical sociologist, Emile Durkheim, the answer to this question must clearly be no. Durkheim's definition of individualism partly parallels that of Lipset, in that both conceptions entail the right of any person to pursue his own goals and interests in society; however, equally central to Durkheim's sense of individualism is an acceptance of the rights of other people, as well as the need to govern individual behaviour according to generally agreed-upon rules of action. Otherwise, there is no real freedom for any individual, only a continual state of war driven by unbridled self-interest, or what Durkheim calls "egoism" (Durkheim, [1893] 1964, p. 203; [1902] 1964, pp. 3–6; see also Baer, Grabb, and Johnston, 1990b, p. 96; Grabb, 1990, pp. 90–93). Thus, higher levels of crime and divorce in the United States may not reflect a higher American commitment to individualism at all; instead, these behaviours may really indicate that Americans have a heightened degree of self-interest or egoism compared to Canadians.

Apart from questioning whether crime rates actually measure individualism, a second problem to note is that there are several alternative explanations of the higher crime levels in the United States, none of which depends on demonstrating that there are differences in Canadian and American values. As has been suggested by other researchers, the higher levels of crime in American society can be partly or mostly explained by structural or situational differences, most notably the greater extremes of wealth and poverty, wider availability of firearms and more deep-seated problems of racial strife in the United States (e.g., Horowitz, 1973; Hagan, 1986; 1994; Baer, Curtis, Grabb, and Johnston, 1994a, p. 7). There is also the question of regional variations within the countries to consider; for instance, some research suggests that the higher American homicide rates are at least partly due to much higher rates in the southern United States, with rates in the non-southern United States somewhat closer to those found in Canada (especially when comparing whites; see Gastil, 1975, p. 116; Nisbett, 1993). The major point here is that without also taking into account these and other potential factors, it is not clear what the crime data tell us about differences in American and Canadian values. At a minimum, both structural factors and cultural (i.e., value) differences should be incorporated into theories for explaining the divergent patterns of criminality in the two societies (Hagan, 1989a; 1989b; 1991).

(iv) Voluntary Association Involvement Basic to the concept of democracy is the idea that citizens are active participants in governing their own and their nation's affairs; such activity, moreover, can and should involve the free association of individuals who may often pursue their own goals as members of organized groups (e.g., Pocklington, 1985, pp. 4, 374–376). Understandably, then, people's involvements in voluntary associations of various kinds have frequently been used as measures of commitment to democratic values.

When comparing the voluntary association activities of different populations, observers have typically concluded or assumed that Americans stand out above all the rest. In other words, the United States is thought to be, more than any other country, a "nation of joiners" (Hausknecht, 1962). This perception goes back at least as far as Tocqueville ([1835] 1954, p. 141), who suggested that Americans "constantly form associations," and to Weber (1911, p. 53), who described the United States as "the association-land par excellence."

A quick review of the literature on voluntary associations, in fact, might leave the impression that Americans are the most likely of all people to join such organizations. Certainly, most of Lipset's commentary on the topic assumes this to be true, especially when comparing Canadians and Americans. He states, for example, that "Americans are more likely to take part in voluntary efforts to achieve particular goals, while Canadians are more disposed to rely on the state" (1985, p. 141; also 1986, p. 135). If true, this assertion would reinforce Lipset's general thesis that Americans are more strongly committed to democratic individualism and self-reliance, whereas Canadians are more collectivist and dependent on state intervention to promote social action and change.

However, a closer examination of comparative studies in this area raises doubts about the conclusion that Americans are more involved in voluntary associations than Canadians or other people. The first study to use representative cross-national sample data to consider this question, found that of the six populations compared, Canadians were actually the most likely of all to belong to at least one association, although Americans ranked about the same as Canadians, if union memberships were excluded, and when multiple, rather than single, memberships were compared (Curtis, 1971, pp. 874–875).

In a more recent study involving fifteen nations, Americans did rank the highest among all the groups when asked if they belonged to at least one voluntary association (Curtis, Grabb, and Baer, 1992; see also Grabb and Curtis, 1992). However, this top ranking was largely attributable to the exceptionally high level of church or religious membership among Americans; with religious affiliations excluded, Canada and several other countries ranked as high as, or higher than, the United States (see also Curtis, Lambert, Brown, and Kay, 1989a; 1989b).

A second finding in this analysis was that the high membership levels in the American sample were far less evident if inactive memberships were excluded. That is, the American respondents in the study were more likely than other respondents to be members of associations, but to take no active part in the work of the organizations. In analyses that included only active or working memberships, Canadians and several other samples had higher levels of association involvement than the Americans (Curtis, Grabb, and Baer, 1992, p. 146). This result seems especially pertinent for assessing the claim that Americans are more democratic or individualist than Canadians, since truly active, rather than simply nominal, membership in voluntary associations would seem to be a more appropriate indicator of commitment to democratic values.

Finally, other research has raised an additional problem in the debate over which of the two populations is more likely to join voluntary associations. These studies suggest that another important factor to consider in any comparison of association involvement in the two countries, is the distinction between English and French Canadians. Findings show that English Canadians and Americans are generally similar to each other on many measures of association involvement, and that it is really French Canadians, not all Canadians, who rank significantly lower than Americans in many cases (Curtis, Lambert, Brown, and Kay, 1989a; 1989b; Grabb and Curtis, 1992). The results of these studies need to be kept in mind when assessing Lipset's argument, which concentrates on the comparison of American-English Canadian differences in values.

As a whole, then, the research on voluntary association memberships in the two countries offers little support for the assumption that Americans are more frequently or more actively involved in such organizations. Partly as a consequence of this research, Lipset has recently softened his views on the subject, and has concluded that, at least in the case of association activity, the claims of Canadian-American differences remain "not proven" (Lipset, 1989, p. 382; 1990, pp. 148–149). In fact, based on our review of the evidence, this same conclusion could be applied to a good deal of the behavioural research that has been done on the value differences between Canadians and Americans.

Research on Attitudes

The last major category of evidence to be considered involves the stated attitudes and perceptions of people in the two countries. Again, the large body of existing research that is potentially relevant cannot be examined in detail here. Instead, our review will concentrate on a reduced set of studies dealing with a few major issues, especially those that seem most relevant to the comparison of democratic values. The studies selected also have the advantage that they are based on representative national sample surveys, which makes their findings more easily generalizable to the entire populations of both countries than is the case for local or community-based studies.

If it is true that Americans have been, and continue to be, different from Canadians in the ways suggested by Lipset and others, these differences should be evident in their expressed opinions on a range of questions dealing with democratic values. Thus, if Americans are more individualist, achievement-oriented, anti-elitist and anti-statist than Canadians, we should find, for example, that Americans are more in favour of equal opportunity for women than Canadians. We would expect, in addition, that Americans are less likely to favour an authoritarian family structure. It should also be the case that Americans are less in favour of more government spending on social services and less trustful of government power than Canadians. In fact, research using national survey data from the 1980s shows the opposite findings on each of these issues (Baer, Grabb, and Johnston, 1990a).

Consider another set of questions, this time dealing with respect for authority and rights of dissent. Given the presumed differences between us, we would expect that, compared to Canadians, Americans should be more suspicious and less accepting of situations where government leaders or other groups have power over them, and should also be more willing to engage in acts of civil dissent or disobedience to oppose such groups. Once again, however, results based on national survey data call virtually all of these expectations into question. One recent study finds that Americans are significantly more likely than both English and French Canadians to respect established authority, both as a general principle and in specific situations, such as in parent-child and employer-employee relationships (Baer, Curtis, Grabb, and Johnston, 1994a). The same study shows that Americans are more likely than English or French Canadians to express a high level of confidence in their government or legal institutions, including parliament or congress, the civil service and the armed forces; on the other hand, Canadians tend to show more confidence in the legal system and the police, and there are no differences in confidence concerning the education system. Finally, in regard to dissent and disobedience, there is consistent evidence in the same study that it is not Americans but Canadians (especially English Canadians) who are more willing to engage in such acts as signing petitions, joining boycotts, attending lawful demonstrations and even occupying buildings for protest purposes. We should note that a few of these patterns vary somewhat if differences in age, education and other background variables are statistically controlled. Whether or not these other variables are controlled, the evidence lends virtually no support to the assumption that Canadians have more docile or passive attitudes about authority than Americans.

As a final illustration, we can consider evidence dealing with child-rearing values. In one international study that included both Canada and the United States, samples of individuals were asked to select, from a checklist provided to them, the qualities that they believed were especially important for children to be taught at home. Some of the qualities listed are consistent with values that we would typically associate with the basic tenets of a democratic society. Among the most notable in this regard are honesty, leadership, unselfishness, determination, imagination, tolerance and respect for other people, independence, hard work, and a feeling of responsibility. An analysis of these data shows some differences between Americans and Canadians, but the patterns are mixed and virtually all of the differences are very minor (Baer, Curtis, Grabb, and Johnston, 1994b). Americans are slightly more likely than English Canadians to choose honesty and leadership as important, while English Canadians are marginally more likely than Americans to choose unselfishness, determination and imagination as important. There are no significant differences between the two groups in their ratings of tolerance, independence, hard work or responsibility. Results are somewhat different when French Canadians are compared to Americans, but again the differences are small and inconsistent. The overall impression from this study and the others, then, is that there is no clear basis for contending that Americans hold more strongly to democratic values than do Canadians.

WHAT DO WE KNOW ABOUT CANADIANS AND AMERICANS?

Now that we have considered some of the major historical analyses and contemporary research comparing Canadians and Americans, a fair question to ask is: what do we really know for certain about this subject? One of the first things to note, no doubt, is that there is much more to know and think about than we have been able to examine in one paper. Even as I write this, more discussions of the issue are regularly being generated in academic books and journals, in intellectual magazines and the popular press and in everyday conversations. The interest in the question is especially high in Canada. We are notorious for wondering about who and what we are, and inevitably seem to define our own identity by comparing ourselves with Americans. More than a few observers have suggested that, in fact, Canadian identity is very difficult to describe or explain, except as a negative. In other words, whatever Canadians are, the one certainty is that they are not Americans (e.g., Clark, 1938; Underhill, 1960; Zelinsky, 1988; see also Maclean's, 1994a).

But even if this is true, we are still left to wonder exactly how Canadians are different from their southern neighbours. As I have tried to show in this paper, one major conclusion to draw is that Canadians may be different from Americans, but not in many of the ways suggested to us by writers like Lipset, or by numerous popular myths and stereotypes. Contrary to some widely held assumptions, Canadians are not unduly enamoured with elites and the maintenance of existing social hierarchies, nor are Canadians particularly respectful or trusting of people in power. This seems especially true of our feelings about government elites and bureaucracy, judging not only from the evidence reviewed here, but also from numerous recent events in Canadian politics. These events include the resounding rejection of the Charlottetown Accord referendum, as well as the rise of the Reform Party and other "populist" opposition to the alleged excesses and complacency of established political parties.

At the same time, there is no question that writers like Lipset are correct in noting that Canadians live with a larger state presence in their everyday lives than do Americans; Canadians are provided with significantly more in the way of health care, social services and other support by government, and, of course, Canadians also pay much higher taxes as a result. In my view, however, it remains debatable whether this structural difference is an accurate reflection of fundamental differences in the values of the two general populations, or is more the result of differences in the values of the elites in the two societies. Given the increasingly negative reactions to government power, certainly in the Canadian populace, there is real reason to doubt, in the current period of our history, whether there is a close correspondence between the values of Canada's leaders and the values of the Canadian people as a whole.

Much of the research we have looked at suggests that, in many cases, Canadians and Americans are not dramatically different from one another. Except for evidence on violent crime, which still shows significant and even larger gaps between the two populations over time, a good deal of what we know seems to suggest that Canadians and Americans have become increasingly alike in many of their behaviours and attitudes. As a result, some writers have perceived a considerable trend toward convergence in national value systems in recent decades, involving not only Canada and the United States, but many other industrialized democracies, as well (e.g., Dogan and Pelassy, 1984; Giddens, 1989; Hofstede, 1980; Horowitz, 1973; Kohn, 1989; Nevitte and Gibbins, 1990).

Some degree of convergence is to be expected, no doubt. We began this paper by noting the longstanding structural linkages between the two countries, especially our close economic and political relations. Such connections seem likely to grow with the increasing "globalization" of the world's economies and political systems, and inevitably must give at least some impetus toward greater national similarity (e.g., Carroll, 1986; Tilly, 1984; 1990; Wallerstein, 1974).

Convergence may also come as no surprise to anyone who is familiar with the diffusion of mass culture in recent times. Probably the principal reason for expecting an increasing resemblance in national values, is the pervasive influence of American culture not only in Canada, but throughout most of the world. The impact of American tastes, outlooks, attitudes and fashions is apparent in all of the popular media of communication — in television, films, music, books, magazines, and so on. The noted British intellectual Malcolm Muggeridge once argued that "a kind of cultural consensus has come to pass in the world, essentially American in all its manifestations." He went on to suggest that, in this respect, the only real difference between Canada and other countries is that, for obvious reasons of geography, history and language, Canadians are more susceptible to the American cultural influence than any other people. Possibly for this reason, some recent research has raised doubts about the significance of the Canadian-American border as a cultural dividing line, since other divisions, such as those between regions within each nation, may be more important (e.g., Baer, Grabb, and Johnston, 1993; Garreau, 1981; Kahle, 1986; Muller, 1989).

Of course, to recognize trends toward greater national similarity on some dimensions is not to suggest that the two countries and their peoples are identical. Some of the evidence reviewed here has shown that Americans and Canadians really are different on some issues (though usually not radically so), and in ways that run counter to the popular wisdom. Two examples we considered include the finding that Canadians are more in favour of gender equality than Americans and also are more likely to engage in various forms of political dissent. Hence, although it is important to recognize our similarities and the various pressures toward convergence, it is also necessary to be aware of our continuing distinctiveness.

One of the areas where Canadians and Americans seem markedly different from each other is in the religious sphere. First, as was briefly touched on in our review of voluntary association research, Americans are more likely than Canadians, and most other populations for that matter, to report that they belong to a church or religious organization (see also Wuthnow, 1991). Americans also report higher levels of church attendance, although some research suggests this may be overstated (Chaves and Cann, 1992; Hadaway, Marler, and Chaves, 1993). In addition, Americans tend to give higher subjective assessments of how religious they think they are, and are more likely to have "fundamentalist" religious beliefs, such as the belief that hell is a real place or that the devil truly exists (see Bibby, 1987; 1994).

Some writers have argued that the high level of religiosity in the United States is related to another central characteristic of the American value system — a strong sense of patriotism and national pride; in other words, American beliefs in "God and country" seem to be closely intertwined (Bellah, 1967; Rokeach, 1977; see Bibby, 1994). Certainly, there is good reason to believe that Americans are more patriotic and nationalistic than Canadians, or at least are more openly so (e.g., Zelinsky, 1988). Those of us who attend Canadian sporting events, or other gatherings where the national anthem is played, know that it is not unusual to find only a few spectators actually singing the words (although some people may hum along). Part of the reason for this may be the Canadian penchant for changing the anthem's words from time to time, something that most Americans would probably find astounding; another reason, however, may be a certain modesty among Canadians about waving the flag too openly. Pierre Berton is one person who believes that Canadians are far more patriotic than they appear, just less flamboyant about it than their American cousins (see Maclean's, 1994a, p. 44). Another view, one that contrasts sharply with Lipset's argument, is that the less demonstrative nationalism of Canadians shows that they are actually more individualist and less bound by collective or group allegiances than Americans (Bibby, 1990, pp. 90–94.)

One speculation I would offer is that the less overt show of patriotism among Canadians is consistent with their generally more moderate outlook and behaviour compared to Americans. My impression is that, with some exceptions, Canadians tend to voice less extreme views than Americans on a variety of issues involving politics, religion, family values and so on. In these and other areas, Canadians seem to exhibit a more understated or "middle-of-the-road" quality in many of their expressed attitudes (see Baer, Grabb, and Johnston, 1990b). More than Canada, the United States also appears to be a nation of structural extremes, where, for example, internationally renowned universities co-exist with ghetto schools and rampant illiteracy, and where untold wealth lives alongside abysmal poverty.

Canadians may indeed be more restrained than Americans in their expressions of patriotism and nationalism; even so, there are reasons for believing that, as a result, Canada is also a more tolerant and forgiving society. More than most other places in the world, Canada is a place where people with differing cultures and belief systems have been able to survive, and even prosper, together. It has been suggested by several analysts, in fact, that our relatively weak national identity, especially among English Canadians, is one key reason why Canada is able to accommodate such diversity in its cultural composition. The acceptance of diversity is apparent from the high proportion of people living in Canada who were not born here. Canada's foreign-born population currently stands at about 16 per cent, which is more than twice that of the United States, and ranks as one of the highest levels among all the nations of the world (Canadian Press, 1992).

Canada's tolerance and encouragement of diversity is also evident in our regional differences. Compared to the United States and many other countries, Canada has frequently been portrayed as more regionally divided, composed of a relatively loose amalgamation of disparate areas, each with its own special character (e.g., Brym, 1986; Coffey and Polese, 1987; Gibbins, 1982; Matthews, 1983; Wien, 1993). For some time now, the federal government has been actively engaged in efforts to preserve this regional distinctiveness, often by funding attempts to create and sustain regionally-based economies in the poorer areas of the Atlantic provinces, Quebec, the North and elsewhere (Brodie, 1991; Bryan, 1986). These efforts have met with limited success at best, and have been the subject of severe criticism, both from those who believe the attempts have been inadequate or half-hearted, and from those who contend such programs are a waste of time and resources. In either event, however, both the image and the reality of regional diversity continue to exist in Canadian society (see Bibby, 1990; Maclean's, 1994b). Moreover, the differences seem likely to persist for some time, in spite of recent moves toward increased regional integration, such as the current attempts to break down interprovincial trade barriers across the country.

Many observers agree, then, that Canadians exhibit a weaker sense of national identity than Americans and that this difference is tied to the greater acceptance and encouragement of both ethnic and regional diversity in this country. However, if there is one clear exception to this assessment of Canadian identity, it appears to be French Canada. In contrast to English Canadians, French Canadians are believed to have a very clear understanding of who they are as a people and, in this way, are much more like Americans in their nationalism and patriotic fervour (see Zelinsky, 1988). Of course, among the French, the "nation" that evokes these sentiments is Quebec, not the country as a whole.

Unfortunately, the strong nationalism shown by many Quebecers, like the intense nationalism to be found in other parts of the world today, can have its darker side. Here I refer to the way in which minorities sometimes have been treated by the Quebec government in our recent history, usually in the name of preserving French culture. Quebec's restrictions on the language and education rights of its English-speaking population, including the infamous Bill 178 outlawing English signs, provide the most prominent illustrations of how nationalism there has led to the undermining of basic democratic principles. The clash between Quebec nationalism and recent aboriginal nationalism, which partly contributed to the Oka crisis in 1990, may also help explain why Native-white relations seem more strained in Quebec than in the rest of Canada these days. A related problem is the evidence of greater ethnocentrism, intolerance of non-conformity and even anti-Semitism among French Quebecers compared to other Canadians (e.g., Brym and Lenton, 1991; Sniderman et al., 1992; see also Richler, 1992). For some French Quebecers, in fact, nationalist sentiments have begun to include the view that an important distinction must be made between a chosen subset of the Quebec populace and everyone else. Those who are "*Quebecois pure laine*" (literally, pure wool Quebecers), especially the descendants of the so-called "*ancienne souche*" (old branch) of French settlers who arrived before the British conquest of Quebec in 1759, should in some people's minds be endowed with special rights and considerations, both to make up for past injustices under English domination and to conserve the future of French Quebec (see Richler, 1992, pp. 13, 103).

Whether or not this special designation will ever be formally recognized in Quebec, and exactly what its establishment would mean for democratic institutions there, are questions that remain to be answered. Even the possibility of such a distinction, however, is a worry for many, given the inequities that already have been entrenched in Quebec society. Creating more policies that assign some rights solely to certain groups can only add to the concerns among those of us who favour the traditional North American conceptions of democracy that have been the subject of this paper.

Similar worries have arisen, not just in Quebec, but in Canada and the United States generally, because of recent attempts by various other groups to obtain special consideration. In both countries, there clearly are those who have experienced (and often continue to face) significant injustices and disadvantages — women and visible minorities, to name just two. But the question that all of us must confront is whether, in the interest of trying to redress the genuine grievances of certain groups, some citizens should be granted special rights or reparations that go beyond and, in many cases, override the rights of other citizens. Some people, in the interest of making up for the past, will say yes to this question; others, however, will see this as a hazardous course to pursue because of its potential to undermine the fundamental tenets of the democratic value system as most of us currently conceive it. Regardless of which position one adopts in this debate, if the drive for special rights continues, in the future, the very meaning of democracy will undergo serious pressures for redefinition, in both Canada and the United States.

REFERENCES

Archibald, W. Peter. *Social Psychology as Political Economy.* Toronto: McGraw-Hill Ryerson, 1978.

Associated Press. "Canada's spending tops 20 countries." In the London Free Press, September 24, 1992.

Atwood, Margaret. *Survival: A Thematic Guide to Canadian Literature.* Toronto: Anansi, 1972.

Baer, Doug, James Curtis, Edward Grabb, and William Johnston. "Respect for authority in Australia, Canada, Great Britain, and the United States." Unpublished manuscript, 1994a.

——— "What values do people prefer in children? A comparative analysis of survey evidence from fifteen countries." In *Values: The Ontario Symposium on Personality and Social Psychology*, vol. 8, edited by Clive Seligman, James Olson and Mark Zanna, Hillsdale, New Jersey: Erlbaum, 1994b (forthcoming).

Baer, Doug, Edward Grabb, and William Johnston. "The values of Canadians and Americans: a critical analysis and reassessment." *Social Forces* 68, 3 (1990a): 693–713.

——— "Reassessing differences in Canadian and American values." In *Images of Canada: The Sociological Tradition*, edited by James Curtis and Lorne Tepperman, Scarborough: Prentice-Hall Canada, 1990b.

——— "National character, regional culture, and the values of Canadians and Americans." *Canadian Review of Sociology and Anthropology* 30, 1 (1993): 13–36.

Bell, David, and Lorne Tepperman. *The Roots of Disunity.* Toronto: McClelland & Stewart, 1979.

Bellah, Robert. "Civil religion in America." *Daedalus* 96 (1967): 1–21.

Bibby, Reginald. *Fragmented Gods.* Toronto: Irwin, 1987.

——— *Mosaic Madness.* Toronto: Stoddart, 1990.

——— "Religion." In *Sociology*, edited by Robert Hagedorn, 401–32. Toronto: Harcourt Brace & Company Canada, 1994.

Bothwell, Robert. "More than kin, and less than kind." In *North America Without Borders? Integrating Canada, the United States, and Mexico*, edited by Stephen Randall, 285–94. Calgary: University of Calgary Press, 1992.

Brodie, Janine. *The Political Economy of Canadian Regionalism.* Toronto: Harcourt, Brace, Jovanovitch, 1991.

Bryan, Ingrid. *Economic Policies in Canada* (second edition). Toronto: Butterworths, 1986.

Brym, Robert. *Regionalism in Canada.* Toronto: Irwin, 1986.

Brym, Robert, and Rhonda Lenton. "The distribution of anti-semitism in Canada." *Canadian Journal of Sociology* 16, 4 (1991): 411–18.

Canadian Press. "Immigration numbers highest since 1957." In the London Free Press, December 15, 1992.

——— "Canada second in university degrees." In the University of Western Ontario Gazette, November 24, 1993.

Carroll, William. *Corporate Power and Canadian Capitalism.* Vancouver: University of British Columbia Press, 1986.

Chaves, Mark, and David Cann. "Regulation, pluralism, and religious market structure." *Rationality and Society* 4, 3 (1992): 272–90.

Clark, S.D. "Canadian national sentiment and imperial sentiment." In *Canada and her Great Neighbour*, edited by H.F. Angus, 225–48. Toronto: Ryerson, 1938.

——— "The post-Second World War Canadian society." *Canadian Review of Sociology and Anthropology* 12 (1975): 25–32.

Coffey, William, and Mario Polese, eds. *Still Living Together.* Montreal: Institute for Research on Public Policy, 1987.

Cross, Michael. "Towards a definition of North American culture." In *North America Without Borders? Integrating Canada, the United States, and Mexico*, edited by Stephen Randall, 303–06. Calgary: University of Calgary Press, 1992.

Crysdale, Stewart, and Christopher Beattie. *Sociology Canada: An Introductory Text.* Toronto: Butterworths, 1973.

Curtis, James. "Voluntary association joining: a cross-national comparative note." *American Sociological Review* 36 (1971): 872–80.

Curtis, James, Edward Grabb, and Doug Baer. "Voluntary association membership in fifteen countries: a comparative analysis." *American Sociological Review* 57 (1992): 139–52.

Curtis, James, Ronald Lambert, Steven Brown, and Barry Kay. "Affiliating with voluntary associations: Canadian-American comparisons." *Canadian Journal of Sociology* 14, 2 (1989a): 143–62.

——— "On Lipset's measure of voluntary association differences between Canada and the United States." *Canadian Journal of Sociology* 14, 3 (1989b): 383–89.

Curtis, James, and Lorne Tepperman, eds. *Images of Canada: The Sociological Tradition.* Scarborough: Prentice-Hall Canada, 1990.

Dogan, M., and D. Pelassy. *How to Compare Nations.* Chatham, New Jersey: Chatham House Publishers, 1984.

Durkheim, Emile. *The Division of Labor in Society.* 1893; reprint, New York: The Free Press, 1964.

——— "Preface to the Second Edition." In *The Division of Labor in Society.* 1902; reprint, New York: The Free Press, 1964.

Eccles, W.J. *France in America.* Vancouver: Fitzhenry & Whiteside, 1972.

Errington, Jane. *The Lion, the Eagle, and Upper Canada.* Montreal and Kingston: McGill-Queen's University Press, 1987.

Foote, Shelby. *Conversations with Shelby Foote*, edited by W.C. Carter, Jackson, Mississippi: University Press of Mississippi, 1989.

Forcese, Dennis, and Stephen Richer, eds. *Issues in Canadian Society.* Scarborough: Prentice-Hall Canada, 1975.

Garreau, Joel. *The Nine Nations of North America.* Boston: Houghton Mifflin, 1981.

Gastil, Raymond. *Cultural Regions of the United States*. Seattle: University of Washington Press, 1975.

Giddens, Anthony. "A reply to my critics." In *Social Theory of Modern Societies*, edited by D. Held and J.B. Thompson, 249–301. Cambridge: Cambridge University Press, 1989.

Gibbins, Roger. *Regionalism. Territorial Politics in Canada and the United States*. Toronto: Butterworths, 1982.

Grabb, Edward. *Theories of Social Inequality: Classical and Contemporary Perspectives*, 2nd ed. Toronto: Holt, Rinehart and Winston of Canada, 1990.

Grabb, Edward, and James Curtis. "English Canadian-American differences in orientation toward social control and individual rights." *Sociological Focus* 21, 2 (1988): 127–40.

——— "Voluntary association activity in English Canada, French Canada, and the United States: a Multivariate Analysis." *Canadian Journal of Sociology* 17, 4 (1992): 371–88.

Granatstein, J.L., and Norman Hillmer. *For Better or Worse: Canada and the United States to the 1990s*. Toronto: Copp Clark Pitman, 1990.

Gwyn, Richard. *The 49th Paradox: Canada in North America*. Toronto: McClelland & Stewart, 1985.

Hadaway, C. Kirk, Penny Long Marler, and Mark Chaves. "What the polls don't show: a closer look at U.S. church attendance." *American Sociological Review* 58, 6 (1993): 741–52.

Hagan, John. "Crime and deviance." In *Sociology*, edited by Robert Hagedorn, 3rd ed., 165–98. Toronto: Holt, Rinehart and Winston of Canada, 1986.

——— "Comparing crime and criminalization in Canada and the U.S.A." *Canadian Journal of Sociology* 14, 3 (1989a): 361–71.

——— "Enduring differences: further notes on homicide in Canada and the U.S.A.." *Canadian Journal of Sociology* 14, 4 (1989b): 490–91.

——— *The Disreputable Displeasures: Crime and Deviance in Canada*. Toronto: McGraw-Hill Ryerson, 1991.

——— *Crime and Disrepute*. Thousand Oaks, California: Pine Forge Press, 1994.

Hagan, John, and Jeffrey Leon. "Philosophy and sociology of crime control: Canadian-American comparisons." *Sociological Inquiry* 47 (1977): 181–208.

Hartz, Louis. *The Liberal Tradition in America*. New York: Harcourt, Brace and World, 1955.

Hausknecht, Murray. *The Joiners*. New York: Bedminster Press, 1962.

Hofstede, G. *Culture's Consequences*. Beverly Hills: Sage, 1980.

Horowitz, Gad. "Conservatism, liberalism, and socialism in Canada: An interpretation." *Canadian Journal of Economic and Political Science* 32 (1966): 143–71.

Horowitz, Irving L. "The hemispheric connection: a critique and corrective to the entrepreneurial thesis of development with special emphasis on the Canadian case." *Queen's Quarterly* 80 (1973): 327–59.

Jones, Elwood. "The Loyalists and Canadian history." *Journal of Canadian Studies* 20, 3 (1985): 149–56.

Kahle, L.R. "The nine nations of North America and the value basis of geographic segmentation." *Journal of Marketing* 50 (1986): 37–47.

Kilbourn, William, ed. *Canada: A Guide to the Peaceable Kingdom*. Toronto: Macmillan of Canada, 1970.

Kohn, Melvin, ed. *Cross-National Research in Sociology*. Newbury Park, California: Sage, 1989.

Lipset, Seymour Martin. "The value patterns of democracy." *American Sociological Review* 28 (1963a): 515–31.

——— *The First New Nation*. New York: Basic Books, 1963b.

——— "Canada and the United States — A comparative view." *Canadian Review of Sociology and Anthropology* 1 (1964): 173–85.

——— *Revolution and Counterrevolution*. New York: Basic Books, 1968.

——— "Canada and the United States: the cultural dimension." In *Canada and the United States*, edited by C.F. Doran and J.H. Sigler, 109–60. Englewood Cliffs, New Jersey: Prentice-Hall, 1985.

——— "Historical conditions and national characteristics." *Canadian Journal of Sociology* 11, 2 (1986): 113–55.

——— "Voluntary activities: more Canadian-American comparisons — A reply." *Canadian Journal of Sociology* 14, 3 (1989): 377–82.

——— *Continental Divide*. New York: Routledge, 1990.

——— "The social requisites of democracy revisited." *American Sociological Review* 59, 1 (1994): 1–22.

Machado, Priscilla. "A comparative analysis of the exclusion of illegally obtained evidence in American and Canadian criminal law." Paper presented at the Facing North/Facing South Conference, University of Calgary, Calgary, Alberta, May, 1991.

Maclean's. "A north-south dialogue." July 3, 1989.

——— "The fear index." January 4, 1993.

——— "The ties that bind." July 1, 1994a.

——— "How we differ." January 3, 1994b.

Malcolm, Andrew. *The Canadians*. Markham: Fitzhenry & Whiteside, 1985.

Matthews, Ralph. *The Creation of Regional Dependency*. Toronto: University of Toronto Press, 1983.

Mauss, Armand, and Milton Rokeach. "Pollsters as prophets." *Humanist* (1977): 48–51.

McRae, Kenneth. "The structure of Canadian history." In *The Founding of New Societies*, edited by Louis Hartz et al., 219–75. New York: Harcourt Brace, 1964.

Merelman, Richard. *Partial Visions*. Madison: University of Wisconsin Press, 1991.

Muller, Thomas. "The two nations of Canada vs. the nine nations of North America: A cross-cultural analysis of consumers' personal values." *Journal of International Consumer Marketing* 1, 4 (1989): 57–79.

Nevitte, Neil, and Roger Gibbins. *New Elites in Old States*. Toronto: Oxford University Press Canada, 1990.

Nisbett, Richard. "Violence and U.S. regional culture." *American Psychologist* 48, 4 (1993): 441–49.

Pocklington, T.C. *Liberal Democracy in Canada and the United States*. Toronto: Holt, Rinehart and Winston of Canada, 1985.

Porter, John. "Canadian character in the twentieth century." *Annals of the American Academy of Political and Social Science* 370 (1967): 48–56.

Reed, J.S. *One South: An Ethnic Approach to Regional Culture*. Baton Rouge: Louisiana State University Press, 1982.

——— *Southerners: The Social Psychology of Sectionalism*. Chapel Hill: University of North Carolina Press, 1983.

Richler, Mordecai. *Oh Canada! Oh Quebec! Requiem for a Divided Country.* Toronto: Penguin Books, 1992.

Russell, Bob. *Back to Work? Labour, State, and Industrial Relations in Canada.* Toronto: Nelson Canada, 1990.

——— "Working class resistance and collective action." In *Social Inequality in Canada: Patterns, Problems, Policies*, edited by James Curtis, Edward Grabb, and Neil Guppy, 2nd ed. 64–74. Scarborough: Prentice-Hall Canada, 1993.

Snidermnan, Paul, David Northrup, Joseph Fletcher, Peter Russell, and Philip Tetlock. "Working paper on anti-semitism in Quebec." North York: Institute for Social Research, York University, 1992.

Stuart, Reginald. "Almost Americans." Paper presented at the Canadian Sociology and Anthropology Association meetings, Charlottetown, June, 1992.

Tilly, Charles. *Big Structures, Large Processes, Huge Comparisons.* New York: Russell Sage Foundation, 1984.

——— *Coercion, Capital, and European States, A.D. 990–1990.* Cambridge, Massachusetts: Basil Blackwell, 1990.

Tocqueville, Alexis de. *Democracy in America.* 1835; reprint, New York: Knopf, 1954.

Underhill, Frank. *In Search of Canadian Liberalism.* Toronto: Macmillan of Canada, 1960.

United Nations. *Human Development Report.* New York: Oxford Press, 1993.

Upton, L.F.S., ed. *The United Empire Loyalists: Men and Myths.* Toronto: Copp Clark, 1967.

Verney, Douglas. *Three Civilizations, Two Cultures, One State: Canada's Political Traditions.* Durham: Duke University Press, 1986.

Wallerstein, Immanuel. *The Modern World-System.* New York: Academic Press, 1974.

Weber, Max. "Deutscher Sociologentag" (German sociology today). *Verhandlungen* 1 (1911): 39–62.

Wien, Fred. "Regional inequality: explanations and policy issues." In *Social Inequality in Canada: Patterns, Problems, Policies*, edited by James Curtis, Edward Grabb, and Neil Guppy, 2nd ed. 449–568. Scarborough: Prentice-Hall Canada, 1993.

Wuthnow, Robert, ed. *Between States and Markets: The Voluntary Sector in Comparative Perspective.* Princeton: Princeton University Press, 1991.

Zelinsky, Wilbur. "A sidelong glance at Canadian nationalism and its symbols." *North American Culture* 4, 1 (1988): 2–27.

QUESTIONS FOR DISCUSSION

1. What examples can you offer to confirm the belief that Americans are more individualistic, anti-elitist, anti-statist and more achievement-oriented than Canadians? Do you agree?
2. To what historical antecedents can differences in individualistic versus collectivist tendencies between Americans and Canadians be attributed? What is your opinion of this presumed causality?
3. What evidence is needed to test for differences in value?
4. What forces are driving the global tendency to converge on values? What are the resisting forces? Which result will prevail? Why?

5. What are "Canadian values?" What are the challenges these values face in today's globalized world?

Edward Grabb received his Ph.D. in Sociology from the University of Waterloo. Much of his early research examined questions of social inequality and ideology in both Canada and the United States. His recent research deals primarily with cross-national comparisons of values and belief systems. He is the author of ***Theories of Social Inequality: Classical and Contemporary Perspectives*** *and co-editor, with James Curtis and Neil Guppy, of* ***Social Inequality in Canada: Patterns, Problems, Policies****. His articles have appeared in a variety of journals, including the* ***Canadian Review of Sociology and Anthropology****, the* ***Canadian Journal of Sociology****,* ***Social Forces****, and the* ***American Sociological Review****. He is currently Professor of Sociology at the University of Western Ontario.*

The Structure of Canada's Economy

TOM WESSON

This article will provide an overview of the structure of Canada's economy. First, we will look at the evolution of Canada's economy from an agrarian to a manufacturing and finally to a service-based economy. Some of the consequences of our new reliance on services will also be discussed. The second part of the article will trace the development of Canada's corporate sector, which is unique in several ways. We will look at why our corporate sector developed in such a unique way, and then at its consequences for Canada and Canadians, focusing on the effects of two key factors: the high degree of concentration of wealth and corporate power within Canada and the high degree of foreign ownership of Canadian businesses.

THE SECTORAL COMPOSITION OF THE CANADIAN ECONOMY

Taken together, Figures 1 (1900–1960) and 2 (1961–1990) show how the sectoral composition of Canada's economy has changed dramatically over the course of the twentieth century.[1] Looking first at Figure 1, we can see that at the turn of the century, there was a degree of balance between employment in the primary sectors of the economy — agriculture, mining, logging, fishing and hunting and trapping — and the industrial and service sectors. Within the primary sector, employment was dominated by the agricultural sector. Employment in agriculture declined more or less steadily until World War II, at which point agriculture's share of Canadian employment began to drop rapidly. In fact, since World War II the absolute number of Canadians employed in agriculture has been dropping. A trend that is closely related to the declining role of agriculture in Canadian employment has been the increasing urbanization of the Canadian population. More and more Canadians now live in cities, as people leave rural areas in search of employment, and cities attract the lion's share of new immigrants.

FIGURE 1
Labour Force Employment by Broad Sector, 1901–1961

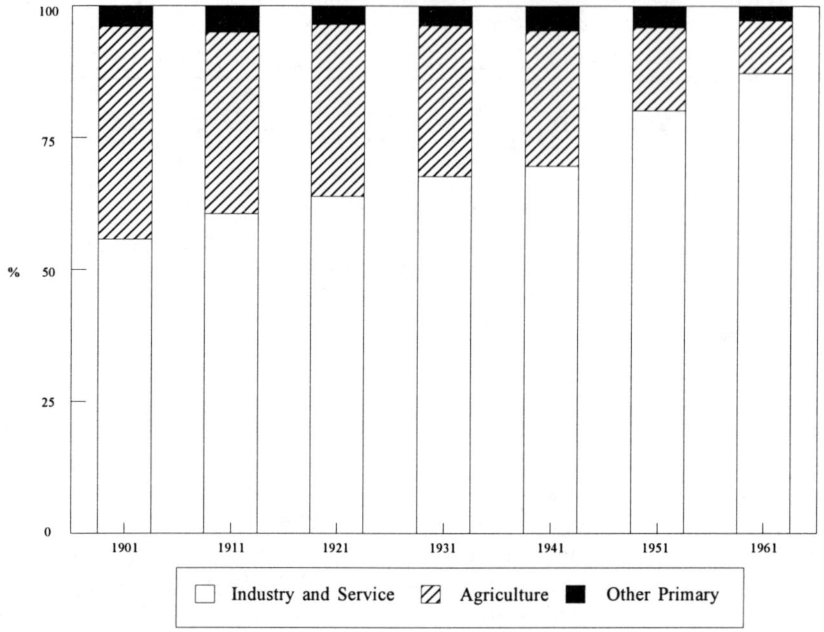

Source: Sylvia Ostry, *The Occupational Composition of the Canadian Labour Force* (Ottawa: Dominion Bureau of Statistics, 1967).

The flip side of the decline in agricultural employment in Canada has been great increases in the share of Canadians employed in goods producing and service industries. Again, this change was most notable in the first 15 years or so immediately following World War II. While it continued through the 1960s, 1970s and 1980s, (see Figure 2) it has slowed somewhat. What is a more significant trend in the later post-war period, is the growth in service employment. While even in 1960, the majority of Canadians workers were employed in services, today, the ratio of service to manufacturing employment is about twice what it was in 1960.

Economists have devoted much effort to explaining these shifts in employment, and have had some success to show for their efforts. First, the shift from agricultural employment can be attributed in large part to an increase in the productivity of agricultural labour: that is, it now takes far fewer agricultural workers to produce the same output. This fact is easily explained by the increasing sophistication and mechanization of agricultural production. Developments from the internal combustion engine powered

FIGURE 2
Labour Force Employment by Sector, 1960–1990

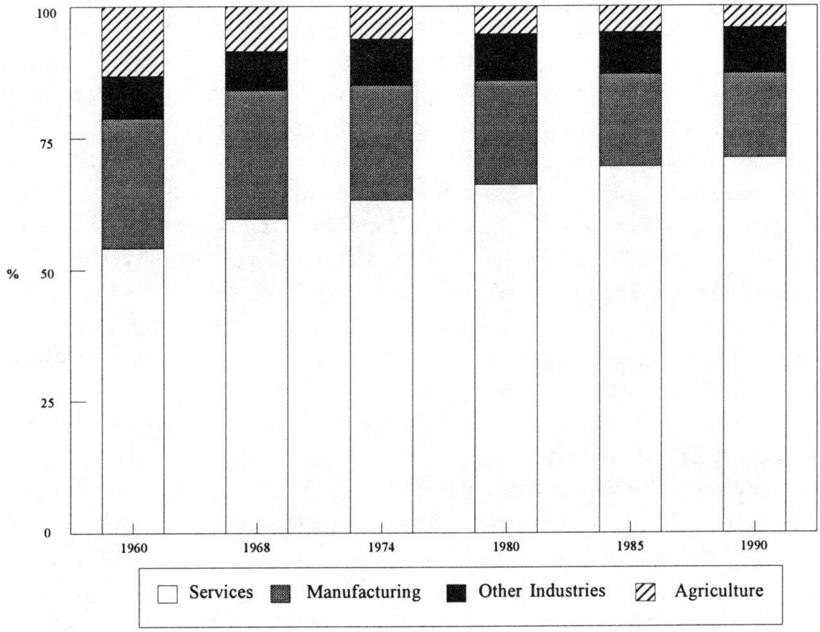

Source: OECD.

tractor to synthetic hormones to boost milk production have all helped fewer agricultural workers to produce more output.

The shift from manufacturing to service employment is not as simple to explain as the shift from agricultural employment. Several explanations have been put forth, and they all seem to have some validity, although none is significantly better than the others when tested statistically.[2] Furthermore, it is especially difficult to test these theories because, in general, available statistics concerning the service sector are much less detailed than those for the manufacturing sector.

One possibility is that the transformation of the Canadian economy into a service one rests, like the shift away from agriculture, on differing rates of productivity improvements. It is hypothesized that labour productivity growth in manufacturing has out-paced that in services, since many service functions (often very simple ones, like waiting tables and very complex ones, like performing heart surgery) do not lend themselves well to mechanization. Thus, productivity growth in these areas is slow relative to manufacturing. The result of this difference in productivity growth rates is that more Canadians need to be employed in services in order to maintain the relative levels of service and manufacturing output.[3]

A second explanation for the shift toward services in the Canadian economy, is a change in consumer demand from manufactured goods to services. The underlying assumption behind this argument is that as incomes rise, people spend more on services than on goods. In other words, it is thought that services tend to be considered luxuries, compared to goods. Since, in general, the incomes of Canadians have been continually rising, this assumptions implies that Canadians' consumption of services relative to goods will also be rising. A related reason why Canadians relative demand for goods and services may have shifted, is the growth in households in which all adults are employed outside the home. This trend has been a boon to such "luxury" services industries as fast-food restaurants and housekeeping services.

Closely related to the hypothesis that consumers are demanding more services today than in the past, is the hypothesis that other industries are demanding more services as inputs, than in past. For example, 30 years ago the information systems consulting industry did not exist. Today, Canadian firms spend millions of dollars annually on this service. Even the demands for traditional services, such as transportation and logistics, may be increasing, as Canadian firms expand the geographic scope of their markets and rationalize production among their plants.

A final reason given for the growth in services in the Canadian economy is the trend toward contracting-out of services by manufacturing firms. For example, if a manufacturing firm contracts out the job of cleaning its facilities, instead of maintaining its own cleaning staff, employment in the manufacturing sector is reduced while manufacturing in services increases. This change occurs without any change in the actual work performed. However, all estimates indicate that contracting out is a relatively small contributor to the growth in service employment in Canada.

Whatever their relative importance in transforming Canada into a service economy, the combined effect of these changes is clear: services are playing a far greater role in our economy than they have in the past. This change, in turn, is significant for several reasons. First, it means that to be successful in the future, Canadians will require different job skills than in the past. Furthermore, in a service economy, an individual's success is more dependant on his skill level than in manufacturing industries. High-paying jobs in the service sector are those which demand greater skill levels, while in manufacturing, labour productivity is often a function of the capital employed. In services, it is the skills of the employee that most often determine her value to the firm. Obviously, this fact has implications for education and training which must be considered by workers, employers and governments alike.

The shift to a service economy has other implications for government policy as well. The mere fact that the data collected by governments on services are sparse and ill-conceived, shows that governments typically focus on manufacturing industries in their economic policy discussions. Governments must realize that service industries have been a major driver of economic growth in Canada during the second half of the twentieth century, and must adapt such aspects of economic policy as industrial, tax and regional policies to reflect this fact.

Now that we have some picture of the sectoral makeup of the Canadian economy, we will turn our attention to the economic actors who actually employ workers and produce output in these various sectors — firms. The rest of this article is devoted to describing what can loosely be called the Canadian corporate sector. Before we go into detail exploring the Canadian corporate sector, however, it is necessary to understand what is implied by the word corporation and what alternative forms of business organization exist.

THE MAKEUP OF THE MODERN CORPORATION

The word corporation is derived from the Latin word *corpus*, meaning body. The essence of a modern corporation is that it is a separate legal body, or entity, distinct from its owners. This legal separation between the corporation and its owners leads, in turn, to the concept of limited liability. This means that any investor in a corporation is risking only the amount of his investment and is not liable for any losses of the corporation beyond this amount. In contrast, in an unincorporated business (known either as a sole proprietorship or a partnership, depending on the number of investors), the firm's owner/managers are fully liable for the firm's debts, up to the full amount of their ability to pay. Thus, for example, if a doctor loses a malpractice suit, not only must he use the assets associated with his practice to pay the settlement imposed, but he must also use his personal assets to whatever extent necessary, as well. In contrast, while the asbestos related lawsuits against the U.S. firm Johns Manville bankrupted the firm, its shareholders lost only the value of their investment, not their personal assets.

The fact that corporations are distinct legal entities has many benefits for them and their investors, as well as the economy as a whole. If corporations were not legally separate from their owners, there could be no capital markets as we know them. Investors would not put money in a business over which they had essentially no control, if their entire worth could be put at risk by poor management decisions. Similarly, the process of trading shares in a corporation would be greatly complicated if every time the corporation's ownership changed, the underlying financial strength of the corporation changed. Furthermore, corporations have a continuity that other forms of business enterprises lack. The Hudson's

Bay Company is about 325 years old and has evolved into a completely different organization than it was originally, with different ownership, goals, activities and so on, yet, it has had a legal continuity over that period which has facilitated its various strategic changes. Finally, but perhaps most importantly, corporations are able to enter into contracts and other legal commitments independently of their owners. Imagine if the workers, suppliers and customers of a large corporation like Bell Canada, all had to enter into contracts with the firm's individual shareholders! The specialization of labour and exploitation of scale economies which drove the industrial revolution in the 19th century, and the growth of the industrialized economies since then, would have been impossible without the corporation.

Of course, incorporation for a business owner is not without its costs, most of which are government imposed. As they do with most other legal entities under their jurisdiction, governments, at both the federal and provincial levels in Canada, tax and regulate corporations. Because of this, incorporation necessarily involves trade-offs which limit its desirability somewhat. However, it is important to note that the vast majority of economic activity in Canada involves corporations.

While corporations were an essential element in the industrialization of world economy, their origins are actually much older. Similar forms of organization have been used since the late middle ages to raise money for such activities as trading, which require large investments up front. Initially, these organizations were created by royal charter to perform some particular function. For example, the Hudson's Bay Company charter gave it the right to trade in all of the territory that drained into Hudson Bay. By 1700, English business people and lawyers had combined aspects of contract and trust law to develop the joint-stock company. Joint stock companies were much like corporations in practice, except they lacked the benefit of limited liability. However, they had a great advantage over charted companies, in that the could be created without a royal decree or an act of Parliament. By the early part of the 19th century, most jurisdictions had enacted legislation which enabled individuals to form corporations without legislative approval, providing certain legal conditions were met.

Only during the late 19th century, however, did the professionally managed corporation that we know today, begin to evolve. As corporations became larger, and involved in increasingly complex activities, their owners found it difficult to effectively mange the activities of these growing enterprises. It also became harder for a small number of owners to meet the equity capital needs of a large corporation as production technologies became more capital and scale intensive. Out of these increasing managerial and financial challenges, together with the expansion of the middle class with funds available to invest, grew the modern structure of the large corporation. Under this structure, the shareholders play no direct role in the operations of the corporation beyond electing a board of directors to represent their interests. The board of directors, in turn, hires a group of professional managers to run the corporation. Typically, some of these managers are also board members. These employee-directors are known as inside directors, while board members who are not employees of the corporation, are called outside directors.

Among the duties required of directors under the *Canadian Business Corporation Act* is to "act honestly and in good faith with the view of the best interests of the corporation and... [to] exercise the care, diligence and skill that a reasonably prudent person would exercise in comparable circumstances..."[4] A corporation's directors do not have the duty to act as the shareholders would like them to, but they do have a clear duty to act in the best interests of the corporation and, therefore, its shareholders. James Gillies has likened a board member to a member of Parliament, elected to represent shareholders' interests, but with their first responsibility being to do what they believe is in the best interest of the corporation.[5]

In recent years, there has been much criticism of the way boards of directors fulfil their fiduciary duty to the corporation and its shareholders. It has been argued, by such authors as Peter Drucker, Irving Olds, the former chairman of the board of U.S. Steel, and Harold Geneen, the former chairman of the board of AT&T, that in many corporations the board is essentially a ceremonial body.[6] It is very difficult for boards to provide an effective check on management activities, for several reasons. First, although board members are normally elected by the shareholders at the corporation's annual meeting, in most cases the meeting is poorly attended, and the election is largely ceremonial. Second, outside directors are essentially dependent on management for the information they use in decision-making, while inside directors obviously cannot provide a effective check on their own activities. Finally, board members often feel an obligation, or at least a practical need, to concur with the views of those responsible for their election. As we will see, in Canada this is often a single large shareholder who controls the corporation, while in the United States it is often the corporation's management which effectively elects the board, since shareholders often assign their proxies to management, giving it de facto control of the corporation without significant ownership.

In fact, today, boards of directors are coming under greater scrutiny, and are being forced to be more responsible to shareholders for several reasons. First, investors are becoming more sophisticated and more critical. As large institutional investors, like pension and mutual funds, expand their portfolios, they are becoming major shareholders of more and more corporations. Unlike large individual or corporate investors, these funds usually wish to play no role in the daily management of the firm's operations. They merely wish to have their interests, that is the shareholders' interests, protected by an effective board of directors to which management is responsive. Because of their size and their ability to influence other investors, many pension funds are able to exert at least indirect influence over such large corporations as General Motors, IBM and Exxon. The rise of large institutional investors means that, for the first time since corporations began to grow so large that no individual could reasonably hope to maintain a controlling interest in them, many of the largest corporations are forced to deal with shareholders whose economic clout is comparable to their own.

Also forcing boards to be more responsive to shareholders is the fact that, to a great extent in the United States and to a lesser degree in Canada, board members are being held legally responsible for their actions and those of the corporation. Shareholders are suing board members who fail to carry out their fiduciary responsibility, while interested parties outside the corporation are suing board members when they feel they have been harmed by the corporation's activities. Shareholder suits have forced boards to look much more critically at the information provided to them by management, especially when issues are involved in which management might have a biased position, such as a takeover.

In many ways, suits by outsiders are the most threatening to boards of directors, since they can involve matters about which the board had essentially no knowledge. For example, an environmental group might sue the board of a corporation which pollutes a waterway, or the employees of a corporation may sue its board if the company pension fund is mismanaged. These third party suits are evidence of a general feeling that, in fact, the board of a modern corporation should be responsible not just to the firm's shareholders, but also to the other stakeholders of the firm as well. In many European countries this recognition has resulted in legislation which gives employees the right to representation on the board, while in the U.S. many states have passed legislation recognizing the general principle that boards should represent other stakeholders in addition to shareholders.

Finally, it is important to recognize another trend that has affected both the role of boards of directors in the modern corporation and the entire way in which corporations are managed. During the 1980s there was an enormous boom in what has been called the market for corporate control, that is, in the market for takeovers, leveraged buyouts (LBOs) and other changes in corporations' ownership structure. Many of the takeovers and LBOs of the 1980s were aimed at breaking down the cosy relationship between the target corporations' management and their boards of directors. It was argued that because boards of directors were not forcing management to operate in the best interest of shareholders, there were profits to be made by taking over the corporation and replacing the existing management team with a new one which would act in the best interest of the shareholders. Often, the process was accomplished by buying a public corporation (that is, one whose shares trade on an established stock exchange) and converting it into a private corporation in which the shareholders took a direct role in its management. This phenomenon was so prevalent that Michael Jensen, a prominent author in the field, wrote of "The Eclipse of the Public Corporation."[7] While the public corporation will probably not be eclipsed anytime soon, it is undoubtedly true that the takeover and LBO booms did serve to heighten boards' awareness of the need to maximize shareholder value.

Now that we understand what a corporation is, and something about how corporations are governed, we will now look at the development of Canada's unique corporate sector.

THE CORPORATE SECTOR IN CANADA

While Canadians often think that our corporate sector is largely similar in structure to that of the U.S., the fact of the matter is, there are profound and important differences between the two nations in the way in which businesses are organized, managed and operated. As Canadians, we have never fully trusted the market mechanism to allocate resources and rewards optimally, and therefore, have not done as much as our continental neighbours either to encourage the growth of what has been called free enterprise, or to discourage conditions which inhibit its growth. The result has been the development of a uniquely Canadian corporate sector, which like many Canadian institutions, is a curious mix of contrasts and contradictions, growing out of a series of historical accidents, poorly co-ordinated government policies and politically, rather than economically, motivated policy decisions.

There are several key aspects to its uniqueness. The first is related to ownership and control. To a significant extent, Canadian corporations are controlled by foreigners. Furthermore, many Canadian-controlled corporations are controlled by a relatively small group of individuals and firms. Next, relating to the competitive environment faced by Canadian corporations, is the fact that Canada often has a relatively small number of corporations in any particular industry. A final unique aspect of our corporate sector relates to the activities performed by Canadian corporations. To a far greater extent than is typical of a nation of Canada's level of wealth, Canadian corporations are involved in the extraction and processing of natural resources.

All of these aspects of Canada's corporate sector have a negative impact on our economic and political well-being. To a large extent, they developed out of a series of poorly planned and co-ordinated government policies, often brought about by the government of the day's unwillingness to make hard political choices (or by the unwillingness of the people of Canada to reelect a government which makes such choices). We will now explore how these policies came about.

Canada, like most nations which began as colonies of the European powers, was initially seen as a source of raw materials for its colonizers, as well as a market for their finished products. This role for Canada is apparent in the early histories of such British-controlled Canadian firms as the Hudson's Bay Company (founded in 1670), The General Mining Association Limited (1825) and the Canada Company (1826). As British-controlled firms in Canada grew, financial firms like the Bank of British North America (1836) and the Trust and Loan Company of Canada (1845) were set up by British investors to serve other British firms operating in Canada.

However, a major local spur to the industrialization of Canada came after the American Revolution, when thousands of United Empire Loyalists came to Nova Scotia, Quebec and Ontario from the United States. The Loyalists were mainly middle class merchants and small businessmen who were opposed to the liberal ideals which motivated the American Revolution. They tended to be politically conservative, but did feel that the state should intervene to protect small businesses from competitive pressures (this would prove to be a very persistent idea in Canadian politics and economics). The Loyalists started myriad small industrial enterprises, especially in Ontario (particularly in the southwest) and Nova Scotia. However, the businesses founded by the Loyalists soon outgrew the financing available locally, and Canada began to rely on British financing not just for British firms operating in Canada, but for indigenous ones as well.

While historical circumstances favoured a Canadian corporate sector with a high degree of foreign ownership and an ambivalent attitude toward competition, government policies, most notably the National Policy introduced by Sir John A. Macdonald's Conservative government in 1878, greatly accelerated these trends. The National Policy, arguably Canada's most important economic policy until the 1988 Free Trade Agreement with the United States, was designed to encourage investment and economic growth within Canada as well as build an east-west flow of goods to tie the country together economically. The policy had two simple components — high tariffs on manufactured goods and an open market for foreign investment. Under the National Policy, the average tariff on Canadian imports rose from 17.5 per cent to 25 per cent between 1878 and 1879.[8]

The tariff was seen as a means of encouraging the growth of manufacturing industries in Central Canada, allowing them to reach a scale that would enable them to compete internationally. The Conservatives were greatly helped in their efforts to sell the tariff to the electorate outside Central Canada, by the fact that the economy had slumped badly under the Liberals in the five years preceding the 1878 election, and by the rejection of Canada-U.S. free trade by the U.S. Senate in 1873.

Those in Canada who might have opposed the tariff were also appeased in several ways. First, for the most part, the machinery needed by Canada's natural resource industries was exempt from the tariff or charged relatively low rates of duty. Second, it was pointed out that the tariff and resulting east-west flow of goods would help make the Canadian Pacific Railway viable. Many Western Canadians were willing to make economic sacrifices in exchange for the railway, since it was seen as an essential means of solidifying Canada's claim to the Prairies in face of U.S. expansionist elements. Finally, Macdonald used what today would be called the "infant industry protection" argument to sell the tariff. He argued that by temporarily protecting Central Canada's young industries from competition from their larger and more fully developed U.S. counterparts, the tariff would give Canada's industries the opportunity to grow and become efficient. Then, the tariff could be removed and Canadians would have access to competitively priced Canadian-made manufactured goods as well foreign goods and would have manufacturers who could compete internationally. As it turned out, this "temporary" protection lasted, at least in part, until 1988 (Figure 3 shows average Canadian tariffs for the period 1971–1985, while Figure 4 shows average Canadian tariffs on various categories of manufactured products for 1987).

The second central element of Macdonald's National Policy was a wide open investment policy. Macdonald described his feelings toward investment this way, "the bigger the capitalist and the more he has invested in the country, the better for the country."[9] The Conservatives felt that one of the factors constraining the Canadian economy was a lack of capital for growth, and hoped to attract both foreign and domestic investors to Canada's protected markets. Under this policy, foreign investment in Canada grew relatively slowly but steadily for about 30 years. Then, during the economic boom of 1908–1922, foreign investment in Canada boomed also. During this later period, however, an important change began to take place in the source and type of foreign investment in Canada. As previously mentioned, most of the early foreign investment in Canada was from Britain, and this was debt, not equity financing. During the early 20th century, however, more and more of the foreign investment in Canada was equity investments by American firms and individuals. In 1900, 14 per cent of the foreign investment in Canada was by Americans. By 1926, this figure was 53 per cent and by 1948, 74 per cent.[10]

To a large extent, these new equity investments were an unforseen consequence of the National Policy, although in retrospect, they were a perfectly logical one. Since foreign firms importing goods into Canada were placed at a great disadvantage by the tariff, but were free to invest in Canada as they saw fit, more and more foreign firms invested in Canadian subsidiaries and/or bought existing Canadian firms in order to produce goods in Canada for the Canadian market. These branch plants typically

FIGURE 3
Canadian Tariff Rates, 1985

Year	*Nominal Tariffs on Imports*	*Nominal Tariffs on Dutiable Imports*	*Per Cent of Imports Not Dutiable*
1971	7.1	15.4	54.0
1975	6.7	15.1	55.9
1980	5.4	13.8	60.6
1985	4.2	11.2	62.8

Source: The General Agreement on Tariffs and Trade, *Trade Policy Review: Canada* (Geneva: The General Agreement on Tariffs and Trade, 1990)

FIGURE 4
Canadian Tariff Rates, 1987

Product	*Average Rate — Import Weighted*	*Average Rate — Production Weighted*
Agriculture	2.8	3.0
Forestry	0.0	0.0
Fishing and Trapping	0.1	0.2
Mining	0.0	0.2
Manufacturing	4.6	5.4
Clothing	22.5	20.3
Tobacco	12.2	16.3
Furniture and Fixtures	18.3	12.5
Electrical Products	6.0	7.9
Metal Fabricating	7.8	7.5
Chemicals and Chemical Products	5.1	6.0
Food and Beverage	4.2	5.6
Machinery	3.1	4.9
Transportation Equipment	1.5	2.8
Petroleum and Coal Products	0.6	0.5
Total Average	4.3	4.6

Source: The General Agreement on Tariffs and Trade, *Trade Policy Review: Canada* (Geneva: The General Agreement on Tariffs and Trade, 1990).

produced a broad product range at a small scale, and, therefore, never became the efficient manufacturers which the National Policy was supposed to foster. Because they were foreign-owned, these firms had no incentive to improve their efficiency and compete internationally, since they would only be competing with their parents. Thus, one of the legacies of the National Policy is what is now known as the branch plant economy — a Canadian manufacturing sector which is a miniature replica of the U.S. manufacturing sector, producing goods for Canadian consumption at an inefficiently small scale.

In addition to encouraging a high level of foreign investment in Canadian manufacturing industries, the National Policy allowed foreigners continued open access to Canada's raw material resources. Macdonald's open policy toward investment allowed firms like the precursors of Inco and the Aluminum Company of America, to invest in Canada to extract ore, and then to export the ore back to the U.S. for processing. Later, large American oil companies were responsible for the development of Western Canada's oil and gas reserves, and American firms opened up Labrador's iron reserves for development.

These foreign firms (usually American) were able to open up Canada's resource frontiers before Canadian firms, because for them, their investments represented opportunities for vertical integration, while for potential Canadian investors, they did not. This meant that for the American investors, these resource developments had a certain market for their output, and were, therefore, less risky than for potential Canadian investors. This pattern of foreign-owned firms exporting unprocessed natural resources, meant that Canada never developed a strong presence in the production of either the manufactured goods which used our raw materials as inputs, or the machinery inputs required by our natural resource industries. Thus, the foreign investment encouraged by the National Policy permeated the Canadian economy.

A second major legacy of the National Policy is the concentration of ownership and market power among Canadian firms. The National Policy made Canadian industries very attractive places to compete. At the time that the National Policy was implemented, supporters of free trade referred to the tariff as the "mother of the trusts."[11] Foreign competition was reduced by the tariff, and domestic competition was often naturally limited by economies of scale and other economic factors. Canadian firms in many industries were, therefore, protected from competition to a large extent and were immensely profitable. Once established, many Canadian firms were able to grow to dominate their market using mostly internally generated funds, allowing the firms' founders and their descendants to retain tight control of their respective organizations. Thus, in industries such as brewing and many types of retailing, the number of major competitors dropped continuously, while the remaining firms stayed tightly controlled and very profitable. Concentration of sales within Canadian industries and

FIGURE 5
Role of Foreign-Owned Firms in Economies of Leading Industrial Nations, 1986

	Share of Foreign-Owned Firms' Sales (%)
U.S.	10
Japan	1
France	27
Germany	18
UK	20
Canada*	25

* 1988.
Source: E.M. Graham and P. Krugman, *Foreign Direct Investment in the United States* (Washington, DC: Institute for International Economics, 1991), p. 33; and Statistics Canada.

concentration of wealth within Canada went hand in hand, as family fortunes grew.

We will now look in more detail at the consequences of the two legacies of the National Policy: a high level of foreign ownership of Canadian corporations, and the concentration of wealth and market power within Canada.

Foreign Ownership in Canada

As shown in Figure 5, in 1986 Canada had a higher level of foreign ownership than any of the Group of Five (G-5) nations, whether measured in terms of foreign-owned firms' share of Canadian corporate sales or assets. Figure 6 shows the level of foreign control of Canadian corporations by industry. From Figure 6 we can see that while the foreign ownership of Canadian industries averages about 21 per cent, very high by international standards, in some industries, particularly in manufacturing, the degree of foreign control of Canadian industries is much, much higher than this average.

What does a high level of foreign ownership mean for the Canadian economy? Macdonald and the Conservatives of his day clearly felt that foreign investment was preferable to no investment, and it is hard to argue with this proposition. Similarly, however, it is hard to argue with the proposition that Canadian ownership and control of corporations is preferable to foreign ownership and control. To understand more fully the costs of foreign ownership for the Canadian economy, we need to move beyond these simplistic propositions and look at what it means to the operations of a corporation for it to be foreign, rather than Canadian, controlled.

FIGURE 6
The Ownership Structure of Canadian Industries by Asset (%)

		Canadian		
	Foreign	*Private*	*Gov't Bus. Enterprise*	*Total*
Food, Beverages & Tobacco	29.5	60.6	9.8	70.5
Wood and Paper	38.7	60.8	0.4	61.3
Energy	20.0	30.7	49.3	80.0
Chemicals, Chemical Products & Textiles	66.0	na	na	34.0
Metallic Minerals & Mineral Products	28.0	na	na	72.0
Machinery & Equipment (except Electrical)	47.1	52.9	0.0	52.9
Transportation Equipment	49.4	na	na	50.6
Electrical & Electronic Products	42.1	na	na	57.9
Construction & Real Estate	11.9	84.5	3.6	88.1
Transportation Services	4.5	65.6	29.9	95.5
Communications	9.4	81.0	9.6	90.6
Deposit-accepting Intermediaries	12.4	81.6	6.0	87.6
Insurers	33.0	63.6	3.4	67.0
Consumer & Business Financing	24.4	49.7	25.9	75.6
Services	15.8	81.6	2.6	84.2
Consumer Goods & Services	21.1	78.9	0.0	78.9
Total Non financial Industries	24.3	58.9	15.9	75.7
Total Finance & Insurance Industries	17.2	75.1	7.6	82.8
Total All Industries	20.8	67.4	11.8	79.2

Source: Statistics Canada, Calura 61–210.

Typically, only about 10 per cent of a Canadian corporation's sales fall to the bottom line as after tax profits. Clearly, for Canadian-owned corporations, these profits go to Canadians and contribute to the wealth and material well-being of Canadians, while the profits of foreign-owned firms do not. However, of much greater significance to the Canadian economy is what happens to the other 90 per cent of the cash the corporation generates through its sales. This money, the lion's share of the corporation's revenue, is spent by the corporation in performing all of the various activities required to design, produce and sell its product: research and development, production, distribution, marketing and so on. Assessing differences in how foreign- and Canadian-controlled firms spend this money is more complex than dealing with corporate profits, but is essential to understanding the effect of foreign ownership on Canada's economic well-being.

Some foreign-owned Canadian corporations design, manufacture and market products for a worldwide market. These firms are often described as having a "world product mandate" for a particular product. For example, ICI Explosives Canada is the worldwide headquarters of its parent's, Imperial Chemicals Industries of the United Kingdom, explosive business.[12] ICI Explosives Canada performs much of the strategic planning, research and development and marketing for its parent's worldwide explosive business. Similarly, although it is 98 per cent owned by the American firm United Technologies, Pratt and Whitney Canada has sole worldwide responsibility for its parent's small turbofan and turboprop airplane engine lines. Pratt and Whitney Canada exports more than 90 per cent of its annual production.

Unfortunately, however, examples like Pratt and Whitney and ICI Explosives are the exception and not the rule for foreign-owned companies in Canada. Many more, and more prominent, foreign firms — the multinational oil companies, the big three automakers and so on — have Canadian subsidiaries which produce products designed and engineered outside Canada, often using imported components.[13] These Canadian subsidiaries have been described as "truncated" corporations, because they do not perform the full range of activities needed to bring a product to market, most notably strategic planning, research and development and product design.[14] These companies are the traditional branch plants which have been the focus of so much attention in Canada.

However, before we vilify foreign-owned firms for not performing a full range of activities in Canada, it is important to realize that the same complaint could be made about an increasing number of Canadian-owned firms. For example, Seagram now produces and blends whiskey in Canada, but performs almost all other functions relating to its whiskey business, including controlling the all-important marketing of its products, in its New York office. Similarly, Northern Telecom's central office switch business is now centred in its U.S. subsidiary, based in North Carolina.

Based on our discussion so far, we can say that being foreign-owned is neither a necessary, nor a sufficient condition for a Canadian corporation to rely on affiliated foreign firms to perform key activities. However, there is significant evidence that, on the whole, foreign affiliates in Canada do tend to rely to a large degree on their parent, or other foreign firms, for important activities and inputs. In their study of 25 Canadian industries, Michael Porter and the Monitor Company found only a few examples of foreign-controlled Canadian corporations which autonomously managed a business unit with responsibilities beyond serving the Canadian market.[15]

Furthermore, foreign ownership is highest in Canadian industries where there are significant extra-plant economies of scale. That is, there is more foreign investment in industries where there are high, firm level fixed costs, like research and development and advertising, which can be shared among several production plants. The accepted explanation for this finding is that foreign firms, coming mostly from nations with larger economies than Canada's, have a clear advantage over Canadian firm's in these industries, since the foreign firms have more domestic output over which to spread their fixed costs before they consider undertaking foreign investment. The implication in this conclusion, is that these foreign firms invest in Canada on the assumption that those activities which provide for the extra-plant economies of scale will be centrally performed, that is, will be performed in the foreign firm's home nation and not in Canada.

This trend toward "truncated" Canadian subsidiaries seems to have accelerated in recent years. Under increasing pressure from Japanese and European competitors, U.S. firms are rationalizing their North American operations and are choosing to eliminate such activities as manufacturing, research and development, marketing and strategic planning from their Canadian operations. Media reports have focused on Canadian subsidiaries of U.S. multinationals being transformed into little more than sales offices, with all of their strategic decisions made by their parent, and all of their high value added activities performed in the U.S.[16]

The Concentration of Corporate Wealth and Power in Canada

The wealth of Canada has always been concentrated in the hands of a relatively small number of individuals and corporations. In 1914, the social critic, Gustavus Myers, contended in his *History of Canadian Wealth*, that "fifty men controlled one-third of Canada's material wealth as expressed in railways, banks, factories, mines and other properties and resources."[17] This one-third figure is even more striking when one considers that about half that amount again was controlled by foreigners. Thus, the remaining 99.99 per cent plus of Canada's population controlled only about 50 per cent of Canada's wealth. Perhaps most surprising, however, is the fact that in her 1985 book *Who Owns Canada*, Diane Francis estimated that 32 families and five conglomerates owned about one third of Canada's non-financial assets.[18] Thus, the concentration of wealth in Canada which had appalled Myers at the time of the great trusts and robber barons in his native U.S., and of similar concentrations of wealth in Europe, had changed little 70-odd years later.

It could be argued that this concentration of corporate wealth in Canada is merely the result of a healthy free-enterprise system. The story could go something like this: those corporations which are well managed, have competitive advantages over their rivals, and are well positioned to take advantage of those advantages, are more profitable than their competitors and naturally grow larger and make their owners wealthier. However, there are several aspects of Canada's corporate sector which do not fit this model.

First, many of Canada's largest corporate empires are conglomerates. They do not participate in just one or a few related industries, where some competitive advantage relating to their core business or businesses could have allowed them to grow rapidity. Rather, these conglomerates participate in many, largely unrelated, industries. For example, Lord Kenneth Thomson controls businesses as diverse as the *Globe and Mail* newspaper, The Hudson's Bay Company, Thomson Travel, and several North Sea oilfields. Jim Pattison built his Pattison Group from a single car dealership in 1960, into a conglomerate which includes, among many other businesses, Canada's largest group of auto dealers, Canada's largest outdoor advertising sign company, a large manufacturer of canned seafood, and the chain of Ripley's Believe It Or Not museums. It is hard to believe that any single competitive advantage has allowed such empires to grow.

It is natural to ask at this point why Canadian business in the 1990s is still dominated by conglomerates at a time when conglomerates have been out of favour in the United States for about 20 years. During their heyday in the 1960s, it was argued that a well organized conglomerate operated an internal capital market which was more efficient than the external one. It was felt that a conglomerate could optimally reallocate assets among its constituent parts, while also offering its investors ready-made diversification, and bring a new external discipline to the corporations under its control. As the conglomerates began to perform poorly compared to their undiversified rivals, however, it became clear that most conglomerates merely added another layer of overhead for their subsidiaries to support, while bringing no real operating benefits. Internal capital markets proved less efficient than external ones, since many decisions were made by managers, not the suppliers of the capital. By the mid-1980s, new fortunes were being made breaking up the conglomerates, which had made their initial investors rich in the 1960s.

If the U.S. markets realized that conglomerates were the proverbial emperor's new clothes, why do conglomerates persist in playing such a key role in Canada? The simple reason is that most of them are not subject to market forces. They tend to participate in concentrated industries, where inefficiencies result in higher prices paid by consumers, not lower profits for firms. Furthermore, Canadian conglomerates are often tightly held, thus they are not regulated by the market for corporate control.

An example illustrates these points well. The late K.C. Irving controlled an empire of over 400 corporations, which all grew out of a single car dealership, founded in 1924, and a small lumber mill. From the car dealership, Irving diversified naturally enough into repairs and gasoline sales. After buying control of the family lumber mill after his father's death, Irving began to acquire timberland and build mills. As his empire grew, Irving's interests expanded to include a construction company, which built his gas stations as well as houses, a shipbuilding company, fleets of barges and tankers, a truck assembly operation, and companies which used his paper and lumber products, including newspapers, hardware stores, building material firms and a pre-fabricated house company.

Irving was able to start or acquire all of these businesses because he had such a high degree of control of all of the markets in which he participated. Obviously, he could not assemble a truck for his own use as cheaply as Ford or General Motors, but this did not matter to him, since he could pass the added costs on to those who purchased gasoline or hardware from his retail outlets. On the other hand, it made sense for him to invest in new businesses in New Brunswick rather than expanding his existing businesses outside the province, because by doing so he increased, rather than lessened, his control over the markets in which he competed. For example, by investing in hardware stores to sell his lumber products and timberlands to supply his sawmills, he was able to build a full vertical monopoly over the entire chain of production. If instead, he had tried to expanded his lumber business into the rest of Canada, he would have exposed himself to competition, and possibly even retaliation in his own tightly controlled New Brunswick market. Similarly, other Canadian lumber firms, even if they could overcome Irving's monopoly of lumber products distribution in New Brunswick, could only enter that market at their peril, knowing it would likely prompt harsh retaliation from Irving. Of course, Irving was protected from U.S. competition by Canada's tariff wall.

Further evidence of the lack of competition in the Canadian corporate sector is found by looking at the list of businesses in which the various Canadian conglomerates have interests. Many of them are in the same industries (e.g., Thomson, Hollinger and Irving in newspapers). In fact, many Canadian conglomerates even share interests in the same firms. For example, at the peak of the real estate market in the mid-1980s, not only did the Reichmann's have their Olympia and York real estate empire, but they also had significant holdings in their major Canadian competitors, Cadillac Fairview, Trizec and Bramalea.

However, perhaps the most damning indictment of the Canadian conglomerates is that many of them do not actually build businesses, but merely buy and sell existing businesses in ever more complicated financial transactions. While the Irvings, the McCains and even the Reichmann's are best known for businesses they created, many other Canadian conglomerates have made most, if not all, of their money merely buying and selling companies. Perhaps the best example of this is Conrad Black, who burst onto the world financial scene when, in 1978, at the age of 33, he convinced the widows of E.P. Taylor and Bud McDougald to sell him a controlling interest in the Argus Corporation, where Black's father had worked. Black raised the money for the purchase from friends and several banks. In the seven years following the Argus takeover, three of the firm's key components — Massey-Ferguson, Dominion Stores and Standard Broadcasting — were losing so much money that Black sold them. Still, although the companies he controlled did not always do well, Black and his partner's did.

We need to be careful, however, not to blame people like Black for making money. We need to concern ourselves with the question of why it is so easy for so-called "paper entrepreneurs" to make money in Canada, while we seem to have so few people who are willing and able to build a business from the ground up.[19] While the American economy has been criticised on similar grounds, it is startling to see comparatively young and specialized companies like Intel, Microsoft and Hewlett-Packard near the top of *BusinessWeek's* list of the U.S.'s most valuable companies.[20] Canada simply does not seem capable of producing new corporate stars at the pace needed to maintain the vitality of our corporate sector.

Concentration in Canadian Industries

The concentration of sales in the hands of a relatively few firms in many Canadian industries, is an issue that, in many ways, is related to the concentration of wealth in Canada. While Statistics Canada, in contrast to its American counterpart, does not collect industry-level concentration data, we can all list many example of a small number of large firms competing in a Canadian industry. From beer (Molson and Labatt), to banks (the big five), to department stores (The Bay and Eaton's), to ice skates (CanStar and CCM), Canadian business abounds with concentrated industries.

Concentration is an important issue, because our entire economic system is predicated on the assumption that prices are set by competitive markets. If the law of supply and demand sets the prices for both buyers and sellers, then, in a free market economy, using the prices set in the marketplace to measure the value of a good or activity, will allocate the economy's scarce resources efficiently. If an industry is too concentrated, however, then the firms in it begin to act as price setters, not price takers. In the extreme, of course, if the industry has only one member (or if its members are able to collude perfectly) then the firm has the absolute power to set its price. Such non-competitive behaviour has two consequences. First, it is obviously going to result in a higher price for the good, and transfer of wealth from the buyer to the seller in the industry. More subtly, however, it can be shown that there is also an overall loss of efficiency in the economy. The perfect allocation of resources achieved by the price mechanism in a competitive economy is distorted, and the economy as a whole is worse off.

Of course, no industry in the real world corresponds to the economists' notion of perfect competition. The policy-maker's job becomes, therefore, to decide how far to allow industries to deviate from pure competition and what to do when an industry crosses that imaginary line. Canada and the United States provide an interesting contrast in their approach to this issue. Canada's competition policy does not treat industry concentration *per se* as undesirable, but rather it aims to prevent the abuse of the power enjoyed by firms with high market share. In contrast, in the United States, legislation has typically been built around the presumption that concentration will always lead to abuse of power, and, therefore, is aimed at preventing concentration.

The makers of Canadian competition policy have traditionally justified their willingness to live with relatively high degrees of concentration in two ways. First, it is argued that because the Canadian economy is quite small, the country cannot support more than one or two competitors in many scale intensive industries, without a great loss of efficiency. Thus, concentration in Canadian industries, which occurs without abuse of market power, might actually be a net benefit to the economy. Second, because the Canadian economy is relatively open, and is highly integrated with that of the U.S., many analysts are not concerned about concentration in Canadian industries, since most are open to competition from abroad. In fact, a high degree of competition from the United States has actually prompted some analysts to advocate that concentration be encouraged in certain Canadian industries. For example, there are those who believe that Canadian travellers would be better off in the long run, if we had only one major international airline centred here.

The principles of competition policy in Canada have been articulated in a constantly evolving series of laws since 1889. In that year, Canada became the first Western industrialized nation to enact legislation aimed at preventing firms from entering into agreements to limit competition. Compared to the legislation soon enacted by other nations, however, Canada's policy was weak and ineffectual, and its enforcement was lax. Over the next century, Canadian competition law evolved, but never gained any real teeth. In fact, it became murkier, as it became abundantly clear that Canadians were ambivalent toward competition. For example, the *Dominion Trade and Industry Commission Act* of 1935, set up a commission to enforce Canada's competition laws, while at the same time allowing businesses to collude when "wasteful" or "demoralizing" competition was occurring.

Canada's most recent pieces of competition legislation, the *Competition Act* and *Competition Tribunal Act*, both of 1986, are perhaps the clearest statements of competition policy in our history, and they are a very lenient statements. For the first time, the *Competition Act* formally recognizes that efficiency gains can be used to justify a merger that otherwise would be prohibited, because it would lead to a high level of concentration in an industry. Another pro-merger provision of the act allow for firms to apply to the Director of the Competition Tribunal for pre-approval of a proposed merger. Pre-approval can significantly reduce the risks and uncertainty involved in entering into a merger, and, thus, make it more attractive to the firms involved. Clearly, 105 years after our first anti-combines legislation was passed, Canada is still without a strong competition policy.

The lack of such a policy can be seen in recent merger activity in Canada. Rogers Communication's acquisition of MacLean-Hunter gave Rogers a dominant position in the cable television industry in several Canadian cities, including Toronto. This position was strengthened by the subsequent swap of licences with Selkirk Communications. Similarly, in recent years, the merger of Carling O'Keefe with Molson, greatly lessened the level of competition in the Canadian brewing industry, and A&P's acquisition of Miracle Mart and Dominion Stores reduced competition in the supermarket industry. Clearly, the legislative changes brought forth in 1986 have not led to significantly tougher competition policy in Canada.

As a final note concerning competition policy, it is worth mentioning one of the key findings of Michael Porter's ten-nation study, *The Competitive Advantage of Nations*.[22] Porter found clearly and consistently that national industries which were successful internationally were characterized by intense domestic competition, and that concentrated industries were highly susceptible to entry by foreign competitors. Porter hypothesized that intense local competition forces firms to be innovative and provide high quality products, while firms without strong local competitors have often been able to survive for long periods without offering good value to their customers. It is interesting to think about Porter's findings as one observes the fear struck in the hearts of many Canadian retailers by the arrival of such U.S. competitors as Wal-Mart and Home Depot.

CROWN CORPORATIONS

While the preceding discussion provides an understanding of the biggest segment of Canada's corporate sector, there is one more element which must be understood if one is to have a full picture the sector. In 1992, 11.8 per cent of the corporate assets in Canada were controlled by government business enterprises — otherwise known as Crown corporations. As Figure 6 shows, these are spread across almost all industries. Not surprisingly, the greatest share of an industry held by Crown corporations is in energy, where the two largest Crown corporations in Canada — Ontario Hydro and Hydro-Quebec — are found. Other industries with high government participation are transportation services (Canadian National Railway, Via Rail, etc.) and consumer and business financing (Caisse de Dépôt et Placement, Canada Mortgage and Housing Corporation, Export Development Corporation, etc.). By 1991, there were about 550 Crown corporations in Canada, with the federal government controlling a little more than a third of them, the Quebec government about a quarter and the rest of the provinces the remainder.

Crown corporations have been used by Canadian governments for a variety of purposes. They have been used to provide services which a private corporation could not profitably provide but which the government feels are needed (e.g., the CBC, Canada Post); to provide services in industries which are natural monopolies (e.g., hydro utilities); to provide services which the government felt in some way reluctant to entrust to the private sector (e.g., the Royal Canadian Mint, Atomic Energy of Canada); and to bail out politically important private enterprises which have run into trouble (e.g., Canadair, Ontario Bus). There is, of course, much debate over whether Canadian governments should be operating businesses in as many sectors of our economy as they do, but examining this issue in detail, is beyond the scope of this article. What we can conclude here, however, is that the role of Crown corporations in Canada's economy demonstrates once again our ambivalence toward the process of free and open competition.

We should also note that Crown corporations have been a factor in the high degree of concentration in Canadian industries. The existence of a large competitor, funded from the nearly bottomless pockets of government, at the very least, acts as a deterrent to potential new entrants in a particular industry. In fact, in some cases, Crown corporations have actually been formed by amalgamating two or more competitors under the auspices of the Crown. For example, Via Rail combined the passenger services of CN and CP Rail to create a single national passenger rail system. Here again, we see government policies acting at cross purposes in shaping Canada's corporate sector. The government enacts anti-combines laws while, in effect, creating combines itself.

Lately, there has been some effort to lower the number of Crown corporations. The federal government has privatized some Crown corporations, including Air Canada and Petro Canada, as have the provinces. Even Ontario's NDP government privatized the Ontario Stadium Corporation (SkyDome). It is argued that privatization benefits the economy because it brings the discipline of the capital markets to the firms involved. In some cases the government makes money by privatization. Of course, because market discipline often means job reductions, employees frequently resist privatizations. Furthermore, just as it is difficult for politicians to resist creating Crown corporations, it is often not easy for them to sell one.

The Caisse de Dépôt et Placement Du Quebec

The Caisse de Dépôt et Placement Du Quebec (the Caisse) is one Crown corporation which is worth special mention. It is unique institution founded in 1965 and now managing over $48-billion in assets. The Caisse manages the funds of the Quebec pension plan and several other Quebec institutions. In this role, its official mandate is to protect the interests of those investing money in the plan. It is prohibited by law from owning more than 30 per cent of the shares in any one company and was envisioned to be a more or less passive investor, as pension funds typically are. Checks were put it place to try to ensure that the Caisse did not become a policy instrument of the Quebec government.

It seems now, however, that the Caisse has moved beyond its mandate to some extent. Since the early 1980s it has provided funds to Hydro-Quebec at less than market rates. It also appears that the Caisse, while keeping below its 30 per cent ownership ceiling, has been able to gain effective control of some of its investments and is using that control to ensure that the firms in question are acting in accordance with the policies of the provincial government. Guy Savard, the President and CEO of the Caisse, recently stated that "while the legislation did not specify it as such in the act, the Caisse was entrusted with a clearly defined mission... [to] achieve an optimal financial return while contributing to the dynamism of the Quebec economy..."[22] If, as it appears, the Caisse has taken an active role in shaping the policies of at least some of the firms it has invested in, it is one further example of a Canadian government not trusting the markets to allocate resources optimally.

CONCLUSION

The structure of Canada's corporate sector, and how that structure developed over time, provide fascinating insight into the evolution of Canada's national economic and political philosophies. We seem torn between a concept of economic collectivism, in which national champions are expected to represent Canada to the world in various industries, while refraining from abusing their economic clout at home, and the strong belief in the power of free markets which spills over our southern border. Those who have been able to play the two concepts of the corporation's role in Canada's economy off against one another effectively have grown very rich doing so. People like Irving, Pattison and Black have been able to use free market mechanisms to build exceedingly strong pockets of economic power around themselves. What we must consider, however, is whether our attempts to reconcile these contradictory views of the corporation's role in our society has created a corporate sector which has served us well in the past, and will be able to serve us well in the future. And then, of course, if we decide that change is needed, we must decide how to implement it.

Notes

1. Because they are based on data from different sources, the numbers in figures 1 and 2 are not completely comparable. However, together, they do show clear trends in the changing makeup of the Canadian economy.
2. The following paragraphs are based largely on The Economic Council of Canada, *Employment in the Service Economy* (Ottawa, The Minister of Supply and Services, 1991), where a more detailed discussion of the causes and consequences of Canada's shift to a service-based economy can be found.
3. In fact, the difference in productivity growth will also result in relative price shifts that will result, in turn, in shifts in relative consumption between

goods and services. This effect will lessen the expected change in relative employment resulting from differences in productivity growth.

4. Canadian Business Corporation Act, RSC, 1985, c.c. 42, sec. 102.
5. James Gillies, *Boardroom Renaissance: Power, Performance and Morality in the Modern Corporation* (Toronto: McGraw-Hill Ryerson, 1992).
6. Ibid.
7. Michael Jensen, "The Eclipse of the Public Corporation," *Harvard Business Review*, vol. 67, no. 5 (September–October 1989).
8. Kenneth McNaught, *The Penguin History of Canada* (Markham: Penguin Books, 1988), p. 168.
9. Ibid., p. 166.
10. A.E. Safarian, *Foreign Ownership of Canadian Industry* (Toronto: The University of Toronto Press, 1973).
11. Michael Bliss, "The Yolk of The Trusts: A Comparison of Canada's Competitive Environment in 1889 and 1989," in R.S. Khemani and W.T. Stanbury, eds., *Historical Perspectives on Canadian Competition Policy* (Halifax: The Institute for Research on Public Policy, 1991).
12. Michael Porter and the Monitor Company, *Canada at the Crossroads* (Ottawa: The Business Council on National Issues and the Minister of Supply and Services, 1991).
13. In the case of the auto industry, the Auto Pact affects U.S.-based firms' sourcing decisions for component parts and finished product, but does not alter the fact that all of the cars assembled in Canada are designed elsewhere.
14. John N.H. Britton, *The Weakest Link: A Technological Perspective on Canadian Industrial Underdevelopment* (Ottawa: The Science Council of Canada, 1978).
15. Michael Porter and the Monitor Company, *Canada at the Crossroads* (Ottawa: The Business Council on National Issues and the Minister of Supply and Services, 1991).
16. John Saunders, "Head Office Flexes Its Might," *The Globe And Mail*, January 18, 1994, p. 1.
17. Gustavus Myers, *A History of Canadian Wealth* (Chicago: Charles H. Kerr and Company, 1914), p. i.
18. Diane Francis, *Controlling Interest: Who Owns Canada* (Toronto: Scorpio Publishing Limited, 1986) pp. 4–5. Francis provides thumbnail histories of many of Canadian business dynasties. These provided much of the detail presented throughout this section of the article.
19. The term "paper entrepreneur" is used by Francis.
20. "The BusinessWeek 1000", *BusinessWeek*, March 28, 1994, p. 63.
21. Michael Porter, *The Competitive Advantage of Nations* (New York: The Free Press, 1990).
22. Guy Savard, "The Caisse: A Balancing Act," *Business Quarterly*, Autumn 1993, p. 30.

QUESTIONS FOR DISCUSSION

1. Suggest how various federal and provincial policies (e.g., tax, industrial, regional, competition, agricultural policy, etc.) might be adjusted given

the major sectoral changes that have taken place in the Canadian economy since World War II.

2. Should boards of directors be accountable to all of a firm's stakeholders, not just its shareholders?
3. What actions, if any, should be taken to lessen the level of foreign ownership of Canadian corporations? What are some of the non-economic implications of this high level of foreign ownership?
4. Will the increasing openness of the Canadian economy increase or decrease the concentration of corporate wealth and power in Canada? Will the effect be beneficial or detrimental to Canadian consumers?
5. What policy changes are needed to create a more dynamic corporate sector in Canada? Given the nature of Canadian politics, is it possible for any government to implement such changes? If so, how?

Tom Wesson is Assistant Professor of Strategic Management at the Faculty of Administrative Studies of York University. Professor Wesson received his Bachelor of Commerce from Queen's University and his Master of Business Administration and Ph.D. in Business Economics from Harvard University. His research focuses on issues of international business strategy and government policies toward business.

The Public Sector in Canada: Structures and Processes

DAVID SIEGEL

This chapter will provide an overview of the structures and processes of the public sector in Canada with a view to assessing their strengths and weaknesses in coping with the global competitiveness and quality of life issues Canada faces in the modern world. Thus, this chapter will describe the workings of the public sector in Canada, with a view to analyzing how well these current arrangements can meet the challenges of the future.

The first section describes the constitutional basis of government in Canada. It begins with a description of the highly visible aspects of the governing system such as the House of Commons and the cabinet. It goes on to discuss the internal workings of government bureaucracy which are much less visible to the casual observer, but are very important to anyone wanting to deal with government on a regular basis. The second half of the article focuses on the financial basis of governments in Canada. It discusses how governments raise money, how they spend it and their current debt situation.

CONSTITUTIONAL BASIS OF CANADIAN GOVERNMENT

The constitutional, legal basis of government in Canada is the Constitution Act of 1982, supplemented by a number of unwritten, but very important, conventions. The Constitution Act is the successor to the British North America Act (BNA Act) which was passed in Britain in 1867 to give Canada its independence.

The structure of government in Canada is very complex. There are three levels of government — federal, provincial and local. The federal and provincial governments are further subdivided into three branches — legislative, executive and judicial.

The legislative branch consists of the Queen (and her representatives in Canada — the Governor General and the Lieutenant Governors), the

Senate and the House of Commons in the federal government. The provincial equivalents to the House of Commons have a variety of names such as the House of National Assembly and Provincial Legislature.

These bodies are the supreme law-making organizations within Canada. There is constant discussion about the appropriate division of powers between the federal and provincial governments, but combined, they are sovereign in all matters.

The executive is composed of the Queen (and her vice-regal representatives in Canada), the Cabinet (i.e., the governments of the day) and the public service. The executive branch actually carries out the activities of government on a day-to-day basis. It has considerable discretion in doing so, but it must always find authority for its actions in some delegation of power by the legislature. To ensure that the cabinet remains accountable to the legislature, the cabinet is responsible in the legislature for all its actions.[1]

The judicial branch of government is responsible for interpreting legislation passed by the legislature, for enforcing that legislation and for settling disputes among citizens.

The role and operation of the executive and legislative branches will be discussed in the following sections of this chapter. The role of the judiciary is very specialized, and will not be discussed here.

THE LEGISLATIVE BRANCH

For the sake of simplicity, this chapter will discuss the legislative branch of the federal government only. Much of what will be said will apply equally to provincial governments with a change of terminology.

The House of Commons

The House of Commons is composed of 295 members elected from ridings or constituencies. Each riding has roughly the same number of residents, with two exceptions. First, some of the smaller provinces are over-represented because of constitutional guarantees provided to them when they entered confederation. Second, some northern ridings contain fewer residents than average because of their vast size.

The House of Commons is the democratically elected legislature. It is an important principle of representative democracy that this democratically elected body should control the activities of the executive and the public service. Whether that control is truly effective or not, will be analyzed later. This section will discuss some of the mechanisms which are available to the legislature to control the executive.

The foremost control mechanisms are the passage of enabling legislation and the approval of the budget. These are really two separate, but related, control mechanisms. The executive must be able to find authority for everything it does in legislation passed by the House of Commons.

The executive cannot spend any funds without parliamentary approval. Conceptually, these two avenues of control should provide strong legislative control over the executive.

In practice, a majority government will almost always have enough votes to prevent the legislature from restricting its actions too much. In reality, the power of the legislature is confined to the ability to delay legislation and to raise an alarm about allegedly bad legislation so that the public can become concerned about it. This power to incite public opinion can be very significant when used forcefully. Even majority governments are sensitive to the fact that they must return to the electorate someday. There have been a number of cases where governments have been dissuaded from doing certain things by the amount of pressure brought by the opposition. The opposition parties have a number of avenues to generate these pressures.

The **question period** is the aspect of the House of Commons which attracts the greatest media attention. For about an hour at the beginning of each day's sitting, members are allowed to ask questions of cabinet ministers. While the rule is that opposition ripostes must be phrased in the form of a question, usually the "questions" are either rhetorical or have long preambles detailing the inadequacies of the current government.

The question period is one of the most important tools at the disposal of the opposition parties because it attracts so much media attention. It provides the short and sometimes witty or caustic thirty-second exchanges which are frequently used by the electronic media. This is an excellent opportunity to hold the government accountable by highlighting its inappropriate policies or its inadequate response to problems.

The unfortunate aspect of question period is that it emphasizes rhetorical flourish at the expense of in-depth analysis. In some cases, the government does not have an appropriate opportunity to explain complex situations. In other cases, the government can easily dismiss a serious opposition concern. The focus is frequently on who can use the media better, rather than who has the better case.

The legislature also has a number of **watchdog agencies** which can provide more in-depth analysis of how the government is managing its mandate. These agencies usually report directly to the legislature rather than through a minister.

The **Auditor General** is a watchdog over the financial activities of the government. The Auditor General of Canada (or the provincial auditor) has two levels of responsibility.

At the basic level, the auditor has the same responsibility as a private sector auditor to perform an attest audit, i.e., review and comment on the accuracy of the government's financial statements.

Most jurisdictions, however, require the auditor to go beyond the straightforward attest function, and comment on whether the government has received "value for money" in its activities. This "value for money" or comprehensive auditing, goes substantially beyond the narrow financial audit to determine how well the organization is using all of its resources (not just financial resources) and to determine whether it is operating with due regard for economy and efficiency.

The auditor produces an annual report which is sent directly to the legislature. In the last few years most auditors in Canada have given their governments fairly high marks, but the reports usually contain some horror stories which delight the opposition and the media. Responsible citizens should read the auditor's report and capture its full flavour before jumping to conclusions about the quality of management in government. Opposition parties and the media frequently use the report selectively.

Another watchdog agency at the federal level is the **Public Service Commission of Canada**. It is a watchdog over the process by which people are appointed to, and promoted within, the public service. Its main role is to ensure that the merit principle is respected in all appointments and to report on what progress is being made in improving the position within the public service of such target groups as women and visible minorities.

The Public Service Commission establishes the rules which govern the appointment and promotion process, and it acts as an appeal body which has the right to intervene in specific cases where the rules are violated. It also prepares an annual report to the House of Commons about its activities which discusses the extent to which the merit system is being respected.

Most provinces have a body with a similar title and somewhat similar functions, usually called a civil service commission. However, some of the provincial agencies do not have the same degree of control over the merit system as their federal counterparts.

Many jurisdictions also have **ombudsmen**. The role of these officers is to listen to any grievance by a resident who feels that the government has acted unfairly. Usually the resident can approach the ombudsmen only after he has exhausted all legal remedies. Therefore most cases handled by ombudsmen are situations where the government has complied with the letter of the law but has acted in a manner which the complainant feels is unfair. Ombudsmen usually try to handle complaints on an informal basis and find some mutually satisfactory compromise solution. They generally have no right to impose a settlement on the government.

However, the ombudsmen's clout comes from the fact that she prepares an annual report commenting on the activities of government. Like the Auditor General's report, this frequently contains much ammunition for the opposition and the media.

The federal government does not have an ombudsman, but it does have a number of specialized watchdogs who could be called mini-ombudsmen. Some of these agencies are:

- Correctional Investigator,
- Commissioner of Official Languages,
- Canadian Human Rights Commissioner,
- Freedom of Information and Privacy Commissioner.

Operation of the House of Commons

The House of Commons is effectively the supreme law-making body of the federal government.[2] However, it is quite clear that in majority government situations, the government party dominates the legislature. Some people wax romantic about the golden days of old when the legislature actually reigned supreme. There is some doubt about whether this golden age ever existed.

The beginning of each session is marked by the Speech from the Throne. While the speech is delivered by the Governor General, it is written by the prime minister and is a statement of the government's plans for the upcoming session of the legislature. It includes a statement of the government's general philosophy and provides an overview of all the legislation that the government will introduce in that session of the legislature.

The Budget Speech is probably the second most important speech delivered in the House. It is prepared and delivered by the Minister of Finance. The budget speech provides the minister's assessment of the future direction of the economy and the government's planned response to that direction. It also outlines the revenue and expenditure budgets for the next fiscal year. It must include reference to any changes in tax legislation which will be introduced in the next year.

In recent years, the budget speech has also been the occasion to present a number of background documents about the state of the economy, discussion papers about alternative tax and expenditure plans and similar documents. The speech itself and these accompanying documents provide a wealth of material for researchers.

There is a long tradition of secrecy surrounding the preparation of the budget speech. This has been deemed necessary because there are items in the speech which could be used unfairly if known in advance. There is a convention that the minister of finance should resign if the contents of the budget speech become known prematurely. This convention has not been followed in recent years when budget documents have been stolen and leaked to the press, or when a long-range camera managed to photograph a page of the budget on the minister's desk.

A general feeling is emerging that the traditional concept of budget secrecy is too extreme. At one point, this convention meant that the minister worked in splendid isolation with her or his staff to produce a document which was a total surprise to everyone else, including members of cabinet. Lately, the thinking has developed that this makes the minister too much of a captive of his or her own department, and isolates the minister from concerns of the business and other interested communities. To remedy this

FIGURE 1
How A Bill Becomes A Law

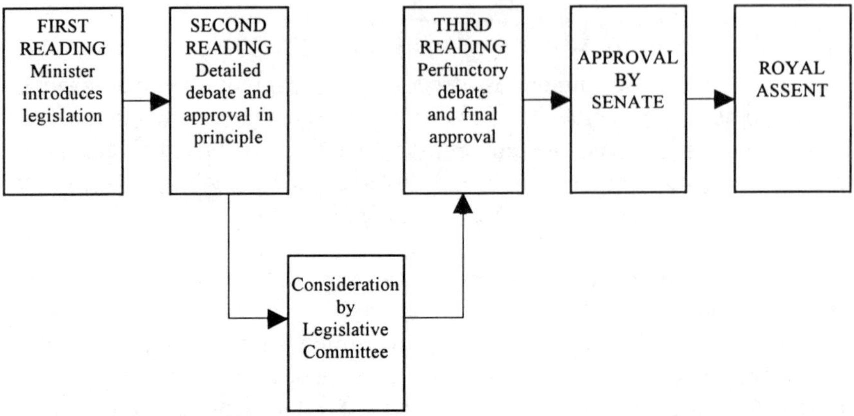

situation, the minister of finance and many provincial treasurers, hold pre-budget consultation sessions with interested groups. It is clear that the conventions of absolute secrecy are changing, but the changes are occurring in a very slow and tentative manner.

There is an emerging tradition that the federal budget speech will be given in February or March, just before the beginning of the government's fiscal year on April 1. Provincial budget speeches follow a month or so later. Provincial treasurers must know what is in the federal speech before they can prepare their budgets.

The Speech from the Throne and the budget speech set the tone for the legislative session, but the real work of the legislature is debating and passing legislation. Figure 1 depicts the normal process by which a bill becomes a law.

Technically, any member of the legislature can introduce a bill and seek its passage, and opposition members and government backbenchers do sometimes introduce bills. However, most legislation is introduced by a cabinet minister. The legislation must pass three readings before it is considered to be passed by the House of Commons.

The **first reading** simply grants the minister leave to introduce the bill and debate it further. The major debate takes place between first and second reading.

Second reading is approval in principle. If the opposition wants to defeat the bill, it will ordinarily try to do so at this point. The debate during second reading can be very extensive. In the federal House of Commons every member has the right to speak for forty minutes, but some provincial legislatures have no such time limit. If all opposition members chose to exercise this right, it would take a long time for legislation to pass. The opposition's most effective way of thwarting a bill is threatening to use this tactic. The opposition seldom defeats a bill, but it can use the threat of extended debate to encourage the government to change proposed legislation or even defer its adoption. An extended debate on one piece of legislation can ruin a government's timetable, so the government will frequently decide not to proceed past first reading with a particular piece of legislation if it knows that it will attract this debate.

The vote at second reading is key. This is approval in principle. Amendments are sometimes introduced before second reading to make the legislation more attractive, but once it clears this hurdle it almost certainly will be passed.

After second reading most bills are **referred to a legislative committee**. Figure 2 contains a list of all House of Commons committees which were active in 1994. These committees are composed of members from all parties, roughly proportional to their representation in the full House. The role of the committees is to apply their specialized knowledge to the proposed legislation to determine whether its passage would be desirable. In the case of high profile legislation committees can hold public hearings across the country to assess public opinion on the issue. The committee can then return the bill to the full House with **recommendations** for amendments. These are recommendations which the full House might or might not accept.

These committees **could** play an important role in the legislative process. Many would-be reformers have focused on re-structuring the role of these committees as one way of improving the operation of the House. However, there are a number of impediments to improving the operation of the committees.

The basic problem is that the bills referred to these committees have already been approved in principle. The committee can recommend minor changes, but if it were to recommend major changes, the revised bill would have to go back through the legislative process again. Therefore, the government members of the committee will usually want to defeat any major amendments — and in a majority government situation they will virtually always be successful.

Many reformers argue that the committees would be more effective if they operated in a collegial, rather than a partisan, manner. However, as long as the composition of the committees mirrors the composition of the House, and legislation is only referred to committees after second reading, this is unlikely to happen.

After the committee stage, the legislation goes back to the House for **third reading**. Since it has already been approved in principle, there is seldom any serious debate at this stage. Any amendments recommended at the committee stage will be discussed and possibly included, and the legislation will then be passed.

FIGURE 2
House of Commons Committees

- Aboriginal Affairs and Northern Development
- Agriculture and Agri-Food
- Canadian Heritage
- Citizenship and Immigration
- Environment and Sustainable Development
- Finance
- Fisheries and Oceans
- Foreign Affairs and International Trade
- Government Operations
- Health
- Human Resources Development
- Human Rights and the Status of Disabled Persons
- Industry
- Justice and Legal Affairs
- Liaison
- National Defence and Veterans Affairs
- Natural Resources
- Official Languages
- Procedure and House Affairs
- Public Accounts
- Transport
- Several Sub-committees of these Committees
- Several Joint Committees with the Senate
- Several Ad Hoc Committees

After approval in the House of Commons, the bill then needs **approval in the Senate** and **royal assent** before it becomes law. Usually both of these stages are formalities. However, the Senate occasionally has delayed government legislation in an attempt to draw attention to alleged problems.

Royal assent is also a formality, but the government controls when it will ask the Governor General to provide this. Since the legislation is not binding until it receives royal assent, the government can decide to delay making legislation effective by simply delaying a request for royal assent.

The Senate

There has always been a certain amount of controversy surrounding the Senate. Originally, it was modelled on the British House of Lords. Both were to be populated by wealthy aristocrats to ensure that an excess of democracy did not endanger the privileged position of the propertied class. As this view fell from favour in the twentieth century, there has been continual questioning about the appropriate role of the Senate.

Members of the Senate are appointed by the prime minister. It has always been clear that most Senate appointments are matters of patronage, i.e., rewards to former politicians or party stalwarts.

Legally, all legislation must be passed by the Senate as well as the House of Commons before it can become law. However, because Senators are appointed, it does not have any legitimacy as a democratic body. Therefore, the Senate will ordinarily pass all legislation submitted to it by the House of Commons.

For many years even the Senate's defenders had great difficulty coming up with strong arguments in its defence. The phrase frequently used was that it was a chamber of "sober second thought." Cynics would then question whether there was much evidence of either sobriety or thought in the Senate.

There is almost no support for continuation of the Senate in its existing form. However, recent constitutional discussions have suggested that a revised Senate could play an important role in representing regional interests. Frankly, the only reason the Senate is maintained is because it could be restructured in the future.

THE EXECUTIVE BRANCH

The Executive branch is made up of the Queen and her vice-regal representatives as head of state, the Prime Minister as head of the government of the day, the cabinet and the public service. Since the Queen's role is largely ceremonial, this section will focus on the cabinet and the organization of the public service.

After an election, the leader of the party which won the greatest number of seats, is asked by the Governor General to form the government. If this party has won more than half the seats, it will form a majority government and will likely have little difficulty maintaining its power.

Minority government situations are more problematic because they require that some arrangement be made among the parties so that one party can form a government and govern with some security for at least a limited period. Canada does not have a history of coalition governments. The usual modus vivendi for minority governments is to tailor legislation to attract the support of other parties and to refrain from introducing legislation which cannot be tailored in this way.

Historically, unstable governments have not been a problem in Canada. With two major parties, we have generally had majority governments or fairly stable minorities. We now seem to be entering a period in which a large number of regionally-based parties will elect members to the House of Commons. This could produce minority governments which would introduce more instability into the system. Some have called this the

"Italianization of Canadian politics," i.e., a situation in which a large number of small parties will require shifting coalitions and could lead to unstable, short-term governments.

The Cabinet

Legally, the prime minister has complete control over the selection of cabinet members, but there are a number of conventions which the prime minister can ignore only at her political peril. Members of cabinet will always be from the prime minister's party and will usually be elected members of the House of Commons. Members of the Senate are sometimes included, and it is possible, although rare, for other unelected persons to be selected.

In Canada, there is a long tradition of having a representative cabinet. This means that cabinet members must be chosen so that a number of different interests are represented. In the early years, this involved a fairly simple balancing of francophones and anglophones and Protestants and Catholics. In more recent years the mix has become more complicated. In addition to a number of other complex balancing arrangements, gender now plays a role, and each province must be represented.

This need for a representative cabinet has two effects. First, the cabinet is larger than it really would need to be otherwise. The size of cabinets grew over the years, until the later Mulroney cabinets had more than forty members. As the size of cabinet became a political issue, Chrétien has reduced his cabinet to twenty-three members. Second, in appointing members to cabinet, the prime minster must consider factors other than just the ability of the person to manage a department. Prime ministers find themselves in the position of having to appoint some cabinet minister because they serve a representative function even though their abilities to manage a cabinet department might be limited. Conversely, some very good people are excluded from cabinet because they are not needed to fill the representative function. In spite of obvious differences in personal capacities and organizational responsibilities, there is a convention that all cabinet ministers are equal. If there were a system of senior and junior ministers, it would be very difficult to develop a representative cabinet.

There are a number of important conventions about the operation of cabinet. Individual ministerial responsibility will be discussed in detail later in conjunction with the operation of operating departments.

Collective ministerial responsibility or **cabinet solidarity** is the concept that cabinet as a collective body will be united publicly in its support of all actions of the government.

This convention, in turn, requires the convention of **cabinet secrecy**. This means that all cabinet deliberations are held in secret and all advice tendered by the public service to cabinet is provided in confidence. Secrecy is an important part of collective ministerial responsibility because secrecy

FIGURE 3
The Cabinet Committee System

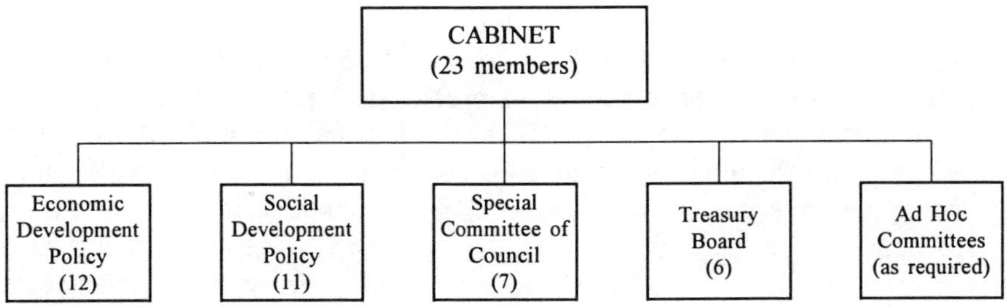

allows cabinet ministers and public servants to discuss issues freely behind closed doors and maintain cabinet solidarity in public.

Until the 1960s most decisions were made by cabinet as a body sitting down and discussing issues. As cabinets have become larger and the process of governing more complex, the cabinet committee system has become more institutionalized and complex. This gradually evolved until in the Mulroney government, most decisions were made in cabinet committees, and cabinet as a body seldom met.

When Prime Minister Chrétien came to power, he both reduced the size of the cabinet and simplified the structure of the cabinet committee system. It is likely that the combination of these two factors will reestablish cabinet as a focus of decision-making.

Figure 3 depicts the cabinet committee system as established by Chrétien after the 1994 election. Some committees focus on particular aspects of public policy. The role of the Special Committee of Council and the Treasury Board will be discussed in more detail later.

The other part of the Executive Branch of government is the public service. The remainder of this section will examine its internal organization. First, some important general issues will be addressed. These are the importance of a professional public service and the differences between the styles and techniques of management in the public and private sectors. The remainder of this section then presents a discussion of the various types of government organizations, e.g., operating departments, regulatory agencies, Crown corporations.

The Importance of a Professional Public Service

Canada prides itself on having a professional, merit-based public service. This means that public servants are appointed on the basis of merit, rather than party affiliation, and that they remain in place after a change in government and can serve governments of any political stripe.

This is in contrast to the situation in countries such as the United States where the senior three or four levels of hierarchy in the administrative apparatus leave whenever there is a change in government and are replaced by adherents of the new party in power.

There are several advantages to a professional or career public service. First, public servants are likely to be more knowledgeable about the operation of their organization. In a professional public service, people tend to start at the bottom levels and work their way up gradually. By the time they reach the top, they will have a considerable amount of experience in managing government organizations. This means that they can be much more helpful to a new government than a group of people holding the appropriate political views but without previous government experience.

Second, it is more likely to be able to attract good, career-oriented employees throughout the organization. Every new employee has the opportunity to rise to the top levels of the organization someday. It would be much more difficult to work in an organization where it was clear from day one that the top echelons of the organization were closed to career employees.

Third, career public servants will find it easier to serve the public interest. If a public servant fears that her or his job will only last until the next election, there could be a temptation to curry the favour of particular persons or groups who could provide future employment. A person in this situation might find it difficult to give proper consideration to the public interest.

The development of a career public service requires public servants to remain politically neutral. The short definition of political neutrality is that public servants do not become involved in the partisan political process and, in return, their career opportunities are determined by merit, not by political considerations. More specifically, political neutrality involves six elements.[3]

1. ***"[P]olicy and politics are separated from administration: thus politicians make policy decisions; public servants execute those decisions"***

This flows from the concept of the politics-administration dichotomy. A traditional principle of public administration is that there is a clear distinction between policy, which is the domain of politicians, and administration, which is the domain of administrators.

This rigid separation is now seen as totally unrealistic. Administrators become involved in policy in at least two ways. In the first place, they provide politicians with advice about what policies to adopt. Ministers at the head of departments can come and go fairly quickly, but the permanent administrators within a department develop a very good knowledge of their policy field. Thus, a wise minister will listen carefully to the advice of her or his experts.

Second, public servants become involved in policy at the implementation stage. Legislatures and ministers determine what policy should be but they are seldom able to anticipate and provide instructions to deal with every situation. Thus, administrators almost always have a certain amount of discretion in implementing policy.

It is quite unrealistic to think there is a policy-administration dichotomy and that administrators can remove themselves totally from anything concerned with policy. However, wise administrators are sensitive to a dividing line between politically-sensitive administrative advice which they can give, and partisan political advice which they cannot. It is true that there is no hard and fast dividing line, but experienced administrators quickly develop a feel for the appropriate limitations.

2. ***"[P]ublic servants are appointed and promoted on the basis of merit rather than of party affiliation or contributions"***

This requires the establishment of a merit system to ensure that all positions are filled on the basis of the ability to perform the tasks required for the job.

Canada's record on this is mixed. In most jurisdictions, the overwhelming number of positions are filled on the basis of merit. However, every jurisdiction has a number of appointments to agencies, boards, and commissions which are made on the basis of the political judgement of the party in power. Usually that means that they are filled by party faithful. This is not ideal but it is not a serious problem as long as it is confined to a limited number of positions which are somewhat peripheral to power.

A more disturbing trend has developed in some provinces. In a few cases, new governments coming to power have resorted to wholesale firings of previous employees and their replacement by party faithful. This does not imply that the new people are incompetent, but it sets a bad precedent because once this pattern starts it is likely to be continued by future governments. Obviously, this is very harmful for the morale of the public service. It is the beginning of the end of a career public service.

3. ***"[P]ublic servants do not engage in partisan political activities"***

If public servants want to be treated as professionals and want to maintain some security of tenure when a new government comes to power, they cannot associate with any political party. They must establish confidence that they will serve any party in power faithfully and they cannot establish that confidence if they are seen as being closely aligned with one party.

This strict rule of no partisan activity by any public servant has been challenged recently because it limits public servants' political rights. Most governments have a two-tiered system. This allows people in relatively junior positions with fairly limited discretionary powers to exercise almost all the political rights available to any other citizen. However, the rights of senior public servants and employees working in sensitive areas such as personnel and purchasing, are somewhat more limited.

The basic principle is that anyone who decides to behave in a politically partisan manner should not expect to be trusted by the other party. The moral is that public servants can exercise political rights but they must recognize that at some point they will have to choose between exercising those rights and moving to the higher echelons of the public service.

4. ***"[P]ublic servants do not express publicly their personal views on government policies or administration"***

This is a corollary to the above principle. Permanent, professional public servants must make it clear that they are able to serve any political party loyally. This means that they cannot become too closely identified with the policies of any party.

In practice, this can pose great difficulties for public servants. They are now routinely expected to explain policies of the government of the day. The dividing line between explaining a policy and defending it can sometimes be a bit difficult to discern.

5. ***"[P]ublic servants provide forthright and objective advice to their political masters in private and in confidence; in return, political executives protect the anonymity of public servants by publicly accepting responsibility for departmental decisions"***

Public servants owe it to their minister to provide the best possible advice. Sometimes this means telling the minister something that he or she would rather not hear. In turn, ministers must respect the confidentiality of the public servant. If ministers do not preserve that confidentiality, public servants will start providing only the kind of safe opinions that they feel the minister **wants** to hear. This will benefit no one, least of all the minister.

6. ***"[P]ublic servants execute policy decisions loyally, irrespective of the philosophy and programs of the party in power and regardless of their personal opinions; as a result, public servants enjoy security of tenure during good behaviour and satisfactory performance."***

This is a summation of the points which have come before. It summarizes the tacit agreement which should exist between politicians and public servants. When public servants behave in a professional, non-partisan manner, their security of tenure should be respected.

Sometimes a new government, unsure of itself as it takes power, is too defensive. New ministers may see public servants as the handmaids of the previous government. Advice which does not rigidly toe the new "party line" is seen as disloyal.

It is important that public servants act in a professional, non-partisan manner, but it is also important that politicians understand that professional public servants can be loyal to the government of the day, even when its stripe is different from the previous one.

Management in Government is Different

There is a common expression in public administration usually attributed to Wallace S. Sayre. "[B]usiness and government administration are alike in all unimportant respects."[4] Superficially it seems that many management techniques from the private sector could be adopted by the public sector, and there are frequent calls to "make government more business-like." Is this realistic?

There are several reasons why organizational structures and operating procedures must be different in the public sector. This section will discuss several of those reasons.[5]

Political Imperatives are More Important than Economic Efficiency In a democracy we require politicians to get elected and re-elected. This frequently requires them to make decisions which have stronger political than economic justifications. This seldom results in the large-scale, crude vote-buying schemes of earlier eras, but there are a number of examples of these kinds of decisions. For example, military procurement contracts are frequently awarded with as much attention to their job creation potential as to their economic efficiency.

Concerns about Ministerial Responsibility and the Need for Fairness Require a Greater Emphasis on Procedural Controls In business, one hears a great deal about emphasis on the "bottom line." Managers are held accountable for delivering high profit levels or meeting established targets, and the process they follow to accomplish this does not matter very much.

In government, the minister is accountable not just for delivering on some bottom line; he or she can get into a great deal of trouble if appropriate **processes** are not followed. Sometimes concern about process actually reduces efficiency, but government managers know that they must protect their minister by following the proper process.

For example, it is very difficult for governments to start a new program quickly. Managers cannot use informal networks to hire good people they happen to know are on the job market. Public Service Commission rules about advertising vacant positions and interviewing qualified applicants must be followed. Similarly, managers cannot make a quick telephone survey and decide where to purchase a product. There are rules about tendering and preparing contracts.

It is important to understand that these rules are not someone's foolish whim; they are there for a purpose. All large organizations need rules to ensure that managers are not engaging in fraudulent activities. But the public expects governments to go beyond avoiding fraud. Governments must be seen to be acting in a manner which is fair to all citizens.

The manager referred to above who used the informal network to hire people might very well end up hiring the best people. But will she be able to **document** that she has hired the best people when someone complains that he was denied a chance to apply for a job? The emphasis on procedural accountability is awkward and cumbersome but it is necessary to avoid embarrassment.

This concern about procedural accountability significantly limits the extent to which governments can employ such modern management techniques as participatory management and empowerment. These techniques are used in some governments, but there must be clear understandings about their limits.

Public administration is also different in the organizational structures that are employed. The next sections of this paper discuss some of these.

Organizational Structures

The public service is organized in a number of different types of structures. Each of these will be examined in turn, moving from those closest to the central operation of government, outward.

Operating Departments Operating departments are the entities which carry out most governmental functions and are closest to cabinet control. Figure 4 sets out a list of departments.

The **Horizontal Policy Coordinative Departments** tend to be fairly small but generally wield a great deal of power because their responsibilities cut across the mandates of many other departments. Most of these departments are central agencies and their roles will be discussed in more detail later.

The **Horizontal Administrative Coordinative Departments** have very important administrative roles within government but are generally not involved in sensitive policy matters. The Department of National Revenue collects most taxes. The Department of Public Works and Government Services provides accommodation and related common services to government departments and acts as the government's central accounting and purchasing agency.

The **Vertical Constituency Departments** are the departments which are most visible in providing services. They tend to be fairly large departments which derive their power from the fact that they have constituencies which depend on them for services.

Figure 5 provides an example of the organizational structure of a typical operating department.

The **Minister** is a member of cabinet who is the political head of the department. The doctrine of **individual ministerial responsibility** holds that the minister is responsible for all activities of the department. The

FIGURE 4
Classification of Federal Government Departments

Horizontal Policy Co-ordinative
- Finance
- Foreign Affairs and International Trade
- Justice
- Privy Council
- Treasury Board

Vertical Constituency
- Agriculture and Agri-Food
- Canadian Heritage
- Citizenship and Immigration
- Environment
- Fisheries and Oceans
- Health
- Human Resource Development
- Indians Affairs and Northern Development
- Industry
- International Trade
- National Defence
- Natural Resources
- Solicitor General
- Transport
- Veterans Affairs
- Western Economic Diversification

Horizontal Administrative Co-ordinative
- National Revenue
- Public Works and Government Services

Source: Based on G. Bruce Doern, "Horizontal and Vertical Portfolios in Government," in G. Bruce Doern and V. Seymour Wilson, eds., *Issues in Canadian Public Policy* (Toronto: Macmillan, 1974), 315–6. Updated by the author to reflect changes.

extreme interpretation of this principle is that ministers must resign whenever serious problems develop in their department. In practice, this seldom happens, but ministers must answer questions about activities of their departments and explain what is being done to correct problems.

Some people incorrectly suggest that the concept of ministerial responsibility is dead because ministers no longer resign their portfolios whenever there is any sort of difficulty. The significance of ministerial responsibility is that ministers are responsible in the legislature for dealing with opposition questions and concerns; that is the essence of ministerial

FIGURE 5
Organization Chart of the Department of Transport

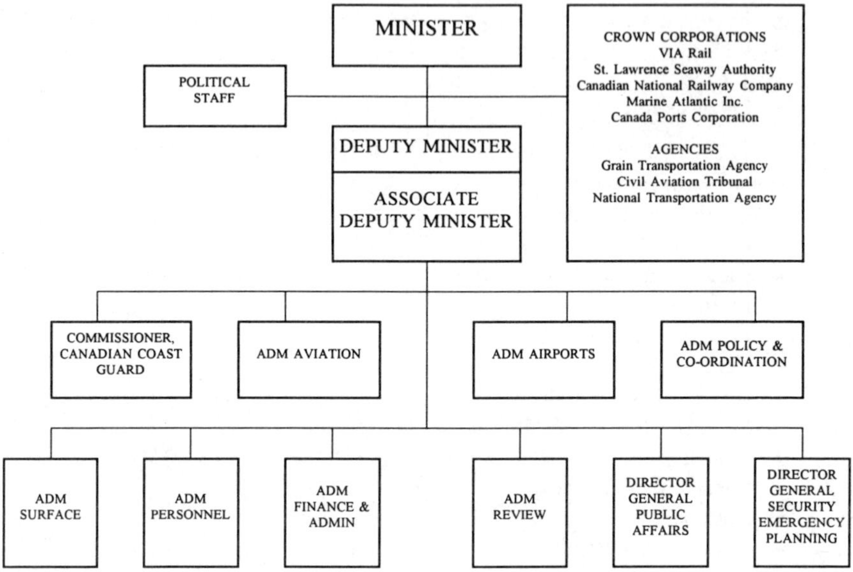

responsibility. It is very important that ministers accept this responsibility in the legislature because the minister forms the only link between the legislature and the operating department. Without that linkage there would be no way for the democratically-elected legislature to hold the public service accountable.

The convention of ministerial responsibility gives rise to the related concept of **public service anonymity**. The minister must accept responsibility for the actions of her or his department, and cannot openly name and attack public servants. This is important because the legislature has no way of holding public servants directly accountable. If the minister denied responsibility and instead shifted it to public servants, then the accountability linkage between the legislature and the public service would be destroyed.[6]

This does not mean that incompetent public servants cannot be disciplined, up to and including removal from office. It just means that the minister cannot publicly shift responsibility to a public servant who does not have any avenue to explain his or her actions or respond to criticisms.

The **Deputy Minister** is the administrative head of the department. While good deputy ministers are sensitive to political issues, they are not political in the partisan sense of that term. Most deputy ministers are career civil servants who have been promoted through the ranks. Legally, they serve "at pleasure" which means that they can be dismissed at any time without cause, but there is a long tradition of deputy ministers remaining in their position and loyally serving governments of different political stripes.

The role of the minister's **political staff** is to provide partisan policy advice to the minister and to enhance the minister's political fortunes. These positions are overtly political; they are not public service positions although incumbents can move into the public service in some circumstances.

The roles of the political staff and the Deputy Minister are meant to be complementary. The political staff provides partisan political advice to the minister and the Deputy Minister provides administrative advice. However, there are stories of tensions between the incumbents in some cases. On the one hand, deputies sometimes accuse political staffers of being gatekeepers who prevent the deputy from having appropriate access to the minister. On the other hand, political staff sometimes see the deputy's administrative caution as evidence that he or she is not fully committed to the minister's program. The relationship between these people is based very much on their personalities and their ability to work out a good relationship.

Beneath the level of deputy minister there are the positions of assistant deputy ministers (ADM), director-general (D-G) and sometimes director. The structure varies quite widely by department and can be very difficult for an outsider to understand.

In sum, operating departments are the large, high-profile government organizations which deliver most services. However, there are a number of other government organizations which are also important.

Central Agencies Central agencies are a type of organizational structure which has no counterpart in most private-sector organizations. One role of central agencies is to ensure that government policies are being implemented across all departments. A second role is to enforce the procedural accountability discussed earlier. "A central agency is an agency that has a substantial amount of continuing, legitimate authority to direct and intervene in the activities of departments."[7] There are usually considered to be four central agencies in the federal government.

The **Prime Minister's Office** (PMO) works directly for the prime minister. Unlike other organizations within the public service, the PMO has an overtly partisan role. The prime minister's principal secretary, as the head of the PMO is called, and the senior employees in the office, are usually not public servants, but are partisan supporters of the prime minister. Their job is to help the prime minister move his agenda forward and to ensure that the media and the general public see the prime minister in the best possible light. In performing these tasks, they interact frequently with deputy ministers and the political staff of ministers to ensure that policy initiatives are properly co-ordinated.

The PMO also advises the prime minister on the large number of appointments he makes to government agencies. In addition, a number of people in the PMO are responsible for such administrative activities as making travel arrangements and responding to correspondence.

The **Privy Council Office** (PCO) works for cabinet. The PCO is headed by the Clerk of the Privy Council, who is officially recognized as the senior public servant. Most people in the PCO are professional public servants, but these are some of the most politically sensitive public servants in government. The PCO provides non-partisan, but politically sensitive, policy advice to cabinet and its committees. It is sometimes suggested that the PCO functions as a gate-keeper for cabinet in that it ensures that all proposals coming before cabinet or its committees are properly prepared. This brings the PCO into contact with every department at some time or another.

The PCO is also responsible to ensure that federal-provincial relationships are operating as smoothly as possible. Since almost every department has federal-provincial programs, the Federal Provincial Relations Office (FPRO) has some involvement with virtually every department.

The **Treasury Board** (TB) is a committee of cabinet which consists of the President of Treasury Board, the Minister of Finance and four other cabinet ministers. It is responsible for preparation of the expenditure budget and for preserving the quality and uniformity of administrative management. Unlike other cabinet committees, it has a relatively large bureaucracy to support its activities.

The **Treasury Board Secretariat** (TBS) is the administrative arm of the Treasury Board. It has a broad range of responsibilities in the areas of administrative management and the expenditure budget.

It has several duties in the area of human resource policy. It is responsible for position classification, i.e., ensuring that all comparable positions in the government are classified in the same way and receive the same rates of pay. As part of the position classification process, the TBS ensures that positions are properly designated for official language purposes. The TBS also represents the employer in the collective bargaining process. This means that the TBS actually negotiates the collective agreement with employee unions and also handles the employer's side of the grievance process.

The TBS also has a number of responsibilities in the general area of administrative management. It sets the rules for financial management, purchasing and contracting. This ensures that uniform administrative standards are followed across all departments and that procedural accountability is maintained. It is also responsible for the overall quality of financial management in the federal government including the internal audit and program evaluation functions.

Finally, the TBS is responsible for preparing the expenditure budget. It receives budget guidelines from the cabinet and negotiates with departments to ensure that the expenditure budget comforms to these guidelines.

The **Department of Finance** advises the cabinet on economic matters. Usually, its advice is of a fairly general nature about the economic stance of the government in terms of overall levels of revenue and expenditure. It also has specific responsibilities for advising about all aspects of taxation policy and federal-provincial financial relations. These responsibilities give it a role in the provision of advice on any new spending initiatives proposed by departments. This obviously gives Finance a significant gatekeeping role in dealing with any new programs.

The general role of the central agencies is to foster procedural accountability and to ensure that government policies are being implemented uniformly across all departments. This frequently brings them into conflict with operating departments which feel that central agencies are hampering them in performing their responsibilities.

The goal in managing this troublesome relationship between departments and central agencies is achieving a proper balance. There is a need for central agencies to ensure uniformity and accountability, but sometimes this results in the agencies becoming too intrusive in day-to-day operations, which restricts the ability of the departments to deliver programs. This has been recognized as a problem and various initiatives[8] have been taken, but much remains to be done.

Operating departments and central agencies are two of the structures of government which are closest to the central organs of government. They are all directly controlled by cabinet ministers. There are a number of other government organizations which are somewhat removed from direct government control.

Public Enterprise Public enterprise is the broad phrase used to cover both Crown corporations and mixed enterprises. A Crown corporation is a corporation which is wholly owned by one government. A mixed enterprise is a corporation which is jointly owned by several governments or a government and private sector organizations.[9]

Public enterprises have a separate corporate status apart from the government which owns them. As will be discussed in more detail later, this means that they operate at arm's length from government, i.e., they are ultimately controlled by government but they have considerable autonomy in day-to-day operations.

Over the years, Crown corporations have become involved in a number of different activities. Historically, they have been used for nation-building activities in the areas of transportation and communication. The high-profile examples are the Canadian Broadcasting Corporation, Radio-Canada and CN Rail. In more recent years, public enterprises have moved into areas of financial activities and economic development, e.g., Export Development Corporation.

An interesting insight into the possible future use of Crown corporations is Quebec's Caisse de dépôt et placement. The Caisse is the depository of all funds collected by the Quebec Pension Plan, the Quebec public servants' pension plan and various other similar funds. The Caisse has invested this considerable sum of money in Quebec-based enterprises to encourage economic development within the province. Some would argue that the development of the confident group of Quebec entrepreneurs referred to as "Québec Inc." is the result of the funds generated by the Caisse.

There are a number of reasons why governments would choose to use the public enterprise form to deliver a service rather than the operating department. One of the classic arguments for the use of the corporate form is to allow the entity to operate in a business-like fashion at arm's length from the political imperatives of government. As discussed earlier, governments are frequently required to engage in certain activities to satisfy political rather than economic needs. A Crown corporation, separated from political control, can behave in a more business-like manner.

Another reason for the employment of the corporate form is to use the board of directors to provide for the representation of diverse interests in the management of the corporation. This is important in such cultural organizations as the Canadian Broadcasting Corporation.

Crown corporations can also be used as "windows" into the private sector. When the federal government established Petro-Canada, one of the rationales was that it would provide the federal government with some insight into how the oil industry operated, so that the government would be able to control this volatile and important industry more effectively.

In recent years, a number of problems have been identified with the corporate form of organization. Some enterprises have been a steady drain on the public purse. Crown corporations are sometimes established when governments are encouraged to pick up the pieces of failed private sector organizations in order to preserve jobs. There are usually great hopes that if government can just bridge the gap for a few years, then conditions will improve and the organization will again become viable. Sometimes it really unfolds in this manner, but too frequently government is simply left picking up the tab into the indefinite future. This is clearly an inappropriate use of the corporate form for a social welfare purpose.

Another difficult problem has been determining whether the corporation ought to be accountable or autonomous. One of the benefits of the corporate form mentioned earlier, was that its arm's length relationship from government allowed it freedom from political interference. Does this autonomy mean that the corporation should be able to simply ignore public policy concerns? Should the corporation be concerned only with businesslike efficiency, or should it be fulfilling some public purpose? It is usually pulled in both directions but it cannot do both. For example, the CBC is frequently criticized because it does not earn a profit, but it is also supposed to be a vehicle to encourage the development of Canadian culture, and so has higher Canadian content requirements than other networks.

As a variety of concerns has developed about the use of the corporate form, interest in privatization of Crown corporations has increased. The Mulroney government pursued a fairly deliberate policy of privatizing as many Crown corporations as seemed reasonable. It privatized such corporations as Air Canada, Teleglobe, deHavilland and Canadair, and sold some shares in Petro-Canada to the general public. It is doubtful that the Chrétien government will pursue privatization in quite the same manner, partly because it is not as ideologically committed to privatization, but also because there are simply fewer attractive candidates for privatization after the sales of the last few years. There are clearly cases where privatization is an excellent idea. However, it is not the panacea that some see it to be. First, privatization should not be pursued for purely ideological reasons. This could result in bad decisions leading to the sale of valuable businesses at fire sale prices. Second, care must be exercised in establishing the terms of sale. There is now a strong argument for selling off assets to reduce the debt. When profit-making corporations are sold, there must be a realization that the government is exchanging a future flow of income over a lengthy period for a one-time payment. Paradoxically, selling profit-making corporations could increase the annual deficit, not reduce it.

Most governments are looking at the idea of privatization but have adopted a cautious approach. There is now a recognition that privatization is not the cure-all it once seemed.

Regulatory Agencies Governments directly provide many services through operating departments and public enterprises, but another important and controversial aspect of government activity is regulation. Government is the only organization in society which has the legitimate right to engage in coercive behaviour. The regulatory function is one manifestation of this power. Regulations can be promulgated by many different kinds of government organizations, including operating departments. However, most regulation is done by regulatory agencies, so this section will discuss their operation.

A regulatory agency is "a statutory body charged with responsibility to administer, to fix, to establish, to control, or to regulate an economic, cultural, environmental, or social activity by regularized and established means in the public interest and in accordance with general policy guidelines specified by the government. This body is under the general direction of the legislature and a responsible minister with regard to policy matters, but possesses relative autonomy of action in making individual decisions within those policy guidelines."[10] Figure 6 provides some examples of regulatory agencies.

Regulation has been divided into two types.[11] **Economic or traditional forms of regulation** are industry-specific rules about pricing, marketing,

FIGURE 6

Some Examples of Regulatory Agencies

Federal Government

- Atomic Energy Control Board
- Canadian Radio-television and Telecommunications Commission
- Copyright Board Canada
- Elections Canada
- Hazardous Materials Information Review Commission Canada
- National Energy Board
- National Transportation Agency of Canada
- Patented Medicine Prices Review Board Canada
- Procurement Review Board of Canada

Typical Agencies Found in Provincial Governments

- Environmental assessment agencies
- Horse racing commissions
- Insurance commissions
- Marketing boards (usually in the area of farm products)
- Municipal boards
- Rent review

Typical Agencies Found in Local Governments

- Bingo and gaming licensing
- Building inspection
- Taxicab and tow-truck licensing

competition, etc. For example, there is a set of rules governing cable television which states how prices will be set, what stations can be carried, etc.

A newer type of regulation, frequently called **social regulation**, cuts across all industries, and deals with such general concerns as occupational health and safety and environmental protection.

Like public enterprise, regulatory agencies operate at arm's length from the political process.

They are created to separate the decision-making process on certain sensitive cases from political considerations. The conceptual arrangement is that the government establishes general policies in a particular area, and the regulatory agency applies them to specific cases. Thus, it is entirely appropriate for the government to specify that any applicant for a broadcast license must provide at least x per cent Canadian content, but it is inappropriate for the government to dictate to an agency that A should get a license instead of B. This spares the government the difficult task of making specific decisions where it could be accused of having political motivations.

Marketing boards are a specialized type of regulatory agency usually found at the provincial level. Their role is to regulate the production, and thus the price, of such commodities as chicken, eggs or milk. The philosophy behind them is that they will control the total production of a commodity by allocating production quotas to each producer in the market. This will stabilize the price by eliminating excessive competition and thus stabilize the supply by limiting the "boom and bust" nature of commodity production. When they work properly the idea is that they will provide a reasonable quantity of the product at a reasonable price.

The argument has sometimes been made that the boards tend to make consumer prices artificially high. There is probably some truth to this, but the trade-off for the consumer is to pay a bit extra for each dozen eggs to ensure that there will always be a reasonable quantity of eggs on the market at a reasonable price.

The difference in the way regulatory agencies and courts make decisions is significant. Courts are generally working with a fairly precise law and their aim is to establish the facts of the case and determine how those facts fit within the law. Regulatory agencies are working with fairly vague laws. Legislation requires regulatory agencies to consider "public convenience and necessity" or "the public interest." Thus, regulatory agencies have the flexibility to apply sometimes vague and changeable public policies to specific situations. This provides them with more discretion than courts have. It also means that regulatory agencies are not bound to follow precedents in the way that courts are.

There have been a number of criticisms of regulatory agencies. One is the same accountability-autonomy conundrum which was discussed with regard to Crown corporations. Regulatory agencies are meant to be autonomous from government, but they are also responsible for carrying out government policies. This can create serious conflict.

Consumers groups complain that regulatory agencies are too sensitive to the needs of the businesses they are charged with regulating. This has been described as the captive agency theory.[12] The idea is that the regulated businesses know more about their industry than does the new regulatory agency, so the industry is able to shape how the agency regulates it. Regulators sometimes say that they are concerned about "the orderly development of the industry" which can frequently be interpreted to mean the protection of all the companies who are currently in the industry from disruptive behaviour like aggressive competitors or overactive consumer groups.

Evidence about the captive agency theory is fragmentary. For example, a recent Statistics Canada report determined that regulated prices had increased about twice as fast as non-regulated prices.[13] Thus, regulation can ensure certain businesses of a price increase regardless of market and economic conditions.

Conversely, businesses sometimes complain that regulatory agencies are too aggressive in enforcing inappropriately high standards in such areas as occupational health and safety and environmental protection. It is fairly easy for agencies which have been charged with certain responsibilities to forget the cost of compliance with their regulations.

The federal government now prepares an annual regulatory agenda[14] which lists the plans of all federal agencies to introduce new, or change existing, regulations. This gives interested groups an opportunity to begin making their case early in the process.

Governments have also investigated the idea of deregulation, which simply means exiting the regulatory environment altogether and allowing the market to determine how services will be provided. The idea is that the "invisible hand" of the marketplace can regulate markets better than government edicts. The word deregulation is generally not used by Canadian governments because it has ideological connections with Ronald Reagan and Margaret Thatcher which are sometimes seen as unattractive in Canada. Governments in Canada have generally not embraced the concept of deregulation in its extreme form, but most governments have adopted a policy of reviewing all existing regulations to determine whether they are still desirable, and establishing gatekeeping organizations to ensure that any proposed new regulations are absolutely essential. In the federal government, this is the role of the cabinet committee referred to as the Special Committee of Council.

The trend to reducing regulation has met with mixed success. There are only certain cases in which it is a viable option. Natural monopolies such as telephone service and cable television cannot be affected by market discipline. It is difficult to see how market forces can replace regulation in environmental protection laws. This leaves areas like marketing boards where the groups which benefit from regulation are so well-organized that governments are reluctant to tackle them. Reduction of the regulatory burden is still on the agenda of most governments, but progress has been very slow.

Advisory councils Organizations discussed to this point have all been geared to providing services. There are some occasions when the government simply needs some advice on how to address an issue. One source of that advice is the ordinary government bureaucracy, and all governments recognize that this is a very valuable source. But governments also feel that they would benefit from having diverse sources of advice before making policy decisions. Therefore, a number of organizational structures have been established as competing sources of information. This section will discuss advisory councils and the following one will discuss royal commissions and task forces.

Governments have established a number of advisory councils. Some examples are:

- Canadian Advisory Council on the Status of Women,

- Fisheries and Oceans Research Advisory Council,
- Social Sciences and Humanities Research Council.

These bodies are funded by government but they are deliberately kept at arm's length so that they are not considered to be government organizations as such.

These councils are governed by people appointed by government, but care is usually taken to ensure that varied interests are represented on the board. There is an obvious temptation for the government to appoint only like-minded people, or even worse, party hacks, to these councils. That temptation is usually avoided because a council constructed in that way would have little credibility with the relevant groups.

Advisory councils function as two-way conduits of information. On the one hand, they advise government about the concerns of the groups they are representing, and pressure government to ensure that their group's interests are properly registered. On the other hand, they are a way for the government to communicate to the interested groups and let them know what it is doing to resolve their problems and concerns. These councils usually do not deliver programs. Their major focus is research and publication to focus attention on the concerns of their group.

Problems sometimes arise around the funding of these agencies. Governments usually provide most or all of their funding. This creates a difficult situation when the organization feels a need to criticize the government. Members of the council are usually concerned about how far they can go in being critical without jeopardizing their very existence.

Royal commissions and task forces Royal commissions and task forces will be discussed together. Sometimes the phrases are used interchangeably, although there is a legal distinction between them. This legal difference does not always result in a difference in the way they function.

The legal difference is that a royal commission is established by an Order in Council, whereas a task force can be established in a much more informal manner. Royal commissions tend to be more formal bodies and engage in lengthier reviews. Royal commissions almost always produce a public report, while task forces frequently report directly to a minister who decides whether the report will become public. However, these differences are not always respected in practice.

Royal commissions and task forces are temporary organizations created to review a particular situation and advise the government on what should be done about it. The focus of the inquiry could be a broad issue such as reproductive technology or a specific incident such as a plane crash.

Historically, these bodies were headed by one person, most frequently a judge. Recent commissions and task forces are more likely to be headed by a panel of people chosen to be representative of the various groups with an interest in the subject under review. This change in the composition of these bodies signals a change in their role from pure fact-finding organizations to a greater emphasis on providing policy advice which almost always involves conciliation and a search for acceptable compromise solutions.

The specific method of operation of the commission will vary depending on its subject matter, but the usual approach is to commission some expert background studies and hold a series of public meetings. The commission will frequently release the background studies and an interim report to stimulate discussion of the topic. It then issues a final report containing its analysis of the problem and its recommendations for solutions. These commissions go out of existence when they have issued their report.

Royal commissions and task forces are sometimes criticized for being devices to defer dealing with a problem, or to divert public attention. These allegations are true in some cases, but these bodies can also have a very significant role to play in resolving difficult issues. It is important not to attempt to deal with complex problems too quickly. There are occasions when taking some time to allow tempers to cool and new ideas to develop can provide a valuable opportunity. Yes, commissions and task forces are sometimes misused, but this should not result in a blanket condemnation. There are situations in which they provide a valuable service.

A Critical Assessment of the Existing Structures

Government in the 1990s is at the crossroads. Canada has developed a very high-quality public service, which delivers a very high quantity and quality of public services. However, the Canadian public sector is a victim of its own success. It has achieved this success usually by tinkering with existing structures. It has never had to stand back, take the long view, and consider basic structural changes until very recently. And even when it attempts to engage in major change, it runs the risk of slipping into incremental adjustments.

Governments in the 1990s are being forced to return to some very basic questions:

- What services should governments provide?
- How should those services be provided? Directly by government organizations or through private sector or not-for-profit organizations?
- Who should pay for the services? Should funding come from general taxes provided by all taxpayers or should the users of the services pay for them directly?
- How should government be organized? Do we need all the existing government departments and agencies or are there more efficient ways of organizing?

One of the key phrases of the 1990s will be "reinventing government," following from the very influential book of the same name.[15] Osborne and Gaebler argue that government must be changed radically so that it can remain efficient in the 1990s. Their basic argument is that government should be steering society, but that in recent years it has become too involved

FIGURE 7
Government Revenue
(as a % of GDP, excluding grants from other levels of government)

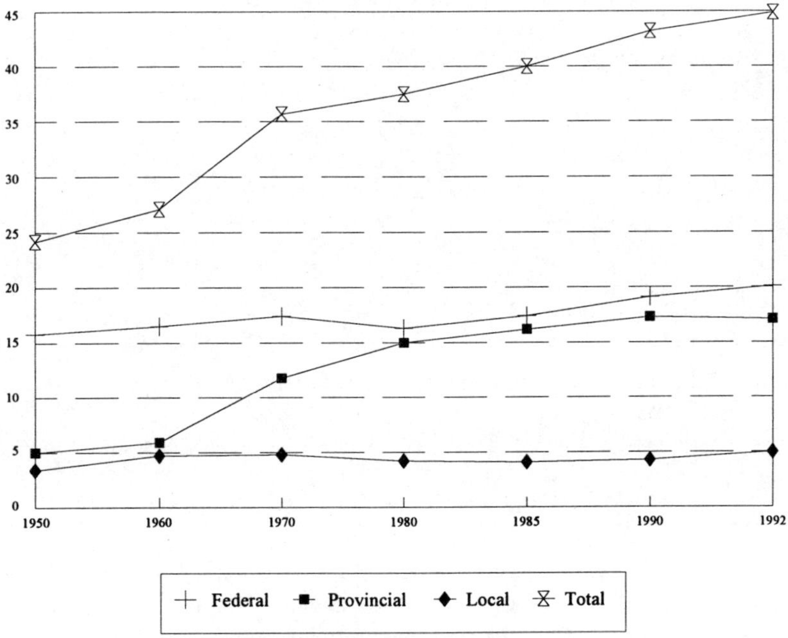

in "rowing," i.e., actually delivering services. The rowing has sapped so much of most governments' resources that they have been unable to steer. Their prescription is for governments to reorganize themselves to accomplish more by actually doing less. For example, they suggest that governments could accomplish more by working in partnership arrangements with private sector and not-for-profit organizations.

Osborne and Gaebler's book has been widely read in government circles in Canada. It is clear that Canadian public servants have heard the message. However, governments are very large organizations and they are very difficult to change. If governments are to maintain their credibility in the 1990s they must change themselves. It is still unclear whether this will happen.

This section has provided an overview of the skeleton of government by examining the operation of various government organizations. The next section puts some flesh on that skeleton by examining the financing of government.

THE FINANCIAL BASIS OF CANADIAN GOVERNMENT

One of the major issues confronting government in the past few years has been the complaint that government revenue and expenditure have been growing too rapidly. Figure 7 shows total government revenue for each

FIGURE 8

Government Expenditure

(as a % of GDP, including grants to other levels of government)

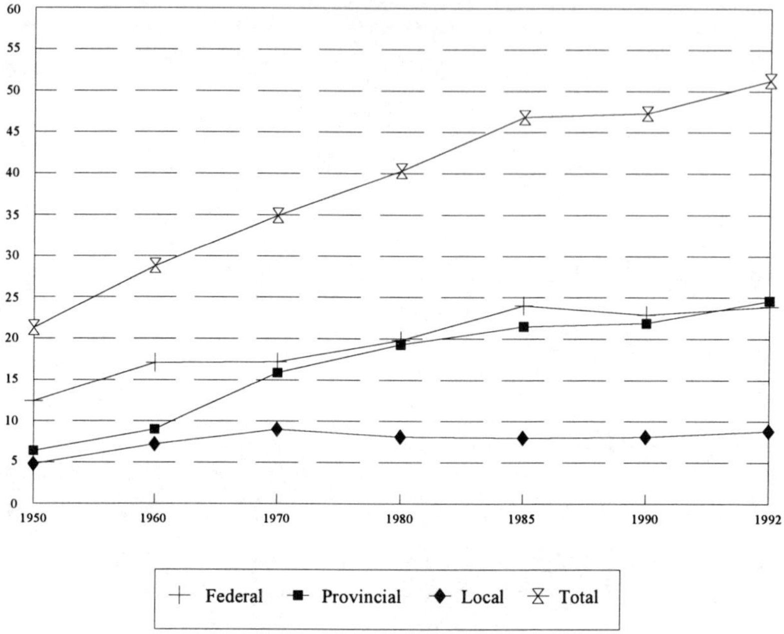

level of government as a percent of gross domestic product (GDP). GDP is a measure of the overall size of the Canadian economy. Measuring the size of government as a percentage of GDP is more relevant than using raw data because it provides a picture of the relative size of government in the total economy.

The chart indicates that total government, as measured by revenue, has been growing fairly steadily over the past forty years.[16] The main level of government fuelling this growth has been provincial, although this has levelled off in recent years. The federal and local governments have remained at roughly the same size over this period. People sometimes have a perception that taxes are growing more rapidly than they really are because they consider the raw numbers, forgetting that a major part of the apparent increase in taxes is caused by inflation. Measuring revenue as a percent of GDP removes the impact of inflation.

Figure 8 shows the expenditure side of the equation. While the graphs are somewhat similar, there are some significant differences. First, federal expenditure increased by a fairly significant amount between 1950 and 1992. Recalling from Figure 7 that federal revenue stayed roughly stable over the same period makes it clear what has caused the federal deficit.

FIGURE 9
Sources of Federal Government Revenue
(1993–94 budgetary estimate)

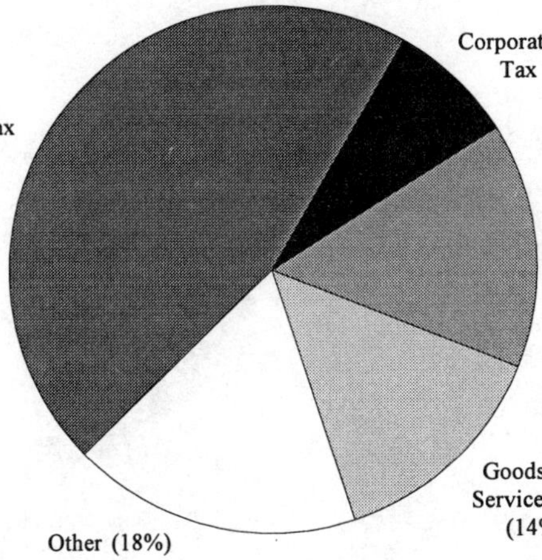

Second, total government expenditure has levelled off in the 1985–1992 period, mainly because of a plateauing of federal expenditure. The provincial and local expenditure trends are very similar to the revenue trends. Provincial expenditure has increased because provincial governments are responsible for what have been the big three items in the post-war period — health, education and social services.

Figure 9 focuses on sources of federal revenue. By far the largest source of federal revenue is the personal income tax, followed closely by unemployment insurance premiums and the goods and services tax. These three sources of revenue have also been the fastest growing in the past few years. The corporation income tax is the fourth largest source of revenue, and has been declining, in relative terms, in recent years.

One reason for the public perception of rapid increases in taxation could be that the burden of taxation has been shifting from the corporate sector to individuals. While the federal government would never admit it, this is likely a conscious policy designed to encourage business investment in Canada.

Figure 10 shows that the largest federal expenditures went to social services and debt charges. The former category has levelled off, but expenditure on debt servicing is still increasing, although this is dependent on the prevailing interest rate.

There is another way of looking at federal expenditure. Figure 11 reports federal expenditure on the basis of national accounts objects of expenditure. It is striking how little money the federal government spends

FIGURE 10
Federal Government Expenditure by Function
(1993–94 estimates)

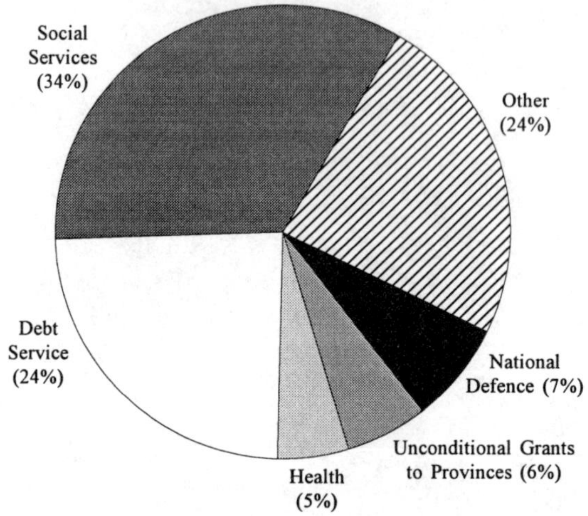

on goods and services. This is called exhaustive expenditure because these expenditures actually consume resources which are then unavailable to other sectors of the economy. Conversely, when the federal government transfers funds to some other entity, no resources are actually consumed.

FIGURE 11
Federal Government Expenditure, 1992
(National Accounts Basis)

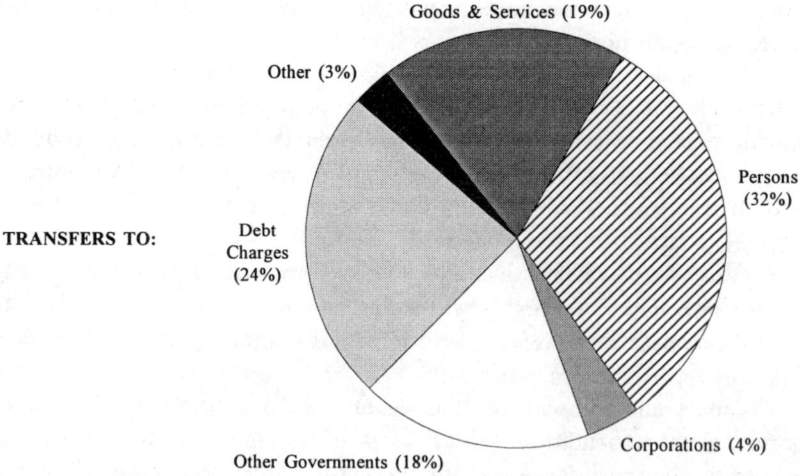

FIGURE 12
Federal Government Surplus-Deficit Position
(as a % of GDP)

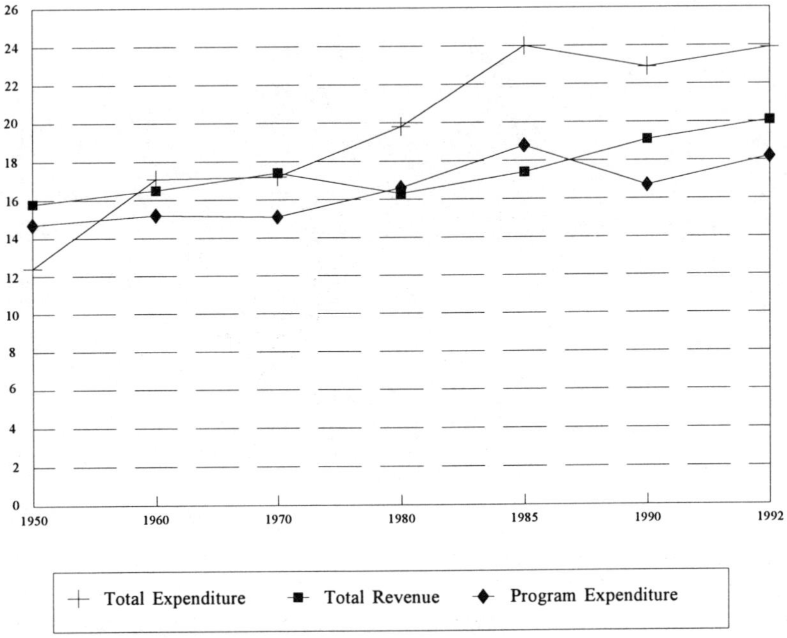

Figure 11 indicates that the federal government's major role in the economy is transferring funds between other entities. In recent years when the federal government has been trying to reduce its level of expenditure and deficit, one of the main areas in which it has cut back is transfer payments, particularly transfers to the provinces. The significance of this will be discussed in more detail below.

The federal government's debt position has been the subject of much attention lately. Figure 12 shows the federal government's revenue and expenditure as a percentage of GDP. This clearly indicates the extent of the gap between revenue and expenditure. It also indicates that the gap closed in the years 1985–90 but seems to be widening again in recent years. The federal government now focuses on the fact that revenues are greater than program expenditure (defined as all expenditures except debt service). This means that if the federal government were not paying to service the accumulated debt, it would actually have a surplus.

Figure 13 illustrates the historical trend of the federal government's debt situation. In 1992, federal debt was 62.7 per cent of the GDP. This is not the worst situation Canada has ever found itself in. After the Second World War, the level of outstanding debt actually exceeded the GDP. Of

FIGURE 13
Federal Debt Position
(as a % of GDP)

course, this was reduced very significantly over the next five years, but it has grown steadily ever since with significant spurts in recent years.

Canada's current debt position needs to be seen in perspective. As the graph indicates, we are not in the worst position we have ever been in, nor are we in a position which is significantly worse than other countries. However, there are two major concerns. First, the trend of the line is bothersome. The debt as a percentage of GDP has climbed steeply recently; if this continues, it will pose serious problems. Second, the percentage of expenditure which must go toward debt service reduces the discretionary funds available to the federal government to engage in new initiatives or deal with unexpected events.

In sum, we are probably not in as serious a crisis situation as many people suggest. However, we are certainly approaching a point of no return. If we do not take decisive action fairly quickly, we will be in a severe crisis.

PROVINCIAL REVENUE AND EXPENDITURE

Figure 14 shows the sources of revenue for all ten provincial governments. It indicates that all receive a significant portion of their revenue from transfer payments and that some receive almost 50 per cent of their total revenue from the federal government. Since these transfers are such a significant

FIGURE 14

Sources of Provincial Government Revenue
(as a % of total revenue, 1991–92 estimates)

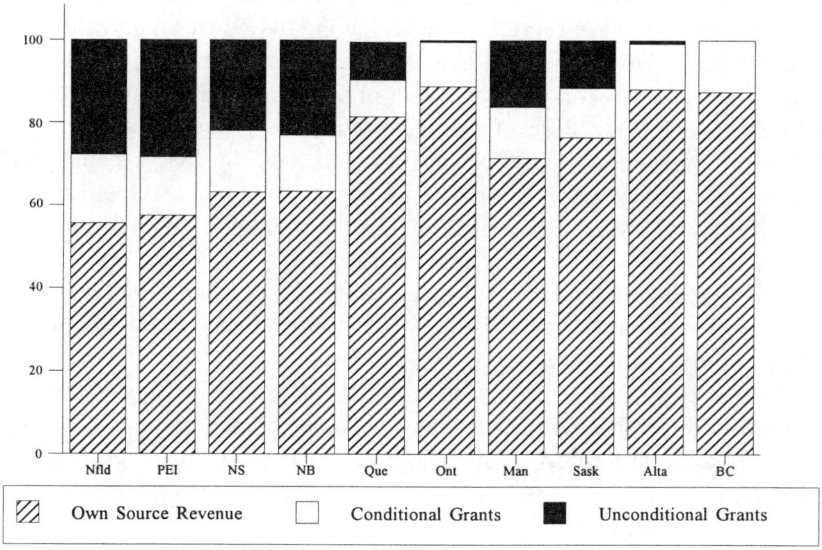

source of revenue for the provinces, it is important to examine how these funds are provided and some of the issues surrounding these transfers.

The federal government provides both unconditional and conditional transfers to the provinces. **Conditional grants** are provided for a particular purpose, and must be spent by the provinces on specified services. There are usually additional conditions with which provinces must comply to receive the funding.

The largest conditional grant is the Canada Assistance Plan (CAP). When originally started, this was an open-ended, shared-cost grant which committed the federal government to provide 50 per cent of the total cost of certain provincial social assistance programs. It was open-ended in that the federal government agreed to match whatever amount the provincial governments spent. This open-ended feature was attractive to the provinces but it meant that the federal government effectively lost control of its own budget.

In recent years, the federal government has attacked its deficit situation by capping the CAP. It now specifies the maximum amount it will pay under the CAP program, regardless of the provincial expenditure. The effect of this has been to require provincial governments to pay **more** than half the cost of social assistance.

There are many other smaller conditional grant programs, but they are generally all being cut back in the same way.

Unconditional grants come with no conditions attached and can be used for any purpose. A major unconditional grant is the equalization grant. This has been both a very important and a very contentious program. Its purpose is to ensure that provinces with a weak tax base will be able to provide a basic level of services without having to impose an unrealistically high tax rate. The details of its calculation are quite complex, but the general idea is that it compares the bases of a number of different tax sources with the average tax base of five representative provinces and provides additional compensation to provinces which have tax bases consistently below the average. Seven provinces usually receive payments under this program — Newfoundland, Prince Edward Island, Nova Scotia, New Brunswick, Quebec, Manitoba, and Saskatchewan.

This program has been a very significant source of revenue for most of these provinces but it has also been something of an irritant in relations between the federal government and the provinces. Although it is usually not considered appropriate to criticise the "have-not" provinces, the provinces which do not receive equalization payments sometimes resent the fact that their tax funds are going to other provinces. The provinces receiving the funds have recently expressed concern that the federal government has been manipulating the formula to reduce its contribution.

The equalization program is a classic example of one of those programs found in federal systems of government which is both absolutely necessary to hold the federation together and a serious irritant at the same time.

The federal government also provides a significant amount of funds to the provinces through the Established Programs Financing (EPF) program. This program replaced previous conditional grants for post-secondary education, hospital care and medical services in 1977. These programs were previously open-ended, shared-cost grants.

The calculation of the EPF in 1977 was based on the amounts of the conditional grants paid in 1976. The federal government agreed to adjust that amount every year at a rate equal to changes in the Gross National Product.

This grant is unconditional in that the provinces can spend the money for any purpose they like, but there are still some conditions attached to the funding. For example, the federal government's prohibition on extra-billing in the health care system is enforced through the threat of reductions in payments under the EPF program.

The provinces were initially concerned about the change in method of calculating the grant because it meant that the federal government's contribution was no longer directly tied to changes in the level of expenditure on these important services. Over time, the federal government has fought its deficit by unilaterally reducing the amount it pays under the EPF. This has angered the provinces because they see the federal government reducing its contribution to these programs at the same time as it continues to impose

FIGURE 15
Consolidated Provincial-Local Expenditure
(per capita $, year closest to December 31, 1991)

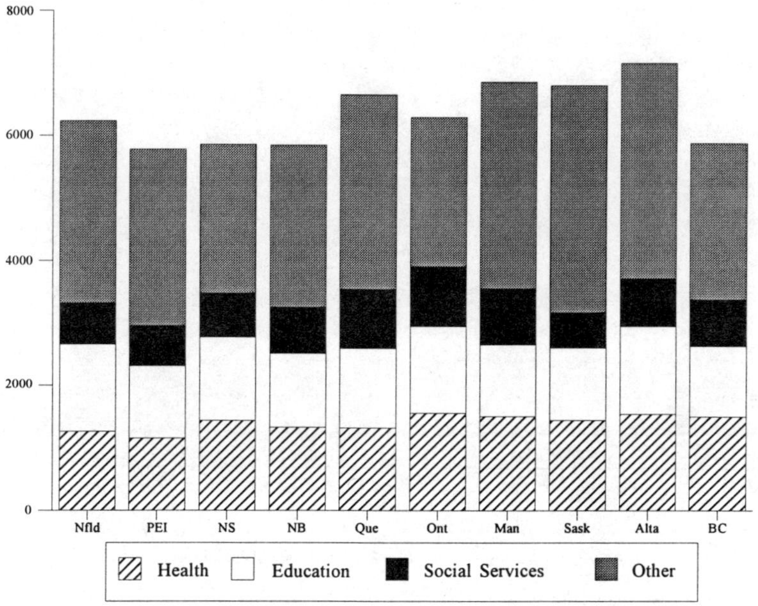

conditions which prevent the provinces from using other methods to reduce their outlays in these areas.

The federal response is that the financial position of the provincial governments is such that they are better able to bear additional expenses than the federal government. In fact, the federal government could even argue that its current serious deficit situation has occurred because it has been **too** generous with provincial governments in the past.

It is clear that there is some validity in both of these positions. Continuing arguments like this are what make federal-provincial relations so treacherous.

Figure 15 shows the major functions to which provincial and local governments devote their resources.[17] The big three items are health, education, and social services. The level of expenditure on health care has been a continuing concern because it has been growing more rapidly than other expenditure and shows no sign of abating. Recently social service expenditure has also been increasing because of the current difficult economic times, but this causes less concern because it is cyclical. The per capita figures also show the different relative levels of spending in the different provinces.

FIGURE 16
Provincial and Local Surplus-Deficit Positions
(as a % of GDP)

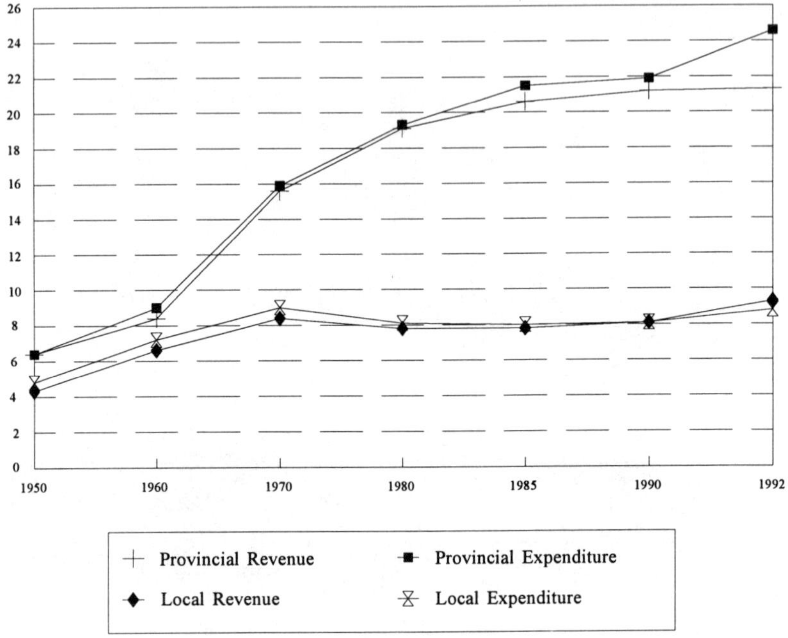

Figure 16 illustrates the surplus and deficit situations of provincial and local governments. The top pair of lines represents the provincial governments and the bottom pair represents the local. Generally, the revenue and expenditure lines are so close together that it is clear that these two levels of government are in a very different situation from that of the federal government. However, a significant trend to be noted is that the provincial deficit has been increasing in recent years. This would indicate that the federal government has been passing its deficit problems down to the next level of government.

It is very important to note that these figures are for all provinces and their local governments combined. Combining numbers in this way can obscure relationships and present very different pictures in different provinces.

It can be dysfunctional to be so devoted to avoiding debt that important expenditures are deferred. Local governments pride themselves on using the pay-as-you-go principle and so avoiding interest charges. However, there can be a cost associated with deferring needed expenditures. For example, the longer infrastructure is allowed to deteriorate, the more it costs to repair. There should be a trade-off between the cost of borrowing and the cost of allowing infrastructure to deteriorate.

CONCLUSION

The purpose of this article was to provide a broad overview of the public sector. The first part described the various organization structures employed by governments and discussed some of the unique problems of managing in the public sector. The second section provided a quantitative overview of recent trends in government revenue and expenditure.

This really just scratches the surface of what the knowledgeable citizen ought to know about government. The list of additional readings that follows this article should be helpful in doing further research or just supplementing general knowledge.

Notes

1. The phrase "responsible in the legislature" is used rather than "responsible to the legislature" to recognize the fact that in parliamentary systems of government, members of cabinet are also members of the legislature.
2. The Senate and the Governor General must both approve legislation, but this is generally a formality after it has been approved by the Commons.
3. These elements are discussed in more detail in: Kenneth Kernaghan and David Siegel, *Public Administration in Canada: A Text* (Scarborough, Ont.: Nelson Canada, 1991), p. 294.
4. Quoted in: Joseph L. Bower, "Effective Public Management," *Harvard Business Review*, vol. 55 (March–April 1977), p. 132.
5. A good discussion of some of the unique problems of managing in government is found in: Timothy W. Plumptre, *Beyond the Bottom Line: Management in Government* (Halifax: Institute for Research on Public Policy, 1988); and "Constraints to Productive Management in the Public Service" in *Report of the Auditor General of Canada to the House of Commons, Fiscal Year Ended March 31, 1983* (Ottawa: Auditor General of Canada, 1983), pp. 53–87.
6. For a contemporary comment on the status of this aspect of ministerial responsibility, see: Sharon L. Sutherland, "The Al-Mashat Affair: Administrative Accountability in Parliamentary Institutions," *Canadian Public Administration*, vol. 34, no. 4 (Winter 1991), pp. 573–603.
7. Kenneth Kernaghan and David Siegel, *Public Administration in Canada*, p. 172.
8. Two of these initiatives are Increased Ministerial Authority and Accountability (IMAA) and Public Service 2000. See: Treasury Board, *The IMAA Handbook: A Guide to Development and Implementation* (Ottawa: Treasury Board Secretariat, 1988; Paul M. Tellier, "Public Service 2000: The Renewal of the Public Service," *Canadian Public Administration*, vol. 33, no. 2 (Summer 1990).

9. A good overview of the universe of federal Crown corporations is contained in: President of the Treasury Board, *Crown Corporations and Other Corporate Interests of Canada: 1992–93 Annual Report to Parliament* (1994).
10. Kernaghan and Siegel, *Public Administration in Canada*, p. 226. Part of this definition was borrowed from: C. Lloyd Brown-John, *Canadian Regulatory Agencies* (Toronto: Butterworths, 1981), p. 35.
11. A good discussion of these two types of regulations is contained in: John C. Strick, *The Economics of Government Regulation*, 2nd ed. (Toronto: Thompson Educational Publishing, 1994), chapter 1.
12. Marver H. Bernstein, *Regulating Business by Independent Commission* (Princeton, N.J.: Princeton University Press, 1955).
13. Alan Freeman, "Regulated Prices Soared in 1991," *The Globe and Mail*, April 17, 1992.
14. Canada, Treasury Board, *Federal Regulatory Plan — 1994* (Ottawa: Minister of Supply and Services, 1993).
15. David Osborne and Ted Gaebler, *Reinventing Government* (Reading, Mass.: Addison-Wesley Publishing Company, Inc., 1992).
16. The graphs in this section are based on data contained in: Canadian Tax Foundation, *The National Finances — 1993* (Toronto: Canadian Tax Foundation, 1994); and Canadian Tax Foundation, *Provincial and Municipal Finances — 1991* (Toronto: Canadian Tax Foundation, 1992). These are annual and biannual publications which are very useful for research purposes.
17. This combination of provincial and local government expenditure is relevant because different provinces allocate different responsibilities to their local governments. Combining the two provides the most meaningful comparison.

Additional Reading

Abele, Frances, ed. *How Ottawa Spends: The Politics of Fragmentation — 1991–92*. Ottawa: Carleton University Press, 1991.

Aucoin, Peter, and Herman Bakvis. *The Centralization-Decentralization Conundrum: Organization and Management in the Canadian Government*. Halifax: Institute for Research on Public Policy, 1988.

Jackson, Robert J., and Doreen Jackson. *Politics in Canada: Culture, Institution, Behaviour and Public Policy*, 2nd ed. Scarborough, Ont.: Prentice-Hall Canada, 1990.

Kernaghan, Kenneth, and David Siegel. *Public Administration in Canada*, 2nd ed. Scarborough, Ont.: Nelson Canada, 1991.

Plumptre, Timothy W. *Beyond the Bottom Line: Management in Government*. Halifax: Institute for Research on Public Policy, 1988.

Savoie, Donald J. *The Politics of Public Spending in Canada*. Toronto: University of Toronto Press, 1990.

Van Loon, Richard J., and Michael S. Whittington. *The Canadian Political System: Environment, Structure and Process*. Scarborough, Ont.: McGraw-Hill Ryerson, 1987.

Whittington, Michael S., and Glen Williams, eds. *Canadian Politics in the 1990s*. Scarborough, Ont.: Nelson Canada, 1990.

Zussman, David, and Jak Jabes. *The Vertical Solitude: Managing in the Public Service*. Halifax: Institute for Research on Public Policy, 1989.

QUESTIONS FOR DISCUSSION

1. What advantages and disadvantage does the federal (vs. unitary) parliamentary (vs. presidential/congressional) system used in Canada offer for decisive politicians who want to experiment and/or make major changes?
2. How is power distributed in a governmental structure and process that features career civil servants and political appointees, numerous multilevel co-ordinating committees with overlapping memberships, and powerful central agencies? How powerful, for example, is a minister? The Prime Minister? Governing Party's caucus?
3. Decisions made by the Department of Finance about deindexing pensions, clawing back social assistance payments, and ending universality of entitlements seem to make it the arbiter of social policy, rather than the Department of Health and Welfare. If this is the case, what does this say about the way government operates?
4. Issues arising from such broad concerns as enhancing competitiveness on a global context, maintaining national identity, and adapting to changing demographics do not map neatly into the mandate of a single department. What organizational mechanisms are governments using to respond to these issues? What inhibits such organizational innovations from working effectively? What else could be done to ensure that appropriate actions are taken?
5. Do the structures and processes of government described in this paper facilitate or inhibit the ability of external stakeholders to influence what governments do?
6. How will settlement of the current constitutional debates change the ways in which Canadian governments operate?
7. What practical limitations impede government from being more effective in intervention to affect day-to-day life. Can these impediments be decreased.

David Siegel is Associate Professor of Politics at Brock University. He has a Ph.D. in Political Science from the University of Toronto, an M.A. in Public Administration from Carleton, and is a Certified General Accountant. He is co-author (with Kenneth Kernaghan) of the book, ***Public Administration in Canada****, co-editor (with Dale Richmond) of the monograph,* ***Agencies, Boards, and Commissions in Canadian Local Government****, and is the author of several articles on public administration and local government.*

The Organized Labour Sector: Structures, Processes and Policies

GRAEME H. McKECHNIE

Requisites for productive, internationally competitive economies invariably include a well-educated, well-trained, industrious labour force, working harmoniously with management. Japanese and European practices are invoked as role models to which North Americans should aspire. Clearly, closing the gaps between contemporary practice and these ideals is one of the most profound challenges facing Canada today. This paper briefs the reader on some of the history, theory and descriptive statistics, and on the institutional framework needed to better appreciate this challenge.

ORGANIZED LABOUR IN CANADA

The Field

The study of the labour movement or, more broadly, of industrial relations, begins with the integration of many viewpoints and strands of thinking. John Dunlop, in his book *Industrial Relations Systems*, began what is now the modern study of industrial relations by looking at the rules of work as the central focal point of the process.[1] Numerous others have refined the Dunlop model. The seminal Canadian work is that of Alton Craig, who put forth a framework for studying labour relations as a complex system of private and public market and institutional arrangements. Stated almost too simplistically, it involves labour, management and government "actors" establishing their goals, values and power within the context of various environmental pressures, among them economics, politics, legal and judicial systems and the social fabric of society.[2] Various mechanisms, such as collective bargaining, strikes or lockouts, arbitration and a variety of co-operative ventures were used by the actors to achieve the outputs of the system. The outputs were the rules contained in collective agreements by which workers and the organizations of labour and management operated, including wages and benefits. Labour economics can be thought of as a subset of the field, concerned with the supply and demand for different types of labour and the resulting wages and productivity levels.

Types of Unions

For ease of discussion, unions can be divided into craft, industrial and white-collar (office, professional and government) unions. The last of these terms is rather all encompassing; however, for purposes of the current discussion it can be used to designate those unions that do not fall into the traditional "blue-collar" areas and that represent employees in the service sector, most often government or "public-sector" work forces. Craft unions represent employees who have an identifiable skill or trade often connected with apprenticeship. These unions are typically smaller than their industrial and service counterparts. Industrial unions represent the traditional shop-floor, blue-collar employees in the manufacturing and maintenance categories. Although they often contain workers who have an identifiable trade or skill, nonetheless these unions are built upon the premise of one job, one worker and therefore tend to be much larger than craft unions. The category of white-collar unions represents an amalgam of different kinds of workers. In the Canadian Union of Public Employees (CUPE), for example, some members are in what could be traditionally thought of as blue-collar occupations, such as sanitation workers. Others fill positions that are white-collar in nature — clerical and professional functions within government administrations. The three categories are broad, but can serve to highlight the varied affiliation of the different kinds of trade-union workers and their skills.

There are also unions that do not fit, precisely, the description above. In Ontario, for example, some university faculties have organized into unions and have the right to strike. Also, the professional engineers at Ontario Hydro have received organizing and bargaining rights. Both groups are made up of "professionals," a label that has often been used to refer to a class of people who were against unions and their attendant strike activities. It must be pointed out, however, that organization and bargaining do not inevitably lead to strikes. In fact, the professional worker often has the power to affect working conditions by virtue of her professional status, without resort to organized pressure. Where such workers have organized into unions, there has been a feeling that collective pressure via bargaining will yield better results than acting alone.

Size and Growth of the Sector

The Canadian trade-union movement represents approximately 30 per cent of the civilian labour force (37 per cent of non-agricultural paid workers), or 4,088,626 workers in 1992.[3] It is important to realize, however, that membership figures understate the impact of organized labour on the Canadian economy. Membership statistics do not tell the full story. The labour movement, through collective bargaining and collective agreements, has an indirect — and, in some cases, a direct — impact on non-union workers and firms by virtue of the spillover of wage and fringe benefit effects.

Although union membership has increased in terms of absolute numbers, the degree of unionization — that is, the percentage of paid workers who are organized — fell slightly in the late 1980s. In the 1980s, union membership proportions in traditional union strongholds such as forestry, mining, manufacturing and transportation, fell or stagnated. By contrast, union membership increased dramatically in public administration, from a low of 28.8 per cent of paid workers in 1961 to 76.3 per cent in 1986. Employees in service industries also turned to unionization — an increase from 8.8 per cent in 1961 to 34.8 per cent in 1986.[4]

Shifting Participation

Union membership figures must be seen against the background of the prevailing economic and labour market climates, public policy and legislative environments, and the reactions of employers to union growth in unorganized plants and offices.

For example, there is still a large proportion of service workers who are not organized, and the service industries are clearly a target for union organizing in the coming years. In addition, future organizing will be directed to the white-collar employees in manufacturing and other goods-producing industries and in the areas of finance and insurance.

Female membership in trade unions has always been less than male membership, although in the last decade female membership has increased dramatically. Approximately 41 per cent of all union members are female; this represents about 31 per cent of female paid workers. With large numbers of female labour force participants in the service sector, it is easy to see why trade unions will be turning their attention to that sector in the coming years for increases in union membership.

It is clear, given the changing structure of the Canadian labour force and the changing labour market, that union organizing efforts will have to be increased dramatically in the nonunion areas if the labour movement is to grow. Indeed, as manufacturing jobs continue to be lost following the 1990–92 recessionary period, unions will be turning to the large pools of unorganized white-collar workers for future growth or even maintenance of current levels of membership.

Types and Sizes of Union Organizations

The size of a typical union in Canada varies according to its type of organization. The average size of Canadian affiliates of international unions (those with headquarters in the United States) was approximately 20,000 in 1989, whereas the average membership size of national unions (Canadian only) was only 11,000.[5]

The largest union in Canada is CUPE, which has a membership of over 400,000 workers. It has been a very active organizer of unorganized workers within the public sector. Also very large is the National Union of Provincial Government Employees (NUPGE), with over 300,000 members, and the Public Service Alliance of Canada (PSAC), with over 147,000 members. These three unions all fall in the category of public-sector white-collar and professional unions, although, in the case of CUPE, members are in a variety of different occupations. In the industrial sector, the Canadian Auto Workers' Union, with approximately 172,000 members, is the largest national union.

The largest international unions in Canada, both of them industrial, are the United Food and Commercial Workers' Union with 174,000 members, and the United Steel Workers of America, with 139,000 members. The largest craft union is the United Brotherhood of Carpenters and Joiners of America, with over 52,000 members.[6]

Union membership is not evenly distributed across the provinces. In 1991 the province with the highest proportion of union membership was Newfoundland, with 53 per cent and the next highest was Quebec with approximately 41 per cent of paid workers in unions. The range of unionization rates lies between 26 per cent (Alberta) and 53 per cent. Ontario, which has suffered losses in the manufacturing sector in the early 1990s, has a unionization rate of approximately 32 per cent.[7]

Although the proportion of Canadian workers who belong to international unions has been declining steadily since 1961, the linkage with unions in the United States remains strong. In 1961, approximately 71 per cent of union members belonged to international unions and 22 per cent belonged to national unions. The remainder belonged to either independent unions or directly chartered local organizations. In 1992, 31 per cent belonged to international unions, whereas 65 per cent of Canadian union members belonged to national unions. International unions lost ground between 1981 and 1992, whereas national unions gained membership. This shift was partly a result of a "Canadianizing" of unions and the growth of public-sector unions.

Institutional Structure

The structure of the Canadian labour movement can be characterized as having three tiers:

- central federation
- national or international union
- local union.

The local union provides much of the action in labour relations. In the Canadian structure, most collective bargaining and collective agreements occur at this level. Although there are independent local organizations, most local unions are affiliated with either a national or international union. The national or international union provides the initiative for organizing, as well as negotiating assistance. These organizations can be industry specific, such as the United Steelworkers (USW), or have broader coverage, such as the Canadian Automobile, Aerospace and Agricultural Implement Workers' Union (CAW). Unions have not hesitated to organize workers outside their more traditional industrial areas. At the apex of the labour movement are the central federations, such as the Canadian Labour Congress (CLC). These organizations represent "Labour" in Canada and attempt to influence government policy in favour of the labour force. As such, it is "the voice of labour." The links between the federations and member unions are not as direct as those between national and international unions and their locals. There are also federations within each province, such as the Ontario Federation of Labour (OFL). These act to represent labour at the provincial level in much the same manner as the CLC does federally.

Agreement Coverage

Size and affiliation (national or international) is one measure of a union's influence. The more important measure, however, is the collective-agreement coverage. In North America, persons who are not members of a trade union may still be covered by the collective agreement that a union in their workplace negotiates. In Canada, it is not strange for a worker to pay dues to a trade union, yet not belong to it. Most labour legislation requires that the trade union represents all workers within the bargaining unit — that is, the group of workers at the plant or office over which the trade union has some responsibility. Right-to-work legislation, which exists in some of the southern United States, guarantees workers employment without requiring them to belong to a union or to pay union dues.

The difference between the proportion of workers who are members of trade unions and the proportion of workers covered by collective agreements is quite dramatic. For example, in 1985 39 per cent of paid workers were members of trade unions whereas 57 per cent of all employees were covered by collective agreements. Those covered, included 69 per cent of all non-office workers and 39 per cent of all office workers. The office sector, even in manufacturing, has been resistant to organizing efforts.[8]

Comparisons with the United States

Union membership in Canada has remained remarkably constant over the past few years; however, union membership in the United States has been declining rapidly. Throughout the 1960s, Canada and the United States had an approximately similar proportion of their labour forces organized. However, beginning in the 1970s, union membership in the United States began to decline dramatically. By 1981 37 per cent of wage and salary earners in Canada were in unions, whereas in the United States the figure had fallen to 23 per cent. By 1985 the proportion in Canada had risen to 39 per cent, whereas in the United States it had fallen to 18 per cent; most recent figures indicate that only 17 per cent of wage and salary earners are now members of trade unions in the United States.

A number of factors have been responsible for this decline in U.S. membership and relative stability or even growth in the Canadian trade union membership figures. R.B. Freeman and J.L. Medoff, in their book *What Do Unions Do?*, indicate that changes in the structure of the economy and in the labour force account for part of the decline in trade-union membership figures in the United States. However, they point out, quite correctly, that similar changes have been taking place in the Canadian labour force: an increasing number of participants in the service sector, which traditionally has been less unionized than the manufacturing and mining sectors, and an increasing number of female participants, who have not shown the same predisposition to join trade unions as do their male counterparts.[9] Industry in the United States has migrated from the northeastern "rust-belt" states to the less-well-organized southern states.

As Freeman and Medoff point out, other factors are at work in the Canadian economy. For example, Canadian labour leaders have been more aggressive in attempting to increase their unions' membership than have their U.S. counterparts. At the same time, the legislative climate in Canada has been more favourable to union membership than that in the United States.[10] This trend is continuing. The changes made to the Ontario Labour Relations Act (OLRA) in 1993 are very favourable towards the trade union movement and its organizing objectives. However, it is too early to tell whether the impact of such legislated changes will be as significant as some business leaders predict.

International Comparisons

Comparisons between Canada and other nations indicate that the proportion of wage and salary earners who are members of trade unions in Canada is significantly lower than in many other industrialized countries. For example, in 1986, in Australia over 50 per cent of wage and salary earners were members of trade unions; this figure is 89 per cent in Sweden. Approximately 43 per cent of West German workers were members of trade unions prior to unification (figures have not yet been published for post-unification Germany). In Japan, slightly under 30 per cent of wage and salary earners were members of trade unions in the 1980s.[11]

HISTORICAL ROOTS

Part of these differences in membership rates is attributable to differing legislative climates and differing philosophies towards unions in various countries, which in turn stem from history.

The Canadian labour movement is an amalgam of British and American trade-union ideas. Trade unionism in Canada is not a recent phenomenon. Beginning in the early 1800s, a variety of "labour circles" and "friendly societies of working men" were formed to discuss working conditions and to give workers support from among their colleagues. It was not until the mid-1800s that trade unions began to form in earnest, and the first congress of labour was formed in the 1870s: the Canadian Labour Union. By 1886, the Canadian Trades and Labour Congress was formed. This body included traditional trade unions but, as well, included the various assemblies of the Knights of Labour, which was founded in Philadelphia in the 1860s. The Knights of Labour was the first major trade-union federation in the United States; it took in all workers whether they were white-collar or blue-collar, skilled or unskilled.

Just after the turn of the century, the first labour-relations legislation was passed in Canada: the Industrial Disputes Investigation Act, which provided for intervention by the federal government into labour disputes. The Trades and Labour Congress (TLC) evolved into a congress of craft unions and was allied very closely with the American Federation of Labour (AFL) in the United States. Beginning in the late 1920s, the All Canadian Congress of Labour (ACCL) was founded; its purpose was to organize workers on an industrial basis rather than a craft basis. As a result, two congresses existed in the Canadian trade-union movement: one representing industrial workers and the other representing craft workers. This parallelled union development in the United States, where the AFL represented the craft workers, and the Congress of Industrial Organizations (CIO) represented non-trade workers.

In 1940, the Canadian Congress of Labour (CCL) was founded. Together with the last vestiges of the ACCL and the industrial unions that were expelled from the TLC, the CCL became a congress for industrial unions parallel to the Congress of Industrial Organizations (CIO) in the United States. During the 1940s and until 1956, the two congresses co-existed in the Canadian trade union movement. In 1956 the two congresses merged, forming the Canadian Labour Congress (CLC), which exists even today as one of the congresses on the trade-union scene. Similarly, a merger occurred in the United States between the AFL and the CIO.

It is fair to say that the underlying philosophy of the Canadian labour movement is a blend of the American and British trade-union traditions. The craft unions have followed the pragmatic philosophy of the AFL. The AFL was founded in 1886 by Samuel Gompers, whose philosophy was very practical: to get "more, more and more." This practical approach has been counterbalanced by the working-class-movement philosophy of the British trade unions, where class distinctions shaped socioeconomic life, and political activism was the route to social change. One writer, Roy J. Adams, indicated that the British link meant that the Canadian labour movement pursued a moderate socialist point of view, but that a great many Canadian trade union members adhered to the more pragmatic U.S. approach.[12]

Labour's role in Canadian politics has tended more towards the British view than the American. The CLC and many Canadian unions actively support the New Democratic Party. Although the American labour movement supports the Democratic Party in the United States, it is fair to say that the direct links between the trade-union movement in the United States and the Democratic Party are not as strong or as obvious as those between the NDP and the Canadian labour movement.

THE COLLECTIVE-BARGAINING FRAMEWORK

The process of organized labour relations — that is, relations between a company's management and a union representing its employees — is governed in Canada by provincial Labour Relations Acts, which regulate the organizing process and set forth the rights and responsibilities of labour and management in collective bargaining. At the federal level, the Canada Labour Code provides a similar function for firms that operate within federal jurisdiction — for example, railways.

Representation

Union activity begins with the certification process by which a bargaining unit is established. Certification involves definition and representation, two steps which, although apparently distinct, are often blurred in reality. The union, by applying for and receiving the rights to bargain collectively, agrees to represent the employees within a well-defined bargaining unit. The steps themselves are distinct in that the determination of a bargaining unit involves a decision concerning which **jobs** are to be covered by the collective agreement. Jobs must be stressed, even though the union represents the **individuals** who hold those jobs. That distinction is most important in craft unions, where the jurisdiction of a union over particular skills and classifications having to do with the nature of the work itself, is often at issue — for example, what are electrical and what are electronic activities? In an industrial union, by contrast, the skills required do not form as important a feature of the jurisdictional process.

Definition of the bargaining unit, therefore, is important because this unit contains the jobs over which the union will claim jurisdiction during the bargaining relationship. Once the unit is determined, the individuals who fill the jobs within it are entitled to vote on whether they want to form a union or be represented by a union.

Representation is the step by which a particular union seeks to represent the workers holding the jobs within the bargaining unit. Such representation may occur by the employer recognizing the union voluntarily as the legitimate bargaining representative of the workers, or the union may apply to the provincial Labour Relations Board to have an election. If an election is held, provincial legislation specifies what proportion of the bargaining-unit members must be in favour for a union to be entitled to represent the employees; traditionally it is a simple majority of those voting. In Ontario in 1993 the NDP government amended the Ontario Labour Relations Act; the Act previously specified that if 45 per cent to 55 per cent of workers in a particular bargaining unit became members of the trade union, the Ontario Labour Relations Board would hold a vote. If over 55 per cent were members, the Board could hold a vote to determine if the employees wish to have a trade union. The government changed the lower limit of 45 per cent to 40 per cent. The impact has the potential to affect the ease of organizing for certain employees.

Bargaining

Once a union becomes established as the bargaining agent for employees within the bargaining unit of the employer, it is ready to assume the responsibility given to it under law. This begins with the union serving notice upon the employer that it wishes to bargain collectively. Once the two parties begin the negotiations process, most labour legislation in Canada steps back from the process and allows the parties to fashion a collective agreement within which they themselves can operate. In other words, the labour legislation does not inject very many requirements into the labour-relations framework between a union, once organized, and a management. The collective agreement becomes the set of rules that will govern the working relationship between the parties in those matters that the parties have chosen to include, and about which they have reached agreement, over the specified time period.

Most labour relations legislation does impose some additional obligations on the actors. For example, in Ontario, legislation requires that the parties must include a dispute settlement mechanism for the resolution of grievances that arise during the life of a contract. A grievance arises when one party believes the collective agreement has been violated. A dispute resolution mechanism begins with a discussion process that can lead to final and binding rights arbitration. There are few other requirements placed on the parties in negotiations. They are free to include the terms and conditions of employment that are most important to their interests in a collective agreement.

The time at which negotiations begin is mutually agreed upon. Formal notice to bargain is usually given 90 days before the expiry of a contract and negotiations begin shortly thereafter. The right to strike or to lock out, however, only arises after the expiry of the current collective agreement. The negotiations process often takes a long time. The legislation requires only that the parties bargain in good faith — that is, with a conscientious objective of reaching a collective agreement. If one party frustrates the process, the appropriate labour relations board adjudicates the matter, and may find the party to be bargaining in bad faith.

The parties negotiate by presenting a series of demands and counter-demands over a period of time. By convention, the union goes first in any negotiating period because it is most often the employees, as represented by their union, that seek to change some aspect of the collective agreement, usually the economic aspect. Management, however, can also present demands arising from its experience under the collective agreement. Over time, the parties become used to operating within the collective agreement; each will have ideas about how to improve the agreement or change it to its own advantage. With few exceptions, parties can bring any issue they wish to the negotiating table. One exception, for example, is in education in Ontario; the Teachers' Superannuation Fund (pension plan) cannot be a subject for collective bargaining between boards of education and the federations representing the teachers.

Conciliation

Should the parties be unable to reach a collective agreement through direct negotiations, most Canadian legislation requires government intervention before any further action can be taken. The generic term for such intervention is conciliation: a process in which a neutral third party (or, in some cases, a tripartite board), requested by either side, chosen and paid by government, enters into the dispute and enquires both as to the reasons for the dispute, and the range of possible outcomes. The conciliation process tries to bring the pressure of public opinion on the parties. As originally conceived, the conciliation process results in a written report containing recommendations for settling a particular dispute. At present, a conciliation officer most often attempts to get the parties to settle, and failing that, recommends that they be allowed to engage in a work stoppage if they wish. In certain high-profile situations, such as Canada Post, a report is issued to inform the public and the parties.

Strikes and Lockouts

Should direct negotiation and conciliation not be successful, the parties may then be free to strike or lock out. (Certain industries, such as fire fighting and police, do not have the right to strike or lock out.) The union, after a vote among its members, may call a strike — either a total withdrawal of services or some other action, such as rotating strikes among various plants — to bring pressure to bear on the employer to make offers that are closer to the union's demands than those made in pre-strike negotiations.

A strike can also sometimes be seen as an end in itself.[13] In Canada there have been a few incidences of strikes with purposes other than solving a collective agreement. For example, following the federal government's imposition of wage and price controls under the Anti-Inflation Board (AIB) in 1975, organized labour staged a day of protest in which workers were encouraged to walk off their jobs for one day.

An employer may bring pressure to bear on the union by locking out the employees in order to force the union and its membership to a more realistic position at the bargaining table, although lockouts are not as frequent as strikes. Under many provincial laws, an employer is free to keep the business in operation even if a strike is in progress. Legislation in the province of Quebec prohibits the use of "scabs" (non-union employees) from operating the struck employer's business. Quebec law is very stringent in this regard and attempts to make certain that when a work stoppage occurs, the company will not attempt to operate. In Ontario, legislation against the use of scabs to do the jobs of striking unionized workers has been less forceful. Ontario law, prior to the 1993 amendments, only prohibited the use of professional strike breakers — individuals whose sole purpose was to break up a strike. The current NDP government, however, amended the Ontario Labour Relations Act and outlawed the use of non-union labour during strikes.

In most cases, a strike results in the total cessation of work by members of the appropriate bargaining unit in the employer's place of business. As a result, in a strike by a blue-collar bargaining unit, the production and maintenance facilities would undoubtedly be closed unless the employer was able to operate some or all of those facilities with managerial staff. In a strike by a white-collar bargaining unit, a company would experience a similar loss of production, although once again, management might attempt to keep that part of the business in operation through the use of management assistance.

Workers on strike are usually provided strike pay by their union, at levels well below the amount usually earned during their regular work week. The company loses production; however, depending on its inventory and the nature of the business, it may not lose sales. A strike at a company that produces a perishable good or service has a much more serious impact than a strike at a company producing durable goods.

Mediation

Both before and during a strike, the parties are not necessarily left alone to attempt to work out a solution. They have access to mediation which, unlike conciliation, is a process designed solely to help the parties reach a collective agreement. The mediation process does not involve either report writing or recommended terms of settlement. Rather, the mediator attempts to discover, through lengthy discussions with each party, what the real issues in the dispute are, and to help the parties in reaching a mutually agreeable solution. The decision to use a mediator is made by the parties, in some cases at the urging of the government. The mediator is chosen and paid by the government. The mediator makes proposals to each party, without prejudice and in confidence. The process is quite informal and relies on the parties' willingness to reach a conclusion, helped by an interested and skilled neutral party.

Essential Services

In the private sector and certain areas of the public sector, should direct negotiations be unsuccessful and mediation not lead to the parties reaching a collective agreement, they could then engage in a work stoppage either through strike or lockout. However, certain areas of the public sector, notably those involving public health and safety, such as fire fighters, police and hospitals, are deemed essential services and work stoppages are not permitted. The parties must submit the outstanding issues to final and binding interest arbitration. Considerable debate has taken place over the meaning of "essential" in this context; however, the standard of public health and safety is generally agreed upon.

The government basically divides essential services into two categories which are treated in different ways. If it is determined that the service itself is essential to the community or to the country (e.g. police, firefighters), no work stoppages are allowed and compulsory interest arbtration is substituted for the right to strike or to lock out. In "quasi-essential" industries (e.g. transit workers, nurses) that are allowed to engage in work stoppages, but where the impact of a work stoppage presents great hardship for the community, the government may enact back-to-work legislation after a stoppage is under way. In 1992, the United States rail strike was halted by the U.S. government for this reason.

Compulsory Interest Arbitration

If a dispute is sent to compulsory interest arbitration, the parties present the issues in dispute, along with the rationale for their positions, to an arbitration board. This "board" can be either a sole arbitrator or a tripartite board consisting of an arbitrator and a nominee from each party.

Although the decision to use this process is made by the government, the parties choose their own members of a tripartite board and, if they agree, the neutral chair as well. In some cases, the government pays the arbitrator(s); in others, the disputing parties do.

The board or arbitrator, upon hearing all of the issues in dispute and the rationale for the positions taken by each party on each of the issues, delivers a final, legal, binding settlement of all items in dispute.

There is a widespread notion that compulsory arbitration should replicate the free collective bargaining process — in other words, that the decisions reached should be the decisions that the parties themselves would have reached had they been able to settle their dispute in a timely fashion. This replication relies primarily on comparability — that is, what other unions and managements in the same industry and in the same geographic area settled on in their collective agreements.

One could argue that such a criterion is not appropriate given that compulsory arbitration has been invoked because the parties in fact **could**

not reach a collective agreement — that replication is therefore an almost unattainable goal.

The replication criterion for arbitration decisions, like the process of binding interest arbitration itself, has both costs and benefits, all of which should be investigated in some detail by parties proposing to use them.

Back-to-Work Legislation

Back-to-work legislation is a technique that most governments are loathe to use for a number of reasons. First, if the government relies on back-to-work legislation frequently, the parties will learn very quickly that a threatened or actual work stoppage will bring government action; the government then becomes a partner at the bargaining table, which politicizes the process. Second, although the politicization of the process is almost taken for granted in the public sector, private-sector agreements are jealously guarded as the responsibility of unions and employers. Intervention by the government is seen as heavy-handed interference.

In the 1980s, back-to-work legislation was used in Canada on 37 occasions out of 7521 work stoppages — a very low proportion. It is interesting to note that of those 37 incidents, 21 involved health services, education or public transit.[14]

However, the threat of back-to-work legislation can be effective. In the 1991–92 bargaining year, the parties in three collective-agreement negotiations — between the Toronto Transit Commission and the Amalgamated Transit Union in the fall of 1991; between the Ottawa Board of Education and the Ontario Secondary School Teachers' Federation; and between the Carleton Board of Education and the Ontario Secondary School Teachers' Federation — were spurred on by the threat of government action to make their own settlements. In 1993, threatened government action was a factor in preventing a strike at Ontario Hydro.

CANADA'S TRACK RECORD

The majority of collective agreements are settled without compulsory interest arbitration. In the private sector, compulsory arbitration is almost unknown, although back-to-work legislation has been invoked from time to time. The vast majority of collective agreements are settled through either direct collective bargaining or collective bargaining with the aid of conciliation and/or mediation. For example, in 1988, 53 per cent of new settlements were reached through direct bargaining, 32 per cent were settled with a combination of bargaining and some third-party involvement such as conciliation or mediation, approximately 8 per cent of the settlements were achieved through arbitration, and 7 per cent were settled only after a work stoppage. In 1990, 58 per cent of settlements were reached through arbitration and 7 per cent involved a work stoppage.[15] In actual numbers, this represents, in 1988, 550 work stoppages — 478 in the private sector and 72 in the public sector. In 1990, preliminary data indicate that there were 420 private-sector and 108 public-sector work stoppages.[16]

Comparing Canada's strike record to the strike records of other industrialized nations reveals a disquieting pattern.

In 1989, Canada experienced 630 disputes, compared with 1229 in Italy, 693 in the United Kingdom and 1402 in Australia. By contrast, there were 51 disputes in the United States and 362 in Japan. Data were unavailable for France, Germany and Sweden.[17] A few years earlier, Australia still held the lead for most disputes, with Italy closely following and the United Kingdom in third place. Canada rests securely in fourth spot, slightly ahead of Japan, but a long way in front of both the United States and Sweden.

The number of work stoppages is not indicative of their impact, however. The working days lost as a result of the stoppages in 1990 was approximately 4-million in the private sector and just over 2-million in the public sector. It is clear that, in Canada, when a work stoppage does occur, large numbers of workers are involved, usually for fairly lengthy periods of time.[18]

If one compares the days lost per thousand employees, one finds that Canada is the "leader," with 326 days lost per thousand employees. Italy follows Canada with 265, whereas Australia and the United Kingdom have just under 190, followed by the United States with 161 and Japan with 5. Therefore, although there were fewer strikes in Canada than in Australia, Italy or the United Kingdom in 1989, in Canada, more employees were on strike for longer periods of time.[19]

While Canada's strike record, both in terms of the number of strikes and the number of days lost, seems at first glance to be a catastrophe, the fact is that the vast majority of collective agreements are settled without either party resorting to a work stoppage. Indeed, the majority of labour-management relationships in Canada take place in the atmosphere of goodwill and harmonious relationships required to forge a successful alliance between management and labour.

Public Attitudes

The Canadian public's attitude towards work stoppages is influenced significantly by the disruptive nature of strikes and the possibility of violence on picket lines. In fact, one of the reasons given for the recent amendments to the Ontario Labour Relations Act, concerning use of non-union labour during a strike, is the prevention of picket-line clashes between strikers and non-strikers. During the strike by the Southern Ontario Newspaper Guild against the Toronto Star in June 1992, there were several incidents of violent activity as non-union workers were transported through the picket lines. In fact, one item of dispute during the strike was management's insistence on discipline for strikers involved in such activity. A second example is the strike by PSAC against the federal government in 1991, which seemed to highlight the concerns of the public. There were supporters and detractors of both parties. PSAC's strike activities angered many; however, the government's position on wages, which were at one point **told** to the union rather than negotiated, inflamed many union members. As a result, each side accused the other of improper behaviour and the public could only look on in disgust.

ACTIVITIES OF ORGANIZED LABOUR

Union-Management Relations

The efforts of trade unions are concentrated in collective negotiations, but they put considerable effort into lobbying activities. Trade unions sometimes secure particular benefits in collective agreements and then, using these agreements as examples, convince governments to enact changes to legislation that will favour larger segments of the workforce. For example, maternity benefits were negotiated in the postal service some years ahead of their enactment in legislation.

One of the significant fears of the Canadian trade-union movement is the whole question of Canadian competitiveness and the pressures placed on workers, both inside and outside trade unions, by industries seeking to compete in a global economy. The increased pressure for competitiveness has led businesses to request or demand concessions in the workplace in order to keep plants operating in Canada. This angers the trade-union movement, which sees this as almost unpatriotic, whereas from the industrial side, the issue is one of keeping plants in operation and competing with firms in countries where labour laws are not as strong and wages may not be as high. There was considerable, often acrimonious, debate among business, government and labour over both the Free Trade Agreement and the North American Free Trade Agreement because of these concerns.

The labour-management debate is important because the changes industry will introduce to increase competitiveness can, at the same time, weaken trade unions. The issue is not simply one of management contracting out work or replacing workers with technology; work may be moved to other countries altogether, or to plants not located in Canada to begin with. The debate over productivity, labour-management relationships and worker efficiency is far from over.

Many observers are beginning to ask whether or not recent initiatives to cope with globalization are coming too late to halt what many see as a decline in the Canadian labour movement's influence, power and membership similar to the one that has already occurred in the United States. As already pointed out, private-sector trade-union membership in Canada has been declining as in the United States, and the large public-sector membership is partly responsible for the Canadian trade-union membership figures.

Labour-Management Co-operative Initiatives

Some quite remarkable labour-management initiatives have taken place in Canada, particularly in Ontario, over the past two or three years. At Algoma Steel, for example, Premier Bob Rae appointed union leaders to the special task force to investigate and arrange for the restructuring of the corporation. Also within the steel industry, the Canadian Steel Trade and Employment Congress, a joint union-management undertaking that has received some federal government funding, has as its major task organizing the retraining of workers laid off in the steel industry.

Other sectors may well follow the lead of the steel industry. In Brantford, Ontario, an air-conditioning manufacturer and its union agreed in 1991 to make a series of changes to work rules, wages and their industrial relations structure in order to continue competing for work. The unionized work force was not an impediment to the process; rather employees, the union and the employer worked together to put a different framework in place.

Political Involvement

Organized labour interacts with government on any number of issues unrelated to the legislative framework or to work stoppages. For example, in Ontario the NDP government has been encouraging work site control by employees. In the case of the Algoma Steel Company, the United Steel Workers and the company recently negotiated an agreement that included wage concessions, but also provided for financing the company through the efforts of workers to restore profitability. It remains to be seen whether such efforts will bear fruit.

The Ontario government has also been directly involved in company financing — for example, it provided DeHavilland Aircraft with the loan guarantees necessary to continue operation. At least part of the reason the government became involved was to save the jobs at the company. Once again, the results will not been seen for some time.

Another disquieting feature of the past decade, beyond the need for bailouts, is the frequency of public clashes between labour and government over such items as the desirability of the free trade agreement and the appropriate mechanisms for solving the recession of the early 1990s. These have increased labour's political involvement.

Labour in Canada has always had a political agenda. Its support for the NDP is well known. The question is whether or not union activities in the political spectrum can positively influence labour legislation, and whether labour should and will join with management and government to meet the global challenge of the 1990s.

Freeman and Medoff state that

> our analysis suggests that despite all of the press given some union lobbying efforts, unions have been unable to win the legislation most important to them as institutions and to their monopoly power.[20]

This statement was made about the American trade-union movement, but it also applies, to a certain extent, to Canada as well. In those jurisdictions where the NDP has gained power, such as in Ontario in the 1990s, the trade-union movement has been able to influence positively certain aspects of labour-relations legislation. However, if one compares the proposed amendments to the Ontario Labour Relations Act, which were signalled in the fall of 1991, with the actual amendments, it becomes clear that substantial changes were undertaken in response to pressures from the business community and a review of the political realities facing the NDP in Ontario. Nonetheless, trade-union lobbying efforts have been effective in a variety of areas, including encouraging governments to consider programs such as pay equity, maternity-leave benefits and pensions.

Historically, labour has not been a willing participant in many government initiatives. One example may serve to illustrate the difficulty in which the labour movement finds itself. In 1975, the federal government's Anti-Inflation Board imposed a series of wage and price controls. In 1976, at the Constitutional Convention held in Quebec City, the CLC published "Labour's Manifesto for Canada." The document attacked the program of wage and price controls and also demanded a tripartite approach to shaping the economic and social policies of the country. At the same time, the CLC withdrew from the Economic Council of Canada as a protest over the wage and price controls. The CLC, however, although it is a voice of labour in the economy, lacks the power that local and national unions have, given their collective bargaining rights.

Perhaps the most startling incident in labour-government relationships occurred in the summer of 1993 in Ontario. The NDP passed legislation, the Social Contract Act, S.O. 1993, c. 5, which was designed to reduce public-sector expenditures while maintaining public-sector jobs. The Act was passed after attempts to negotiate a social contract between the government and the various employers and unions in the broader public sector failed. The broader public sector encompassed not just the government, but health care agencies, schools, municipalities and other agencies that received government funds. The labour force that was affected comprised approximately 900,000 workers. The negotiations failed — in fact some unions walked out of the negotiations — and the government then enacted the legislation. The public-sector unions and employee groups raised strong objections to the legislation, especially the provision that some employees could be required to take up to 12 unpaid days in each year of the three-year life of the legislation, an approximate 4–5 per cent reduction in wages. For all employees covered by the Act, compensation was frozen at the levels in effect in June 1993. So serious was the opposition to the Act and the government, that a split between public and private unions occurred within the Ontario Federation of Labour when the public-sector unions wanted the OFL to voice its opposition to the NDP government and the private-sector unions did not support the proposal. The legislation is very complex and the ramifications for relations among labour, management and government will not be known for some time, at least until the termination of its provisions in 1996.

Too often, the labour movement views government initiatives as weakening the power both of the trade-union movement and of worker input into decision making. Often, it sees the government's political agenda as an overriding force, even in programs in which labour would have a legitimate interest and legitimate input. When that occurs, the labour movement tends to back away from co-operation and, as a result, does not share in the decision making. One could argue that operating from within the power structure would be a much more appropriate strategy to follow, and that if the labour movement does not begin to co-operate in initiatives between business and government, the trade-union workers will simply lose their ability to influence decisions affecting their working lives.

It is interesting to note that when Bob White was elected president of the CLC in June 1992, he indicated that the labour movement would be taking part in discussions with the government, and that it was in labour's best interest not only to criticize government policy, but to attempt to formulate constructive policies of its own, which the government would have to consider. If the labour movement does in fact assume this stance, it will go a long way towards silencing the critics who indicate that labour is mainly a reactionary and negative force.

STRUCTURAL ADJUSTMENTS

If labour does become more politically involved, its first task will be coming to grips with the various structural adjustments taking place that will have an impact on the labour force. To do so, it must investigate both the initiatives that are going on at the level of the whole economy, as well as at the industry and local level.

The increased awareness and concern about training arises, in part, from the increased competition brought on by the North American Free Trade Agreement. However, the issue is more complex. The labour market has undergone significant changes over a period of time and technology has moved quickly, whereas skills training has not. In addition, educational programs have been unable to keep pace with changing labour-market demands.

For example, there are concerns, both in Canada and in the United States, over increasing rates of illiteracy and of dropping out at both the elementary and, especially, secondary levels. If such matters are not addressed, young entrants to the labour force will be totally unprepared for the demands that will be placed upon them. At the same time, workers currently employed with skills that are not easily adaptable to the changing labour market will find themselves in great difficulty as the year 2000 approaches.

Fortunately, labour-market adjustment issues have received heightened attention in the past few years. In the summer of 1989, the Canadian Labour Market and Productivity Centre, a joint labour-management organization funded by the federal government to discuss problems and search for solutions to labour-market problems, held a variety of consultations, which led to the establishment of the Canadian Labour Force Development Board. This is a non-governmental institution for developing national training goals, strategies and standards.

A paper delivered by P. Kumar at the 1991 conference of the Canadian Industrial Relations Association set forth a number of reasons for the recent increase in concern about labour-market adjustments. Among others, Kumar mentions the higher unemployment rate, regional disparities in labour-market performance, deteriorating job quality and a growing mismatching between jobs and skills. Kumar outlines the labour movement's position on training and the various other issues as follows:

1. Training is a basic worker right
2. Training is a fundamental part of a job
3. Training is a tool for equity
4. Workers and their unions must have a central role in determining the direction of training[21]

At the same conference, Gordon Betcherman of the Economic Council of Canada reviewed recent labour-market policy in Canada. He raised the issue of the Premier's Council in Ontario, which is composed of leaders of government, industry, labour and education, and out of which should come a blueprint for education, training and labour adjustment in Ontario.[22] One of its initiatives is the Ontario Training Adjustment Board (OTAB), an independent, self-governing organization with the responsibility for workplace and sectoral training, apprenticeship, labour-force adjustment and labour-force entry and re-entry. This board will deal with programs for older workers, student training and sheltered workshops, among others. Its governing body will be made up of: eight business leaders; eight labour leaders; four people from social-action groups representing women, people with disabilities, racial minorities and aboriginal people; and two representatives from the education and training sectors. OTAB, although an agency of the Ontario government, will operate independently. It will have one representative each from the provincial and federal governments as ex-officio members. A concern that has been raised is whether or not the equal representation from business and labour will simply lead to a constant debate concerning priorities and directions to be taken, rather than a comprehensive program of action.

Experience from the de Grandpré report (a labour and business investigation into the adjustments needed in light of the Free Trade Agreement) suggests that local or regional initiatives will become more important in the coming years. The result of the de Grandpré report was increased activity by the private sector and a corresponding decrease in federal government intervention in training. With the discussions of provincial jurisdiction over labour-market activities as part of the constitutional debate, provincial initiatives such as OTAB will take on an increased importance and could heighten the tensions between labour and management over this issue.

Betcherman's paper states that: "...labour and management have two quite separate agendas regarding training and labour-market policy more generally."[23] The difficulty that may emerge is the difference between "macro" discussions and "micro" implementations. In other words, while labour leaders and business leaders may be able to agree on some philosophical and general programs, union-management relationships in Canada take place most frequently at the shop-floor or office-desk level, rather than the national or international level. Industry and trade-union leaders in organizations such as the Canadian Steel Trades and Employment Congress operate at an industry level. Often it is easier for them to reach agreement on broad issues, but these may not address the day-to-day problems faced by individual managers and individual workers.

While one does not wish to underestimate the power of the national union, nonetheless, the pattern in Canada is for collective agreements — and therefore, discussions of internal labour-market activities — to take place at the local union level. This will mean that unless labour and management can get together in their discussions, an initiative such as OTAB may not in fact be able to function as effectively as it might.

An example can serve to illustrate the potential difficulty. The goals of efficiency, competition and productivity may best be served by changing the structure of job classifications and job duties within a firm or industry. However, workers who have negotiated collective agreements containing various job-protection clauses may not be able to see any immediate or even long-term value to changes that will affect their employment status. Arbitration cases are often undertaken because a worker's job has been changed or a job classification has been rearranged. This occurs within the company where the collective agreement is in operation. It directly affects particular workers at their job site. It is one thing to argue that workers will have to adopt very flexible skills; it is quite another to tell an individual worker that the requirement of flexibility has now removed a particular employment position or opportunity for advancement.

It is clear that there will have to be some job flexibilities negotiated that will allow industries and particular companies to adapt to the changing labour-market structure. At the same time, workers need employment security; this may include some job protection, but undoubtedly will include job training and retraining, so that workers and their unions will not only accept the changes, but in fact will welcome even more changes as the decade proceeds.

What, then, is a potential blueprint for this area of structural adjustments? In part, there may be some ideological conflict as the labour movement may see the government's intervention as part of an overall political agenda. Part of the conflict may be in the labour movement itself, however, since it takes the stand that the government must play a more proactive role in labour-market adjustment problems. Yet the labour movement has not been a willing participant in some governmental undertakings. There may have to be a significant change in the way these undertakings are conducted, and in the labour movement's position within them, if success is to be achieved in labour market adjustment.

Labour-Management Co-operation

If a goal of the labour movement is to help increase competitiveness, productivity and efficiency, it will, at the same time, insist on accomplishing the social goals of retaining the employment security of those who currently have jobs, as well as increasing the number of jobs within the economy. The labour movement has staunchly supported various equity programs and will continue to support such programs; however, both industry and labour will have to come together with a renewed spirit of co-operation and a determined effort to achieve a meeting of the minds, both at the industry and the sector level. These shared goals will then have to filter down to the local level, where collective agreements are negotiated.

This co-operation will not come easily. In a paper delivered to the 1989 conference of the Canadian Industrial Relations Association, B. Bemmels and Y. Reshef indicated that collective bargaining, in fact, was a defensive mechanism to protect workers from technological change and labour-market adjustments.[24] It should be expected, therefore, that unions will attempt to affect the implementation of technology, and to structure appropriate retraining programs to enable workers to take part in whatever benefits flow from technology. If employees and their unions are to take part in the discussion at the firm level, then the question is one of where in the decision-making process the union and the employees will participate.

Bemmels and Reshef put forward the following hypothesis:

> That all else equal, the greater the employees' participation in the decision-making process over technological changes, the more supportive the employees will be of the technological changes.[25]

Their study, the two authors conclude, does lend some support to this hypothesis; they further conclude that a union presence itself does not automatically affect the workers' impact on decisions with respect to technological change. This means that as technology proceeds throughout this decade, workers and managers should be able to sit down and discuss reactions to the current technological change and begin to propose new programs to take advantage of new technology and new skill development.

This shared decision making will not come easily in a nation in which management has had the right to plan, direct, manage and control the work force, especially in the matter of decisions relating to technological change. This is different from the situation in, for example, Norway in which work councils allow the opportunity for employees to participate with management. Martin Serediak, in a paper presented to the same conference, stated that, although Norwegian workers had only consultative powers, their system was a more effective mechanism than the Canadian one.[25] He found that worker participation in Canada was very limited.

This finding echoes what is found in Canada in collective bargaining and grievance and arbitration processes. At the local plant or office level, the collective agreement specifies work rules and working conditions, and unions and their members jealously guard the ability to negotiate those kinds of items in a collective agreement. Management also protects the right to negotiate and to make decisions with respect to the work force. At this micro level, therefore, shared decision making is a radical departure from the status quo and change will not come easily.

There are numerous examples of how joint determination and shared responsibilities can present problems. For example, in occupational health and safety legislation, Ontario employers must take every reasonable precaution to ensure the health and safety of employees. There is no reciprocal requirement for employees. Legislation compels employees to wear safety protection if required, and not to make that equipment ineffective, or to engage in dangerous operation of machinery. At the same time, employees are protected from discipline or discriminatory action for exercising their right to refuse unsafe work. Employees may refuse to do work which, in fact, is safe, and thus disrupt the production operation. Nonetheless, no one would deny that if unsafe work conditions exist, an employee must have the right to refuse to work. This requires a balancing of interests, and employers and employees are going to have to work very hard at it.

This lesson from occupational health and safety legislation has general applicability. At the level of the local union, where most collective agreements are negotiated, workers and managers are going to have to change the way they approach industrial relations, if a spirit of co-operation is to begin to build. Fortunately, in Canada, the industrial-relations arena is not a constant battleground. Too often, the media report only the "newsworthy" occasions on which open conflict has occurred. The impression is often created that all industrial-relations activities are at an impasse the majority of the time. This is not the case; in many locales, labour and management work harmoniously together and, in fact, are working toward a new structure. More initiatives demonstrating co-operation between labour and management, in a unionized setting, will be needed to ensure a healthy Canadian work force and, from the trade-union movement's perspective, a healthy labour movement.

CONCLUSION

What role will the Canadian trade movement play in the 1990s? There is no need to ask if there should even be a role for it to play, because a trade-union movement that has organized over 30 per cent of the labour force is a labour movement that, although it may be in some decline, must be given credibility in discussions concerning economic programs. Anthony Giles and B. Sharma, in a paper delivered to the 1991 conference of the Canadian Industrial Relations Association, concluded an investigation of unions, strikes and competitiveness in the following way:

> Broadly, the results suggest that patterns of industrial relations do have an impact on the economic competitiveness of nations. However, the popular view that unions damage the competitive performance of nations has been shown to be overly simplistic. The important factor is not the extent to which a nation's firms and industries are unionized, but rather the organizational and political nature of the union movement, especially its strategic orientation. In short, strongly organized trade unions which have the organizational capacity to direct their efforts to the political arena are not harmful to international competitiveness.
>
> Perhaps the key implication of our findings is that trade unions do not necessarily have to wage a defensive campaign against those who would weaken them in the name of international competitiveness. On the other hand, trade unionists and their leaders, especially in those countries where the labour movement is decentralized, must come to terms with an unpleasant fact: trade union activity, that is, primarily economic and fragmented, does seem to damage competitiveness. For labour movements that find themselves in this situation, a long and hard self-appraisal should be made of their organizational structures and political role.[27]

What this means, therefore, is that in Canada, where collective bargaining is fragmented and carried out at local levels, the trade-union movement will have to make a decision with respect to its long-term goals and the manner of achieving them. The trade-union movement cannot simply become defensive and view all undertakings by either business or government, separately or in concert, as actions to be criticized rather than joined in a concrete and constructive way. The Canadian industrial-relations system, as detailed by Alton Craig, in which the various actors — labour, management and government — attempt to achieve their own particular goals in light of a series of economic, political, legal and societal pressures, is still a viable framework.[28] However, the self-interest of trade-union members and local unions will have to be re-examined in light of the demands made by the labour market and by a growing global competitiveness challenge, if trade unions, as they are now known, are to survive the 1990s.

This may dictate a shift in the way in which unions and managements approach one another, either at the bargaining table or in terms of looking at a company or industry, or indeed, broader still, a sector of the economy.

The trade-union movement does not have to retreat, however; the managerial side of the negotiating equation cannot also insist on having its own way in terms of direction and control. Both parties will have to share in the decision making and this will require an enhanced spirit of co-operation that has not yet been seen at the local level.

What will be needed over the next few years is renewed effort. In some cases what will be needed are discussions of a broad scope, combined with a willingness to include some form of security for workers whose jobs will change, and may even be lost. At the same time, initiatives in training and education will be needed to prepare the new, young labour force entrants for a labour market that is vastly different from the one in which the trade unions of today began.

Notes

1. John T. Dunlop, *Industrial Relations Systems* (New York: Holt Rinehart and Winston, 1958).
2. Alton J. Craig, *The System of Industrial Relations in Canada* (Scarborough, Ont.: Prentice-Hall, 1990), chapter 1.
3. *Directory of Labour Organizations in Canada, 1992–93*, Labour Canada.
4. Mary Lou Coates et al., *The Current Industrial Relations Scene in Canada* (Kingston, Ont.: Queen's University, Industrial Relations Centre, 1989), 33–34.
5. Ibid., 24.
6. Ibid., 27.
7. Corporations and Labour Unions Returns Act (CALURA), Statistics Canada, 1991.
8. Coates, 37.
9. R.B. Freeman and J.L. Medoff, *What Do Unions Do?* (New York: Basic Books, 1984), chapter 15.
10. Ibid.
11. Coates, *Industrial Relations Scene*, 21.
12. Roy J. Adams, "Industrial Relations in Europe and North America," *Union-Management Relations in Canada* (Don Mills, Ont.: Addison-Wesley, 1982), 461.
13. See Craig, *Industrial Relations*, chapter 1.
14. P. Kumar et al., *Canadian Labour Relations: An Information Manual* (Kingston, Ont.: Queen's University, 1991), 349.
15. Ibid., 225.
16. Ibid., 337.
17. Ibid., 346.
18. Ibid., 347.
19. Ibid., 348.
20. Freeman and Medoff, 192.
21. P. Kumar, "Labour Market Adjustment Issues in Canada: An Industrial Relations Perspective," in *Proceedings of the 28th Conference of the Canadian Industrial Relations Association, 1991.*

22. G. Betcherman, "The Recent Labour Market Policy Debate in Canada," in *Proceedings of the 28th Conference of the Canadian Industrial Relations Association, 1991.*
23. Ibid., 231.
24. B. Bemmels and Y. Reshef, "Manufacturing Employees and Technological Change," in *Proceedings of the 26th Conference of the Canadian Industrial Relations Association, 1989*, 205.
25. Ibid., 207.
26. M. Serediak, "Employee Participation in the Implementation of Technological Change: A Three Country Comparison," in *Proceedings of the 26th Conference of the Canadian Industrial Relations Association, 1989*, 234.
27. A. Giles and B. Sharma, "Unions, Strikes and International Competitiveness: A Ten Country Comparison," in *Proceedings of the 28th Conference the Canadian Industrial Relations Association, 1991*, 51.
28. Craig, *Industrial Relations.*

QUESTIONS FOR DISCUSSION

1. What are the types and sizes of unions operating in Canada? Which are growing and which are declining? Will the labour movement grow and, if so, where will the new growth come from?
2. Outline the stages through which labour and management proceed before a strike/lockout decision is made. What weaknesses, if any, do you see in this process? Which side, if any, has the advantage?
3. Do the European and American roots of the Canadian Labour movement still influence how it operates today? In what ways?
4. What are the objectives and the components of Labour Relations Policy? Is it more than just the Labour Relations Act? Can this policy be shaped to improve a jurisdiction's international competitiveness and whether it is perceived as a place in which to invest?
5. Are there any significant Canada-U.S. labour relations differences? If so, do they threaten the Free Trade Agreement in any way? How do your answers differ for Mexico?
6. Should labour be more or less active in Canadian politics? What are the benefits and costs of your beliefs?
7. The Japanese have an incentive for the unemployed to become reemployed as fast as possible. They pay a reemployment bonus (one third to one half of the remaining entitlement) to those who start a new job within the first half of the period of unemployment insurance entitlement. Why do you think there are not similar programs in Canada?
8. To adjust to the recession, Japanese companies have begun deep staff cuts, affecting mostly women. The move is justified because, in the words of one spokesman, "...they tend to quit sooner anyway." Although Japan has an equal employment law, it tends not to be enforced. Men are reassigned and retrained; women are just let go.

(Toronto Star, July 20, 1992) Does this practice give Japanese industry an unfair advantage? Why could it not happen in Canada?

9. The Ontario NDP government is seeking jurisdiction in the constitutional debates over job training. Unions oppose this move stating that Canada needs a national job retraining program, not ten provincial ones, and that it threatens Canada's unemployment insurance program. The federal government now funds retraining out of unemployment insurance funds, so that transferring training responsibility to the provinces would allow the federal government to downsize, and perhaps even exit one of Canada's most important social programs. Since business funds part of the UIC premiums, it favours Ottawa's exit. What is your view? Give full support for your stated preference.

Graeme McKechnie has mediated and arbitrated labour disputes in the public and private sectors since 1975. He is a co-author of the 1973 book, ***Federalism and Policy Development: The Case for Adult Occupational Training in Ontario****. Graeme McKechnie is Associate Professor of Economics at York University, Co-ordinator of the Business and Economics program in York's Faculty of Arts, and Area Co-ordinator of Organizational Behaviour and Industrial Relations at the Faculty of Administrative Studies.*

The Financial Services Industry

PETER A.T. CAMPBELL

The financial services industry performs three basic economic functions. First, it provides the payments mechanism for the economy. By interfacing between buyers and sellers of real goods and services, the industry lubricates and depersonalizes economic transactions. At its most primitive, the payment structure mechanism is a barter system. At the other extreme, it is a sophisticated system of electronic funds transfer, known as Interac. The industry is an integral part of the electronic highway.

Second, the industry facilitates the saving and investment process, providing a link between those with excess funds and those who have a need for funds. By creating acceptable substitutes for legal tender, the industry provides a mechanism for converting savings into bricks, mortar, processes, distribution systems, etc. This is referred to as the capital formation process. An efficient financial sector, such as the Canadian one, automates the saving and investment process.

Third, the financial industry provides the pricing mechanism for capital — both existing and newly created financial assets. This price mechanism allocates capital based on relative rates of return, subject to certain other factors such as risk, liquidity and time horizon.

Figure 1 provides a snapshot of the size of the financial services industry by institution and by number of establishments in 1965 and 1993–94.

This paper assesses the performance of the Canadian financial services industry. Strategically, the industry is part of the new economy; it is characterized by globalization and heavy reliance on communications, telecommunications and technology. Moveover, it is being rapidly transformed into one of the most innovative, technologically-advanced and globally-competitive Canadian industries. Hence, an appreciation of the industry's characteristics, the basics of its operations and an awareness of the events that have shaped its evolution are prerequisites to beginning the assessment.

The topics discussed in this paper include the process of financial intermediation, the formation of prices, the range of financial instruments and global and national institutions. Once these topics are presented, the discussion then turns to the structure of the industry, the impact of regulation, how the industry has performed recently and where it stands today.

FIGURE 1
Size of Financial Services Industry

	Assets ($Billions)		*Establishments*	
	1965	*1993–94*	*1965*	*1993–94*
Chartered Banks — Schedule I	23.4	522.3	8	7
Chartered Banks — Schedule II	0.0	62.7	0	55
Credit Unions	2.6	113.7	4128*	2586
Investment Dealers	0.6	6.8	na	151
Life Insurance	12.0	156.1	146	148
Mutual Funds	1.6	132.0	39	681
Property & Casualty Insurance	1.8	36.4	350	234
Trust Companies	3.5	83.5	78	60
Trusteed Pension Funds	6.6	234.0	3778*	3397

* Note these figures are for 1973, not 1965.

FUNDAMENTAL CONCEPTS AND CHARACTERISTICS

Some Basic Concepts

Before embarking on an in-depth assessment of the Canadian financial services sector, a brief discussion of a few of the concepts according to which industry functions, is in order.

First of all, the financial industry functions according to a unique concept of time. Essentially, all values are present values. Yields in the fixed income markets, price-to-earnings ratios in equity markets, capitalization rates in real estate and rates of return on real investment projects are all valued on a "time-now" basis. This imparts a sense of immediacy and urgency to the élan of the financial industry.

The concept of the franchise is also very important to constituent parts of the Canadian financial industry. A franchise holds forth the promise of delivering excellence on a consistent basis — colloquially, this is known as the "confidence-factor." If a financial organization does not enjoy the confidence of the public, either because it is not well known or because of its performance, then the survival of that organization is threatened.

The necessity for the shotgun marriage of the Royal Trust Company with the Royal Bank in 1993–94 resulted from a severe deterioration in the confidence factor in the trust company. The absorption of the Central Guaranty Trust Company in 1992 by the Toronto Dominion Bank is another case in point.

Industry Characteristics

The financial industry is both dynamically innovative and imitative. At its core are highly skilled, computer-oriented knowledge workers. They work as a close-knit entrepreneurial cluster, almost akin to a cottage industry. From these clusters emerge a never-ending stream of financial innovations: new twists on old financing instruments, or even entirely new instruments. These new products are then immediately replicated by competing entrepreneurial clusters. What was new yesterday becomes common practice today.

Because the industry is computer dominated, there is constant need to convert procedures and instruments into simplified, almost commodity-like products. The driving force is cost reduction. Once systems are in place, their costs "flatten out"; marginal costs can often be eliminated. The difference between processing a ten-dollar transaction and a ten billion-dollar one for example, is negligible.

The industry is entrepreneurial, performance-oriented and greedy. The high rate of innovation spawns entrepreneurship. Compensation becomes performance oriented with no upper limit. And greed pervades. Because the industry deals in money, its visible reward is more money — hence greed. Greed motivates the humblest depositor stretching to earn a higher interest rate just as it does a conglomerate giant maximizing its leverage using other people's money.

The industry is risk-oriented. There are six basic kinds of risk that need to be understood in this context. Credit risk related to the borrower's ability to pay back. Market risk involves the improvement or depreciation in the value of existing assets as a result of market forces. Liquidity risk relates to the ready disposability or marketability of existing assets. Solvency risk relates to the equity base of an organization and its ability to meet commitments. Systemic risk relates to the confidence factor in the financial system or in a sub-group within it. If confidence evaporates, then the ability to perform the economic function disappears as well.

The industry is borderless. Innovations such as currency swaps and the multi-jurisdictional financing prospectuses make national borders irrelevant. Thus, the industry is at once both globalized and globally interdependent.

The industry is highly mobile. Because of its global reach and emphasis on modern telecommunications, capital can easily seek out the most attractive investment opportunities anywhere in the world. At the same time, entrepreneurs and the knowledge workers, on whom the industry depends, themselves become very mobile.

The industry is highly volatile. The compression of time brought on by globalization and modern telecommunications means that all participants who matter are aware of the same events simultaneously. Collective response to these events generates high volatility in asset prices. The senior financial officer of an industrial corporation in Winnipeg, for example, has a desktop video monitor that informs her of events at the same moment that the capital market entrepreneur in Zurich is informed, or the banker in Frankfurt, or the foreign exchange trader in Tokyo, the trading company in Hong Kong, and so on.

Management in the industry today focuses on risk management, cost control and market share, in that order.

Power Centres

Power within the financial system as a whole is continuously shifting over the course of the economic cycle. Power sometimes relates to the market share or assets controlled by firms or institutions. Sometimes it depends on whether there is a buyers' or sellers' market. There are, however, two almost absolute sources of power in the financial system. One emerges as dominant in the inflationary zone of economic expansion: the Bank of Canada, Canada's central bank. The other tends to dominate the recession phase of the economy: the credit-rating agencies.

Through aggressive action in forcing interest rates higher, the Bank of Canada can materially control the performance of the financial sector and, in turn, the economy. A determined central bank can wield absolute power in an inflationary environment. On the other hand, when the economy is in a recession, the credit-rating agencies can wield absolute power. Placing a borrowing entity on credit watch can effectively eliminate the capacity of an organization to acquire new funding and to refinance maturing obligations.

There are two Canadian and two significant rating services in the United States: Dominion Bond Rating Service Ltd., Toronto; Canadian Bond Rating Service Inc. of Montreal; Standard & Poor's Corp. of New York; and Moody's Investor Services Inc., also of New York. Until recently, the Canadian rating services focused on Canadian ratings, and the U.S. services focused on U.S. pay issues of Canadian debt. The U.S. services now also rate Canadian debt and preferred shares and have established themselves in Canada.

Financial Intermediation

A debt obligation incurred in an economic transaction can be discharged directly by proffering the appropriate amount of legal tender. Obviously, however, when substantial sums are involved, more practical alternatives are needed. The financial services industry intermediates between transaction parties by creating acceptable substitutes for legal tender — the process of financial intermediation. There are seven main types, which are discussed below.

Payments intermediation has come to be identified with deposit-taking institutions, who confer the ability to transfer ownership of deposits through checking. Banks, trust companies, caisses populaires, credit unions and cash management accounts of securities dealers perform the payments intermediation function. These institutions perform this function so effectively that legal tender has all but become the petty cash in the economic system.

Denomination intermediation refers to the process of gathering liabilities in small lots from the general public and acquiring assets in large pieces. Almost all intermediaries offer liabilities in small denominations, but deal in wholesale or large denominations in the financial markets. In effect, the efficiency of the intermediary process enables primary securities from large borrowers to be broken into small lots.

Default risk intermediation enables the intermediary to interpose its credit rating between acquired assets and the liabilities offered to the public. The public, in effect, has an indirect claim on a portion of a portfolio. This provides diversification for the public. Mutual funds are the most aggressive marketers of this form of intermediation, but diversification is a feature of all well-run financial intermediaries.

Maturity risk intermediation refers to the preference of the majority of savers to have access to their monies on demand or short notice, while the majority of borrowers prefer longer time horizons for their liabilities. Once again, the financial intermediary interposes its credit rating between these differing lender and borrower time preferences. By relying on its fund-gathering efficiency, the intermediary bears the risk of the time differential. All deposit-taking institutions engage in this form of intermediation.

Credit-rating intermediation relates to the perception that a financial institution has superior credit-rating strength. The institution can then interpose its credit rating between primary savers and those borrowers who have a lesser credit rating than the institution itself. The institution matches the maturity or duration of its liabilities with those of its assets. Because of its superior credit rating, the cost of its liabilities is less than the return on its assets. The difference becomes profit for the institution. Most deposit-gathering institutions engage in this form of intermediation, as do pension funds and insurance companies.

Capital-value intermediation focuses on the stability of liability value in the face of volatility of asset values. Institutions that engage in this kind of intermediation offer diversification and professional management to minimize risk and thus enhance the capital value stability of their liabilities. Mutual funds are dominant in this field.

Liquidity-risk intermediation relies on the marketability of the underlying security in asset portfolios. The security for bank loans, for example, is often property or equipment, which are not easily disposable in most market settings. The bank interposes its efficiency in fund-gathering between the demand nature of its liabilities and the non-liquid nature of its assets.

The creative goal of financial intermediaries is to establish unique marketing niches for their products. The resulting product mix is normally a variant of the major forms of intermediation. In all cases, they attempt to create an acceptable alternative to legal tender as a store of value and, in many cases, an acceptable alternative to legal tender as a payment mechanism.

Price Formation

The core of the price formation process is dominated by securities dealers. Dealers buy and sell securities on behalf of clients and for their own account. The two traditional forms of market structure are over-the-counter and auction.

Over-the-counter markets involve dealers in their offices communicating with clients and competitors by telephone or electronically. The money, bond and foreign exchange markets are the principal illustrations of this market form.

An auction market is located in a specific place where dealers meet face to face and bid orally for securities. Most stock exchanges have taken this format.

Rapid advances in telecommunications technology are tending to blur the distinction between auction and over-the-counter markets. All market forms are rapidly adopting screen-trading techniques. Bids and offers are recorded systematically in video-based communication networks; and business is initiated on the basis of information received via the telecommunications network.

The price structure in the Canadian financial sector is transmitted to, and influenced by, the global financial sector through a process known as "passing the book." Major firms deal in several different countries. As normal business hours come to a close in one time zone, the firm's securities position, or "book," are sometimes passed on to an affiliate in another time zone, usually in a different country. After Canadian markets go to bed, Asian markets are becoming active in Hong Kong and Tokyo. When Tokyo is winding down, Europe is opening. North American markets open when Europe is past mid-day. Firms' positions get passed around the world during the relevant working time zones. Markets are literally never closed and are always being materially influenced by events around the globe.

The entire term structure of interest rates in readily marketable debt instruments is determined by this never-closing electronic price formation process. This price structure serves as a price leader for less marketable forms of securities such as the mortgage and loan portfolios of major lending institutions. It is through actions taken to influence the structure of the Canadian interest rates that Canada's central bank, the Bank of Canada, transmits its monetary policy.

A shorthand form of viewing the price structure in financial markets is known as the yield curve. The government bond market has maturities ranging from a few days, in the case of maturing issues, to about 30 years. If you plot the yields on these maturities on a graph, with the vertical axis representing yield and the horizontal axis representing remaining term to maturity, the pattern that emerges is known as the yield curve. This pattern is used as a proxy for the price formation process in the entire capital market.

The government bond market is viewed as being a sufficient proxy since the credit of the federal government is considered the prime credit in the system. Because the federal government has the sovereign right to print legal tender, it is not possible for the government to fail to meet a maturing obligation in its own currency.

The value of all other credits in the system is based on a spread above the government credit. These spreads are determined by the relative creditworthiness of the borrowing entities and are examined and recorded publicly by credit-rating agencies. These spreads from the government credit narrow and widen as the fortunes of the entities improve or deteriorate over time. Because these relative credit spreads relate to Government of Canada yields, movement in government yields are automatically transmitted to non-government yields, reinforcing the usefulness of the proxy value of the government market.

Values in the stock market are determined by myriad microeconomic factors. Unlike bonds, stocks have no maturity. Historically, equities have yielded in the vicinity of 12 per cent, assuming that all dividends are reinvested and that a representative basket of companies is reflected in the sample. In effect, this 12 per cent return becomes a benchmark yield for the latest maturity item in the yield curve.

The disciplines of economics and finance contain many theories to explain both the shape of the yield curve and its height. Among the more prominent of these are the loanable funds (supply and demand) theory, the real interest rate theory, the liquidity preference theory, market segmentation and expectations theory. Each of these theories provides a partial explanation of what goes on in the real world.

The yield curve is a convenient way of describing price transmission effects among both market-determined and administered prices, or between the two, within a capital market — or between two different national capital markets.

For transactions between national capital markets, the foreign exchange market becomes an important vehicle for transmitting price influences.

Cross-border financial transactions are served by an efficient foreign-exchange market that has market depth in both spot (now) and forward (future) contracts. The existence of this foreign exchange market is prerequisite to an integrated global financial sector.

FINANCIAL INSTRUMENTS

Intermediation opportunities and pricing mechanisms shape and value many financial instruments. Financial markets involve three basic kinds of instruments for transferring purchasing power: debt, equity and foreign exchange. Debt instruments are promises to pay. Equity instruments represent ownership. Foreign exchange facilitates cross-border economic activity by transferring purchasing power from one currency to another.

Innovation in the financial services industry creates a wide variety of financing forms within each of these instrument groups. There are also hybrid forms that span groups, and synthetic instruments (called derivative securities) based on widely-recognized industry benchmarks such as stock indexes.

FINANCIAL INSTITUTIONS

Institutions structure financial dealings in any society. There are four sets of financial institutions that play prominent roles in the financial services industry: public institutions, balance-sheet-dominated private-sector organizations, service-function-dominant private-sector firms and various institutes representing segments of the financial sector.

Public Institutions

The principal public institutions are the Bank of Canada, the Bank for International Settlements (BIS), the International Monetary Fund (IMF) and the World Bank. Additional special-function organizations play important roles in their fields: the Canada Mortgage and Housing Corporation (CMHC) provides guarantees and credit in the housing field; the Farm Credit Corporation (FCC) supports the agricultural industry; the Export Development Corporation (EDC) provides guarantees and credits in the export field; and the Federal Business Development Bank (FBDB) provides assistance to small and medium-size businesses.

The Bank of Canada is the source of legal tender in the system and provides ultimate liquidity as the lender of last resort to the banks. The BIS, located in Basel, Switzerland, was originally established to manage war reparations payments following the First World War. It has evolved into a truly international regulatory agency focusing on the capital adequacy of banks that operate internationally.

As the Second World War was winding down, world opinion was optimistic that international order could be established without the grievous economic and political wrangling that characterized the depressed 1930s. The United Nations was established as a forum to resolve political disputes. The General Agreement on Tariffs and Trade (GATT) was set in process to promote the reduction and eventual abolition of restrictive trade barriers among nations. What has come to be known as the World Bank was established to assist in closing the wealth gap between the rich and poor nations. The IMF was established to bring stability to currency markets.

The IMF system was known as the gold-exchange standard. The price of gold was pegged in terms of the U.S. dollar. All other currencies then established values in terms of the U.S. dollar, and all countries agreed to intervene in their currency markets to maintain these values. The IMF provided credits and advice to countries experiencing balance-of-payment difficulties that threatened their ability to maintain the value of their currency.

The gold-exchange standard lasted until the early 1970s, when the United States found it beyond its political will and economic capacity to serve as the centrepiece of the world monetary system. Since that time, world currencies have operated on what has come to be known as a floating currency system. The values of each currency is now determined by market forces, not by government fiat.

Thus the IMF's original role no longer exists. The organization carries on, however, serving as a technical bureaucracy that provides assistance when called upon by international agencies and various governments. The World Bank is still active in international development.

Private Sector Organizations

Financial institutions in the private sector are divided into those that are balance-sheet-dominated and those that are service-function dominant. The first group includes deposit-taking institutions, insurance companies, pension funds and mutual funds. Service-function-dominant organizations include actuarial advisors, financial planners, financial holding companies, investment counsellors, merchant banks, securities dealers and venture-capital companies.

Industry Associations

Each major financial-service industry subgroup has established an industry association or organization. The purpose of these associations is to develop educational programs for industry members; to set standards for business conduct, to serve as a lobby group to further the collective interests of its members and, in some cases, to regulate member activities.

THE STRUCTURE OF THE INDUSTRY

The organization of the financial services industry has always been shaped by regulation. In general, the object of regulation has been to achieve allocation, operational and social efficiency. Allocation efficiency involves allocating financial resources to the areas of highest expected economic rate of return. Operational efficiency means delivering financial services at the lowest possible cost. Social efficiency refers to maintaining the confidence factor in the system, ensuring competition and maximizing the industry's accessibility to the general public.

A number of other, more specific, objectives have always influenced the formulation of public policy. Consumer protection through full, true and plain disclosure of all material facts has been the watchword of provincial securities commissions. To enhance the smooth functioning of the payments mechanism and provide an effective milieu through which monetary policy can be implemented, is also important to many. Ensuring the stability of financial institutions, while at the same time fostering active competition among them, is regarded as a high priority. Concern over undue concentration of economic power is never far from political attention. Additional social goals, such as fostering housing or supporting the farming industry, often intrude into the regulatory debate.

A final goal of financial service regulation is harmonization — a uniquely Canadian phenomenon. Because some areas fall under federal jurisdiction, others are a provincial responsibility and still others are matters of overlapping responsibility between federal and provincial jurisdictions, it is crucial that the various governments harmonize their activities. This is necessary, on the one hand, to minimize bureaucratic strangulation of the entities being regulated and on the other, to prevent problems from "slipping between the cracks" when one authority falsely assumes that the other is on top of the situation.

The Four-Pillar System

Until the middle of the 1980s, the modern Canadian regulatory system was known as the four-pillar system. The "four pillars" of the financial services industry were as follows: the banks, whose primary responsibility it was to administer the payments mechanism; the trust companies, whose primary responsibility was the fiduciary business — the discretionary management of other people's money; the insurance industry, whose business was the protection of life, health and property; and the security dealers, who performed both the underwriting function — marrying up primary savers with borrowers — and the market-making function in outstanding financial claims. Banks were the exclusive preserve of federal regulation, and security dealers were provincial. Trust and insurance companies could be either provincial or federal, depending on how they were incorporated.

Regulation of the four-pillar system was designed to foster competition within each pillar, but not among them. At the same time, there was a very strong bias against foreign ownership and control where it did not previously exist.

The separation of the pillars resulted from a blend of three forces. Separation meant a minimum of conflict of interest. At the same time, undue concentration of economic power was limited. Separation was also a function of effective lobbying by the three non-bank pillars. The bias against foreign ownership was both a function of the notion of nationalistic preservation of key industries, and the product of effective lobbying.

The four-pillar system was in place for roughly 25 years. Through the 1980s, however, events and public debate successfully challenged the validity of the system. By the early 1990s, it had been swept aside and broadly-based new legislation had been set in place to regulate the financial industry.

The Transformation of the Four-Pillar System

Many themes dominated public debate about financial services in the 1980s. Some were related to weaknesses in the four-pillar system itself, some to the political clout of those demanding change, and some to the revolution in telecommunications technology.

The four-pillar system did not adjust adequately to the development of new centres of power in the financial system. These included pension funds, investment counsellors, mutual funds and financial planners. These subgroups thrived almost without reference to the system. At the same time, the role of trust companies changed dramatically. Initially, their fiduciary business drove their fortunes. Later, their deposit-taking business came to dominate. In effect, the trust-company industry became just as expert in administering the payments mechanism efficiently as the banks.

Finally, through a process known as "securitization," the securities dealers began to strip away the prime assets of the banks, forcing them to move downmarket into lesser credits to survive. Securitization is the process of converting non-marketable financial assets into marketable assets or securities. Banks, for example, have viewed providing working capital lines of credit to strong corporations as one of their prime functions. Security dealers created markets for commercial paper — promissory notes of prime corporations — which became a perfect substitute for working capital loans at the banks. European bond markets developed a taste for high-quality corporate debt. Security dealers met this demand by encouraging corporations to finance directly in these public markets. This reduced the need for corporate term-loan facilities at the Canadian banks. Security dealers made further inroads into the loan business of the banks, by creating asset-backed securities (financial assets backed by other securities) to finance the mortgage portfolios and receivables of finance companies. The rigidities of the four-pillar system made it impossible for the banks to compete directly with the securities dealers to get their prime business back. Something had to give.

The New Regulatory Environment

As in all policy discussions, the financial-industry regulation issues debated during the 1980s, were always couched in terms of the national interest. Only by accident did the furtherance of a position happen to also advance the interests of the specific industry, subgroup or corporation supporting it. Principal among the issues discussed were the level playing-field concept, globalization, foreign ownership, commercial links, concentration and competition.

The concept of a level playing-field means organizations performing similar functions should be playing by the same set of rules. The banks argued effectively in favour of such a system. It was noted, for example, that the trust companies, through their deposit-taking operations, competed directly with the banks in administering the payments mechanism, but the banks were prohibited from operating in the fiduciary business. The securities dealers were securitizing the banks' prime assets, but the banks could not compete in the securities field in order to retain their clients' business. Through margin- and cash-management accounts, the dealers were, in effect, invading the personal loan and payment roles of the banks. The savings component of life-insurance policies competed with the deposit business of the banks. In order for the playing field to be level, the banks felt they should have direct access to the other pillars.

Overlooked in the banks' arguments were the questions of size and power. Canada's largest bank, for example, is larger than the entire life insurance industry combined.

The globalization of the financial industry meant that Canadian financial organizations were faced with tough foreign competition in every sphere of activity. Canada is a small country in global terms, and its financial institutions are, as well. In order to compete effectively on the international stage, it was argued that fewer, more powerful, financial organizations would be necessary in order to withstand foreign encroachments within Canada, and enable Canadians to compete effectively abroad. The four-pillar system was viewed as fragmenting the Canadian financial industry, leaving it vulnerable to globalized competitive pressures.

The issue of foreign ownership was debated primarily in terms of reciprocity of treatment. If Canadians wanted the freedom to establish abroad, then foreign organizations should be afforded similar treatment in Canada. Only in this way, would Canadian financial institutions be able to serve their clients abroad effectively.

Commercial links were another issue. The term refers to the commingling of ownership of financial organizations and commercial companies. Historically, commercial links were viewed as bad because they could lead to abusive self-dealing, particularly if the commercial corporation was in trouble. Initially, the debate favoured the abolition of commercial links. By the mid-1980s however, the federal government had reversed its position on this issue.

This change of heart turned on two sets of events. First, Quebec regulators were in favour of holding companies that combined strong commercial companies with full-service conglomerates. This was part of Quebec's corporatist élan. The federal government was extremely reluctant to take on Quebec in this issue, given the fragility of Quebec's position in Confederation at the time. Second, through the financial holding company technique, a number of major corporate groupings had already been formed with a strong flavour of commercial linkage. For example, the three largest trust companies were parts of holding-company empires. These organizations lobbied effectively for the right to retain their commercial links. They argued that the linkage strengthened the ability of the financial service arm to meet foreign competition, reinforced their capital base, created economies of scale in management expertise and enhanced shareholder values.

In the end, the negative implications of the potential concentration that would ensue from eliminating the four pillars, gave way to the perceived need for concentration **now** in order to meet international competition head on.

The four-pillar system crumbled in 1986 when ownership of securities dealers was thrown open. By the end of 1991, legislation was in place for promulgation in the middle of the following year, that would reregulate the rest of the financial system.

The new system of regulation was presented as having a consumer focus. By eliminating the four pillars, competition would be enhanced. Greater competition meant that financial services would be delivered to consumers at lower cost. Consumer protection would be strengthened by the establishment of a new federal regulatory agency — the Office of the Superintendent of Financial Institutions (OSFI). Measures were included to encourage widely-held ownership of financial organizations. And the federal government made harmonization of regulation between the federal regulatory agency and its provincial counterparts, an essential objective.

The key change between the new system and the four-pillar system was dropping the restrictions on ownership of more than one pillar by one firm. Cross-pillar diversification was now allowed.

The potential for conflicts of interest arising from commercial links was dealt with by banning non-arm's length transactions, establishing conduct review committees for permitted transactions and requiring that certain transactions obtain prior approval from the OSFI.

Two peculiarities remain. Banks are not permitted in the auto-leasing business, nor are they able to sell insurance through their branch systems. These anomalies are a tribute to the grass-roots political clout of automobile dealers and independent insurance agents across the nation. The upshot of financial reregulation is that any financial organization can now be in anyone else's business. Five of the six major banks bought controlling interest in large securities firms almost immediately, in order to staunch the securitization haemorrhaging.

The collapse of the commercial real-estate market from 1990 on, fed into a serious deterioration of asset values in the portfolios of all financial intermediaries. What began as serious defaults in the development industry — Campeau Corporation, Olympia & York — quickly spread to financial intermediaries in the trust company field — Standard Trust, Central Trust, First City Trust, and in the insurance field — Les Coopérants and Sovereign Life.

The sorting out of other intermediaries, weakened by deterioration in the real-estate-asset class, provided strong organizations with remarkable opportunities for cherry picking and accelerating growth of the strong at the expense of the weak. In the insurance field, Great West Life picked up Confederation Life and North American Life picked up First City Trust. The Royal Bank acquired Royal Trust. The Bank of Nova Scotia acquired Montreal Trust and the Toronto Dominion Bank absorbed Central Trust.

The impact of reregulation of the financial-services industry has been swift and brutal in the face of the collapse of the real-estate-asset class. The upshot is a concentration of economic power in the hands of the Canadian banks as they become owners and marketers of the full range of financial services.

SAFETY NETS

In many respects the real test of the viability of a financial system is how it performs when the chips are down, particularly during a prolonged recession or when the system goes into shock for some reason. When a specific financial institution gets into trouble from time to time, only that institution must go under, not the whole class of organizations. When the confidence factor evaporates for a particular institution, leading to its demise, then how the financial system limits damage control to that organization, isolating it from the system as a whole, is a critical test of the system.

Since World War II, the Canadian system has experienced a number of recessions and financial failures. The recessions of 1981–83 and 1989–92 provided the greatest challenges to the system. The two major shocks — the oil crisis in the mid-1970s when the Organization of Petroleum Exporting Countries (OPEC) raised the price of energy sharply and the stock market meltdown in October 1987 — were taken in stride by the financial system. In addition, structural change in the relative clout of major trading nations — resulting in massive currency realignments and significant shifts from creditor to debtor nation status — have also been readily absorbed and facilitated by the financial system.

Each recession, each shock and each fundamental realignment of economic power, teaches the financial sector more about how to deal with such events, while, at the same time, preserving and improving the performance of the industry's essential functions. In the face of such adversity, the Canadian financial sector has developed five clear safety nets: a central bank sensitive to systemic issues; deposit insurance; protection for securities investors; insurance within the insurance industry itself; and regulatory intervention.

Each of these is discussed in turn below. It should be noted, however, that the system is constantly in flux; any analysis of these safety nets is therefore a shot at a moving target.

The Central Bank

The ethos of central banking has historically been acting as a lender of last resort to the banking system. Traditionally, banking systems based on a fractional reserve system have been subject to periodic crises of confidence — known as runs on the banks — where depositors want instant conversion of their deposits to legal tender. So long as the central bank has the authority to create legal tender and is willing to provide unlimited amounts to a bank experiencing a deposit run, then the central bank is said to be performing the lender-of-last-resort function.

In a financial system that is highly integrated, where prices are very sensitive to changes in the yield curve, the central bank's lender-of-last-resort function gets extended throughout the financial sector at a time of crisis or shock, merely by operating as the liquidity base of the banking system. When a central bank operates in this manner, it is said to be providing systemic relief, unrelated to whatever the prevailing monetary policy of the day might happen to be. When confidence in global equity markets evaporated in October 1987, leading to massive price changes and gaps in market continuity, Canada's central bank moved very quickly to liquify the base of the financial sector so as to provide a cushion to the system. Short-term interest rates fell sharply, confidence returned, equity markets stabilized and the Bank of Canada went back to whatever it was doing before. Its swift and decisive action provided systemic relief to the entire financial sector.

Deposit Insurance

Deposit insurance in Canada is provided and funded by all deposit-taking institutions and is administered by the Canada Deposit Insurance Corporation (CDIC). The genesis of deposit insurance is the grass-roots political idea that the "little guy" should be protected from big financial interests. The present ceiling in deposit insurance is $60,000, depending on how the ownership of the deposits is structured.

The economic impact of deposit insurance has a somewhat perverse aspect known as the "moral hazard" problem. In effect, deposit insurance nationalizes the liability side of the deposit-taking institutions, but is silent on the prudent use of deposits by those institutions. The higher the insurance limit, the more open to abuse the system becomes. A depositor who is protected by insurance, for example, is indifferent to the quality of the institution to which she lends. Thus, relative price becomes the only guideline. Weak financial organizations that offer deposit insurance, need only pitch their interest rates slightly above the prevailing market in order to attract funds. In effect, the existence of deposit insurance presupposes a strong regulatory presence. The higher the deposit-insurance ceiling, the greater the need for effective surveillance by regulatory authorities.

In the early 1980s in the United States, the insurable deposit ceiling was raised to $100,000, while the prevailing legislative ethic was for less regulation. The combination attracted a plethora of unscrupulous buccaneers who hid behind the insurance ceiling on the liability side of their operation and committed grand larceny on the asset side. What has come to be known as the bailout of the savings and loan industry, is estimated to have cost U.S. taxpayers $500-billion.

Protection for Securities Investors

The Canadian Investor Protection Fund (CIPF) provides insurance against losses incurred against funds and securities left in safekeeping with securities dealers. The insurance limit is $500,000, which some firms increase by way of additional private insurance, to more than $1-million. The CIPF provides industry surveillance and undertakes executive action when necessary under the authority of its board of directors, which includes both industry and public representation.

Insurance for the Insurers

The insurance industry provides consumer protection through two compensation entities — one for life and health insurance companies, and one for fire and casualty — which are together known colloquially as CompCorp. The insurance limit is $60,000.

Three Kinds of Protection Compared

The three insurance entities discussed above — the CDIC, the CIPF and CompCorp — are quite different. CompCorp operates on the "insurer is first out" principle. Insurance claims are paid up to the insurance limit in the event of failure, but if upon subsequent litigation, funds become available, CompCorp stands first in line to recapture what is paid out. Because the CIPF insures losses, it is the last out in the event of subsequent litigation. The CDIC shares pro rata on subsequent recoveries with the insured.

Unlike the CIPF, where regulatory authority and protection responsibility are in one pair of hands, the CDIC has a split personality. Regulatory authority is vested in the OSFI, in the case of federal organizations, and in various provincial ministries, in the case of provincially-incorporated ones; the insurance function is a separate entity. The CDIC thus has responsibility but no authority.

This separation of authority and responsibility is a faulty principle. If the regulatory authority is not responsible for paying the damage if things go wrong, then there is no sense of an urgent need to make certain things go right. At the same time, without a sense of urgency, regulators tend to overlook the needs of uninsured creditors and contributor of capital. Given deposit insurance, the regulators should only need to focus their attention on the other elements of the balance sheet.

Regulatory Agencies

The final safety net consists of the enabling legislation governing each financial organization and the power provided to the regulators under these acts. If the regulators are alert and do their jobs well, then their surveillance activities serve as an early warning system within the financial sector. Arrayed against their efforts, however, are powerful legal and accounting brains acting on behalf of financial entities, attempting to minimize the discretion of the regulators. On balance, this creative tension is a positive force.

The Safety Nets in Action

The 1981–83 recession led to the failure of regional banks, sideswiped some institutions that relied on interest-sensitive wholesale deposits rather than stable, service-related retail deposits, threatened the fire and casualty industry, and flushed out some dubious trust company activities. This set the stage for the entire reregulation debate of the 1980s. It led to the establishment of the OSFI, which consolidated the federal regulatory powers in one set of hands, and to provincial regulators having a say in the regulation of any non-bank financial organization carrying out business in that province. While the CDIC has been around since the 1960s, the CIPF, in its present form, and CompCorp, are products of the 1990s. In a real sense, they are a response to the perceived need for safety nets to strengthen and ensure the smooth functioning of the financial services industry.

The 1989–92 recession also flushed out many significant failures throughout the financial sector. Each of the five safety nets has been called into action; the system remains intact. The essential functions performed by the financial services industry continue in place.

AN ASSESSMENT OF THE CANADIAN FINANCIAL SERVICES INDUSTRY

An assessment of the strengths and wellnesses of the Canadian financial services industry and of the opportunities and threats it faces, tends to be a moving target because of the rapid pace of change that characterizes the industry.

Strengths

The strengths of the Canadian financial sector include the following: a nationwide branch-banking system; a successful conversion from an establishment mentality to a meritocracy of professionals; a number of thriving, entrepreneurial, cluster-style cottage industries; and an ability to adjust rapidly to fundamental changes in the economic environment.

Stable Branch System Since Confederation, the Canadian banking system has operated through a federally-regulated branch system, which grew nationwide as the country developed. The branch system provided geographic diversification for both its deposit base and its loan opportunities. This diversification reduced the system's vulnerability to regional-economic problems.

The stability of a national banking system contrasts with the vulnerability of regional banks and a system of unit or state banking, such as exists in the United States. In Canada, regional banks come and go, usually being blown away by the regional concentration of their assets. This was the experience of Alberta banks in the mid-1980s when the ill-conceived National Energy Policy demolished the energy business and the value of its real-estate infrastructure. In the United States, the absence of a national banking system rendered the entire system extremely vulnerable to recession, particularly the weak real-estate-asset class.

Meritocracy Until the past decade or so, the financial services industry was establishmentarian. The owners worked in close networks, provided employment for their own and hired a few "worker bees" to execute the transactions consummated on the golf course or in the clubs. Business was dominated by relationship management, not by performance.

As the seventies became the eighties, the pace of business accelerated, and volatility and risk came to dominate financial markets: the need for professionalism and performance rapidly overtook established connections. Establishment networks were replaced by desktop video monitors for keeping financial officers up to speed on all markets and relevant news events. The best deal for the corporation, whatever its source, became paramount — not dealing with people one dealt with previously.

Entrepreneurial Spirit The rapid emergence of the performance cult within the financial sector created thriving entrepreneurial clusters within many organizations. These either won authority and a piece of the action from the establishment owners, or broke away and set up their own firms. The rapid emergence of the investment-counselling industry out of the fiduciary business of the trust companies, is a spectacular illustration of such a success from the early 1980s, as is the explosive growth of the mutual fund industry in the 1990s.

In a few short years, the ethos of the financial services industry went from "What have we done together in the past?" to "What can you do for me today?"

This entrepreneurial and innovative ethos is self-reinforcing, and has accelerated the pace of change in the industry. It has transformed the competitive instincts of large financial organizations, and laid the groundwork for continuous renewal. At the same time, it has become the source of new firms and new industry subgroups, which serve as a counterweight to the dangers of the economic concentration that could result from the reregulation of the financial industry.

Rapid Adjustment The ability of both the Canadian and the world financial industries to adjust rapidly to economic change, and even to facilitate it, is a profound strength. The collapse in the early 1970s of the Bretton Woods agreement which had created the IMF and the U.S.-dollar-based gold-exchange standard, led to a system of freely-floating foreign-exchange rates. The financial services industry rapidly met this challenge by creating interest-rate and foreign-currency swaps that permitted economic units to manage more effectively the increased risk inherent in foreign business.

Conflict in the Middle East in the early seventies, led the OPEC countries to exert cartel-pricing on oil, driving the price from a few dollars, to more than $30 a barrel, by the early 1980s. The balance of payments impact was to suck huge balances out of oil-importing countries and place them at the disposal of the oil exporters. Hundreds of billions of dollars were destined to pile up to the credit of the oil producers, who did not have an immediate need for funds. The international financial sector stepped in and recycled these balances away from the surplus countries to those that had a need. The Euro-markets served as the recycling milieu, the principal instruments being Euro-dollar deposits and bonds. A Euro-dollar deposit is a U.S.-dollar deposit owned by a non-resident of the United States. International banks bid for these deposits at market rates from the OPEC countries, such as Saudi Arabia and Kuwait, then reloaned the deposits to others.

The Euro-markets were truly offshore markets and were not subject to national banking or securities regulations. So long as a bank was deemed credit-worthy, funds would flow to it. There was no regulatory limit, such as a cash reserve ratio, to which the banks need adhere. In effect, the recycling process was an infinite credit deposit multiplier. The world became awash with liquidity. The explosive growth of the Euro-markets, outside any regulatory constraint, is a tribute to the efficiency of the global financial services industry.

Pursuant to the creation of this infinite credit multiplier and the rapid escalation in world energy prices, serious price inflation became a worldwide concern through the 1970s, which was ended only by co-ordinate draconian central bank interest-rate policies leading to the 1981–83 recession. Again, the financial sector played a leading role in balancing inflationary pressures against the real needs of the various economies. The price structure, or yield curve, rapidly adjusted to sustain real rates of interest, creating extremely high nominal interest rates. These high nominal rates were the focus of central banker activity designed to break the inflation psychology that had come to grip the world economy.

By the 1980s, the shift in economic power from the United States to Japan was complete from a balance-of-payments point of view. In addition to having an incredibly high internal saving rate, Japan was piling up massive current-account surpluses. Again, the global financial sector stepped in to recycle these balances. This time, the Japanese securities industry took the lead in the recycling process, emerging as the dominant force in the world capital market.

The Canadian financial sector was a key player in the development of the Euro-markets and in the techniques to mitigate interest rate and currency volatility. However, during the 1980s, as economic power shifted away from North America and managers of Canadian financial institutions became more concerned with profits than with global market shares, the role of the Canadian financial services industry on the world stage shrunk on both a relative and absolute basis.

Weaknesses

While its central strength is efficiency, in many respects the main weakness of the Canadian financial services industry is its effectiveness. The capacity of the industry to direct funds to areas of want, is awesome, but its ability to assess adequately the risks involved in its lending practices, however, is often found wanting. Three modern illustrations of this weakness have been the proliferation of Third World loans during the 1970s, the apotheosis of the leveraged buy-out along with its accomplice, the junk bond, during the 1980s, and a relaxation of credit standards with respect to the commercial real-estate business in the 1990s. A final weakness, which stems, ironically, from efficiency, is the system's ability to provide modern governments with an almost unlimited capacity for deficit financing.

Effectiveness and Risk Assessment When they were recycling the OPEC balances in the 1970s, the international banks found a very willing user of these funds: the governments of Third World countries, either directly in their own names, or through the intermediation of the World Bank and regional development banks. For a dangerous moment in history, the rationale for these massive loans was that sovereign powers were good credit risks. After all, these loans were backed by the country's assets.

The global financial system made the same mistake it had made at the end of the First World War when it insisted on reparations payments from Germany, noting that the real-estate value of Berlin alone far exceeded the value of the required payments. A fixed asset is one thing, and cash flow is another, and the availability of foreign exchange to service foreign debt is yet another. At the same time, many of the governments to whom the bankers lent, did not have any legitimacy beyond the power of the prevailing whim of the military establishment. The business ethics of these cabals were suspect at best.

The upshot of the massive infusion of liquidity into the Third World from the infinite credit multiplier of the Euro-markets, was that the income from the investments these governments made was inadequate to service their debts. What income there was could not be converted from domestic currency to strong, internationally-acceptable currencies, because of inadequate balance-of-payment flows. The house of cards collapsed in the early 1980s, starting with Mexico. The international banks had to take very large write-downs on their balance sheets and severe hits on their earnings statements to reflect the reality of sovereign government default.

Although default is a reality, it is not a word commonly used in the financial service industry. Loans "experience temporary moratoriums." "Creative creditor/debtor/international agency discussions" get held. Loans are "rescheduled." Loan payments are "suspended with clawbacks," — that is, when you can pay, you will. And so on.

All but one of the major Canadian banks was caught in the game of internationally-syndicated loans to sovereign governments. A tight-fisted approach by the OSFI has enforced appropriate write-downs of these losses in the order of billions of dollars.

A leveraged buy-out occurs when one company acquires another by using debt rather than equity financing. The more debt involved in relation to equity, the more the transaction is said to be leveraged.

During the 1980s in the United States, it became common to use less-than-investment-grade debt to finance mergers and acquisitions. Investment-grade debt is graded by credit-rating agencies as to the probability of the instrument meeting its ongoing interest or debt-service payments, and ultimately repaying the debt at maturity. Less-than-investment-grade debt is that which is not rated by the agencies. This form of debt is known colloquially as "junk bonds."

The rationale for acquiring junk bonds had two elements. First, junk bonds had a higher yield than investment-grade debt. Second, junk bonds as a class had a small failure rate historically. The excess yield on junk bonds more than made up for the failure rate. Therefore, a broadly based portfolio of junk bonds enhanced the yield of an investor's portfolio.

Corporate asset value inflation was the story of the 1980s. The use of junk bonds as a financing vehicle gave effect to the ambitions of corporate raiders in the mergers and acquisitions field. Financial engineering became the dominant theme of American business and attracted the best brains in the country into the related investment banking and legal fields.

The ease with which this process was financed indicates the efficiency of the industry. The magnitude of the entrepreneurial rewards that were being achieved attracted fraudulent practices. The major acquisitions in the U.S. retailing field by Canadian real-estate developer Robert Campeau, burst the bubble of junk-bond unreality. The resulting asset deflation now threatens the existence of major segments of the U.S. savings and loan industry, the life insurance industry and significant portions of the commercial banking system. These were all major players in the junk-bond business, either as end buyers or as interim financiers involved prior to junk-bond-funding take-out. The courts have dispatched the founder of the junk-bond market and many other key players in the game to significant jail terms. The other weaknesses in the financial services industry pale in significance before the excesses of infinite credit multipliers running amok without the checks and balances of adequate risk management.

Deficit Financing in Government The efficiency of the financial sector has also enabled governments to finance deficits almost without limits. The continuous availability of funding somewhere along the yield curve has proven to be irresistible to the political system. The ability to provide a good, service or some other freebie to an electorate now, through deficit financing, overrode any concern about who ultimately would pay; that concern, after all, is beyond the time horizon of the next election.

Insufficient Regulatory Surveillance Regulatory agencies are normally at a disadvantage in their surveillance of those being regulated, simply because the latter are compensated on an entrepreneurial basis. One tends towards inward-looking caution, while the other thrives on designing a better mousetrap and beating the system. The result is a calcification of the existing regulatory process and an inability or unwillingness to comprehend and deal with accelerating change.

Apart from the banks (which are federal) and securities (which are provincial), regulation in Canada is divided according to whether an organization is provincially or federally incorporated, or is shared between the two jurisdictions, depending on the aggressiveness of the relevant provincial ministry. On the surface, this diffusion of responsibility could be viewed as a weakness in the system. In international forums, for example, when the Securities and Exchange Commission speaks, it is clearly stating the American point of view. When Canada speaks, eleven different governments express their views.

Until recently, the international capital market was unregulated. Within the BIS, it was agreed to co-ordinate and apply capital adequacy ratios for international banks in 1992. This was an attempt to rein in the excesses of the wanton international credit multiplier.

Difficulties in Managing Entrepreneurial Clusters The successful management of performance-oriented entrepreneurial clusters is difficult in corporate settings, which emphasize conformity and efficiency. Almost by definition, entrepreneurial activity is centrifugal. It takes a remarkable corporate culture to allow entrepreneurial clusters to exist side by side with the massive standardizing force of commodification, relentlessly imposed by computer systems.

Excessive Competition The efficiency of the financial services industry has reduced profit margins, inducing rapacious loss-leader market-share competition in some arenas and leading to the relaxation of prudent practice in others. Those with deep pockets prevail in the market-share games, as was illustrated by the entry of the Japanese securities dealers into the Eurobond underwriting business to recycle Japan's large current accounts surpluses in the 1980s. Those who relax prudent lending standards eventually experience life-threatening losses such as those experienced by the international banking community with their Third World loans, and by some sectors of the Canadian trust company industry, when they shifted their focus from the residential mortgage market to the real-estate development business in the late 1980s.

Poor Risk Identification Risk identification and actions to reduce the effects of risk do not seem to be the long suit of many Canadian financial managers. The international banks failed to account for country risk. Regional banks failed to diversify or even acknowledge the risk inherent in the concentration of their assets. Failure to hedge position or market risk leaves many organizations vulnerable to the volatility of asset prices. In essence, the quality of risk management, generally speaking, appears weak throughout the financial industry.

Poor Conglomerate Ethos Finally, one of the main ideas behind financial reregulation in Canada was tested and found wanting during the 1989–92 recession. It was argued that diversification among the four pillars through the use of the conglomerate holding-company format would strengthen the financial system. Yet, the many problems that occurred, such as Central Capital, Co-opérants, First City, Olympia & York and Standard Trust — all resulted from a single basic cause. Although the strong elements in the portfolio were supposed to help the weak ones ride out storms, in fact, the weak elements dragged down the strong. In case after case, the good assets were sold to bail out the bad. In the end, only the bad assets were left — a situation that doomed many financial service firms.

Opportunities

The reregulation of the Canadian financial services industry has generated the opportunity for a significant reshaping of the business, which will challenge managers and regulators for as far ahead as one cares to look. A principal theme will be applying modern marketing techniques to the industry. Other themes include further integrating the global capital market, dealing with the new reality of location irrelevance, and creating a new international medium of exchange and standard of value to replace the U.S. dollar-based gold-exchange standard, given that Japan has chosen not to assume the mantle of international financial leadership.

Modern Marketing Techniques Applying effective marketing techniques and developing powerful distribution systems will require dramatic changes in corporate culture within the financial sector. Yet most branches of deposit-taking institutions, for example, are still dominated by the old mores. One challenge is to convert branches from transaction processors to sales outlets. Typically, about 10 per cent of the space in a branch was for customer use; the balance was used for processing, storage and staff.

In effect, the interests of the client were of low priority. Technology has eliminated the need for that 90 per cent of administrative space.

A second major marketing challenge is to either reconcile differing distribution systems operating under one roof, or commit to one form of distribution system and run with it. For example, life insurance has traditionally been marketed across the kitchen table, with the focus on customer bonding. In contrast, the imperatives of computerized systems, stress the commodity-style product lines and marketing to the masses. The wherewithal **is** in place to reconcile these seemingly incompatible distribution systems. The automated banking machine (ABM), for example, could be easily adapted to deal with commodity-style products driven by mass-marketing techniques. At the same time, specialist enclaves focusing on customer bonding have been developed to service the heterogeneous product needs of the high end of the market — known as private banking.

Clearly, the elimination of the four pillars provides the opportunity to develop cross-selling techniques among quite different product lines. Although a life-insurance salesperson is working on death and protection, while a stock salesperson is focusing on growth and wealth creation, for example, the techniques of the financial planner can reconcile these differences. How to orchestrate this cross selling becomes a key strategic question. Now that the payments mechanism function has been fully automated by ABMs, eliminating the need for clients ever to enter a financial service establishment, all other financial service product, have to be sold; they will not simply be bought. Those organizations that are most successful at matching effective marketing with the appropriate distribution system, will emerge as the winners.

Integration of the Capital Market The further integration of the global capital markets provides additional opportunities. For example, as the multi-jurisdictional prospectus becomes accepted in more jurisdictions, this process will join foreign currency swaps as another integrating force among national financial sectors.

Location Irrelevance Technology has eliminated location as a determinant in the financial services industry because ABMs can be installed anywhere, and facsimile machines and modems solve the logistics of documentation. Of even greater impact is the fact that screen trading diffuses the market-making function. In effect, there is no longer a need for a "critical mass" of skill sets to be concentrated at one location. The economic rationale for established financial centres such as London, Toronto or New York has been rendered obsolete by technology. This creates an opportunity for the financial service industry to diversify its marketing and operations bases fully throughout the entire economy.

A New Base Point: The Securities Market More by accident than by design, the U.S. government securities market appears to have become the centrepiece of the world financial system. This market has depth, breadth and resiliency. At the same time, the inexorable growth of the U.S. government's debts has made this market a growth industry. Surplus countries can come and go in the U.S. treasury market with minimal transaction costs. In effect, the treasury market has become both the base point for the global yield curve and the medium of international exchange. The U.S. treasury market thus provides the world's financial system with the opportunity for continuous flexible change.

Threats

Management Incompetence The major threat to the Canadian financial service industry is incompetent managers who cannot withstand the downdraft of a severe recession. This threat is of systemic-crisis scale. The 1989–92 recession tested the basic strength of the system, including its safety nets. Looking back, we can see that the well-managed companies such as SunLife and Canada Trust survived quite handily, while there was a weeding-out of the weaker organizations — without triggering a systemic crisis. This is the way the capitalistic system is supposed to operate over the economic cycle.

Increased Concentration The concern over concentration usually focuses on the banking system. The countervailing forces are competition within the banking system for market share; the growth of non-bank intermediaries such as pension funds, mutual funds and merchant banks; the allocation of capital to those financial intermediaries that exhibit the highest potential rate of profitable growth; and the creative centrifugal force of entrepreneurial clusters.

Powerful Foreign Intermediaries The entry of foreign organizations into the Canadian financial sector is sometimes viewed as a threat because of their sheer relative size. Major foreign securities dealers have taken a big run at the Canadian market, failed and left. Similarly, several ambitious major foreign banks have retreated, to become marginal players in most instances. Foreign successes seem to be focused on niche activity such as cross-border mergers and acquisitions, offshore financing and global fund management. In those areas where Canadian firms are active, they seem to be able to hold their own. In the life insurance field, for example, Canadian firms have a dominant share of the Canadian market and are expanding rapidly abroad, particularly in Asia.

Insufficient International Regulation The lack of effective international regulation has encouraged some international financial organizations to incorporate in "soft" jurisdictions, allowing their activities to slip between the cracks of national regulators. The 1991 fraudulent failure of a very large Third World international bank, BCCI, registered in Luxembourg and the Cayman Islands, illustrates this point. The BIS capital adequacy rules, established during 1992, should mitigate this type of threat and set the tone for international regulatory co-operation in other areas.

Foreign Ownership of Canadian Debt The growth in foreign ownership of Canadian debt has created an Achilles' heel for the Canadian financial system. The possibility that foreign firms could liquidate these holdings, or even cease to participate in new financing, threatens the value of the Canadian dollar and the structure of Canadian interest rates. Canada's vulnerability to foreign creditors poses a continuous threat to the formulation of Canadian economic policy.

THE CURRENT ENVIRONMENT

Financial historians will probably put an asterisk beside 1992 as a watershed in the evolution of the financial services industry. The promulgation in mid-year of sweeping financial reform legislation in Canada will be the focus of attention, as will the adoption of common capital adequacy standards among the international banks under the aegis of the BIS.

It is worth remembering that change does not come in discrete time capsules. The BIS agreement was in process for almost 20 years and financial reform rattled around the corridors of power for almost 10 years. What looks like a new set piece is really only a reflection of the evolutionary past, and has little to tell us about the future.

Without getting into the forecasting game, there are some additional bits and pieces that can be noted. One relates to the mopping up of the carnage of the 1989–92 recession, particularly with respect to real-estate assets. The recession created the opportunity for some banks and life-insurance companies to kickstart their entry into the trust company business through the acquisition of the franchises, technology and assets of existing but troubled companies.

The treatment of risk will continue to be the central challenge for the financial services industry. Current issues, such as access by deposit-taking institutions to federally-sponsored deposit insurance, but lack of access by life-insurance companies — or the lack of understanding of the risks involved in the derivative securities business — will continue to concern regulators and challenge management.

QUESTIONS FOR DISCUSSION

1. What role does the financial sector play in helping or hindering a country's economic growth?
2. Why was the four-pillar system a sound and effective structure to aid Canada's development? What forces led to its demise?
3. What has transformed the financial sector into a globalized industry?
4. What evidence can you provide that the financial sector is entrepreneurial and innovative?

5. The Canadian financial sector pales in international comparisons. At the peak of the late 1980s, the Tokyo securities market was one third larger than the New York Stock Exchange; the thirteen largest Japanese banks were four times larger than the fifty largest U.S. banks. One Japanese security dealer, Nomura, controlled enough capital to buy out all of the investment on Wall Street. Do scale disadvantage seriously hinder the Canadian financial sector?
6. In 1960, the Royal Bank of Canada was, in terms of assets, the 7th largest in the World. In 1987 it was 51st, moving to 44th in 1991. What explains these changes?
7. What criteria would you suggest for the regulation of Canada's domestic financial industry given its openness and its interconnections with the rest of the world?

Dr. Peter A.T. Campbell received his Ph.D. in Financial Economics from the London School of Economics (England) in 1963. He began his career in the financial services industry in 1960 at the Bank of Canada, Ottawa. Except for two years at the LSE, he remained in the financial industry until 1989. He spent 22 years at Wood Gundy Inc., involved in all aspects of finance within Canada and around the world, achieving the rank of President and CEO of Wood Gundy Holdings Inc. (New York). From 1986–1989, Dr. Campbell was Chairman, President and CEO of Midland Doherty Limited, Toronto, a national securities dealer. From 1989, Dr. Campbell has been a consultant in the financial sector, a financial columnist with the ***Financial Post, Financial Times*** *and the* ***Toronto Star****, and an entrepreneur in the industrial and commercial real-estate industry. In addition, he is presently Editorial Director of* ***Mergers and Acquisitions in Canada****, a professional journal devoted to the merchant banking industry. He lectured from 1964–74 at York University and at the University of Toronto Business School in the evening programs. He was also a visiting lecturer in the Management of Canadian Financial Institutions at York in 1990–92.*

Technology and Competitiveness: A Canadian Strategy

CHARLES J. McMILLAN

> Technological Innovation is not a priority with Canadian business executives.
>
> — the de Grandpré Report

Canada's technological lag stems from two decades of relative neglect.[1] In both basic and applied research, Canada trails behind all the advanced western countries. The result is a growing trade deficit in technology-intensive manufacturing.

Canada's fundamental challenge is to shift from a resource- to a knowledge-based economy. To many people, this transformation implies abandoning raw materials and primary industry — trading coal, oil and gas, aluminum, nickel, copper, gold, fisheries, agriculture, hydro, uranium etc. — for the new world of high technology — electronics, computers, aerospace and advanced information systems. In truth, nothing could be more unrealistic.

Canada's economic future is predicated on the very foundations of its economic history — its natural and human resources, and its infrastructure (transportation and communications), developed to commercialize them. Public opinion tends to revolve around several false contrasts:

- raw materials versus human resources
- low technology versus high technology
- domestic economy versus export economy
- primary resources versus manufacturing
- manufacturing versus service economy

Evidence from international trade statistics and from company data, clearly reveal that all the concern about these issues is seriously misplaced. Canada's problem is not its dependence on raw materials, but something much more fundamental. It is the growing dependence on undifferentiated commodities, which are sold purely on the basis of price. Canada is locked out increasingly of the high-value-added sectors of raw materials, where technology, marketing prowess, quality and labour skills combine in an organizational package to produce real wealth. This pattern of investment, management and strategy, implicit or otherwise, has left the vast bulk of Canada's resource firms still in their historic roles as hewers of wood and drawers of water.

The real debate must, therefore, centre on the difference between low- and high-value-added goods, low and high export intensity, and competitive and uncompetitive sectors and products in the international economy. At the root of all these issues is the question of technology.

Technology — The Key

Why are science and technology so important in the modern industrial economy? Traditional economics has placed technology in a black box or treated it as a residual, with the major emphasis on the mix of labour and capital inputs. In the past two decades, however, as entire industries have shifted to new "knowledge inputs", the role of technology has been identified as the leading indicator of growth and the ratio of exports over imports. For example, in a study of some 22 nations in the Organization for Economic Cooperation and Development (OECD), Dosi et al.[2] found that technological innovation, measured by patent grants received by national firms in the United States, between 1963 and 1977, was the leading determinant of whether exports exceeded imports in a national industry. Company and industry case studies clearly point out the effects of innovation: a complex, highly dynamic shift in superiority away from the United States among firms, industries and countries, as witnessed by Japanese automobiles or European radial tires and aerospace products. These shifts raise serious questions about Canada's ability to compete against aggressive foreign rivals.

International comparisons expose Canada's weak position in science and technology measured by a range of indicators. For instance, in the number of domestic patents granted to residents per 100,000 population, the number of patents filed within the country, and the number of scientists and engineers per 1,000 people in the labour force, Canada has one of the lowest ratings among industrialized nations. More tellingly, Canada's weak performance in research and development (R&D) directly relates to its future trade patterns. Compared to its global competitors, Canadian private firms rank last in company-funded R&D; only a tiny fraction undertake any R&D at all. Of the leading industrialized countries, Canada's position is least favourable, especially compared with the United States and Japan. Yet those two countries are Canada's most important trading partners, together accounting for almost 90 per cent of Canada's trade.

Canada is experiencing an increasingly negative trade balance in R&D-intensive industries. In 1980, the deficit was $4.6-billion; it rose to $7.1-billion in 1987 and $12-billion in 1991. Moreover, none of Canada's science-intensive sectors are in the traditional resource industries, where Canada supposedly has an international comparative advantage. The danger is that Canada will be caught in the middle, between the growth sectors represented by high-technology trade fostered by the United States and Japan and the low-cost sectors, increasingly dominated by Asia, where labour costs and engineering applications are key to competitive success.

Why does Canada trail so badly in science-and-technology-related competitiveness? Canada is not a poor country. It has a rich tradition of invention and discovery, from telephones to jet engines, kerosene lamps to insulin.[3] Canada spends an enormous amount of money on education; indeed, it spends considerably more per capita on it than any other advanced countries. And as an immigrant nation, Canada, like the United States, is a net recipient of a hugely rich stock of human capital from other countries, especially of talented professionals and well-educated entrepreneurs.

Three observations help answer the question why Canada lags in technological innovation. First, Canada is not well organized for science and technology co-ordination. Federal efforts are widely dispersed; central agencies compete for resources regardless of either achievement or effort; and key instruments of science policy are saddled with ambiguous mandates. Second, Canada's federal system, in which education is a provincial responsibility and economic policy is a mixed federal-provincial mandate, creates a natural tendency towards program duplication, budgetary paralysis and policy ambiguity. Politicians and bureaucrats alike find this situation more comfortable than one of strategic focus, policy co-ordination, and results-oriented implementation. And third, until recently, science and technology policy has not been a central part of the national agenda of either the federal or provincial governments, or the private sector.

The reality is that Canada lacks the dynamic "critical mass" in industry, academe or government to be a significant global player in the R&D game. Facing that reality requires a strategy, a commitment and resources (including people, money and specialized talent). Canada does not lack any of the specific elements, but strategy and commitment remain in short supply. Science and technology have received mostly lip service and none of the understanding that wealth creation warrants.

This paper examines three issues that are critical to developing the needed policies:

- the organization of Canadian science and technology
- linkages between education and the economy
- government leadership, including new mechanisms for improving science-and-technology performance

Before discussing these issues, the next section provides an overview of the new economics of science-based innovation.

THE ECONOMICS OF SCIENCE-BASED INNOVATION

Although its theoretical constructs may be remote to most people, the products of science-based innovation — from pharmaceuticals to computers, advanced materials in ski equipment, to electronics in home stereos — illustrate what is clear from empirical evidence: consumer value and quality are ever improving. Underneath these simplistic observations are some profound realities about the nature of innovation in the economic system and the role of knowledge creation and competitive advantage in firms, to be sure, but also in entire industries and countries, which can be seen as a portfolio of industries. What is behind this new way of looking at economics and competitive advantage?

The classical theory of factor endowments as the centrepiece for international comparative advantage has been challenged. Classical economics focuses on the three factors of production: land (God-given), labour (skilled and unskilled) and capital (physical as well as technological). Some countries have comparative abundance in land and natural resources (Australia, Canada, Saudi Arabia, Argentina, the United States and Russia, to cite obvious examples). But contrast their economic performance with that of resource-poor countries like Germany, Japan or Switzerland. Clearly, other factors are at work.

Anecdotal and case studies of companies and industries all point to the link between technological innovation and industrial growth. Unfortunately, theorizing and theory development in this area — in economics, business strategy and management — is still in its infancy and lacks an empirical base. A possible reason is that technological innovation occurs in a wide variety of forms: changes to products and processes, major and minor breakthroughs, linkages between public policies and industry activity etc. Discovery sets in motion fundamental changes, causing the knowledge base of a company, an industry sector, or an entire economy to be revolutionized by technology changes. Witness the impact, beginning a century ago, of the industrial revolution on a single sector: shipping. Technology radically changed the nature of construction materials and methods of propulsion from sail and wooden ships, to coal and iron ones, and now to oil, nuclear power, and steel ships.

Labour, or more generally, human capital (workers and managers), has also made a significant difference, as contrasts between otherwise comparable countries readily show: consider Britain and Japan, or even Korea and Argentina. This view coincides with a classic study by Nobel economist Wassily Leontief, who discovered in the early 1950s that, contrary to expectations that American export success would lie in capital-intensive goods, U.S. trade surpluses existed in sectors with labour-intensive products.[4] One explanation is the level of skill requirements in the production process.

There is no question there is a need for additional qualitative and quantitative assessments that leads to a theory explaining precisely how technological change impacts on economic outcomes. What is undeniable, however, is that in the last 25 years, the determinants of industrial success and wealth creation have altered as economies changed their competitive abilities. The primary reason is knowledge.

In the past generation, largely as a result of the staggering research budgets in the United States, but also of those of Europe, Japan and elsewhere, there has been a quantum leap in new knowledge (including underlying theories, engineering and commercial applications) in three generic technologies: biotechnology, electronics and advanced materials. In this respect, the technological frontiers have moved dramatically into new theoretical directions, to be sure, but especially into new commercial applications.

Canada's industrial structure is increasingly dependent on low-value-added, price-sensitive commodities, while technology-intensive products increasingly dominate Canada's imports. Although the new strategic technologies all effect Canada's primary sector, too little use has been made of them by Canadian companies.

Yet consider the case of Japanese investment in Canada's resource sector. The Japanese are heavy investors in Canadian raw materials — forest products and coal in Alberta and B.C., aluminum in Quebec and hydrocarbons in the Arctic. They are also active in overseas purchases of farmland, wineries and specialized fisheries in the United States. However, Japanese companies also conduct major research efforts at home, especially projects in aquaculture, superconductivity, ocean research, deep-water robotics, new ceramics, high-quality crystals and high-performance ocean chemicals. Japan's vision is in the potential for transforming resources into new products. The production of higher-value-added products is at the heart of a knowledge economy.

From a worldwide competitive perspective, these trends represent dramatic, new and challenging implications. Innovations are occurring both in products (such as semiconductors) and in production processes (such as electric arc mini-mills in the steel industry, or digital and fibre-optic technology in telecommunications). New technologies are evident in products as common as tennis rackets, the Pill or satellite television. Winning and losing firms vary in size, industry structure, management, government support and innovative entrepreneurship. Consider some examples: U.S., tire makers against Bridgestone of Japan or Michelin of France; Caterpillar against Japan's Komatsu in earth-moving equipment; Detroit's "Big Three" against Japan's car sector; America's fast food giants (McDonald's, Pizza Hut etc.) against Europe's traditional food sector. No industry is immune; no country can escape the global impact of new knowledge, changed production processes and new skills.

Clearly both the level and composition of R&D expenditures do count, a point that is especially relevant in assessing U.S.-Japan rivalry, since Japan's research does not have anything equivalent to the military focus of the United States. Moreover, there are additional factors that economists are now only starting to recognize. What are these factors?[5]

First, technology and knowledge are central to the economic growth process, in workers as well as managers. Second, knowledge inputs can lead to a growth spiral — knowledge creating new investment, leading to new knowledge. A corollary is that, once ahead, a firm or country can stay ahead of rivals. Third, despite classical economic theory, inputs to production do not produce a fixed rate of return to scale. Rising inputs lead to increasing returns, despite cuts in prices or rising outputs.

In this non-linear world, these factors lead corporate strategists to focus on being first to market with technologies, and relentlessly pursuing improved production processes in order to maximize returns. Unlike traditional, resource-based industries such as mining, forestry and fisheries, the new knowledge-based sectors have developed a qualitatively different industry logic, where the process of knowledge creation and knowledge commercialization are inextricably combined in production and organizational methods. In this game, commercial and engineering concerns — production cycle times, resource use (minimization of waste) and consumer needs — require continual organizational innovation. In short, the new economics means new management strategies, corporate skills and organization designs, a point as true for government as for private firms.[6]

CANADIAN ORGANIZATION FOR SCIENCE AND TECHNOLOGY

Canada produces, at best, three per cent of the world's stock of scientific knowledge, relying on the world community for the 97 per cent sourced from external countries. Yet Canada's basic science organization and policy apparatus are oriented as if Canada were a major science creator, rather than importer.

Canada's science infrastructure — key institutions, scientific personnel and modus operandi — is almost an exact transfer of the British model.[7] Canada's Royal Society, established in 1882, is a direct copy of the British model of bringing scientists into a united stream of study and exploration towards national efforts. The formation of a national government in 1867 led to the establishment of such institutions as The Dominion Experimental Farms System (1886) and, later, the Biological Board of Canada (1912) and the Honourary Advisory Councils on Scientific and Industrial Research (1916).

One of the most important advances in scientific institution-building was the establishment of the National Research Council (NRC). Set up originally as part of the network of laboratories of the Advisory Council on Scientific and Industrial Research, it then became the basis of all federal government pure and applied research activity. Indeed, for 60 years, the NRC has been a link between the scientific community and the application of science to industry. However, in its evolution, the NRC became the basis of important spin-off creations, including the Defense Research Board (1947), Atomic Energy of Canada (1952), the Medical Research Council (1960) and, more recently, the Natural Science and Engineering Research Council (1978).

The structure of the National Research Council and the role of the funding councils point to a central dilemma facing government-sponsored, science-based innovation in Canada: is the mandate to support primarily basic research, to assist industry in applied, commercially-driven research, or to do a mixture of both?[8] Despite the success of the much-lauded Industrial Research Assistance Program (IRAP) which focuses on direct technological improvements to industry performance, historically, NRC activity has focused on purely scientific research. Typical of most government-department labs, NRC research activity has not been driven by industry and commercial applications, and has not been targeted to potential commercial clients. This pattern of development neglected the vital relationship between research institutions and industry, thereby inhibiting scientific tools and resources from contributing to Canada's commercial innovative capacity. The result is that, over all, Canada's post-war record in basic science is weak, and its comparative performance in technological innovation is weaker still.

International comparative data reveal just how much Canada trails other Western nations in terms of R&D spending — a key measure of innovation capacity. In the 1993 World Competitiveness Report, Canada ranks 16th. Of the top 200 private sector firms engaged in R&D, only one — Bell Canada — was Canadian. Indeed, Canada's industry base in science and technology is exceedingly small. In 1991, only 0.4 per cent of Canadian firms engaged in R&D; of these 3,566 firms, 25 accounted for 48 per cent. Total commitment to R&D expenditures (as a percentage of GNP) remained essentially unchanged from 1.41 per cent in 1984 to 1.49 per cent in 1993. In 1991, Japan spent 2.87 per cent, the United States 2.75 per cent, Germany 2.66 per cent and Britain 2.08 per cent. Canada's public sector research funding accounts for about 50 per cent of the $10.56-billion total national spending on R&D. The federal government directly funds $1.67-billion and the provinces $323-million. The higher-education sector spends some $2.8-billion, funded by both levels of government. However, these data contain overlaps.

The 1993–94 *Federal Scientific Activities Report* issued by Statistics Canada breaks down federal funding into 58 per cent in-house, 18 per cent to educational institutions, 16 per cent to industry, and the balance to foreign and other recipients. Totals given are in the $5.9-billion range in 1993–1994, so the figures do not reconcile exactly.

FIGURE 1
Top R & D Spenders Around the World, 1992

	Latest Spending (millions)	*Per cent Change*	*As Per cent of*		*Number of Companies*
			Sales	*Profits*	
Japan	$35,035	9%	5%	109%	75
Germany	14,402	7	5	149	19
France	9,103	8	4	66	22
Britain	8,098	10	3	33	29
Switzerland	5,206	10	6	90	11
Italy	3,781	5	4	558	8
Sweden	3,500	15	6	283	10
The Netherlands	3,104	–8	6	187	6
Canada	2,474	3	5	74	7
Australia	466	0	2	23	3
Belgium	445	1	5	100	2
Finland	384	99	4	NM	3
Norway	96	29	11	48	1
South Africa	95	17	NM	33	1
Austria	65	0	4	310	1
World Composite	87,951	8	4	81	200
U.S. Composite	79,439	7	4	67	900

SOURCE: Global Vantage (Standard & Poor's Compustat Services)

Analysis of R&D spending is complicated in Canada by the fact that the source of funding, be it the federal government, a provincial government, industry or a foreign firm, is often different from the agency doing the spending — a government in-house agency, a university, industry etc. The data are further muddled by imprecise provincial reporting and inconsistent classifications. These difficulties are compounded when attempts are made to secure disaggregated international comparative data.

Yet Canadian industry's position in science and technology, whether measured by domestic patents, by scientists and engineers in the labour force or by sectors with a positive trade balance, is weak. The low level of private sector R&D expenditures tells much of the story. Within corporate Canada, only Northern Telecom, which is increasingly run from the United States, has a big R&D budget comparable to those of European, American and Japanese companies. There is simply no large sector — for example, mining in advanced materials, food or agribusiness in biotechnology — to provide an engine of development equivalent to the pharmaceutical industry in Switzerland or the electronics sector in Japan.

Foreign ownership plays a role, as illustrated by the automobile sector in Ontario. But foreign ownership is as much a symptom as a cause.

Although as a general rule, Canadian-owned firms spend more on research and development than foreign-owned firms operating in Canada, their actual expenditure levels compared to their U.S. or Japanese counterparts, are very low.[9] In 1981, American private sector companies spent about $36-billion of R&D, compared to about $20-billion in Japan. In 1986, Japanese companies spent some $41.5-billion on R&D, compared to $58.2-billion in the United States. In the 1990s, private sector research in Japan is expected to equal, or exceed, that in the United States, even though the American population and economy are double the size of Japan's.

Clearly, spending on research and development per se is not a panacea. Other factors are at work. For one, Canada has an anemic record in applying existing technology for competitive gain. For six advanced manufacturing technologies — computer-aided design, NC-CNC machines, program controllers, inter-company links, LAN for technical data, and LAN for factory use, Canadian usage is not only significantly less than American firms, the gap in technology application is the greatest among small firms, i.e., those with fewer than 500 employees. This is, in part, a reflection of how few engineers and scientists occupy prominent executive positions in Canadian firms; it is also a result of the low priority given to on-the-job training. Over half of Canada's spending on research goes outside the commercial market for tradable goods and services. Canada, like all other western nations, must import technology as part of the global marketplace. The problems is that other countries do it more effectively. As Japanese government support for R&D demonstrates, it is not the amounts governments spend — 80 per cent of Japanese spending in science and technology comes from the private sector — but what they spend it on. What counts is the commercial leverage that can be gained; private sector spending can be leveraged by rapidly diffusing research output, or by developing commercial prototypes for new products, identifying new markets, or both.

A generation ago, commercial success did not depend on scientific output; German chemistry, British engineering and American electronics all preceded codification of scientific analysis and theory development. In certain areas, that remains true today. But in all the new technologies — biotechnology, advanced materials, electronics and their applications — real progress comes from the long-term work of basic science and the desire to move the technological frontier forward. But this is not a short-term process, nor a field where quick gains are likely without a highly educated management cadre and a well-trained work force.

Historically weak linkages between Canadian universities and the private sector only compound the problem. Few Canadian universities enjoy the level of funding, either for research or overhead support, that their U.S. counterparts do; further, inter-provincial rivalries, excessive duplication and lack of institutional specialization have decreased the potential for large concentrations of scientific talent, as well as for budget levels comparable to their counterparts in other countries.

Emphasizing Commercialization

In applying technology, a country's engineering infrastructure — software and hardware, people and machines, as well as the facilities for their interaction — can be more important than the technological idea itself, or even how it is marketed. It is a balance of strategic functions and their integration that leads to commercial success in science-based innovation, not emphasis on any one area. Indeed, this latter point explains why being on the technological frontier of scientific work does not, in itself, bring commercial success.

The need for commercialization accentuates the importance of the innovation cycle. The conventional view of science-policy analysis is science innovation as a chain of separate but distinct activities forming the basis of a dynamic innovation cycle.[10] The chain starts with basic research for new knowledge, and proceeds through a sequence of activities from the general to the specific, from the basic and non-proprietary, to the applied and proprietary. The next stages involve specific management functions linking the early stages to such "downstream" areas such as engineering, tooling, production and marketing.

This conventional perspective applies to the vast majority of science-based innovations, although in many instances, it has been significantly accelerated. Many product cycles are becoming shorter and shorter, and management is placing a premium on reducing them even more. Some of the Japanese-inspired innovations in the automobile industry (in inventory management, quality, quick-die change, and plant layout) are the most notable examples of reducing the time cycle. These new corporate capabilities also reflect another fact: imitators can often learn from, and even surpass, product leads of innovating firms. The American economist, Edward Mansfield, estimates that companies can, on average, imitate a new product for only two-thirds the time and cost of pioneering one.[11] Nonetheless, the chain from basic research to commercial applications can still be as long as 10 years or more, a requirement which dictates a strategic blend of patient capital, constant effort and a supportive research culture.

A second consideration is the multiplier effect of breakthrough research. In some areas, such as superconductivity, biotechnology and advanced materials, the cost of doing research is so astronomically high, and the impact of breakthroughs so pervasive, that the traditional innovation cycle may not hold. For instance, the changes introduced by the microchip, first developed in the Bell labs in the early 1950s, were so dramatic that the commercial opportunities flowed not from the royalties of the discovery, but from the multitude of applications inherent in the technology. Hence, commercial innovation became the key, rather than technological research per se. A parallel example in industry today would be advances in high-definition television.

The third important factor in commercializing innovation is that the requirements for successful innovation do not apply equally across technologies or products. In electronics, for instance, the real cost is not labour, but research and technical equipment. In steel, the significant costs are in advanced capital equipment. In automobiles, labour costs are below 15 per cent of total costs and falling. This suggests that "process technology" — how something is made — can be as important as what is made. Japan's enormous emphasis on process technology is what has led to better strategies for commercial use of breakthrough scientific knowledge.

New Role for Policy

Every advanced industrial society has had a public policy vehicle to promote technological development, both direct or indirect, publicly owned or publicly regulated. Americans continuously point to the monolith of "Japan Inc.," and to the pervasive powers of its Ministry of International Trade and Industry (MITI), ignoring all the while, the fundamental pluralism of modern Japan. To be sure, the Japanese have their own vast web of industrial networks, public-private vehicles such as MITI, NTT, Technopolis Centres and strategic grants to support science and technology strategies into the next century.[12] In the United States, military spending, defense procurement, space development, agricultural support systems, and a huge complex of government-business-university spending take a central role in supporting American technological development. There are now similar networks in Europe — in space, computers, biotechnology and aerospace, to name a few sectors.

The question for Canada is simple: what master instruments does Canada have to reshape its science and technology organization to meet the needs identified, given that defense research is practically non-existent?

The weakness of the industrial base for R&D is compounded by political pressures to dispense scarce research funds across the country. This dispersion approach has inhibited the development of either a critical mass of research talent (universities, research centres or companies) or a degree of specialization in universities or research laboratories that fosters world-scale talent, research and focus. (Canada's National Research Council has won one Nobel Prize in a generation; Germany's equivalent has won 23.)

Geography and politics, in other words, play a big role in science and technology in Canada. The cards are rarely on the table. True, federal and provincial governments have taken steps to overcome political parochialism, but their efforts remain insignificant, especially in the current political climate.

Is the answer long-term, national mega-projects involving public and private sector collaboration, such as developing the Arctic? Is it a 21st century national telecommunications network? Government infrastructure in electronic transportation control systems? Or an international initiative in biotechnology fields, such as preventive medicine, AIDS or population aging? Japan has its fifth-generation computer thrust; Europe was successful in developing the AirBus; the United States has NASA. Such mission activity is a big-country game, risky and limiting in its deep but narrowly focused, allocation of resources. Canada does not have infinite research resources, nor has it the talent base to compete against other nations across the board. Specialization and focus — on an appropriate scale — are key.

Canada's response is hampered as much by structural problems as by money. Bear in mind that there is a difference between who funds research and who spends the money. Recall that Canada's public sector research funding accounts for about 55 per cent of total national spending on R&D. From a competitive perspective, Canada devotes too much of this to non-commercial sectors that involve no tradeable goods or services. These sectors are also largely outside the mainstream of international scientific research and the professional mechanisms for publications and peer review, and thus independent of both scientific and commercial accountability.

Clearly, in all sectors of the economy, Canada needs improvement in adopting and applying technology, regardless of its source. In relative terms, Canada's record in the commercialization end of the innovation cycle is weak. From a perspective of economic growth, it is not theoretical knowledge alone that drives industrial innovation, but the capacity to develop industrial applications. Even the United States, despite its national excellence in higher education and postgraduate research, has trailed Japan's enormous resources for process technology and first-to-market innovation skills.

Recent changes at the federal level have started to realign budget allocations in Canada, particularly in such flagship institutions as the National Research Council.[13] The NRC is in the process of shifting its focus from its scientific origins to the industrial community, and serving as a bridge between basic and generic research, undertaken in concert with the universities and technological applications in the commercial world. Unfortunately, strategic assessments of research work undertaken in line departments — federally and provincially — are substantially underdeveloped, despite the unusually large proportion of funds devoted to government labs. Here again, the challenge is to develop better linkages to commercialize products and services in the global marketplace.

Even at the provincial level, the outlay of research dollars is relatively high, but the quality and quantity of commercial payoffs — in products and in processes — remain underdeveloped, a challenge now recognized by governments and companies alike.

Canada's record in scientific research by university researchers stands up well by international criteria. Yet there are many barriers to further progress, including aging plant and equipment, low levels of funding, a lack of openness to commercialization and a complete reliance on peer review for judging performance. These institutional barriers now combine with two other problems in Canada: demographics and education-funding levels. The average age of Canadian research scientists in both universities and government labs is climbing steadily. At the NRC the average age is about 49 compared to Bell Northern's 28. Per-capita spending on higher education trails that in the United States by a growing margin; the evidence is particularly noteworthy in science and engineering, precisely the areas where fundamental research is most likely to lead to subsequent commercial production. Moreover, the vast majority of workers who will be in the labour force in the year 2000 have already left school.

EDUCATION AND THE ECONOMY

Some 200 years ago, Adam Smith wrote "the wealth of a nation depends upon two inherent determinants: first, the fraction of population gainfully employed and second, the skill, dexterity and judgement by which labour is generally applied." Smith foresaw the central role of education and training in an advanced economy.

Education in advanced industrial countries is big business, accounting for perhaps 10 per cent of employment in the United States. It is increasingly seen as the basis of lifetime learning and the key to the continuous development of specific skills and credentials necessary for an advanced economy. Indeed, the evidence clearly shows that the basic "mismatch" between demand and supply for specialized skills is increasingly exacerbated in all Western countries — a sign of serious imperfections in the labour market. Countries like Britain, Canada and France, despite enormous unemployment, rely on immigration to supply workers with particular job skills. In the United States, the Carnegie Foundation estimates that more than one million new teachers will be needed in the 1990s — over 300,000 in mathematics and science alone — a figure larger than the entire current teaching force. In Japan, the Council of Science and Technology estimates a shortage of one million computer programmers and systems engineers by the turn of the century, despite the fact that 40 out of every 1,000 Japanese students are studying engineering, compared to 7 out of every 1,000 American students.

The relationship between education and a society's industrial performance has long been a preoccupation of social scientists in general, and economists in particular, and the abundant literature on the subject has owed much to the theoretical contributions of Canadian economists, notably the late Harry Johnson.[14] Much of this theoretical and empirical work has focused on two basic linkages: the levels of educational attainment on the one hand, and on earnings and career performance in the economy, on the other. Clearly, for the individual and for society at large, there are major social benefits to be had from public expenditure on education, both in terms of a future flow of educational payoffs through salary and earnings (where society reaps rewards or returns through taxation on earnings) and through society-wide benefits, such as having a more literate work force, specialized skills and mobility in the job market. All Western countries — especially Canada, the United States, Sweden, Japan and France — have increased their public-education spending greatly since the 1960s. Yet many education systems are in peril. Even the very largest, the U.S. system, is recognized as being in trouble. Literacy and dropout levels, school-leaving rates, student truancy — all the basic indicators — are raising the spectre of educational stagnation. The U.S. Education Secretary, Lauro Cavosoz, summarizes the situation in that country as follows: "The good news is that the schools are not worse. The bad news is that we are not making progress."[15]

Increasingly, the focus on the educational system, particularly in light of detailed comparisons between the U.S. and Canadian systems with that of the Japanese, brings forward a basic conclusion. In North America, the emphasis is on the "E-E" relationship: that between education (and all its forms, programs, institutions and curriculum) and the economy. The Japanese emphasis is on the "F-E-E" relationship: among family, education and economy. In Japan, where education and learning are social obsessions, the starting point is the family unit and, in particular, the role of the mother as a special link between student and the school.

Illiteracy

Illiteracy is a particularly important concern. Canada has been slow to face up to the crisis that low literacy attainments impose on an advanced economy.[16] The challenge of literacy is related to education and training and also to learning skills. It is the capacity of an individual to cope through reading and writing, with the changes in an information-based economy, including the skills needed to operate well in the home or at work. One 1987 Southam newspaper national survey found that 8 per cent of Canadians are unable to read and write at all, with another 16 per cent functionally illiterate. Studies in the United States suggest that illiteracy there is at the same level — that is, 60-million adult Americans, one quarter of the population, are unable to adequately function.

Obviously, no single factor can explain Canada's illiteracy problem. Domestic studies and international reports all agree on the evidence of its effects in at least the following two areas:

- The fastest growing jobs in the economy are those that have the highest skills levels in basic mathematics and language capabilities.
- Literacy skills are directly related to a country's productivity and international competitiveness. Illiteracy levels have been shown to

correlate closely with levels of poverty, crime and other social problems in local communities.

There is a pervasive presumption that the problem of illiteracy can be solved in the schools, or somehow by the education system, generally. However, studies in both the United States and Japan provide ample evidence that this presumption is false. Literacy must be tackled in the home, the family and the community. Fortunately, there is a growing awareness in Canada of the problems of illiteracy, and a host of voluntary organizations have sprung up to cope with the ongoing challenges. More significantly, the efforts of groups such as ABC Canada, a private-sector foundation promoting literacy, have active support from business and labour alike.

Educational Performance — Cost Relations

Recent U.S. experience in education has raised serious doubts about existing education policy. Not only is a huge percentage of the U.S. population functionally illiterate, but there are growing bottlenecks in the labour market owing to skilled labour shortages. Yet U.S. spending on education is enormous, and the heterogeneity of schools, the quality of the elite schools, the spending on research, the richness of diversity, all reflect well on U.S. education vis-à-vis the Canadian and European systems.

The unease within American education has never been greater.[17] Even academics openly question the payoff of such enormous spending. The interest in the "expenditure-performance" relationship — from grade schools to business schools — has never been higher. Indeed, academic research on the factors underlying educational performance, show some remarkable challenges to orthodox policy conclusions. Spending more does not necessarily pay off. Moreover, Canada and the United States have school systems with far fewer days spent in school — about 180 days per year, compared to about 240 in Japan, 235 in Germany, 195 in Hong Kong or 190 in England and France.

Nowhere is the evidence of unease more obvious — because of the abundance of comparative data — than in scholastic performance in America's public schools. The standard measure of educational performance — imperfect and incomplete though it may be — is the Scholastic Aptitude Test (SAT), which tests for skills in language and literacy, as well as in mathematics. U.S. scores on the test have risen marginally since 1980, but average scores have actually fallen below those of 25 years ago. Worse, the actual number of high-scoring students (above 600 out of a possible 800) has declined: it fell by 40 per cent between 1971 and 1982, then rose slightly between 1972 and 1988. The number of students scoring above 600 in mathematics fell from 1972 to 1981, but increased by nine per cent between 1981 and 1988, ironically, in part, because of the number of Asian Americans taking the SAT.

The International Association for the Evaluation of Educational Achievement reports that the average Japanese student outscored the top five per cent of U.S. students enrolled in college-prep mathematics courses. In chemistry and physics, advanced science students in U.S. high schools performed worse than their counterparts in almost all countries studied. In biology, they ranked dead last, behind such nations as Singapore and Thailand.

American and Canadian educators offer abundant reasons for their weak performance compared to Japan. The arguments often centre on a critique of Japanese educational methods, the punishing rate of learning and the examination system and the desire of the Japanese educator to enforce conformity, rigidity and student passivity:

> Japan's educational system has gained a reputation overseas as one of the best, if not the best, in the world. This reputation rests partly on the high (often highest) scores Japanese school children attain in international mathematics tests and on the presumed connection with Japan's' economic success. It is backed up by remarks of specialists impressed by the discipline in Japanese schools, the commitment of mothers and the ability of pupils to absorb masses of facts...[18]
>
> The overriding purpose of the Japanese educational system was summed up by an authority on the subject as "shaping generations of disciplined workers for a techno-meritocratic system that requires competent individuals capable of performing reliably in a vigorous, hierarchical and finely tuned organizational environment.[19]

Other Problems

Other problems cannot be overlooked. Consider the case of computers in U.S. and Canadian universities. There is a huge disparity in both the number of computer systems and their value, on leading U.S. campuses compared to Canadian ones. Indeed, the University of Texas, the leading U.S. school, has more invested in its computer base, than all of the top ten Canadian schools combined! Moreover, U.S. schools have a higher percentage of mainframe and minicomputers, while Canada relies on a higher lever of personal computers (55 per cent).

In Canada and the United States, the high school dropout rate is extraordinarily high — as much as one-third of the total, and even more in certain provinces and among certain groups. High school dropout rates signal a future problem in the labour market, where low skills begin the cycle of dependency on low-skill jobs and vulnerability to technological change. In the end, the unemployed increasingly face the prospect of being unemployable.

Spending priorities are also coming into question. Canada spends about $50-billion per year on education — $45-billion for formal education and $5-billion for adult training. Big firms undertake the largest proportion of adult training. Yet Canada's overall spending on adult education is only a fraction of other industrialized countries: total share of GDP in industrial training is 0.3 per cent, half that of the United States. Japan spends five times more than Canada on adult training; Germany spends eight times more.

GOVERNMENT LEADERSHIP

A historic weakness in Canadian science policy has been the absence of a clear structure and of government leadership in promoting science-based innovation in industry, co-ordinating government-funded science, and developing a science culture in Canada. Unfortunately, Canada has no institutional base that can undertake long-term science policy and research. The Science Council of Canada, set up in the 1970s, served as a public-sector think-tank, but its influence rarely matched its promise, and it was abolished in 1992. The U.S. Congress has a highly influential American Office of Technology, Japan has its Science and Technology Agency and has launched a new initiative, the National Institute of Science and Technology Policy. Among Canadian universities, there is no equivalent, for example, of the Science Policy Research Unit at Britain's Sussex University. Science policy-making has been dispersed, and instruments of science development have been given ambiguous mandates. In the competitive world of the 1990s, where technology is the key to shaping international competitive advantage, some priority-setting mechanisms must be established at the national level.

Canada has only recently raised the priority of its science and technology policy agenda. Although many think-tank groups — the Economic Council of Canada, the Science Council, the C.D. Howe Institute, The Hudson Institute and some business advisory groups — have attempted to promote the role of science and technology in Canadian public policy, but over the past two decades, their actual impact on policy has been minimal. The recently launched federal "prosperity" initiative is the public manifestation of new policy directions. There are three thrusts to this: reorganizing the federal government departments involved, establishing science and technology advisory councils, and facilitating research consortia and strategic alliances.

Department of Industry, Science and Technology

A major starting point for new initiatives came in the 1986 federal Throne Speech, which established a new government department: Industry Science and Technology Canada (ISTC). It was formally legislated and approved in Parliament and given a clear mandate to:

- elevate science and technology to the top of the government's agenda
- encourage a commitment to international competitiveness and excellence
- create new attitudes towards commercially exploitable science and technology

- promote a technologically sophisticated industrial base
- coordinate policies and programs among industry, the science community and the government

To date, the new department has been slow to demonstrate either a definite mission or a workable structure. Some outsiders see ISTC as a Canadian-style equivalent of Japan's MITI. Clearly, this is not the case — Ottawa combines the "trade" function of government within the Department of External Affairs, with technology and industry operating as a separate departmental mandate. Over 20 years, these responsibilities have been the subject of extensive bureaucratic review and reorganization. The acronyms of successive organizations — DREE, DRIE, MOSST and now ISTC — represent a depressing litany of attempts to balance the outward-looking supportive functions needed for growth in the sunrise sectors of the economy, with the politically expedient focus of job protection, government bailouts and subsidy support for sunset sectors. Moreover, to such an extent that it has been a plague to the department's functioning, ISTC also operates with a mandate to promote regional development, with all the attendant biases to support uncompetitive enterprises and direct scarce financial resources to sectors without a strong technological future (such as low-value-added textiles, shipbuilding and some sectors of aerospace).

What is clear from the operating structure at Japan's MITI, and increasingly from other jurisdictions such as Britain's Department of Trade and Industry, or France's Centre Français de Commerce Extérieur, is that the key building blocks for ISTC must be strong sector-by-sector analysis, possibly modeled on the 15 Sectoral Advisory Groups for International Trade (SAGITs), first instituted in 1986 for the U.S.-Canada free trade talks. The intent was to develop a strong policy framework in such areas as trade, technology, procurement, small business and industry structure, with in-depth performance analysis at the sectoral level. The challenge is to develop and integrate the policy instruments and to achieve growth, increase the value-added on goods and encourage exports.

Under this approach, public- and private-sector groups can work together to build the statistical analyses, data bases, assessments of comparative industrial structure, technological forecasting and various other tools that can serve as the basic input necessary to build a supportive climate for private-sector development and growth. The emphasis must be on continuous benchmarking, i.e., on international comparative performance, especially in the vital areas of productivity, technology innovation and export competitiveness. Public policy instruments, such as the Federal Business Development Bank, Investment Canada, the NRC and sectoral advisory boards on international trade, are all potential vehicles for developing a long-term planning framework, as well as specific tools — such as memoranda of understanding (MOUs), research consortia, R&D vehicles or international agreements on industrial R&D.

Advisory Councils

Complementing these developments is a more dramatic, influential and long-term trend, namely the advent of science advisory councils reporting directly to political leaders. This idea was opposed by the senior echelons of the federal bureaucracy — a telltale sign of the traditional low priority given to science and technology in Ottawa, a preference for non-intervention in the economy and a concern over possible subsequent spending requests. The genesis of this lay in the policy commitment of Prime Minister Brian Mulroney. In another bold move, in the Throne Speech of 1986, he introduced a National Advisory Board of Science and Technology (NABST), an initiative that, at a stroke, moved science policy from the periphery of the nation's policy agenda, to the very centre of the federal government. The high profiles of its members, chosen on the basis of merit rather than political affiliation, were the most telling signal in a generation that science and technology issues now counted.

This Canadian initiative has parallels in other jurisdictions. In 1987, for instance, shortly after her third electoral victory, British Prime Minister Margaret Thatcher, established a new Advisory Committee on Science and Technology, which reported directly to the prime minister via the cabinet office. That committee was in part a result of a report from the House of Lords criticizing British science for underfunding, lack of direction, and fragmentation of effort. Another Thatcher innovation was the new Centre for the Exploitation of Science and Technology, funded mainly by large corporations, but also by three government departments. The centre focuses on medium-term research priorities, as well as areas where research efforts should be reduced or even abandoned.

The formation of external advisory boards and the new ministerial initiatives at the centre of the science policy process, has also extended to Canada's provincial governments. While Quebec had a science advisory board dating back a generation, Ontario was the first province to establish one with a major political leader in the chair, as in Japan. The initiative, known as the Premier's Council on Science and Technology, was announced in the April 22, 1986 Throne Speech, as being designed "to steer Ontario into the forefront of economic leadership and technological innovation." Since 1986, every province has set up its own equivalent advisory council, each with a specific mandate to deal with public policy issues and develop science and technology plans, in both the short and long terms. In June 1989, all members of Canada's science advisory councils met for the first time, as part of a Nova Scotia initiative supported by the ten provincial premiers and the prime minister. Since then, these annual meetings have been the centre-piece of science and technology policy-making in Canada.

Research Consortia

Provincial research organizations do not have large budgets, but their local impact can be significant.

To compete in a global economy with rapidly changing technology, Canada needs to husband scarce resources and avoid wasteful duplication. Canada's companies are mostly too small to undertake generic research on their own. Few industrial research labs in Canada are of sufficient scale and quality to follow, let alone lead, global technological trends. The only viable alternative is research consortia — what some call strategic alliances — to drive the technology-commercialization cycle.

The new ISTC is a natural vehicle for initiating and funding a series of strategic technology alliances involving Canadian industry and universities. Funds could be reallocated from in-house government programs to non-government researchers committed to the types of investigations needed. Agreements have already been arranged in such areas as plastics and information technology, but the approach can be extended to robotics and artificial intelligence, aquaculture, advanced materials, biotechnology and flexible manufacturing, to cite obvious examples. Agreements such as the one reached with the Canadian Plastics Institute are serving as a prototype for a number of other sectors — for research, training and technology diffusion.

Many points of leverage are available. The Canadian Institute for Advanced Research (CIAR), one of the most important science initiatives undertaken in Canada in a decade, has assembled networks to develop a critical mass of researchers in strategic technologies. Recent initiatives such as the federal and Ontario Centres of Excellence programs are a natural complement to the CIAR, because these centres bring together the best researchers in Canada to focus on real problems.

Consider Figure 2, which depicts the research-commercialization process. At the lower left is the generic and basic research block. This is where a country's basic technological infrastructure feeds into its industrial infrastructure. Support for basic research leads to pre-competitive, non-proprietary research. At this stage, the aim is to support strategic technologies — those that are key to a wide band of industries and products — such as semiconductors. Physical infrastructure is important, but so too are the tools that build science infrastructure, such as access to advanced computer technology, journals and technical data, measuring and control instruments, and the like. For instance, the Japanese government translates over 20,000 technical journals and makes them available to Japanese and foreigners alike. The U.S. Congress supports Internet, a vast electronic web of some 2,000 computer networks linking U.S. universities and research labs both domestically and internationally.

Alliances can play a key role here. Research consortia are neither novel nor confined to big markets like the United States or Japan. Denmark pools resources for export and technology studies, translation, industry fairs and overseas promotion of export sectors such as furniture. In Germany, the textile machinery association develops collective strategies

FIGURE 2

The Research-Commercialization Process

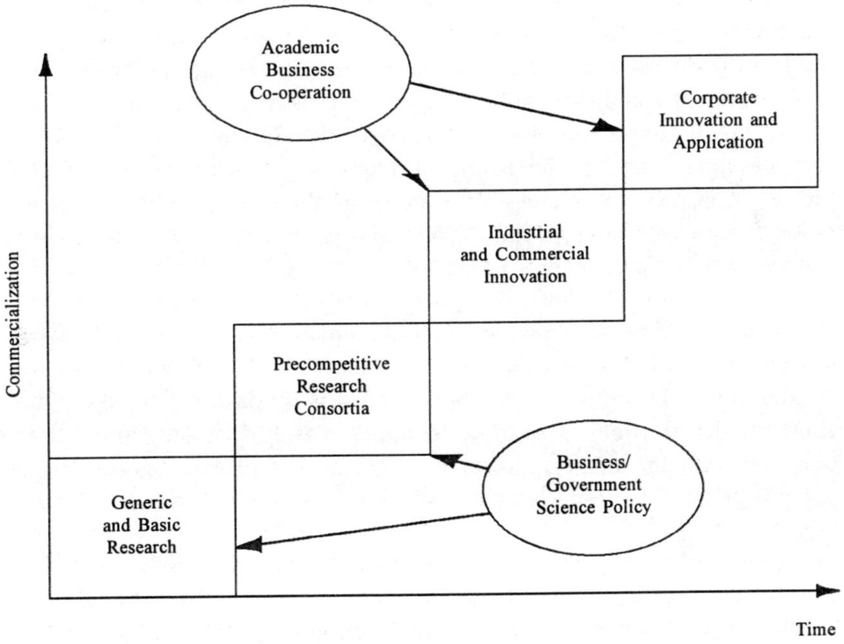

for advertising, overseas markets, links to trade schools and research with technical institutes.

The Japanese are the leaders in research and technology consortia, yet even American companies are now looking with favour on this approach.[20] The Reagan and Thatcher administrations were supportive, and U.S. anti-trust obstacles to industry consortia have been lowered by new congressional initiatives. Electronics and computers have been at the vanguard of the strategic-alliance approach. The first major U.S. initiative was the Semiconductor Research Cooperative, founded in 1982, with 35 sponsoring companies. It funds research, acts as a clearing house for technical literature, provides a first right to members for copyright and patents and funds up to 300 research students on priority projects. Equivalent consortia have sprung up in chemicals (the council for Chemical Research, sponsored by 43 companies and 142 universities) and television (the Center for Advanced Television Studies, sponsored by four networks, five TV manufacturers and MIT). Detroit's Big 3 have 12 research consortia working on such areas as electric cars and parts recycling.

Basic research provides the ideas for corporate research. In between are long-term applied research and specialized short-term applied research.

The research-commercialization process (shown in Figure 2) is an evolving chain in which the institutional support for the research changes over time. In generic and basic research, funding typically involves close business-government collaboration, often with the government taking the lead in order to lever the private sector and to assume a portion of the front-end risk. This, of course, has been the strength of Japan's MITI and its Science and Technology Agency. It is not the level of funding per se that is important, but the speed of developing research consortia and the commitment to long-term horizons, say of 10 years or more. At the other end of the chain is the more applied side, where the key is closer business-university links, particularly for highly skilled personnel and mobility of personnel between companies and academic settings.

These efforts have two key goals: to bridge the gaps in the research-commercialization process and to build up a critical mass of first-rate personnel. They are succeeding, particularly in Japan, but also in the United States. Despite the perception that it is the Japanese who are most comfortable with the research consortia approach, it is the United States that has been the most aggressive in promoting research consortia, especially those involving companies and universities. Europe has a mixed record.

Canada has experimented with three large initiatives in research consortia. Precarn, a joint industry-government initiative focussing on robotics, semiconductors and artificial intelligence, was launched in 1986. It is a pioneering effort to link diverse private-sector firms to pool R&D risk capital, develop common know-how and share patents and royalties across the research network.

Ontario's 1987 Centres of Excellence program, literally forced institutions, by the incentive of research dollars, to combine forces and work together with industry to develop consortia to promote pure and applied research goals. This initiative, launched by the Ontario Government under the auspices of the Premier's Council, was a $204-million program of seven Centres of Excellence in such advanced, multi-disciplinary sectors as space, lasers, telecommunications, advanced materials, information technologies, manufacturing and groundwater. The open competition, involving some 28 proposals and including input from 28 hospitals, universities and colleges, six industry associations and over $2-billion in proposed funding, gave a unique kick start to federal initiatives, and marked an unusual business-university research collaboration.

In 1989, the federal government adopted the same approach, establishing a program of National Centres of Excellence with a budget of over $250-million, a carrot simply too large to ignore. It involved 14 Centres of Excellence, selected through a peer-review process from 158 major proposals. Like the Ontario initiative, the federal Centres of Excellence were largely divorced from politics. They engage university-industry collaboration and involved the Prime Minister's National Advisory Board for Science and Technology as a key decision-making component. In 1994, the federal government announced an additional allotment of $48-million for a new "Networks of Centres of Excellence" in five target areas: materials and software engineering, environment, health research, technology-based learning, and trade, competitiveness and sustainability. Although the federal initiative has been weak on private-sector support, given the history of non-communication between universities and business in Canada, both the Ontario and federal approaches have truly changed the ground rules for science and technology policy, and these changes are sure to make a difference in the years ahead.

A novel Canadian research consortium is the Northwest Biotechnology Consortia Inc., founded in 1992 to promote management in biotechnology firms, assist financing and promote corporate networking and strategic alliances. An interesting mix of larger, publicly-listed firms, and small start-up enterprises, the research consortia's aim is to build up a critical mass of technological and management skills with a view to attracting financial support for marketing growth and additional research.

Other federal initiatives — in copyright and patent legislation and support for science and engineering scholarships — reinforce the commitment to commercial R&D. But are they enough when other nations are devoting ever more resources to promote their knowledge-based industries? More radical proposals, such as privatizing governmental laboratories or deregulating university graduate programs, are not yet on the national science and technology policy agenda. Nor have serious moves been made towards using the tax system to promote equity infusions into technology-intensive innovations, especially in small companies. However, the Liberal government elected in Ottawa on October 25, 1993, made this issue a highlight of their election promises.

THE CHALLENGE

Canada faces key challenges at both the national and the industry/firm levels.

For the Nation

At the national level, resolving the following issues over the next few years is particularly important:

- a corporate culture that is woefully weak in the areas of technological innovation and worker training
- a labour-management climate that pays only lip-service to technological change and to science policy in general
- a university system too often disdainful of commercial and private-sector linkages, precisely at a time when public spending on university education is well below comparable U.S. levels

- a federal bureaucracy seized with angina over the embarrassment of the 1980s scientific research tax credit (SRTC) fiasco, incapable or unwilling to devise an effective instrument to put Canadian technology companies on par, in terms of cost of capital, with industrial competitors in the United States, Japan and Europe
- a tax regime more accommodating to the real estate industry than to knowledge-based research talent and innovative small companies

Another relative weakness of Canada's industrial structure can be succinctly summarized: the ratio of business start-ups to failures is too low. Too few start-ups are spin-offs from universities, large firms or research centres. Too few small firms emerge as medium-sized firms. Too few medium-sized firms become large companies, with appropriate strengths in finance, production, management and technology. Mitel, Lumonics and Geac are three examples of companies that stumbled dramatically, underscoring the management pitfalls along the growth curve.

The problems appear almost insurmountable. From where will innovation come? With a few notable exceptions, the truly innovative ideas do not flow from large resource companies, or from the foreign-owned sector (much of it under competitive pressure from Japan and Asia), or from universities and government laboratories.

From where will the required investment come? Funding inadequacies cannot be blamed on inadequate R&D tax incentives. It is widely believed, especially in the federal Department of Finance, that by all measures of tax credits, Canada is second to none in the world. Recent studies show that the issues are more complex: macroeconomic considerations, such as price stability and productivity, must be related to the capacity of the economy to produce the investment, and the capacity of the financial system to direct the funds towards growth enterprises developing science-based innovations.

Will Canada ever have a coherent strategy? There is no broad-based consensus underlying an industrial strategy, however defined. There is not even a general belief that realistic levels of resources must be devoted to developing one over the next five to 10 years.

Contrast these uncertainties with the situation in Japan, which is the model for all of Asia.[21] The most dramatic of new Japanese initiatives is a nation-wide system of technopolis centres, linking private capital, research consortia and universities, to long-term research goals. Technology continues to be emphasized as the life-blood of its advanced economy. Japan is the centre of all major auto-based technological changes. It is revolutionizing Western concepts of mass production, including the use of robotics, computers and management software, as regards quality, inventory management and distribution. Japan holds about 50 per cent of current global patents, a key to subsequent product commercialization. The Japanese dominate foreign patent listings in the United States — 21 per cent versus 9 for Germany and 3 for France and Britain.

The Japanese know the challenge of becoming a world-scale science innovator. Few foreigners appreciate how well Japan can afford to pay for a science-based economy. It outspends all Western countries in civilian research: 20,000 Japanese study in U.S. universities; Japan rivals the United States in research employment, with about 65 researchers for every 10,000 workers. By the end of the next decade, Japan will be world leader in the next century's technologies: unmanned space systems, artificial intelligence, biotechnology, advanced materials, high-energy physics, media power and many commercial applications of advanced pharmaceuticals.[22]

For Industries and Firms

By a number of indicators of the technological intensity of industry, Canada is among the lowest ranked: in the number and level of applications in information and computer technology; in new methods of production, such as computer-assisted design and manufacturing (CAD/CAM) and robotics; and in various modes of "mechatronics." These are all indicative of the importance of process technology — the special skills and engineering applications transforming the production process to increase flexibility and reduce cycle times. Other measures include how closely the production process is being linked to the firm's strategic requirements, how many workers are skilled, how outward-looking is management and whether or not state-of-the-art capital equipment is being used. By most such measures, either on the input or output side, Canada is a serious laggard country.

New ways of thinking about individual organizations are required. In fact, the traditional stand-alone company research laboratory operating on "technology-driven" principles may well be obsolete, even in the United States and Japan. The alternative is a "business-driven" approach to research laboratories. As Drucker notes:

> The research lab may become a free-standing business, doing research work on contract for a multitude of industrial clients. Each client would then need a "technology manager" rather than a "research director" — someone who can develop business objectives based on the potential of technology and technology strategies based on business and market objectives, and who then defines and buys the technical work needed to produce the business results.[23]

The point is that science-based innovation requires different management strategies from those practised by Canada's traditional resource companies. Linkages with universities, strategic alliances for markets, venture capital for funding and public policy support for market entry and trade are central concerns. The style of management and the corporate values are outward oriented and growth demanding. Few Canadian firms match this profile.

CONCLUSIONS

The new game of science-based innovation represents a qualitative change in the ground rules of international competition. In many ways, it is a game of "chicken" economics — the basic decision is to play or not to play. It is like riding a roller coaster — once you have started, it is impossible to exit gracefully. It is a game of fierce stakes, of huge payoffs for winners and huge losses for losers — a game akin to Japan's sumo wrestling.

Science-based innovation, while still confined to only a few industrial sectors, turns the traditional wealth-creation theory on its ear. Firms on the leading edge of the technology frontier are not price takers; they are price leaders (and temporary monopolists, because of superior technology). Returns to scale are not constant. They can be infinite, since the marginal cost of reproducing knowledge is theoretically zero. Imitators and followers are at a real disadvantage; to fall behind may imply staying behind. Product innovation is closely linked to process innovation. The question of what to produce is linked to that of how to produce it. And finally, the complex interactions of customers, market rivalry and educational resources, centre on the need for constant and relentless change, including cost-cutting innovation and technological upgrading.

In this sense, science-based innovation has become a never-ending match of wits, much like a championship game of contract bridge. There are three identifiable variables. The first, akin to the perspective of classical economics (land, labour, capital), is the lay of the cards. The player can only deal with the cards in the hand — in this sense, governments and industries are at the mercy of uncontrolled market forces and national resource endowments.

To this orthodox perspective is added the second tier of the bridge analogy: how players play the cards. Here, strategy, cunning and guile all play a role (surrogates for international trade policy, political pressure groups and management processes and capabilities). But that relates to the third tier: how the competition plays the game — in the context of the cards played, of the competition's guile and strategy, and also of self-interest.

In a knowledge-based economy, it is the production of ideas that propels growth. While the role of the private sector is important, so too, is that of government, through direct funding, but also through indirect aid, such as tax and research support, and incentives for university-industry co-operation. This approach amounts to what has been called an industrial policy. It implies a model of an economy that is a far cry from the invisible hand of Adam Smith, or the laws of comparative advantage: it is a strategy for creating competitive advantage.

Technology-intensive exports are the key to economic growth; that is why trade in knowledge-intensive industries is so competitive. Performance in trade reflects the effectiveness of a wide range of policies that form the basis for the new economics of wealth creation, and most of the countries of the developed and undeveloped world recognize it. This is the context that will determine Canada's future.

What matters is not only how Canadians play, but also how others play. That's one reason why *Business Week* in the U.S.A. and Britain's Department of Industry produce an annual R&D scoreboard. Most Canadians (and governments) still believe a science and technology culture comes from public policy and government-spending programs. In fact, all the evidence from the world's most technologically advanced industries indicate that the key imperatives involve a judicious mixture of technologically literate employees, relentless adaptation to competitive forces in unfettered markets and managerial and financial strategies that mix long-term and short-term horizons.

Only recently has science and technology moved to the centre of Canada's public-policy agenda. International competitiveness and prosperity issues are clearly driving the need for a fundamental rethinking of Canada's traditional approach to science manpower, science and technology priorities, funding allocations, the relative merits of competing institutions and the role of the public and private sectors. Fortunately, the debate has moved beyond pointing fingers at past failures or inadequacies. Recent reports by the Conference Board of Canada, the Canadian Manufacturers' Association, Canada's provincial science advisory boards and industry associations, have provided new impetus for a more coherent approach. Important federal programs have changed the national policy mix and improved the science-and-technology climate. New federal initiatives (such as the Canadian Space Agency), new approaches to intellectual property (such as an updated patent policy, plant breeder's rights and software and book copyright), the Centres of Excellence program, a national program for science and engineering scholarships, and tax incentives for business-university linkages, all add up to a very new approach to science policy.

For Canada, the familiar obstacles remain — low managerial recognition of the issues, interprovincial trade barriers and private sector inertia — in the resource sector, in manufacturing and in banking. Canada's resource sector, the traditional cash cow for wealth creation, has never been more challenged: the East-coast fisheries are all but bankrupt; more than a third of Canada's pulp and paper plants are almost 50 years old and technologically obsolete; rents from mining, oil and gas are at historic lows in real terms; and farm staples, like wheat, are at depression levels. Even the industrial base of Canada's heartland — automobiles and steel — is severely challenged as the new base of global competition, especially from Japan and Asia, alters these capital and technology-intensive sectors.

Whether Canada's public- and private-sector leaders are willing to seize the fundamental need to make science and technology a national priority, remains an open question. The 1989 conference of Canada's science advisory committees produced an important document, *The Halifax Declaration: A*

Call to Action. It expressed the sense of urgency and the need for action this way:

> No one seriously doubts the essential message. Canada is not maintaining its position. Canada is, in fact, slipping. No political rhetoric can disguise this fundamental reality.
>
> The strong consensus of the Halifax Forum was to adopt a real target, to accept a figure as a national goal, where all Canadian partners can and must play. A 2.5 per cent of GNP expenditure, achievable by the end of the century, would not be a federal target, a provincial wish or an industry approach. It would be a national target, involving real commitment, applicable to public and private sectors as well as to the Federal Government and to each Province. Further, it is necessary for the private sector to accept this national goal and to make the necessary commitments to create a strong industrial base around science-based innovation. A public announcement of agreement on the target is, more fundamentally, a clear statement of national will and long-term commitment on the part of Canada's political leadership.

Notes

1. For an overview, see the Economic Council of Canada, *The Bottom Line: Technology, Trade and Income Growth* (Ottawa: Ministry of Supply and Services, 1983). See also the Annual Report, Catalogue 88–201, "Science and Technology Indicators," published by Statistics Canada.

   Obtaining reliable, consistent, comparable R&D data remains difficult, especially for up-to-date information. The situation in Canada is not helped by cutbacks to budgets for the Science and Technology Section of Statistics Canada, moves that will reduce the information available, and slow down the timing of publications.
2. G. Dosi et al., *The Economics of Technical Change and International Trade* (London: Harvester Wheatsheaf, 1990).
3. J.J. Brown, *Ideas in Exile* (Toronto: Penguin, 1965).
4. Wassily Leontief, "Domestic Production and Foreign Trade: The American Capital Position Reconsidered," *Proceedings of the American Philosophical Society* 97 (September 1953): 332–49.
5. *Technology and the Economy: The Key Relationships*. Paris: OECD, 1992. For a precise summary, see "Economic Growth: Explaining the Mystery," *The Economist*, 4 January 1992, 15–18; and "Innovation: The Machinery of Growth", *The Economist*, 11 January 1992, 17–19.
6. Charles J. McMillan, "Japan's Contribution to Management Development," *Business and the Contemporary World*, 4 (Winter 1992): 21–33.
7. M. Thistle, *The Inner Ring: The Early History of the National Research Council* (Toronto: University of Toronto Press, 1966).
8. Premier's Council on Science and Technology, *Competing in the New Global Economy* (Toronto: Queen's Printer, 1988). See also *Adjusting to Win*, Chapter 4.
9. National Research Council, *A Practical Perspective* (Ottawa: Ministry of Supply and Services, 1987).
10. Raymond Vernon, "International Investment and International Trade in the Product Cycle," *Quarterly Journal of Economics* (May 1966): 190–207. See

also Michael L. Dertorizon et al., *Made in America: Regaining the Productive Edge* (Cambridge, MA: MIT Press, 1989): 40.

11. Edward Mansfield, *R&D and Innovation: Some Empirical Findings* (Chicago: University of Chicago Press, 1984).
12. Sheridan Tatsuno, *The Technopolis Strategy* (New York: Prentice-Hall, 1986); Daniel I. Okimoto, "Regime Characteristics of Japanese Industrial Policy," in *Japan's High Technology Industries*, eds. Hugh Patrick and Larry Meissner (Seattle: University of Washington Press, 1986): 41–42; Charles J. McMillan, *The Japanese Industrial System* (New York: de Gruyter, 1989), Chapter 5.
13. *Revitalizing Science and Technology in the Government of Canada* (Ottawa: Supply and Services Canada, 1990).
14. Harry G. Johnson, *The Canadian Quandary* (Toronto: McGraw-Hill, 1963); for a thorough overview of the literature, see M. Blaug, ed., *Economics of Education*, Vol. 1 and 2 (Middlesex, U.K.: Penguin, 1969); Gary Becker, *Human Capital* (Chicago: University of Chicago, 1975).
15. Lawrence A. Uzzell, "Education Reform Fails the Test," *Wall Street Journal*, 10 May 1989.
16. See "Review of Education and Training,: *Quarterly Labour Market and Productivity Review* (Spring 1989): 19–29.
17. Allan Bloom, *The Closing of the American Mind* (New York: Simon and Schuster, 1987); David Harmin, *Illiteracy* (New York: Columbia University Teacher's College, 1986); Jack E. Bowsher, *Educating America* (New York: Wiley, 1988).
18. Karel Von Wolferen, *The Enigma of Japanese Power* (New York: Alfred A. Knopf, 1989), Chapter 3.
19. Charles J. McMillan, *The Japanese Industrial System* (New York: de Gruyter, 1994), Chapter 5.
20. See "Industrial Policy" *Business Week*, 6 April 1992, 70–76.
21. Charles J. McMillan, *Investing in Tomorrow: Japan's Science and Technology Strategies in the 1990s* (Ottawa: Canada-Japan Trade Council, 1989), chapters 4 and 5; Charles Ferguson, "Computers and the Coming of the U.S. Keiretsu," *Harvard Business Review* (July-August 1990); 55–70.
22. David H. Brandin and Michael Harrison, *The Technology War: A Case for Competitiveness* (New York: John Wiley, 1987), Part III; Andrew J. Pierre, ed., *A High Technology Gap* (New York: Council on Foreign Relations, 1987).
23. Peter Drucker, "Best R&D is Business-Driven," *Wall Street Journal*, 10 February, 1988, 18.

QUESTIONS FOR DISCUSSION

1. Is the importance of technology overemphasized in discussions of international competitiveness and industrial growth? Does technology affect all sectors of an economy equally?
2. What are the components of science and technology policy? Should government become actively involved in establishing and implementing such policies in Canada? Why?
3. Is GERD (Gross Expenditures on Research and Development) potentially misleading if used as an indicator of innovativeness or

technological intensity? What other measures would you suggest to complement or supplement GERD measure?

4. What is it about the Japanese system of bringing technology to market that makes it so effective and so difficult to compete against?
5. How should the alleged problem of illiteracy be defined and attacked? In your opinion, what are its causes? Can high school dropout rates be reduced? What really is a knowledge worker?
6. What are the components of Professor McMillan's recommended science and technology strategy? What are the strengths and what are the weaknesses of his approach? Do you believe it could be implemented in today's socio-political and economic environment?
7. In what ways do individual Canadian companies have to change if they are to make better use of technology? What is preventing them from changing?

Charles J. McMillan is Professor of International Business in the Faculty of Administrative Studies at York University, Toronto, Canada. He is the author of eight books and monographs, including ***The Japanese Industrial System****, now available in English, Japanese, Malaysian and Russian editions. He serves as North American Editor for the journal,* ***Business in the Contemporary World****, as well as a member of the Editorial Board of* ***Journal of Far Eastern Business****, published by the University of London, U.K. His latest monograph,* ***Building Blocks or Trade Blocs: NAFTA, Japan and the New World Order****, is published by the Canada-Japan Trade Council (Ottawa, 1994).*

Active in public affairs, Dr. McMillan has served as Senior Policy Advisor to the Prime Minister of Canada, consultant to numerous national and international companies and agencies, and director on such bodies as the National Ballet School of Canada, Nova Scotia's Council of Applied Science and Technology, the Asia Pacific Foundation and the Canadian Children's Foundation. His report, "Standing Up to the Future: The Maritime Provinces in the 1990s," has become the blueprint for economic co-operation and development in Atlantic Canada. In 1991, he produced the Economic Development Plan for the Republic of Kyrghyzstan, a former Soviet Republic in Central Asia, and serves as Founding Dean for the Bishkek International School of Management and Business. In 1993, he was appointed as Special Advisor to Goskominvest, the Kyrgyz State Commission on Foreign Investments and Economic Assistance.

In the private sector, among his directorships include Chairman of the Midas Group, and director of P.E.I. Trade Enterprises Inc., Nu-Stadia Inc., and Yamaichi International (Canada) Limited, one of Japan's largest investment banks.